DON ISAAC ABRAVANEL

For the complete list of books that are available in this series,
please see www.brandeis.edu/tauber

Cedric Cohen-Skalli
Don Isaac Abravanel: An Intellectual Biography

ChaeRan Y. Freeze
A Jewish Woman of Distinction: The Life and Diaries of Zinaida Poliakova

Chava Turniansky
Glikl: Memoirs 1691–1719

Dan Rabinowitz
The Lost Library: The Legacy of Vilna's Strashun Library in the Aftermath of the Holocaust

Jehuda Reinharz and Yaacov Shavit
The Road to September 1939: Polish Jews, Zionists, and the Yishuv on the Eve of World War II

Adi Gordon
Toward Nationalism's End: An Intellectual Biography of Hans Kohn

Noam Zadoff
Gershom Scholem: From Berlin to Jerusalem and Back

*Monika Schwarz-Friesel and Jehuda Reinharz
Inside the Antisemitic Mind: The Language of Jew-Hatred in Contemporary Germany

Elana Shapira
Style and Seduction: Jewish Patrons, Architecture, and Design in Fin de Siècle Vienna

Don Isaac Abravanel

An Intellectual Biography

CEDRIC COHEN-SKALLI

TRANSLATED BY AVI KALLENBACH

BRANDEIS UNIVERSITY PRESS *Waltham, Massachusetts*

Brandeis University Press
© 2021 by Cedric Cohen-Skalli.
Originally published in Hebrew as *Don Yitzhak Abravanel*
(Shazar Center for Jewish History, 2017).
All rights reserved
Manufactured in the United States of America
Designed by Richard Hendel
Typeset in Arno by Integrated Publishing Solutions

For permission to reproduce
any of the material in this book, contact
Brandeis University Press, 415 South Street, Waltham MA 02453,
or visit http://www.brandeis.edu/press

Library of Congress Cataloging-in-Publication Data

Names: Skalli, Cedric Cohen, author. | Kallenbach, Avi, translator.
Title: Don Isaac Abravanel : an intellectual biography / Cedric Cohen-Skalli ;
translated by Avi Kallenbach.
Description: [New edition]. | Waltham, Massachusetts : Brandeis University Press, 2021. |
Series: The Tauber Institute series for the study of European Jewry | Includes bibliographical
references and index. | Summary: "An intellectual biography of Don Isaac ben Judah
Abravanel, a 15th century Portuguese rabbi, scholar, Bible commentator, philosopher,
and statesman"—Provided by publisher.
Identifiers: LCCN 2020031446 (print) | LCCN 2020031447 (ebook) |
ISBN 9781684580231 (hardcover) | ISBN 9781684580248 (ebook)
Subjects: LCSH: Abravanel, Isaac, 1437–1508. | Rabbis—Spain—Biography. |
Jewish philosophers—Spain—Biography.
Classification: LCC BM755.A25 S55 2021 (print) | LCC BM755.A25 (ebook) |
DDC 296.3092 [B]—dc23
LC record available at https://lccn.loc.gov/2020031446
LC ebook record available at https://lccn.loc.gov/2020031447

CONTENTS

Preface *vii*

Acknowledgments *xiii*

PART 1: DON ISAAC ABRAVANEL IN PORTUGAL (1437–1483)

1. The Kingdom of Portugal and the Abravanel Family *3*

2. Isaac Abravanel and Iberian Court Culture *20*

3. Isaac Abravanel as a Jewish Leader in His Hebrew Epistles *36*

4. Isaac Abravanel: Philosopher and Theologian *54*

5. Don Isaac's Fall from Grace in Portugal *76*

PART 2: DON ISAAC ABRAVANEL IN CASTILE (1483–1492)

6. Don Isaac Abravanel Immigrates to Castile *85*

7. Isaac Abravanel's Historical and Literary Approach
to the Books of the Former Prophets *98*

8. The Figure of the Leader in Abravanel's Commentary
on the Former Prophets *118*

9. Don Isaac's Republicanism *138*

10. Success at the Courts of the Catholic Monarchs *156*

PART 3: DON ISAAC ABRAVANEL IN ITALY (1492–1508)

11. Abravanel's Arrival in Naples *167*

12. Commentary on Kings as a Response to the Expulsion *174*

13. Solomon: The Ideal King *186*

14. The Temple: Construction, Glory, Destruction *200*

15. The Military Crisis in Italy at the End of the Fifteenth Century *213*

16. A Defense of Judaism in the Midst of the Storm *219*

17. Messianism 243

18. The Last Years in Venice (1503–1508) 265

Afterword: Don Isaac Abravanel in the Twentieth Century 282

Notes 291

Bibliography 321

Index 337

PREFACE

Don Isaac Abravanel (Abarbanel, Abrabanel, Bravanel, Brauanel, or Braunel) was born in Lisbon in 1437 and died in Venice in 1508. He was active during a period of great changes and crises that shaped not only the course of his own life and thought but also, to a large extent, the face of the early modern era as a whole. This book presents an intellectual biography of Isaac Abravanel while at the same time exposing readers to the great historical drama taking place behind the development of his philosophy and thought. To begin, I would like to briefly acquaint the reader with the man and the subjects that constitute the backbone of the present biography.

Don Isaac's seventy-one-year-long life can be divided geographically into three periods: the Portugal phase (1437–83), the Castile phase (1483–92), and the Italy phase (1492–1508). The present book is similarly divided into three sections, each dedicated to one of these periods. As will be explained, in every phase of his life, Don Isaac Abravanel enjoyed impressive successes. And in every phase, these were snatched away from him by the hand of fortune—or, more precisely, by the tides of history. Isaac Abravanel was born and grew up in Lisbon, in a family of rich Jewish bankers and merchants who had immigrated from Castile to Portugal in the aftermath of the pogroms of 1391. During his forty-six years in Portugal, he became one of the richest Jewish merchant bankers in the kingdom, as well as a community leader and an intellectual who actively participated in both Jewish and Christian discourses in Portugal. He also enjoyed close ties with the nobility and King Afonso V. He served the nobility by giving loans, taxing their lands, and conducting trade. In exchange he received privileges and large estates—as well as the title of don. For many years he gave lessons on Maimonides's *Guide of the Perplexed* from his house in Lisbon. In addition, he wrote several works and carried on correspondence with both Jewish and Christian scholars. If testimonies are to be believed, his views and ideas on various issues were held in high esteem. It seemed that nothing could cast a shadow on this economic, intellectual, and social prosperity. But in 1481, with the death of King Afonso V, his good fortunes would come to an end: Over the course of just two years, the new king, João II, managed to reverse and eliminate all of the achievements of the Abravanel family in Portugal. Don Isaac was forced into exile to Castile.

Arriving in Castile in 1483, Don Isaac, by then no longer a young man, was forced to rebuild his reputation in a new, if nevertheless somewhat familiar, environment. Documentary evidence demonstrates that within two or three years, Don Isaac had once again resumed his role as a community leader and a court Jew—now serving the Castilian nobility. The scope of his writings during this relatively short Castilian period (nine years in total), as well as the sums of money that he lent and the scope of his activity as a tax farmer, all point to his talent for surviving and his exceptional creativity and initiative. For the second time in his life, Don Isaac managed to climb the ladder of Jewish and Christian society, all the while weaving together a unique synthesis of Jewish and Christian thought. But a new and unexpected trial would soon irrevocably change the course of his life—not to mention the lives of thousands of his coreligionists.

In 1492, the Jewish status quo in Castile and Aragon collapsed. King Ferdinand and Queen Isabella signed the expulsion edict, bringing an end to the largest and most important Jewish community in Europe and scattering it across the Mediterranean over the course of a mere three months. Don Isaac did his utmost to avert the harsh edict. But when he realized that the court Jews in Castile and Aragon would be unable to change the decision of the rulers who were later called the Catholic monarchs, he—unlike many other Jewish courtiers—resisted the temptation to convert to Christianity and departed with his family and coreligionists for exile. At age fifty-five, Don Isaac was forced to abandon his historical environs and the cultural and political world in which he and his family had succeeded in establishing their status over generations.

In the last sixteen years of his life on the Italian peninsula, Don Isaac searched for a new home—for himself, his family, and some other members of his community. At first, he was greeted with open arms in the city of Naples. But in 1495, the French invasion of the Italian peninsula and the Italian wars that ensued put an end to his plans to make the southern Italian kingdom his new home. For eight years he wandered between Sicily, Corfu, and the Venetian port city of Monopoli. He finally settled in Venice, where he died in 1508.

The instability that characterized the last years of Don Isaac's life was a fate he shared with many Iberian exiles. But this did not stop his literary creativity, business ventures, or political activity. On the contrary: Don

Isaac composed the vast majority of his exegetical oeuvre under the specter of uncertainty and itinerancy. During these years, Don Isaac succeeded in making a place for himself in the historical and religious consciousness of the Sephardic exiles. His literary activity and political endeavors toward the end of his life made him the hero of these exiles and their descendants, as well as elevating him to the status of a historical and spiritual figure who continues to attract profound interest from Jews and Christians alike. His successes in the face of harsh conditions and international turmoil are an impressive testament to his talents at survival and resistance, the nucleus around which his legendary image as both a leader and a writer was created.

The full and active life led by Isaac Abravanel in no less than four states and four courts (Portugal, Castile, Naples, and Venice) brought him into close contact with great developments, innovations, and crises in the realms of economics, politics, religion, literature, philosophy, and geography. He was not simply a courtier and merchant who participated in the social and economic life of his time. He was also a scholar and an author who responded to the historical shifts that affected his life and that of the Jewish community, both in the Iberian peninsula and, after the expulsion of 1492, in the Jewish communities in Italy and the Sephardic diaspora. It is true that Don Isaac was a wealthy merchant and moneylender who served noblemen and kings alike. But at the same time, he was an intellectual with an extremely diverse education: Jewish, Christian, Islamic, and classical. He was a teacher and exegete who composed an impressive series of commentaries—on scripture, rabbinic literature, and Maimonides's *Guide of the Perplexed*—as well as philosophical tracts.

These are just some of the factors that made Don Isaac one of the most exciting Jewish personalities of the late Middle Ages and the early modern era. The historical line that defined the contours of Don Isaac Abravanel's life begins with the pogroms and mass conversion of 1391 in Castile and Aragon that displaced his father, continues through the internal changes within the Iberian kingdoms that led to the expulsion and forced conversion of the Jews, and reaches to the great Italian crisis that began at the end of the fifteenth century. Abravanel was the son of an immigrant, who himself immigrated time and time again due to events that convulsed the Christian kingdoms in the Iberian and Italian peninsulas throughout the fifteenth century. In this sense, but also in a more positive sense that we will discuss in this book, Don Isaac was the product of a period of flux—a period that brought an end to existing structures and institutions and saw the rise of new world powers and new modes of behavior and thought.

Two different portraits of Don Isaac Abravanel have been etched into Jewish collective memory and the memory of modern scholars, respectively. The first is that of a leader of exiles during the period of the expulsion at the end of the Middle Ages and the end of Iberian Jewish history. The second is that of an innovative Jewish thinker who adopted modern republican views drawn from the literature of humanism and the Renaissance. The gap between the traditional image of Abravanel and his image in modern scholarship points to the difficulty in pigeonholing him in a single period, movement, or role. Don Isaac's loyalty to his religion and community gave him legendary status and turned him into a symbol of Jewish resistance and survival, even in the era of the expulsion. By contrast, his innovative political views and economic success in the courts of Iberia and Italy prompted some scholars to see him as a new sort of Jewish figure, a forerunner of the modern Jew of the eighteenth and nineteenth centuries. The question thus arises: Was Don Isaac a hero who defended Judaism and Jews as the modern era dawned, perhaps protecting Judaism from modernity itself? Or perhaps was he a Jew imbued with the spirit of modernity (or early modernity), who internalized new conceptions and new modes of behavior and expression?

The question of Don Isaac's conservatism or modernity has occupied scholars of Abravanel since the first studies dedicated to him, and even today, scholars continue to debate the issue. In some senses, Don Isaac remains a mystery and a challenge for historians and readers alike. Is this mystery bound up in the complicated period in which he lived, a period of great innovations and discoveries but also of expulsions, forced conversions, discrimination, and severe violence? Do Don Isaac, his life, and his works reflect an ambivalence that challenges our ideas about the relationship between Jewry and modernity? In this book I hope to answer these questions by describing both the course of Abravanel's life and the literature he produced. However, this book also aspires to share with its readers the irresolvable complexity of Don Isaac Abravanel. To this end, I have endeavored throughout to allow different voices to speak from his work as well as from the cultural environment in which they emerged.

In every part of the book, I have tried to understand the unique and exciting connection between Don Isaac's life as a merchant and court Jew and his career as a philosopher, exegete, and writer. My goal has been to combine a description of his economic and literary activity with an understanding of his personality and the trends of his time. My choice not to sharply separate discussions of Don Isaac the merchant and community leader from those of Don Isaac the thinker and author is born of a view that sees the social and literary dimensions of his life and works—even though tensions do exist—as complementary facets of his personality, each one shedding light on and enriching our understanding of the other. It bears mentioning that the information available about the first period in Abravanel's life in Portugal is the most detailed, allowing us to more precisely describe his cultural and social profile at that stage. For this reason, I have put greater emphasis in this first section on sociopolitical issues as a context in which to understand his literary, exegetical, and philosophical writings. These discussions are introduced with a historical overview of Portugal at the end of the fourteenth century and the beginning of the fifteenth. In providing this context, I hope to give the reader a better understanding of the political and cultural framework to which the Abravanel family immigrated and in which they thrived and prospered.

In the second part of the book, I emphasize the literary and social paths traversed by Abravanel in his efforts to overcome his harrowing flight from Portugal and rebuild his status in Castile from scratch. These efforts are the background for Don Isaac's first achievement in this period, a commentary on the Former Prophets that includes innovative historical, political, and literary ideas. The third part of the book is focused on the many commentaries composed by Don Isaac after the expulsion. The reason for this is not just the sheer scope of his writings during this period but also the dearth of documentary evidence that can give us a glimpse into his personal life— with the exception of his autobiographical accounts in the introductions to his works. In our discussion of Don Isaac's commentaries after the expulsion, we will see how his writings combine an aspiration to reestablish his personal status with the goal of reviving Sephardic Jewry as a whole. Adopting the role of a leader, in the last years of his life he composed numerous commentaries and works, many of which included various apologetic defenses of Judaism. At the end of this impressive, sixteen-year-long literary effort, Don Isaac had managed to establish his place as a great apologist for Judaism among the Sephardic exiles. The path leading from a rich and learned merchant in Lisbon to an advocate of Judaism after the expulsion in Italy is the story I wish to tell in this book.

ACKNOWLEDGMENTS

I would like to express my appreciation and thanks to the many amazing people who have supported me through the years in my studies of Don Isaac Abravanel.

First and foremost, I would like to thank Sylvia Fuks Fried and Eugene Sheppard, who agreed to include my book in the prestigious Tauber Institute Series for the Study of European Jewry and afforded me a wonderful opportunity to reach an English-speaking audience.

I would like to express my deepest gratitude to Avi Kallenbach, the translator of this English edition, for using his literary and scholarly talents to craft the perfect translation. I am also most grateful to Adrian Sackson for his wonderful editing work and to Avi Staiman, the CEO of Academic Language Experts, who is responsible for making this translation project possible.

This book was published with the support of the Israel Science Foundation. I am very grateful for this support. I want also to thank the team at the Zalman Shazar Center, who assisted in the preparation of the original Hebrew edition of this book.

I am most grateful to my former dissertation advisor, Menahem Loberbaum, who believed in me from the beginning and helped me develop and grow under his amazing tutelage.

I would like to also express my appreciation to Claude Stuczynski, Ram Ben Shalom, Zeev Gries, Robert Bonfil, Moshe Idel, the late Michele Luzatti, Maurice Kriegel, Giancarlo Lacerenza, Giuseppe Veltri, Javier Castaño, Avraham Melamed, and Menahem Kellner. Their scholarship and discussions have guided me for more than a decade, providing an invaluable contribution to my research.

My thanks and appreciation to my colleagues in Haifa—Gur Alroy, Marcos Silber, and Micha Perry—for assisting me in preparing the Hebrew edition of this book and encouraging me to work on translating it into English.

And finally, I must give my most sincere thanks to my beloved wife, Sophie; my children, Eytan and Yoel; and my parents, Hélène and Edgard. Their daily support, encouragement, and advice are the only reason this book exists.

DON ISAAC ABRAVANEL

Part One

DON ISAAC ABRAVANEL

IN PORTUGAL

(1437–1483)

1 : THE KINGDOM OF PORTUGAL AND THE ABRAVANEL FAMILY

Although his ancestors hailed from the Kingdom of Castile in Spain, our author was born in the metropolis of Lisbon in the Kingdom of Portugal. Due to some persecution, [his family was] impoverished and forced into wanderings that brought them from Spain to Portugal, where he was born in the year [5]197 after Creation and where he was raised to have good discernment, knowledge and fear of the Lord.[1]

This short biographical introduction, penned by the Italian Jewish scholar Barukh Forti (Hezqeto) in 1551, discloses the details of Isaac Abravanel's place and date of birth.[2] We thus know that Isaac Abravanel was born in 1437 in Lisbon to Don Judah Abravanel. Forti also makes vague reference to "persecution" looming in the background in the years leading up to Isaac's birth, a series of dramatic events that forced his family to abandon their ancestral homeland of Seville and seek their fortunes in Portugal. Isaac Abravanel was born and grew up in an era steeped in turbulence and upheaval. As the fourteenth century made way for the fifteenth, new dynasties arose in Iberia, and grievous attacks were perpetrated against Jewish communities throughout Castile and Aragon. This combination of destruction and renewal lies behind Forti's description of the persecution that precipitated the wanderings of the Abravanels "from Spain to Portugal." In many senses, Don Isaac was influenced by historical circumstances set in motion before his birth.

The Rise of the Avis Dynasty and Its Conception of Rule

In 1383, following the death of King Dom Fernando I of Portugal's Dinis dynasty, the king's daughter, Dona Beatriz, and her new husband, King Don Juan I of Castile, were crowned king and queen of Portugal.[3] Many members of the nobility and the urban bourgeoisie opposed this dynastic union, which would spell the end of Portuguese independence. Led by Dom João—head of the Knights of Avis and illegitimate brother of the deceased monarch—the people of Lisbon rose up in revolt against the queen and supporters of the Castilian union. The queen fled and called for her husband's aid. In response, King Don Juan invaded Portugal. However, Dom João and his allies proved themselves on the battlefield, successfully removing the Castilian army from its siege of Lisbon. Beyond the battlefield, Dom João conducted a legal war, endeavoring to have the Cortes (Portugal's assembly of the three estates) confirm him as the rightful king of Portugal, Dom João I (1385–1433). In 1385, after defeating the Castilian army at Aljubarrota, Dom João I was able to declare victory on both the military and the legal fronts—marking the foundation of the Avis dynasty, which would go on to rule Portugal for the next two hundred years. To the best of our knowledge, the Abravanel family arrived in Portugal some decades after the new dynasty's creation.[4] Their integration into the royal court was influenced by the political circumstances surrounding the dynasty's ascent, as well as by the cultural model forged and embodied by its monarchs.

The establishment of the Avis dynasty was facilitated by a large group of learned men, including jurists, who articulated the legality of Dom João I's royal succession, presenting him as a more suitable candidate for the throne than more direct heirs. These scholars found in the new king a patron who, in many ways, embodied the ideal of the learned knight. Dom João I had certainly received an excellent education. At a young age, he composed a treatise on the art of riding, one in a long series of books written by members of the Avis dynasty during the fifteenth century. These books served as a means of consolidating their hold on the throne and were part of the Portuguese literary renaissance of the late Middle Ages and early modern era. Dom João I and his wife, Dona Filipa, had eight children, including five sons: Dom Duarte, Dom Pedro, Dom Henrique, Dom João, and Dom Fernando—collectively known later as *inclita geração* (the illustrious generation). These five men perpetuated the model of the learned ruler embodied by their father, and in action and writing they traced the contours of Portuguese statesmanship, culture, and historical memory for generations to come.[5] In addition to the cultural and political dimensions of the Avis dynasty, Dom João I, his children, and his grandchildren all knew how to secure their rule by cultivating and supporting groups of university scholars. Serving in various legal roles, these men of learning became a sort of clerical aristocracy and often served as agents of the monarchy, supporting royal interests against those of the old nobility.[6] In light of the strong affinity between the Avis dynasty and men of learning, it is no surprise that the well-educated Abravanel family found fertile ground for their scholarly talents on Portuguese soil.

The Avis dynasty's complex relationship with the nobility also played a significant role in Isaac Abravanel's life.[7] The dynasty saw a gradual, and certainly not seamless, transition from feudalism to a more centralized form of monarchy.[8] After his military victory at Aljubarrota in 1385 and his confirmation as king by the Cortes, Dom João I allowed neither his allies from the nobility nor representatives of the church and the people to put checks on his rule or to impose upon him a constitutional monarchy balanced by the power of the Cortes. Moreover, even in the last years of the fourteenth century, Dom João I began reassessing royal properties that had been granted to the nobles in the past. These included lands recently awarded to nobles during the war against Dona Beatriz and the king of Castile. Dom João I sought to reclaim royal lands for the king and thus strengthen his position against powerful nobles with large estates. Naturally, many noblemen opposed the policy. This continued to be a thorny issue throughout the fifteenth century, leading nobles into open conflict with the king and often forcing them flee to Castile, despite having fought the Castilian alliance in the past. These tensions left their mark on Isaac Abravanel's life. Like his noble patrons, he too was eventually forced to flee Portugal for Castile.[9]

During his short reign (1433–38), Dom João's son Dom Duarte continued—and even expanded—his father's policies, passing a law meant to curtail the transfer of royally endowed properties to heirs. According to this new legislation, such properties were not to be bequeathed but rather returned to the king. Ironically, this attempt at asserting monarchical power actually highlighted its limitations: Dom Duarte was forced to waive the law for the high nobles, such as his illegitimate brother Dom Afonso, the Count of Barcelos, who would become the Duke of Bragança (and one of Isaac Abravanel's patrons).[10]

During his reign, Dom Duarte composed a philosophical-ethical treatise entitled *Leal conselheiro* (The loyal counselor), in which he expounded an influential conception of rulership that Isaac Abravanel, like many of his contemporaries, absorbed.[11] According to *Leal conselheiro*, it is not enough for a king to rule and administer his kingdom. Instead, he must also instill loyalty among his subjects—courtiers as well as the people—cultivating proper social, moral, and cultural norms to this end. Through this conduct, the king strengthens the connection between himself and his subjects, forging a mutual, contractual bond based on loyalty. In the introduction to his work, Dom Duarte summarizes this conception of loyalty as follows:

In the name of our Lord Jesus Christ, with His grace and the grace of His most holy mother, our Lady Saint Maria. I begin this tract named *The Loyal Counselor* which Dom Eduarte [Duarte], King of Portugal and Algarve and Lord of Ceuta, has composed with the grace of God by request of the excellent Queen, Dona Leonor, his wife. . . .

If it so pleases you, you may call [this book] *The Loyal Counselor*, because, while I would not dare to guarantee that it gives good advice on every matter, I at least know that everything in it was written with complete faithfulness[12] and sincerity as much as my limited knowledge allowed me. . . . I have conceived it as an "ABC" of loyalty. It was written primarily for the lords and [the members of their] entourage who in [their ignorance of] the theory of these [loyal] deeds, are to be considered like children when compared to sages. And indeed, like children, proper instruction [begins] with the ABC. More precisely: the letter A can be understood as the faculties and passions which every one of us possesses; the letter B can be understood as the great good which the followers of virtue and goodness receive as recompense; [and] the letter C can be understood as the rectification of our evils and sins. . . . Since in this time, God, by His mercy, has granted this virtue [of loyalty] to the lords and servants, husbands and wives of this kingdom in so perfect a measure that I neither know nor hear of another [kingdom] in which it is exercised more or with greater perfection, and since among [these people], God, by His good grace, bestowed upon me kingship, therefore, I feel myself bound to conserve and keep this virtue for [the benefit of] all, and for you, [my wife].[13]

In 1438, a year after Isaac Abravanel's birth, Dom Duarte passed away. While he had held his brother Dom Pedro in the highest esteem, even relying on him for political counsel more than once, Dom Duarte did not name him successor. Instead Queen Dona Leonor of Aragon was appointed regent until Dom Duarte's six-year-old son, Dom Afonso, came of age.[14] This decision was fraught with controversy and marked the fault line between two opposing political approaches. On one side was Dom Pedro, considered the political genius among Dom João I's five sons. Dom Pedro represented the continuation of the policies of his father and brother Dom Duarte—strengthening the power of the monarchy against the nobility and adopting a less accommodating and more conservative approach toward the crusades in Morocco led by his brother, Dom Henrique.[15] Opposing him were supporters of Dom Henrique's crusades (considered a continuation of the Reconquista, the wresting of the Iberian lands from the hands of the Muslims). Among these were the majority of the nobles, including the Duke of Bragança—an outspoken critic of the king's centralized monarchism and a defender of aristocratic interests.

After Dom Duarte's death these two camps vied over the regency. Dom Henrique and the Duke of Bragança supported the queen. Dom Pedro; his brother, Dom João; and the urban elites in Lisbon maintained that the right to confirm a regent should be returned to the Cortes. After a decade (1438–48) of alternating conflict and compromise between the two sides, the Duke of Bragança—along with the young king, Dom Afonso V (1448–81), and a group of nobles—went to war against Dom Pedro. At the battle of Alfarrobeira on May 19, 1449, they routed his army, killing him and most of his men. The chronicler Rui de Pina recounts that shortly after the battle, riots and plundering broke out in the Jewish quarter of Lisbon.[16] The young king intervened and arrived to punish the perpetrators.[17]

Portuguese historians are divided over the extent to which this victory can be considered the nobility's reaction to the centralization policies initiated by the founder of the Avis dynasty and his successors, Dom Duarte and Dom Pedro. Many modern historians have portrayed Dom Afonso V as a monarch who, more than any of his predecessors, pursued a policy based on appeasing the high nobles by giving them privileges and favors.[18] While this policy certainly secured his rule, it also empowered the nobles (mainly those related to the king by blood) and afforded them a greater measure of independence. The fact that Dom Afonso V rose to the throne as a friend of the nobility and a supporter of Reconquista in Morocco and North Africa would significantly dictate his policies during his thirty-year reign—and especially his relationship with the Dukes of Bragança, Dom Afonso and Dom Fernando. It was during the same years that Isaac Abravanel was beginning to make a name for himself in Portugal. Sponsored and protected by the house of Bragança, Don Isaac naturally aligned himself with the political agenda of the nobility, whose support significantly contributed to his success while Dom Afonso V reigned. However, after

Dom Afonso V died in 1481, he was succeeded by João II, who was far less accommodating toward the nobility. Don Isaac and his family suddenly found themselves backing the wrong side and were forced to flee for their lives.[19]

However, before moving on to discuss Portuguese Jewry, which flourished during these years, we must first focus on Dom Pedro's important literary legacy, which would influence Isaac Abravanel's writings. Between 1417 and 1429, Dom Pedro—in collaboration with the monk Frei João Verba—composed *Livro da vertuosa benfeytoria* (The book of good virtues).[20] The book includes Portuguese translations of Seneca's Stoic treatise *De beneficiis* (On favors [or benefits]) and other classical and medieval works, a discussion of the nature of giving and receiving favors, and an exploration of the social bonds they forge. Continuing the conception developed in Dom Duarte's *Leal conselheiro*, Dom Pedro and Verba described human relations (specifically, those between the monarch and his subjects) as relations that ideally imitate God's bestowal of favors on mankind. Dom Pedro defined two types of social bounds: the giver, who gives freely and liberally, and the receiver, who seeks favor and repays the benevolence bestowed upon him. This model of benevolence is meant to turn the relationship between ruler and subject into one of contractual and mutual responsibility. Explaining why he composed the book, Dom Pedro writes:

> The wicked error and guilt to which our natures fell in the beginning is the reason for our propensity toward ignorance and malice. For this reason, our deeds sometimes lack the virtuous perfections with which they should be endowed. Already in antiquity, sages were aware of this flaw, and therefore exerted great effort to provide men with teachings which would help them [in this regard]. Among them was the great moral philosopher Seneca, who observed the errors to which men are prone in deeds of benefaction. Indeed, many do not perform these actions as they should, and do not know how to give favors, how to receive them, or how to give thanks for them. As a consequence, many are responsible for severely devaluing deeds of benefaction. Endowed with a great desire to correct this state of affairs so that a deed so noble and so perfect as benefaction would not vanish, he composed in Latin seven short books to teach men who wish to perform deeds of benefaction rationally. Taking these sentences and compositions [of Seneca], which are brief, ob-

scure, and written in an obsolete language, I have endeavored to combine them with other matters which were necessary [to add] for the understanding of the subject. Thus, I created a new compilation profitable for me and for all those who are obliged to wield power but should nonetheless do good works.[21]

In his Portuguese and Hebrew writings, Isaac Abravanel liberally quotes Seneca alongside medieval sources. As we will see below, Don Isaac adopted the style and literary tastes of Dom Pedro.

The Jewish Community in Portugal

The Jewish presence in Portugal began with the kingdom's formation from the territories taken from the Muslims in the Reconquista, a process that extended from the mid-ninth to the mid-thirteenth century. During the reign of King Dom Afonso Henriques (1140–85), who looked favorably on the arrival of Jewish immigrants from Castile and Al-Andalus, Jews lived in Lisbon and other cities such as Porto, Santarem, and Beja. In broad terms, the development of Jewish communities in Portugal was fueled by the monarchs' need to settle the new territories acquired during the Reconquista and by waves of Jewish immigration. Jews sought refuge in Portugal when conditions deteriorated in neighboring kingdoms, arriving from Al-Andalus with the Almohad invasion in the 1240s and from Castile and Aragon following the massacres of 1391. The monarchs' financial interests also influenced their favorable policies toward the Jews: from the late thirteenth century, Jews were subjected to an impressive array of taxes—ranging from poll taxes and property taxes to food taxes, military taxes, royal taxes, and more.

In the mid-twelfth century Jews began to serve as financiers and doctors in the royal court. They had the privilege of a *rabi-mor* (a chief rabbi of sorts) who served as the main representative of the king's Jews specifically in matters related to taxes and law. In exchange for these services rendered to the king, Jewish courtiers were granted properties and privileges denied to their coreligionists. The members of the Ibn Yahya family (whose name was Negro in Portuguese) dominated the position of rabi-mor until the end of the fifteenth century. Due to their lofty status, Jewish families who served the king or nobles would intervene in royal politics, choosing sides in succession crises and political disputes. This Jewish interference in court politics often served various political actors as a pretext for launching anti-Jewish campaigns.

By the fourteenth century, Jewish communities were spread throughout most of the kingdom. The Jewish community in Lisbon, the largest in the kingdom, numbered approximately 1,000 individuals in the fifteenth century. Jews constituted 3 percent of the Portuguese population, and their total population was between 22,000 and 30,000.[22] Throughout the thirteenth, fourteenth, and fifteenth centuries, the relationship between Jewish communities and the crown and Christian society as a whole was enshrined in law, specifically in the *Ordenaçoens do senhor rey D. Affonso V* (The ordinances of Afonso V). Promulgated in 1446, this was a codex compiled from royal decrees from the reign of Afonso II (1211–23) to King Dom Duarte (1433–38). However, alongside these positive trends were the opposing agendas of ecclesiastical powers—especially the Franciscans and Dominicans—whose activities compounded the negative repercussions of anti-Jewish regulations formulated in the Fourth Lateran Council, in 1215. These tendencies, when combined with the anti-Jewish predilections of certain kings, could lead to a deterioration in the quality of Jewish life, such as the curtailment of Jews' right to conduct trade or the imposition of limitations on their settlement. That being said, it should be borne in mind that laws do not necessarily reflect reality. The clergy in fact complained throughout the fourteenth and fifteenth centuries that anti-Jewish regulations were not effectively implemented, let alone rigorously enforced. Thus, despite real challenges, the status of Portuguese Jews until the end of the fifteenth century was far superior to that of their coreligionists in Castile and Aragon.

The Jews of Portugal worked as farmers, craftsmen, tailors, cobblers, ironworkers, metalworkers, and textile workers as well as professionals such as doctors, merchants, moneylenders, and tax farmers. This wide spectrum of professions is indicative of the extent to which Jews were integrated into the Portuguese economy and society. The historian Maria José Pimenta Ferro Tavares has shown that alongside this professional diversity, Portuguese Jews were particularly prominent in certain important trades, such as metalworking (producing weaponry), tanning, and the textile and clothing industries.[23] Many Jews also worked as manual laborers for Christian nobles or local authorities. Some even built ships and cannons. However, if this broad spectrum represents integration, it also reflects unambiguous social gaps: most Jews worked in agriculture, crafts, or local trade and were therefore subject to Jewish laws and taxes. By contrast, a number of families (the Ibn Yahyas, Latams, Abravanels, Palaçanos, and others) worked in international trade, medicine, and money lending. By virtue of their direct relationships with the king, nobles, and urban economic elites, they enjoyed certain privileges and exemptions.

Starting at the end of the fourteenth century, a number of factors converged to facilitate the rise of Christian and Jewish merchant bankers. The development of maritime trade with northern Europe, North Africa, and Italy over the course of the fifteenth century; the crusades led by the Avis dynasty in North Africa; the Portuguese discoveries on the African coast; and the settlement of Italian, Flemish, and Catalan merchants in Lisbon and Porto all played a part.[24] At the same time, the anti-Jewish riots throughout Castile and Aragon in 1391 prompted wealthy Jewish families working in trade, money lending, and tax farming—such as the houses of Latam, Abravanel, and Palaçano—to immigrate to Portugal. Upon their arrival, these families made inroads into maritime trade, sometimes in collaboration with foreign Christian merchants. This led to tensions between local Portuguese merchants and their foreign competitors, both Jewish and Christian.[25] If we also consider the traditional services that court Jews rendered to the king and nobles, and the need of the latter for loans and tax collection, we can understand the impressive economic and social rise of certain Jewish families in the fifteenth century.

An echo of the integration of Castilian Jewish families into Portugal's international maritime trade is preserved in an interesting and important document from 1453. Don Judah Abravanel, Isaac's father, was asked (apparently by Dom Afonso V) to submit (in collaboration with another Castilian Jew) a recommendation for a royal monetary policy that would combat the devaluation of the Portuguese currency and correct its detrimental effects on the population.[26] The document proposes the adoption of three main measures: to prohibit, as much as possible, the export of valuable Portuguese currencies (that is, silver and gold); to prevent Italian merchants, particularly those from Genoa, from settling in the kingdom and conducting trade therein; and to outlaw "superfluous trades such as silk-working embroidery, and expensive shoe-making which result in a bad behavior and lead the people to disorder and unnecessary expenses."[27] Toward the end of the document, the two authors assert that the wealth of Portugal and the king's personal wealth are linked to the well-being of the people and the just management of the kingdom. In their opinion, extensive social inequality should not be permitted, as it detracts from the wealth of the people and mars their relationship of trust with their monarch. The king's wealth is based on the relative wealth of the entire nation; his financial prosperity is responsible for maintaining the proper relationships between the kingdom's different components (the king, the nobility, and the people). This is reminiscent of Dom Duarte's and Dom Pedro's conception of the relationship between the people and the ruler, mentioned above.

This rare document highlights the role played by Castilian Jewish families in the Portuguese economy in the mid-fifteenth century and especially the status of the Abravanel family. Their recommendations attest to the knowledge, extensive trade experience, and broad economic worldview of Castilian Jews. The document also reveals an extensive network of contacts and a deep familiarity with economic and political figures active both in the kingdom and outside of it. We can also assume that Judah Abravanel and his friend were consulted precisely because their connections and economic expertise were known to the royal court, nobles, and merchants. It can be argued (based on this source and other details that we will discuss below) that the Abravanel family, like other affluent Jewish families, benefited from financial experience and economic knowledge that gave them an advantage in their dealings with the nobility, the king, and their competitors—foreign and local Christian merchants. The recommendation to forbid the activity of foreign merchants in Portugal shows that the members of these families also sought to improve their position vis-à-vis other merchants, identifying their own interests with those of society as a whole. While the king did not ultimately accept it, this bold proposal exhibits the power enjoyed by Jewish families in the Portuguese economy and court in the fifteenth century.

The Immigration of the Abravanel Family to Portugal

In his first work, ʿAteret zeqenim (Crown of elders) written in the mid- or late 1460s, Isaac Abravanel introduces his father as "a valiant man, of mighty deeds, the prince Don Judah Abravanel, a pure Sephardi."[28] In the autobiographical introduction to his commentary on the Former Prophets, which he wrote almost twenty years later, he portrays his connection with his father (who had passed away in the meantime) as part of a house whose ancient roots stretch back to the house of King David himself:

> I am the man [Lam 3:1] Isaac, son of a valiant man who has done mighty deeds [2 Sam 23:20], his name is great in Israel [Ps 76:2], Sir Judah son of Samuel son of Joseph son of Judah of the Abravanel family, all of them were leaders of the children of Israel [Num 13:3],

from the seed of Jesse the Bethlehemite [1 Sam 16:1], from the house of David prince and commander of the people [Is 55:4]. May the memory of my father be blessed.[29]

In both cases, Isaac Abravanel celebrates the status of his father and their ancestors. However, he deftly evades the crisis lurking behind this formidable lineage and the continuity of the Abravanels' social position. Forti's 1551 biography of Don Isaac provides a glimpse into a family rift that was associated with Don Judah's move from Seville, Castile, to Lisbon, Portugal. Forti writes: "Due to some persecution [they] were impoverished and forced into wanderings that brought them from Spain to Portugal."[30] In Abravanel's commentary on the twelve Minor Prophets (on the verse "The Lord also shall save the tents of Judah first, that the glory of the house of David and the glory of the inhabitants of Jerusalem be not magnified above Judah" [Zech. 12:7]), we see again how the departure of the Abravanels from Seville marked the end of the family's ancient presence in the city. According to Abravanel, his family had resided in Seville ever since the destruction of the First Temple:

> The House of David, mentioned here, has been interpreted by the exegetes as referring to the seed of David and his family. And R. Abraham Ibn Ezra wrote: "House of David"—until this day in Baghdad in the Muslim kingdom, they are the exilarches . . . and Benjamin [of Tudela] wrote in his *Travels,* that he saw them. He did not write that they were a large family but rather a few exceptional men. And in Spain also, after the destruction of the First Temple, R. Isaac Ibn Ghiyyat wrote that two families from the House of David arrived there—the Daud family . . . and the Abravanel family which settled in Seville, of which is my humble family.[31]

What then caused such a well-entrenched Sevillian family to abandon its home? The "persecution" referred to by Forti, while chronologically close to the riots and persecution of 1391, is not identical to it. In a document dated 1388, Isaac Abravanel's grandfather, Samuel, is referred to with a Christian name, Juan Sanchez de Sevilla, and described as the chief treasurer (*tesorero mayor*) of King Don Enrique III (1390–1406).[32] Scholars have shown that even before his conversion to Christianity, Samuel Abravanel was a prominent financier in Seville. It seems that he was driven to conversion out of fear of losing his properties and status in the wake of the religious and social pressures exerted on Spanish Jews in the years leading up to the riots of 1391. It did not help that Samuel may have grown disillusioned with the Spanish Jewish communities in Castile, following a successful plot (hatched by Jewish conspirators) to have Samuel's fellow Jewish financier, Joseph Pichon, executed as an informer.[33]

These are the known reasons for his conversion. In *A History of the Jews in Christian Spain*, the famous historian Yitzhak Baer was quick to condemn Samuel for his actions:

> Samuel Abravanel . . . seem[s] to have anticipated that trouble lay ahead and saved [himself] while it was still possible to arrange such matters conveniently and advantageously. A new type of apostate now emerged. Previously, Jewish apostates had entered their new faith as penitents. . . . Now, change of religion was prompted by political considerations.[34]

Alongside Baer's explanation of the conversion, we have another document that casts a somewhat different light on Samuel's complex personality. The document was written by Rabbi Menahem ben Zerah, who experienced well-nigh intolerable conditions in Alcalá de Henares during the civil war between Dom Pedro and Dom Enrique, who fought over the crown of Castile. He explains how Samuel Abravanel saved him and supported him when he settled in Toledo:

> The esteemed Don Samuel Abravanel, may God protect him, a resident of Seville, helped me escape the upheaval . . . and I found him to be a man who loves learning, patronizes scholars, is concerned for their welfare and who, whenever he is relieved from the turbulence of the times, is possessed of a desire to delve into the works of the famous authors and philosophers.[35]

However, immediately after these accolades, the author adopts a cooler tone, implicitly criticizing Samuel's lax religiosity:

> And then I saw that [Jews] who walked in the court of the king, may his grace be exalted, served as a shield and shelter for the rest of their people, each according to his rank and position. Indeed, in the turbulence of the times and the enjoyment of luxuries and unnecessary things, they vacillate in their [observance] of obligatory commandments, especially emissaries, servants, and those who attend

to the king. And due to my love of the esteemed [Don Samuel], I exceeded myself, making myself the target of teachers and great ones . . . and for him I have composed a book and have called it *Tsedah laderekh*.[36]

In this testimony, Samuel Abravanel is cast as a complex and ambivalent character, his loyalties torn between the royal court and the Jewish community.

In any case, hiding behind the name Samuel Abravanel—whom Isaac lists in a family pedigree presented in his commentary on the Former Prophets (1483–84)—is a story of a family drama and a difficult past. Even if there was no direct connection between Samuel's conversion and the religious persecutions of 1391, historical memory could not help but associate the apostasy of a socially and economically prominent Jew with the mass conversions to Christianity that took place during the massacres of 1391 and in their aftermath.[37] The crisis of the Abravanel family in Seville in the late fourteenth century should, therefore, be seen as part of the broader crisis that befell Castilian Jewry, as a result of an unstable monarchy in the second half of the century, the growing use of incitement and violence against Jews as an accepted gambit by competing political camps, and the social transformations taking place within Jewish communities.

At the end of the fourteenth century, the house of Abravanel was split in two. The Christian branch remained in Castile, while the Jewish branch emigrated to Portugal. This divide, as we will see, had considerable repercussions on Isaac Abravanel's historical outlook. Even if Abravanel covered up the details of his divided family—and in his first book even called his father "a pure Sephardi," despite his grandfather's apostasy—there is no reason to doubt the basic historicity of his account. Isaac Abravanel belonged to an ancient Iberian Jewish family that, over the centuries, delineated as its areas of expertise trade, money lending, and tax farming and that developed a sociocultural profile based on literary education, patronage, and community leadership.

The Abravanels were "forced into wanderings that brought them from Spain to Portugal."[38] These words, written by Forti in 1551, are the only record of Judah Abravanel's immigration with his family from Seville to Lisbon. The first texts documenting the presence of the Abravanel family in Lisbon date back to the 1430s.[39] In them, Don Judah Abravanel is featured as the financier of the "Infante" Dom Fernando, brother of King Dom Duarte, who died in captivity after the Portuguese defeat at the battle of Tangier in 1437.[40] Such documents show that immigration to Portugal did not change the Abravanel family's trade or sociocultural profile. The recommendations sent by Judah Abravanel and his coauthor to Dom Afonso V in 1453 reveal, as we saw above, not only extensive economic knowledge but also philosophical and literary proficiency.[41] All in all, the sense of continuity that Don Isaac emphasizes again and again in the presentation of his pedigree is not unfounded. Both his grandfather Samuel and his father, Judah, were figures who consciously combined economic acumen with literary knowledge. Like Don Isaac, they were courtiers and merchants, as well as community leaders. However, Don Isaac's family legacy was not free from blemishes. He well knew the familial and historical crises that had dislodged his family from Castile and forced them to seek their fortunes in Portugal.

Abravanel's Integration into the Royal Court and International Trade

As we have seen, Isaac Abravanel's birth and childhood in Lisbon were closely intertwined with the upheavals and persecution that befell Castilian Jewry in the fourteenth century, the political struggles surrounding the accession of Dom Afonso V, and the development of his family's social and economic position upon arriving in Portugal. However, besides this context attested by historical records, the childhood of Isaac Abravanel—inasmuch as his education and social profile were concerned—can be patched together only from an examination of the literary and financial documents he wrote in his adulthood. What did Don Isaac study? Who educated him? And how did he enter the business of his father and other relatives? Only by collecting references from later documents and sources can we answer these questions. And even though we know very little, we can sketch with broad strokes the social and cultural curriculum of the boy who would grow up to be Don Isaac Abravanel.

In extant contemporaneous economic documents, Don Isaac's name first appears in the mid-1460s, then more frequently in the 1470s and 1480s.[42] Thus, for example, in two letters penned in 1463 and 1464, respectively, the king confirms Abravanel's privilege not to wear the Jewish badge and his right to ride a donkey, lodge in Christian inns, and carry a weapon. In the first letter, Isaac is described as the merchant (*mercador*) of "Dom Fernando Count of Guimarães, our much beloved nephew, who has requested this favor for him." In the second letter he is described as "our [the king's] servant (*noso seruidor*)." In 1472, the king confirmed Abravanel's right to live outside of Lisbon's Jewish quarter "in compensation for his special services (*especiaees serviços*). . . . [W]e wish that henceforth, he shall enjoy and benefit from all the honors, privileges, liberties and franchises which the Christian neighbors and inhabitants of this city [Lisbon] enjoy and should enjoy." Eight years later, in another letter, Dom Afonso V ratified the Duke of Bragança's gift to Abravanel of an estate in the city of Queluz, near Lisbon, "with all its lands." The letter describes the reason for the gift: "Dom Fernando Duke of Bragança and Guimarães . . . in view of the many services (*muitos serviços*) he has received and hopes to receive in the future from Isaac Abravanel his servant (*suy servydor*), wished to reward him."[43] These three letters show that Isaac Abravanel was not just a member of the Duke of Bragança's court. He was also connected—directly or through the duke—to the king. In other words, in exchange for financial services rendered to the duke and the king from about 1460 to 1481, Isaac Abravanel was an important participant in the alliance between Dom Fernando and the king. This was the same alliance that had paved Dom Afonso V's path to the throne. Isaac's brother, Samuel, and Samuel's son also appear in contemporaneous documents. They are described as the financiers of other prominent nobles during Dom Afonso V's reign: the Dukes of Viseu, Dom Henrique and Dom Diogo.

What are the special services referred to in these documents? They could refer, among other things, to the large loans made to the nobles and the king. For example, in 1430 Isaac's father provided several loans, totaling 97,100 *reais*, to Dom Henrique.[44] In 1478 Don Isaac with Gedalia Palaçano lent the king 3,834,615 reais.[45] We also know of a loan of 950,000 reais made to the Dukes of Bragança and Viseu in the early 1480s.[46]

To complete this picture, it is important to note that the members of the Abravanel family were given tax-farming agreements for noble and even royal domains, sometimes in exchange for providing loans. For example, in 1454 Judah Abravanel, Isaac's father, appears alongside prominent merchant families like Beleagua and Lomellini on such an agreement for the king's domains. Twenty years later, in 1477, we find the signatures of Isaac Abravanel and Moshe Latam on similar agreements with the king.[47]

However, the financial documents bearing the Abravanel name are not limited to agreements with the king and the nobility. Other documents tie the house of Abravanel to various groups of foreign merchants (Italians, Flemings, Catalans, and others) engaged in international trade.[48] Along with the Italian merchants—at first mostly from Genova, and later from

Tuscany—the Abravanels also participated in the trade relations with North Africa and the Madeira Islands, as well as with Flanders and northern Italy. These trade relations were facilitated by groups of merchants who could raise the capital necessary to transfer goods by sea. Because of this system, we sometimes find the name Abravanel alongside the names of prominent families of international merchants, such as Flemings and Genoese. Even though it is difficult to know the extent to which Don Isaac was personally involved in these maritime ventures, we see that he maintained contact with these countries, participating in international trade and developing partnerships with foreign merchants who lived in Lisbon (as well as their partners in Italy and Flanders). Thus, for example, we know that Isaac's father had a direct relationship with the representative of the Portuguese merchants in Flanders in the late 1460s and early 1470s.[49] Likewise, we know that Don Isaac had an account with the Florentine bank of Francesco and Bernardo Cambini in the 1470s.[50] From these documents, we can conclude that Isaac Abravanel was involved not only in the management of the wealth and properties of the house of Bragança and the king himself but also in the financial and trade ties prevailing between Portugal, Flanders, North Africa, and Italy.

It is notable that in financial documents bearing Isaac Abravanel's name, he is associated with a number of different groups: the Abravanel family; other wealthy Jewish families (the Palaçanos, Latams, Ibn Yahyas, and others); families of international merchants in Lisbon, Flanders, and northern and central Italy; and the courtiers and servants of the nobility and the monarchy. Isaac Abravanel's integration into these circles indicates, without a doubt, his economic and social rise in Portugal during the 1460s and 1470s. On the one hand, Don Isaac's meteoric rise was the perpetuation of his family's business; but on the other hand, it was based on new relationships he forged with merchants and aristocratic families.

In poems from the period that inveigh against Don Isaac and his wealth, we see that he was generally identified with the other members of his class. For example, Isaac Abravanel's name appears alongside those of members of the Jewish economic elite in the following poem, included in a collection of Portuguese poetry from the fifteenth and sixteenth centuries titled *Cancioneiro Geral*, edited by the poet Garcia de Resende and printed in 1516:

These are the men filled with pains,
Useless to negate it.

They are the eight great sirs of this anxiety.
The first is Latam,
The second Samuel,
The third Salomon.
The fourth will be Fayam,
The fifth Abravanel.
In love [with wealth] are also Palaçano
Gualyte and Jaçee.[51]

These stanzas are part of Resende's larger poetic composition on the pains (*cuidar*) and sighs (*soupirar*) of love. In this poem, he describes the different psychological and physiological effects of love on men and women, distinguishing between pain (an internal state of suffering and anxiety) and sighs (which create the possibility of an outpouring of the soul). In this excerpt, the eight rich Jews serve as examples of unrefined people whose love is expressed only in the form of anxiety and is directed not at a beloved other or salvation, but rather at base needs such as bread (*pano*), annuities (*arrendamento*), and percentages (*perçento*). In contrast to this caricature of the Jew whose love is characterized by pain and anxiety in pursuit of wealth, Resende presents the sighs of love as proof of sincerity and humanity:

He who sighs
Sighs only out of pangs of love,
And the sighs which come out of the soul
Never lie.[52]

2 : ISAAC ABRAVANEL AND IBERIAN COURT CULTURE

While the economic documents discussed in the previous chapter provide important information about Isaac Abravanel's financial and commercial dealings, they say nothing about his own thoughts on his status and activities. Luckily, four personal letters penned by Isaac Abravanel—one in Portuguese and three in Hebrew—are extant, and they shed important light on the development of Abravanel's sociocultural outlook as he gradually found his place in his father's dealings and relationships with the royal court and groups of international merchants.[1] The letters—especially those in Hebrew—also highlight the Jewish aspects of Isaac Abravanel's socioeconomic rise in the 1460s and 1470s. They show how an ideal of Jewish leadership was developed by affluent Jewish merchants in the second half of the century in the context of the Iberian peninsula's cultural atmosphere at the time, drawing inspiration from its literary models of leadership.

The move away from the external elements of Isaac Abravanel's life evinced in his financial records to the internal perspective provided by these personal letters necessarily raises the issue of Don Isaac's literary knowledge—in Hebrew, as well as in European languages such as Portuguese, Castilian, and Latin. While little is known about Don Isaac's educational upbringing (apart from some mentions of a relationship with Rabbi Joseph ben Avraham Hayun), the letters allow us to partially reconstruct the Iberian literary atmosphere in which Isaac flourished.[2] We have already seen how Rabbi Menahem ben Zerah praised the literary knowledge of Don Isaac's grandfather, Samuel Abravanel. We also have seen evidence of Judah Abravanel's literary education in his recommendation to the king about royal monetary policy. But despite the impressive legacy of Abravanel's ancestors, none of them was particularly renowned for their literary accomplishments, and it was only Isaac who would become famous as a writer. As we broach the subject of Don Isaac's letters, we will see for the first time one of the qualities that distinguished Isaac from the other members of his family—that is, his unique literary capacity and sensitivity.

In this chapter, I will begin with Abravanel's Portuguese letter, written in

1470 or 1471 and addressed to the Count (Conde) of Faro.[3] The letter was included in an impressive sixteenth- century literary manuscript anthology featuring essays and letters from the Iberian peninsula's most prestigious authors and political figures in the fifteenth and early sixteenth centuries.[4] The compiler of this anthology titled the document "A Letter That Abravanel Sent to the Count of Faro Concerning the Death of the Count of Odemira, His Father-in-Law." The fact that a Christian copyist was willing to include a letter from a Jew in his collection is testament to the high esteem in which its literary quality was held.

The Count of Faro was Dom Afonso, uncle of the third Duke of Bragança, Dom Fernando—the same duke who awarded Don Isaac an estate in Queluz in exchange for his "many services."[5] In the years following King Afonso V's victory over Dom Pedro, the young king awarded Dom Afonso the title Count of Faro in gratitude for his support. The count's deceased father-in-law was Dom Sancho de Noronha, Count of Odemira. Dom Sancho was known for his participation in the Portuguese crusades in northern Morocco between 1425 and 1465. Moreover, he was one of King Afonso V's most prominent supporters during his war with Dom Pedro, for which he received important titles and offices (for example, the military governorship of Ceuta, in northern Morocco). The fact that Dom Sancho's daughter was wed to the Duke of Bragança's son shows that Don Isaac served a well-defined group of nobles who particularly benefited from Afonso V's reign.

As Don Isaac was an important figure in the economic administration of the properties and wealth of the house of Bragança, his letter—filled with praise of the Count of Faro's father-in-law—is not surprising. However, besides pointing to Abravanel's social and political affiliations, this rare document illustrates another aspect of the Abravanel's relationship with the Portuguese aristocracy: his affinity for their culture and literature. The letter highlights the literary context of Abravanel's relationship with the Portuguese aristocracy, as well as providing some insight into Don Isaac's learning.

Literary Context

The professed purpose of the letter is to console Dom Afonso for the loss of his father-in-law, Dom Sancho, who had died just a few days earlier. The letter belongs to the literary genre of consolation (*consolatio*), a popular style during the Renaissance. The genre has its roots in antiquity, hailing from the classical literatures of Greece and Rome. While the genre was never forgotten in the Middle Ages, the renaissance of Latin literary learning would push it onto center stage in the thirteenth century (and even more so in the fourteenth and fifteenth centuries), and it was given expression in consolatory letters, eulogies, and ethical essays composed during the period. It is true that within the consolatory genre, certain Judeo-Christian texts played their part as well. For example, the theme of consolation plays a major role in the Hebrew Bible (for example, in Job, Isaiah, Ezekiel, and Psalms) and is featured in the New Testament and patristic literature. Nevertheless, even if biblical and Christian sources informed consolatory literature during the Renaissance, it was the writings of Cicero (43–104 BCE) and Seneca (4–65 CE) that proved most influential.[6] The appearance of their names in Abravanel's Portuguese letter to the Count of Faro is, therefore, far from surprising.

In the third book of Cicero's *Tusculanae Disputationes,* Cicero conceives of philosophy as foundation of the consolation rhetoric, portraying it as the cure for the passions of the soul:

> Seeing, Brutus, that we are made up of soul and body, why is it that for the care and maintenance of the body there has been devised an art which is so useful that its very discovery is attributed to the immortal gods ... while conversely, the art of healing for the soul (*medicina animi*) has not been felt so deeply before its discovery, nor has it been studied so closely after becoming known. ... Assuredly there is an art of healing the soul—I mean philosophy. ...
>
> For pity, envy, exultation, joy, all of these the Greeks refer to as "diseases," that is, movements of the soul which are not obedient to reason. ... For the soul which suffers from some disease—as I have said, the philosophers apply the term disease to these disordered movements—is no more sound than the body which is diseased. It follows that wisdom is a sound condition of the soul (*sanitas animi*), unwisdom on the other hand, unsound health (*insanitas*) and also aberration of mind (*insania, dementia*).[7]

Having thus defined philosophy as a medicine, or a means of restoring rational balance to an ailing soul, Cicero delineates at the end of book 3 the relationship between rhetoric and philosophy, defining consolation discourse as a literary method for treating various patients depending on their condition:

These, therefore, are the duties of the consolers (*officia consolantium*): to root out distress, or allay it, or diminish it as much as possible, or stop its progress and not allow it to extend further or divert it elsewhere. There are some who think it the sole duty of a consoler to insist that the evil has no existence at all, as is the view of Cleanthes; some, like the Peripatetics, favor the lesson that evil is not serious. . . . There are some too in favor of concentrating all these ways of administering consolation—for one man is influenced in one way, one in another. . . . But it is necessary in dealing with diseases of the soul, just as much as in dealing with bodily diseases, to choose the proper time.[8]

Cicero proposes treating each philosophical view of suffering as a distinct rhetorical tool, each one being administered by the consoler to his patient at the proper time. Thus, he defines the proper attitude toward different philosophical approaches not as an issue of abstract theory, but rather in terms of their rhetorical and practical effects. No opinion should be rejected based on its verity. Rather, each approach should be properly implemented according to rhetorical principles that dictate which view to administer to which individual and under what circumstances.

In his famous *Ad Lucilium Epistulae Morale* (Moral letters to Lucilius), the Stoic philosopher and playwright Seneca developed a conception of consolation that had a significant influence on philosophers and authors in Abravanel's period. Seneca calls for a sharp distinction between those things that are independent of man and those that depend solely on him, especially activity and the passions of one's soul. For Seneca, purifying the realm of the soul and separating it from the realm of natural events goes hand in hand with the cultivation of literary, moral, and philosophical abilities, allowing a person to preserve her soul from external influences. Molding the soul's disposition to face the blows of fate is an integral part of the arts of rhetoric and literature: it is chiefly through speech that the soul becomes aware of its own internal causality. In the following excerpt, Seneca applies this principle to death:

And what difference does it make how soon you depart from a place which you must depart from sooner or later? We should strive, not to live long, but to live rightly; for to achieve long life you have need of Fate [*fatum*] only, but for right living you need the soul [*animus*].

> A life is really long if it is a full life; but fullness is not attained until the soul has rendered to itself its proper Good, that is, until it has assumed control over itself.[9]

Fear of death is a typical example of conflating the physical with the psychological. In his letter, Seneca teaches Lucilius to separate these two spheres: through this act of demarcation, the soul can reclaim itself and thus attain perfection.

In summary, the literary and philosophical message of Cicero and Seneca, the conception that so captivated the hearts and minds of Abravanel's contemporaries, is as follows: after the soul has been plunged into insanity by the heavy blows of fortune, it can regain self-control through rhetorical means. Abravanel was not only well versed in the intricacies of commerce and banking. He was also intimately familiar with the new literary norms of early humanism, a literary movement first developed in the fourteenth century in Italy and then in the Iberian peninsula.[10]

Isaac Abravanel's Use of Consolatory Rhetoric

Don Isaac's Portuguese letter is a paragon of early Iberian humanistic writing, and its historical importance cannot be overstated: this letter is one of the earliest (if not the first) examples of a composition written by a Jew with a command of the new style of the humanistic epistolary writing.[11] Just as economic records attest to Don Isaac's integration into the politics of the royal court and his participating in international commerce and trade, this letter is evidence of his integration into the court's culture and his adoption of Iberian literary styles.

Don Isaac's letter to the Count of Faro has a tripartite structure, following a clear rhetorical scheme. In the first section, Abravanel reacts to Dom Afonso's letter, justifying the latter's sorrow despite the fact that it is his father-in-law, not his father, who has passed away. In the second section, Don Isaac seeks to convince the mourner—with numerous references to philosophy, classical literature, and the Hebrew Bible—that one must not indulge in one's sorrow when faced with the death. In the third and final section, Abravanel calls upon the count to return to public life and make efforts to advance his political status. The letter thus has a well-developed rhetorical structure: it begins by justifying the recipient's distress; it then tries to persuade him to change his conception of death; and finally it offers him advice, recommending more fitting behavior. This is a clear application of Cicero's and Seneca's "medical" conception of rhetoric—that it is a process by which the soul is cured of its sickness and restored to health.

Abravanel opens his letter as follows:

> As with the beginning of all illnesses, the remedies of medicine often fail, and nature refrains from obeying them, so that when the pain of the death of relatives is fresh, one ought to abstain from offering words of consolation. The strength of the pain and the excessive mourning prevent their being heard. In Job, chapter two, one reads that when his friends came to console him and found him so distressed, they refrained from speaking to him, not even one word, for seven days and seven nights, while his pain was so strong. They waited until he began to voice his pain. Fearing to write to your Lordship in your time of distress, and not feeling myself wise enough to offer counsel, I therefore permitted the first few days of your mourning to pass.[12]

Already in his opening words, Don Isaac shows Dom Afonso that he is well aware of the comparison drawn in classical literature between the illness of the body and the illness of the soul.[13] Through this literary allusion, Abravanel presents himself as versed in this "medicine" (the Stoic rhetoric of Cicero and Seneca) and thus as particularly suited to console the grieving count. He is, in other words, the count's advisor not only in financial matters but also in psychological ones.

This opening is not, however, drawn solely from the classical theories of the Stoics. It is also rooted in a mature humanistic tradition developed in the fourteenth and fifteenth centuries. This conception can be seen in the first lines of a consolatory epistle written by Francesco Petrarch (1304–74), one of the fathers of Renaissance humanism, to his friend the bishop of Cavaillon. The letter was penned in 1337 after the death of the bishop's brother:

> Your virtue removes from me the enormous difficulty of having to write to you now. For just as the cure of a bodily affliction is more difficult the more serious it is, so it is with the mind. For both, a healthy condition requires no cure or a very light one. And just as with the former there is little or no need for a doctor, with the latter there is little or no need for a consoler.[14]

(25)

From this example we can see that the style of the opening of Don Isaac's letter was already an accepted literary convention in his time, a means of signaling one's knowledge to one's reading audience.[15]

However, Abravanel does more than simply emulate this Stoic notion of consolation. He qualifies it, explaining that healing words are effective only under certain circumstances and at specific times—that is, only after the first stage of distress and sadness has come and gone. Thus, he refers to the account of Job and his companions, justifying waiting for a few days to pass before sending his letter as opposed to dispatching it immediately after learning of Dom Sancho's death. Like the imagery of grief as a disease of the soul, invoking the book of Job as a primer on consolation was a widely used theme in the literature of the time. For example, in a treatise on consolation composed between 1422 and 1424, the Castilian humanist Enrique de Villena explains how the book of Job can be used as a model for offering consolation:

> The [consolatory] method employed by [the friends of Job], after having arrived at Job's place, is divided into three parts, according to the biblical text. First, when they saw him disfigured, they tore their robes, threw dust in the air onto their heads, and sat down with him. Second, they remained in silence for seven days allowing him to express his complaints and resentments. Third, each one gave words and advice of friendly consolation.[16]

We cannot know if Abravanel read Enrique de Villena.[17] Nevertheless, his use of Job in the context of consolation once again points to his familiarity with the literary conventions associated with the genre. By alluding to the famous story of Job, Abravanel once again presents himself as a doctor of the soul, experienced in treating psychological ailments with proper timing.

Abravanel continues, commiserating with the count on his pain, offering his support, and justifying his distress. As befits a good advisor, he does not criticize the behavior of his patron. On the contrary, he encourages and supports him, but with a purpose: to draw the count's attention to the second part of the letter:

> Many believe, as do I, that your magnificent Lordship has more space in his noble and human heart for pain and sorrow for the death of the illustrious Count, your father[in-law], than for the new

glory resulting from your succession and the honor of the inheritance you have received from him. I believe your attitude to be the correct one and I would not reprove your great mourning and bitter sorrow, but rather find reasons to support this mourning.[18]

Attitude toward Death

In the second part of the letter, Abravanel embarks on a philosophical discourse with the aim of changing the count's attitude towards the death of his father-in-law—healing him by transforming his emotional response into a rational outlook. Abravanel writes:

Sir, although humanity feels great pain upon the death of such relatives, it cannot find any just cause for lamentation, because by nature, according to philosophy and following the sin of Adam according to faith, we all have an obligation to death. The debt itself is so imperative that we should not exacerbate this debt as we honor it. Because, as Seneca writes in *The Remedies against Fortune*, we enter life with the condition that we also leave it. We receive this soul and this life as treasurers who must account for it. And concerning the date when payment is due, there is no fixed time. It occurs when the King, whose officers we are, desires it. In his letters, Seneca maintains that we must wait for death like a table prepared for a host who, if he does not come for lunch, will arrive in time for dinner, and so on from day to day. In fact, as lawyers say, nothing is more certain than death, and nothing is more uncertain than the hour when it will take place. Hence, it is mentioned in the first tragedy that God was never so inclined toward someone that He promised him one day of life, whereas chapter 38 of Isaiah, which Seneca could not know, relates that God promised to King Hezekiah, when he was at the point of death, fifteen more years of life.[19]

Having gained the count's confidence with words of encouragement, Abravanel proceeds to broach the count's succumbing to an emotional perspective unbefitting a nobleman. As Petrarch writes to the bishop of Cavaillon: "It is human at the death of one's dear ones to shed tears as evidence of one's devotion; it is manly to place a limit upon them and to control them after they have flowed for some time."[20] An emotional connection to the deceased harms the intellectual capacity of the mourner. Mired in this irrational perspective, the count expresses *querella* (complaints or lamentations) in response to the death of his father-in-law. However, as Abravanel takes pains to demonstrate, marshaling an eclectic mixture of Stoic and biblical sources, no lamentation in the face of death is justified.[21] On the contrary, death is something necessary that we must accept if we wish to develop a rational understanding of ourselves and the world.

The theme of the "querella" with which Abravanel opens this section was a common motif in humanistic literature. It appears for example in Petrarch's abovementioned letter:

> You lost a brother; you would not have lost him unless he were mortal. The complaint [*querela*] therefore is not about the death of one man, but about the mortality of nature which introduced us into this life subject to the rule that we must exit at the command of the one who calls us back.[22]

The same term also appears in Seneca's famous letter of consolation to Marcia, an inspiration and model for Petrarch:

> We have, therefore, no grounds for making ourselves believe that we are surrounded with the things that belong to us; we have them merely as a loan. The use and enjoyment are ours, but the dispenser of the gift determines the length of our tenure. On our part we ought always to keep in readiness the gifts that have been granted for a time not fixed and, when called upon, to restore them without complaint [*sine querella*]; it is a very mean debtor that reviles his creditor.[23]

Seneca's complaint motif—which reached Abravanel via the revival of Stoic consolatory literature by Petrarch and Iberian writers[24]—states that man should conceive his life and his relationship to his surroundings (his relatives and his property, for example) as temporary, as given to him on loan. This is the same motif that we encountered in chapter 1 in the descriptions of Dom Duarte and Dom Pedro of the political relationship between God, the king, and his subjects.[25] The uncertain certainty of death distances man from both himself and his surroundings. This distance can devolve into complete detachment at any moment and into a final farewell when death inevitably arrives. From a rational perspective, man's relationship to himself and his environment can be likened to a loan with an unknown date of repayment that may arrive at any time. Humans and their surroundings should, therefore, not be viewed as complete entities that have been unjustifiably harmed by external forces. The mourner's lament for his loss is the consequence of his blindness to the human condition; he mistakenly views life as "owned" as opposed to "borrowed." The consoler must, therefore, coax the mourner from the sickness of lamentation to the health of acceptance. Through a psychological shift in one's attitude toward oneself and one's surroundings, the mourner can reintegrate himself into the cosmological order of being. The shift entails the recognition of time as an essential part of man's relationship to himself and to the world. Abandoning the mistaken and intransient notion of "ownership" in favor of the more dynamic notion of "loan" is the purpose of the rhetorical act of consolation. In the vein of neo-Stoic consolatory literature, Abravanel seeks to change the Count of Faro's understanding of the ontological status of subjects and objects: they are not static entities, but rather natural processes of appearance and disappearance. At the end of the process, the mourner develops a new state of mind, a consciousness of "readiness." Readiness is the proper mind-set for accepting the existence given to us on loan—taking advantage of it, but eventually parting from it.

Isaac Abravanel's Literary and Humanistic Learning

Abravanel presents the religious and Stoic philosophical belief in the inevitability of death as a matter of general consensus: "because by nature, according to philosophy and following the sin of Adam according to faith, we all have an obligation to death."[26]

However, later in the letter, Abravanel compares Seneca's tragedy, *The Mad Hercules* (*Hercules furens*) to a case "unknown to Seneca"—the biblical account of Hezekiah's prayer—understanding that he needed to produce a solution to the conceptual tension between these two accounts.[27] In Seneca's tragedy the choir states:

> The Parcae [the Fates] come at the set time.
> None may delay when bidden
> none postpone the appointed date.[28]

In the book of Isaiah, by contrast, one reads:

> In those days was Hezekiah sick unto death. And Isaiah the prophet the son of Amos came unto him, and said unto him, Thus saith the Lord, Set thine house in order: for thou shalt die, and not live. Then Hezekiah turned his face toward the wall, and prayed unto the Lord,

and said, Remember now, O Lord, I beseech thee, how I have walked
before thee in truth and with a perfect heart, and have done that
which is good in thy sight. And Hezekiah wept sore. Then came the
word of the Lord to Isaiah, saying, Go, and say to Hezekiah, Thus
saith the Lord, the God of David thy father, I have heard thy prayer,
I have seen thy tears: behold, I will add unto thy days fifteen years
(Is. 38:1–5).

These two sources are in sharp contrast: The former presents death as
inevitable, as lying beyond man and his influence. The latter portrays death
as something that can be deferred: by praying to God, one can delay a divine death sentence. Abravanel resolves this contradiction by casting the
two accounts as a rule and the exception to the rule, respectively. As a rule,
death is beyond our control, as maintained by the Stoics. The exception to
the rule (which proves the rule) is a case of divine intervention in the natural order of being, which can delay what would otherwise be inevitable.

The juxtaposition of Stoic and biblical sources shows how Abravanel, in
his correspondence with a Christian nobleman, sought to use the Stoic conception of fate as common ground to unite them. The way Abravanel resolves the conflict between biblical and Stoic sources represents an attempt
to blur the religious line of demarcation separating him and Dom Afonso.
To promote fruitful communication between a Jewish courtier and a Christian nobleman, Abravanel conceals his Jewish identity and the Hebrew
Bible behind the veil of Seneca. From this seemingly minor episode, one
can understand the cultural adaptive practices Abravanel needed to employ
to take part in the humanist Christian epistolary literature of the period.

How did Abravanel study Seneca's writings? While it seems that he was
versed in Latin, as indicated by his numerous references to Christian literature in his exegetical writings, it is likely that he read Seneca in the translation and adaptation composed by the Infante Dom Pedro in his *Livro
da Vertuosa Benfeytoria* or in the Castilian translations of Fernán Pérez de
Guzmán (1378–1460) and Alonso de Cartagena (1385–1456), two major
Iberian literary figures in the first half of the fifteenth century.[29] In his letter,
Abravanel refers to *De Remediis Fortuitorum* (Remedies for fortune) a work
then attributed to Seneca but now known to be an anthology of excerpts
from his writings, which was translated into Castilian during the fifteenth
century. *The Mad Hercules* was translated along with Seneca's other tragedies into Catalan in the late fourteenth century and into Castilian in the

fifteenth century.[30] Abravanel's citations of Seneca show the extent of his integration into the Iberian circles of high culture and learning in the Iberian peninsula. Like the other members of those circles, he adopted the practice of reading and imitating Seneca and employing Stoic conceptions to his own ends.

Besides referring to Seneca, Abravanel also quotes Cicero, who served in the fifteenth century (due in no small part to Petrarch's influence) as a literary model for many humanists.[31] Abravanel's quotations of Seneca and Cicero show once again that he was well versed in the literary trends of his time—especially humanistic trends that sought to imitate the styles and conceptions of Seneca and Cicero and apply them to new contexts. Thus, for example, later in the letter, Abravanel refers to the augurs of death that are clearly visible to every person, the reminders of death's imminence, and the necessity of preparing oneself for it. Abravanel mentions these "ambassadors of death," which appear in Genesis 3:20 and Cicero's *De Senectute* (On old age):

> When [God] found Adam naked, He commanded at once that he be given clothes made of the skin of dead animals, and He immediately dressed him with dead bodies. . . . Thus, we do not have any just cause to lament death—it does what it must do—nor can we aver that it takes man by surprise, because it dispatches its ambassadors in advance. It first sends youth, so dangerous and ardent, and then, so close to death the tortured and ugly old age, the pains, the pangs, and the martyrdom, and much else that relates to death. The white banners of death come, as Tulio writes in his book On Old Age.[32]

On Old Age was translated into Portuguese in the fifteenth century by the Jewish converso Vasco Fernandes de Lucena and into Castilian by the humanist Alonso de Cartagena.[33]

Like his previous citation from Seneca's *The Mad Hercules*, here too Abravanel marries Stoicism with the Hebrew Bible. Regardless of one's perspective, be it the biblical notion of Adam's sin or the Stoic view of humanity's inherent nature, humans are constantly surrounded by death, in both time (any moment could spell man's end) and space (man is surrounded by reminders of death such as Adam's garments, created from the flesh of dead animals). Humanity's proximity to death reminds it of the ephemeral nature of existence, and it leaves its mark on the objects with which man has a relationship. The augurs of death—such as the death of one's relatives—

are recurring reminders of this. It behooves us to develop a rational and positive attitude when facing this reality. In the passage quoting Cicero, we see again how Abravanel weaves Stoic sources into a Judeo-Christian context, the latter being represented by the Hebrew Bible. Abravanel was aware of Christian literary trends in the fourteenth and fifteenth century that emphasized the possibility of reconciling the teachings of Cicero and Seneca with Christianity.[34] However, he limited his own discussion to the Hebrew Bible, allowing him, as a Jew, to participate in this nascent literary discourse.

The Moral and Political Lesson of Death

Abravanel writes: "If one ought not to feel deep sorrow regarding natural events, how could one experience deep sorrow about death, which is more natural than anything else?"[35] However, he does not make do with demonstrating and preaching about death's inevitability. In his approach, this insight about death is only one stage that the count must pass through to receive the positive message that death provides—a lesson that is moral though primarily political. Morally and even religiously speaking, death is the cure to all of life's suffering. As Seneca writes in his letter to Marcia: "O how ignorant are they of their ills, those who do not laud death and look forward to it as the most precious discovery of Nature."[36] It is not enough to view death as inevitable. The desired shift in mind-set, the true goal of Stoic consolation, is the conception of death as something positive, as a sign of a person's healthy relationship with herself and her surroundings. Thus, Abravanel writes:

> Beyond death as the just and natural outcome for the body, and a useful one for the soul, the memory of death is a remedy for the many unconsoled; for those who might otherwise believe that their misfortune has neither conclusion nor end, and so would live in great pain and continuous despair, as Job himself laments. Death is also a deterrent against all the vices for the one who keeps it constantly in his memory. Remember death, says Ecclesiastes, and you shall not sin. Socrates taught us to despise the material possessions of this world.[37]

The same rhetorical method is employed by Petrarch in his consolatory epistle to the bishop of Cavaillon. Having proved the inevitability of death, he continues: "If you consider the destiny and variability of human affairs, not only will you not mourn, but perhaps you may even rejoice that he [the bishop's brother] is dead."³⁸ Death ends the body's suffering and liberates the soul from the tyranny of fortune (*fortuna*). However, the true moral lesson from death pertains to man's ability to perceive the world as essentially temporary, a perspective that only death affords. Only thus can a person detach herself from the currents of good and evil prevailing in this world and curtail fortune's ability to pain his soul. The scorn expressed by Socrates, Ecclesiastes, and Job for every ephemeral thing is the true means of teaching humans how to behave toward themselves and their environment.

But what political message can be gleaned from death? Turning to Aristotle's *Ethics*, Abravanel explains to the count the political utility of death—specifically, how death regulates the behavior of a state's political and aristocratic leaders. Abravanel thus alludes to the fact that death is beneficial not only to the deceased Count of Odemira but also to his grieving son-in-law. Death teaches the Count of Faro how to behave like a political leader:

> Aristotle highlighted another principle in the first [book] of the Ethics. All consider death to be a very appropriate means of removing envy, greed, and all other vices. Its effect is so strong that the best and most honored king or nobles of the world must die as the lowest of mortals. In the first day of life which is birth, and at its end which is death, all are equally born. There is no power, no property, no merit. It is written that there was a custom in Persia, when upon crowning a new king, the honors and ceremonies included bringing a bricklayer who came bearing different kinds of stones. The king was asked in front of the assembled crowd from which stone he wished his sepulcher to be fashioned. So that even in his moment of triumph he should not forget death. In remembering death, he temperately disdains all that we borrow for such a short period of time.³⁹

Abravanel concludes his philosophical discourse by reminding the count that death is not only inevitable and not just the comforting conclusion of one's life, but also an important lesson for the living—provided that they are emotionally and intellectually receptive to it. This is the receptiveness to and readiness for the lessons of death that Abravanel's neo-Stoic discourse was meant to engender. Now he can impart to the Count of Faro wisdom that will prove vital for the rest of his life. Both birth and death represent moments of transition, to and from the blows of fortune, respectively. These two liminal moments of transition draw the boundaries in which human and social differences are able to develop. However, as can be seen from the account of the coronation ceremony in Persia, these differences cannot efface the equal origins and destinations of all humans. Every political power is working with borrowed time. However, this should not be construed as a sign of weakness or a fault but as essence. This being the case, the death of relatives can serve as a reminder of humanity's state, providing a periodical, natural lesson about the limits of power. Power is not part of a ruler's essence; it is a borrowed capacity. Death teaches the ruler that he neither owns his reign nor can control its circumstances; it is simply given to him on loan. He who forgets death or wallows in grief cannot rule, for he has not yet developed the proper approach toward ruling. In summary, the political message that Abravanel gleans from death is that the correct attitude toward power is not strength but rather the utilization of external and passing opportunities.

The Ideal of Active Life

At the end of his letter, Don Isaac offers the count some practical words of advice, calling on the count to apply the Stoic principles that have been discussed and to return to public life:

> One does not even need these examples, when one witnesses through one's own eyes today the death of my father, yesterday that of my brother, another day the death of my son or my friend, and tomorrow I will die myself. You see, nothing remains from the Count of Mira, nor from others who have died, but their celebrated actions in this world and the merit of their virtuous accomplishments before God. Why mourn that which cannot be recovered?[40]

According to Abravanel, only political action affords man the ability to suspend, if but for a short period of time, the crumbling and erosion of human things. Only by exploiting the time that is left can the nobleman reintegrate himself into the rational, albeit ephemeral, order of the cosmos. Abravanel is adopting here the humanistic ideal of active life (*vita activa*)— that a ruler must pursue his good fortunes and, through valorous actions, garner for himself glory that will endure even after his death. Abravanel concludes the letter by encouraging the count to assume the position of his deceased father-in-law. Through a smooth succession, the cycle that began with the Count of Odemira's death will come to a close.

Isaac Abravanel's letter demonstrates the social function of consolation letters during this period. On the one hand, we see that composing such a letter required extensive literary knowledge and a high level of reading and writing. This is why this letter is important for our understanding of Don Isaac's non-Jewish learning: it shows how he assimilated the Christian literary culture of his time. On the other hand, in addition to constituting a literary work, the letter serves as a social tool: in elite circles, it is a medium for the expression of feeling and for giving voice to emotional turmoil after the death of a relative. At the same time, it is a means of overcoming excessive grief that could hinder the nobles from properly functioning on a social level. As becomes clear from the letter's conclusion, Abravanel's purpose was to help the count make peace with his sociopolitical role, ensuring the continuity of his house. Just as we learn from Abravanel's economic documents about the "special services" provided to the house of Bragança, in this letter—which was certainly just one of many—Don Isaac serves the members of the house in another way, using epistolary literature to help them conduct their personal lives. Abravanel's integration into the management of the family properties went hand in hand with his integration into the literary discourse developed among the Christian Iberian elites, along with providing psychological and literary care for his patrons.

In light of these two types of services rendered by Abravanel to the house of Bragança, I wish to reevaluate the motif of borrowing, which was meant to portray the nobleman's attitude toward his existence and status as something random, beholden to the tides of fortune. On the one hand, the motif draws attention to Isaac Abravanel's background and his economic pursuit of lending money. On the other hand, it demonstrates his integration into the Stoic discourse of the time, that developed both by the Avis dynasty and Iberian and Italian humanists. Abravanel's letter shows, in other words, that Don Isaac's economic activities went hand in hand with a well-developed literary and social outlook.

3 : ISAAC ABRAVANEL AS A JEWISH LEADER IN HIS HEBREW EPISTLES

Having described Don Isaac's secular literary learning and integration into the high culture of his time, I wish now to address the Jewish component of his literary knowledge as evinced by his Hebrew letters. While we can assume that someone boasting as prominent a social status and as extensive a literary knowledge as Isaac Abravanel found time to write more than a few Hebrew letters during his forty-six years under Portuguese rule, only three are extant.[1] All are addressed to Italian Jewish banker Yehiel ben Isaac da Pisa.[2] From what we know about the relationship between Don Isaac and Yehiel, these letters are certainly only a small remnant of their personal correspondence as well as the correspondence between their respective families. From other extant documents we learn that the two families had a deep and long-lasting relationship that spanned almost one hundred years, from the mid-fifteenth to the mid-sixteenth century.[3]

The Portuguese Isaac Abravanel and the Italian Yehiel da Pisa certainly had much in common. Yehiel was born at the beginning of the fifteenth century and died in 1490. He was a member of the fourth generation of a prominent Roman family that had settled in Tuscany at the end of the fourteenth century and remained there until its expulsion in 1570.[4] Throughout this period, the da Pisa family could boast a long history of success. Over the course of two centuries its members combined the successful creation of a flourishing banking network in Tuscany with Jewish political and cultural leadership. Yehiel da Pisa was an emblematic representative of this familial paradigm and could count among his accomplishments the extension of his family's banking network to the city of Florence. Due to his economic activities, Yehiel also enjoyed the protection of the Florentine statesman (and de facto ruler of the city) Lorenzo de' Medici, a relationship that would prove eminently beneficial. Lorenzo de' Medici shielded Yehiel from the machinations of the Franciscan friar Bernardino da Feltre, who delivered sermons inciting the Christian populace against Jewish loan bankers—especially Yehiel da Pisa.[5] In addition to his economic and political activity, Yehiel was also renowned for his patronage of Jewish men of learning, developing relationships with Jewish scholars from Portugal (Abraham Hayun and Don Isaac Abravanel), Italy (Yohanan Alemano) and Castile (Moshe ben Joseph).[6]

The correspondence between Abravanel and Yehiel da Pisa provides an illuminating perspective into the economic and cultural bonds that united the elite Jewish families from different communities in two different countries, Tuscany and Portugal. If Abravanel's letter to the Count of Faro allowed us to reconstruct the Iberian cultural atmosphere that permeated his economic relationship with the house of Bragança, his letters to Yehiel da Pisa serve to complete the picture: they teach us about the Jewish conceptions that pervaded Abravanel's relationship with other members of the Jewish elite.

To preface this discussion, I wish to draw attention to the difference between the 1472 letter to Yehiel da Pisa and the one discussed in the previous chapter, the consolation letter addressed to the Count of Faro. The most obvious difference, of course, is language. However, the distinction between them cannot be reduced to this point alone and runs far deeper. Each letter represents a separate channel of communication and an independent mode of discourse, their respective contours being defined by distinct norms formulated in two separate, albeit interconnected, cultural spheres in the Iberian peninsula: the Christian and the Jewish. These two cultures developed distinct epistolary and literary norms. This is the second most prominent difference between Don Isaac's Portuguese and Hebrew letters. While in his letter to the Count of Faro, Don Isaac cites extensively from classical Latin literature and its Iberian translations and literary imitations, in his Hebrew letters Stoic sources are notably absent. Instead, he adorns his Hebrew letters with ornate prose, cobbled together from contiguous snippets from scripture.

In 1472, Isaac Abravanel sent a letter to Yehiel da Pisa, around the same time as he wrote to the Count of Faro. In the letter to his Italian friend, Abravanel discusses a number of subjects: Yehiel's misfortunes in Florence, the liberation of Jews captured and sold into slavery with the fall of Arzila in Morocco to Portuguese conquerors, a secret message to be delivered to the pope, the exchange of Hebrew manuscripts, and a gift to Yehiel's wife. Each subject is a window into Don Isaac's life as a community leader, not to mention the way he conducted himself and justified his behaviors.

Consolation for Yehiel's Troubles in Florence

The years 1469–72 were troubled by much commotion related to the question of the renewal of the *capituli* (terms of agreement) of 1459 that fixed the terms of Jewish loan banking in the city of Florence. Although we possess very little evidence of it, it seems that Yehiel and other Jewish loan bankers were the targets of the accusations of a Jewish converso and were threatened by the Florentine mob with having their homes looted and being expelled. As a result, the activity of the Jewish loan banks was apparently suspended during the years 1469–71. On June 8, 1471, their activities were allowed to resume, but with interest rates cut in half.[7]

This is most probably the historical background of the letter that Yehiel sent to Don Isaac around Passover 5231 (April 1471), as Abravanel refers to it and dates the beginning of his epistle with "at this season, the other year." In response to Yehiel's depiction of his worries, Don Isaac begins his letter with words of consolation:

> The letter you wrote telling me of your situation has arrived one year ago. My ears have heard and understood your fury in the midst of a people of impure lips. . . . I was alarmed when I understood your concern. I heard and I trembled. . . . I was distressed to hear your misfortune.[8]

As he did one or two years earlier in his letter to the Count of Faro, Don Isaac begins his letter with words of sympathy. Exemplary of Abravanel's empathy with Yehiel's misfortunes is the use of Habakkuk 3:16: "I heard and my bowels quaked, my lips quivered at the sound; rot entered into my bone, I trembled where I stood." Passing to the second step of the consolation (the rationalization of the sorrow), Don Isaac explains to his friend that he was the victim of the shared destiny of Jews who live as members of a minority within Christian states:

> Worry cried out in my heart to see that Jews should be prepared, wherever the soles of their feet shall tread, to come to the cleft of troubles and to the holes of torments, that every Jew-baiter would make himself a Lord over them and over their offspring. For the wicked does attack the righteous.[9]

Abravanel depicts the situation of Jews in exile with two plays on words with the verses Exodus 33:22 and Isaiah 7:19. Instead of "cleft of the rock [*tsur*]" (Ex. 33:22) and "the holes of the rocks [*selayim*]" (Is. 7:19), Don Isaac writes "the cleft of troubles [*tsarot*]" and "the holes of torments [*met-siqot*]." He thus suggests that instability and constant exposure to injustice characterize the Jewish exile.

At the same time, he is showing that Yehiel's personal misfortune is but one of the many consequences of the historical condition of Jewish exile. This rationalization is a rhetorical tool, used to diminish Yehiel's sorrow and integrate it into the normal order of Jewish life in exile.

After the consolatory rationalization, Abravanel encourages his friend to pursue his mission as a Jewish leader:

> You have seen those who follow the teaching of the Lord and trem-
> ble at His word, passing through the valley of Baca. . . . These peo-
> ple are our friends, the Lord watches over them. They shall enter
> into His sanctuary, be near Him, and be blessed. You too are one of
> them, you who fear the Lord and are fervently devoted to His com-
> mandments. . . . Though you walk through the valley of the shadow
> of death, and see misery and distress from an ungodly nation, for all
> your labor under the sun, for the Lord and His anointed, your re-
> ward shall be very great. . . . For the wrong they committed against
> you and which you endured, you shall obtain gladness and joy. Jus-
> tice shall precede you . . . and those who sow mischief shall reap
> their just deserts.[10]

Facing the historical condition of exile and its grievous consequences for Yehiel, Don Isaac affirms a certain political and religious ideal of Jewish leadership. He demands that Yehiel accept the weakness and contingency entailed by exile, promising him political and religious rewards for his capacity to face its misfortunes. The "valley of Baca" (Ps 84:7) through which the Jewish leader has to pass becomes a privilege and a merit in front of God but also within the Jewish society, as suggested by Abravanel's use of Ez 44:16: "they shall enter into My sanctuary, and they shall come near to My table, to minister unto Me, and they shall keep My charge." The exemplary attitude of the Jewish leader is rewarded not only by a religious promise, but also by the strengthening of his leadership within his community.

The Liberation of Arzilan Jewry

After offering words of consolation for the looting of Yehiel's properties in Florence, Don Isaac proceeds to recount the liberation of Arzila's Jewish inhabitants, an undertaking in which he played a pivotal role. As I will show below, Abravanel's telling of these events, while based on well-known historical facts, is intentionally tendentious and colored by deliberate rhetoric. Abravanel begins by describing to Yehiel the conquest of Arzila at the hands of the Portuguese forces:[11]

> Our Lord the king [of Portugal], may God prolong his days in his kingdom, he who stands and shakes the earth, the leader of many people. . . . He gathered the ships of the sea with their mariners, all that handle the oar and all that pilot, and crossed over to Africa to possess dwelling places that are not his. He encamped there against the city of Arzila, the city of kings great among the nations, he shot their arrows and laid siege against it. Not one man withstood them. The people went up into the city, every man straight in front of him, and they took the city and plundered all of it. They kept the silver and gold and took cattle and herbs as their booty. The king and those who have access to the royal presence did not lay hands on the spoil. See, the gentiles were ill tempered and complied with every man's pleasure. They utterly destroyed all that was in the city, both man and woman, ten thousand of souls, those destined for captivity, to captivity, and those destined for the sword, to the sword.[12]

On August 20, 1471, Dom Afonso V's royal fleet approached the shores of Arzila. According to the royal chronicler, Rui de Pina (1440–1522), the fleet numbered 477 ships and 30,000 troops. After four days of intense battle, the Portuguese forces finally took the city, capturing 5,000 prisoners. In his account, de Pina confirms Abravanel's portrayal of the conquest as particularly cruel and violent:

> And so finally, thus were the Moors of the city and the citadel attacked, that they were all killed or made prisoners without any exception, according to the common estimation, the number of dead reached up to 2,000 and the number of prisoners up to 5,000. And a very large and rich booty was found and taken in the city, which was estimated at eighty thousand gold *dobras*, of which total, the king granted an exoneration to the plunderers and did not even reserve for himself a fifth of it, nor any other right whatsoever.[13]

On August 25, the archbishop of Lisbon held a celebratory mass in the city's central mosque, which was converted into the Church of São Bartolomeo. At the end of the ceremony, the king knighted his son João. The knighting took place alongside the corpse of another brave knight who had fallen in battle, whose body was displayed at the center of the church with a cross laid upon his chest. Without a doubt this was a poignant moment, the climax of a stirring victory mass. As de Pina vividly describes it, "both of them wearing victorious arms, at the end of this pious and glorious scene, the king said to the prince, not without shedding a few tears: 'Son, may God make of you a knight so good as the one lying here!'"[14]

The conquest of Arzila—which was followed a few days later by the conquest of Tangier—was a celebrated event in Portugal and Christendom as a whole. It eclipsed the Portuguese defeat in 1437 and was deemed a fitting revenge for the death of Infante Santo Dom Fernando.[15] Large tapestries were commissioned to commemorate this dual victory, describing the conquests and depicting Dom Afonso V as a victorious military commander.[16] After his death, Dom Afonso V would be awarded the title "Africano," commemorating his conquest of several cities in North Africa—and imitating the title of the Roman conqueror of Carthage, Scipio Africanus, a reflection of the classicist tastes of the Avis dynasty.

After his sympathetic account of the city's conquest, which reflected the contagious air of victory that was circulating at the time,[17] Abravanel moves on to a sobering description of the fate of Arzila's Jewish inhabitants who, after the city's fall, were sold into slavery:[18]

> Since the community of these unfortunate Jews lived in Arzila, scattered and dispersed within the city, one on the one side and the other on the other side; although a great number were slain with the sword among the children of Kedar [Muslims] that went into captivity before the enemy, the Lord being merciful, He singled out the faithful. From His dwelling place He hovered over His young and none of the children of Israel died. Then were the chiefs of Edom alarmed when they saw that from the babes suckling at the breast, to the elderly dim with age, not one was missing. All the souls that came out of the city in captivity, both young and old, daughters of Israel and the children of Israel: two hundred and fifty men, faint with hunger, thirsty, naked, and lacking everything. We saw the precious sons of Zion, the people of the God of Abraham once valued as gold, now sold as bondsmen and bondswomen, in the furnace of affliction, shackled in iron.[19]

While acknowledging the political importance of Arzila's conquest for the kingdom of Portugal, it is this that most concerns Abravanel: the Jewish population of Arzila who, along with five thousand Muslims, were sold into slavery.[20]

Don Isaac draws a sharp contrast between the fate of the city's Muslims, many of whom were put to the sword, and its Jews, who—though taken captive—were at least left alive. Abravanel attributes this bittersweet salvation to religious causes: the Jews' survival is a sign of divine providence, a power that cast its aegis over the Jews of Arzila and the Jewish Diaspora as a whole. It is also the result of the dispersion of the Jewish population within the city, a fact that prevented the Jews from being annihilated in one fell swoop.

Having discussed the circumstances of their survival, Abravanel describes the dire fate suffered by his captive Jewish brethren, as well as the ransom mission he conducted to save them:

> Our eyes looked unremittingly, straining to see them. We, the leaders of the community, decided to proclaim release for the captives and liberation for the imprisoned, to offer a ransom for their souls. . . . I, your servant, and other leaders who are more just and better than I, selected twelve chiefs from the community, corresponding to the number of tribes of Israel, to perform the tasks of righteousness, and to release the prisoners from the dungeon. I and someone else from among the leaders were sent from one city to another, men who continually traverse the land to deliver the children of Israel from Egypt and pay the ransom for their souls. So those who remained told us: . . . Take double money in your hand and bring all your brethren out of all the nations as an offering unto the LORD, that they shall be redeemed by money. The LORD has led us both on our paths for the sake of the glory of His name, and He inclined all their captors to be kindly disposed toward us. For the full price, within a few days or ten, we ransomed one hundred and fifty men, and so here in the city, and in all the other cities, the people of that land [Arzila] are now many, the ransomed of the LORD, through us and thanks to the benevolent care of the LORD for us, two hundred and twenty persons and the cost of the ransom of their souls—ten thousand doubloons in gold.[21]

According to Don Isaac's testimony, he was one of two Jewish leaders chosen to locate and free the Jews of Arzila. The successful ransoming of

220 of the 250 prisoners sold into slavery is a testament to the role of these Jewish elites not just as merchants, but also as leaders and deliverers of the Jewish people.

Besides demonstrating Abravanel's economic and political prowess, this passage is also notable for its elegant rhetoric. Weaving a textual tapestry from threads of scripture, Abravanel articulates not only the sense of responsibility the Portuguese Jewish elite felt for the Jews of Arzila, but also the pivotal role played by wealth in rectifying this injustice. It is through their economic power that the elites were able to play a concrete role in history, taking on the mantle of saviors. Of course, by describing how he had been selected as an emissary to liberate the Jews of Arzila, Abravanel wishes to project a specific image to Yehiel da Pisa—that is, to present himself as a prominent leader belonging to the Portuguese Jewish elite. However, he also voices here a clear conception of the role that such elites are expected to play. The division of financial and mercantile capital among a small number of related Jewish families represents to Abravanel a nexus of economic and political power with the ability to act as a counterbalance to historical forces that often seek to overpower a Jewish minority. This positive conception of the wealth of the Jewish elite pervades Don Isaac's description of how the ransom money was collected. Particularly notable is Abravanel's adaptation of the verse "You were sold for naught; and you shall be redeemed without money" (Is. 52:3), which he actually inverts: "you shall be redeemed *with* money." Unlike the redemption in the messianic future, in which God will redeem Israel without money, the redemption wrought by Jewish elites was completely dependent on their financial and mercantile capital. To some extent, this opposition parallels the role played by the Jewish economic elite for their communities vis-à-vis divine providence guiding Jewish history as a whole. This parallelism represents an important expression of an Iberian Jewish elitist mentality that viewed political and economic power as a secondary form of providence, operating under the universal providence of God.[22]

If one follows the rhetorical thread in Don Isaac's account, one can identify a narrative composed of three factors: the history of gentiles (the conflict between Christians and Muslims over a city); the universal providence of God that protects the Jews in the Diaspora (the salvation of the Jews from death during the city's conquest); and the responsibility, or secondary providence, of a Jewish elite that has the ability to use its wealth to correct local injustices, as it did for the Jews of Arzila.

Abravanel ends this account by adapting passages from the Passover Haggadah, describing an imaginary seder that will soon be held by the redeemed Jews of Arzila:

> And on this night which is a night of vigil, in their villages and encampments, they shall praise the LORD for He is good. Together they shall lift up their voices and all the sons of God shall shout for joy: we were slaves for a short time and the LORD led us out of slavery into freedom and out of bondage into redemption, and now we are, as all of the multitude of Israel, free.[23]

At the hands of the Jewish elites' providence, the Jews of Arzila reexperience the liberation from Egyptian slavery described in the Haggadah. Through the image of this fictional Seder, Abravanel shows that the protection provided by Jewish elites reinforces the Jewish people's connection to the divine. Indeed, the Jews of Arzila do not thank their immediate saviors during their seder—rather, it is the God who brought the children of Israel out of Egypt who merits their words of praise. This was a social and religious effect that the Jewish economic elite had an interest in cultivating.

This dramatic envisioning of a seder held by ransomed prisoners paints a vivid picture for Yehiel. It emphasizes the importance of the hegemony of the Jewish economic elite in Diaspora communities as well as the reciprocity between divine providence and the providence of Jewish leaders. The victory of this elitist ethos is, of course, an echo of Dom Afonso V's military victory over the Muslims of Arzila and Tangier. In Abravanel's narrative the grand Christian victory is accompanied by a small Jewish one—the Jewish elite's ability to ensure Jewish continuity within the kingdom of Portugal.

Don Isaac's Politics of Friendship: A Royal Delegation to the Pope

Isaac Abravanel moves on to a new topic: a diplomatic delegation composed of the royal dignitaries Lopo de Almeida and João Teixeira, who have embarked from Portugal for Rome to greet the new pope, Sixtus IV. In addition to his royal mission, Teixeira also served as Abravanel's emissary to Yehiel da Pisa: it was he who brought Yehiel this letter. In a relatively long passage, Isaac explains to Yehiel the political significance of Teixeira's mission, both for the king and the Jews of Portugal. It should be borne in mind that the pope, who had been elected during the conquest of Arzila and Tangier, had praised the king's crusade in a public letter, even offering economic rewards in the form of exemptions from paying taxes to the Church.[24] The delegation to the pope was dispatched in the aftermath of fall of Arzila and Tangier, the source of the strengthened connections between the king and the pope. Abravanel explains the role of the two emissaries:

> Our Lord the king . . . sends his messengers before him to the Pope to bow down to him. . . . His messengers are the greatly exalted Prince Lopo de Alemeida, and a wise, perceptive and good man, Doctor João Teixeira, who brings this letter to you. Both have access to the royal presence and are closest to him. The doctor in his goodness knowing how to distinguish between good and evil, interceding for the welfare of all our kinsmen, always seeking our peace and prosperity because his hand is guided by God, wonderful is his love for me.[25]

The friendship described here between Isaac Abravanel and Teixeira, the humanist scholar, sheds important light on the sociocultural context of Don Isaac's activities, illuminating yet another facet of his integration into Portuguese humanist circles.

The second emissary mentioned, Lopo de Almeida (1416–86),[26] was one of the most prominent noblemen in King Afonso V's court. He joined most of the king's royal delegations to foreign states—for example, accompanying the king's sister Leonor to her wedding to the Holy Roman Emperor Frederick III (1452–93), which took place in Rome in 1454. During his journey through Italy, de Almeida sent four letters to the king, keeping him informed of the events that had taken place and depicting the character, customs—and even clothing—of the Germans and Italians. These letters, characterized by stark realism and subtle humor, are considered landmarks in the history of Portuguese literature. A passage from the first letter, in which de Almeida mocks the Holy Roman Emperor's thrift, is illustrative of their unique style:

> I swear to you, my Lord . . . that he [the emperor] is petty and stingy beyond compare. For example, in Florence, he wanted to buy a damask of white brocade from Cosimo de' Medici. He asked [de' Medici] to bring the cloth and show it to him. He was bargaining [so hard] over a large piece [of cloth] with Cosimo's men that they refused [to agree] and took it with them. Afterward, [the emperor] ordered [his servants to inform] Cosimo that the latter's men had

asked an exorbitant price for the piece of cloth. He asked Cosimo to order them to sell him the piece for a better price. Cosimo, who was lying ill at that time, said to his business agents that he understood the kind of "deal" the emperor sought. Cosimo asked his men to give him the piece for free. The emperor accepted, taking the gift for granted.[27]

Teixeira, whom Abravanel portrays as a close friend, was another figure who combined noble virtues with literary learning. Teixeira was a doctor of law. He sent his children to study in Florence under the tutelage of the famous humanist Angelo Poliziano (1454–94).[28] In a speech Teixeira composed in 1489, we can see his fluency with humanistic literature, the likes of which we encountered in Abravanel's Portuguese letter. Cicero, Seneca, Plato, Aristotle, Livy, Virgil, and other classical authors make appearances throughout the speech, sharing the stage with excerpts from the Bible and patristic literature. Besides making an impressive display of his literary sagacity, Teixeira promotes in this context the image of the learned nobleman and ruler, bearing a strong resemblance to the conceptions pervading Abravanel's Portuguese composition. Thus, for example, Teixeira addresses King João II (successor of Afonso V) in his speech:

> And you, mighty King, you had the Prince, our Lord your son, taught by a very expert master in your house. You will see how much, thanks to the liberal arts, the learning is increased. This is what caused Alexander to have the nickname "the great" in the entire world. At the same hour he was born, King Philip, his father, wrote to Aristotle a letter in the following manner:
> "Philip to Aristotle, may you be in good health,
> My son is just born, and you shall know that I am grateful not only for this birth, but also for its taking place during your lifetime. I hope that being taught by you, he shall merit being my son and the heir of these kingdoms."[29]

As I noted in chapter 1, the kings of the Avis dynasty cultivated a learned aristocracy of civil officers, composed of figures such as Lopo da Almeida, João Teixeira, and others. They revived literary and humanistic activity in Portugal, while justifying their new position by propounding the humanist ideal of the learned ruler and noble—values that the Avis monarchs were claimed to embody. The fact that Abravanel associates himself with a prominent member of the administrative and learned nobility of the Portuguese court further demonstrates his integration into these circles, which led in turn to his assimilation of their literary knowledge and political ideologies. Because he was part of the king's circle of learned courtiers (though, being a Jew, he was accorded a lower status than his Christian colleagues), Abravanel could turn to a Christian friend who belonged to the same social class and request help—in exchange for a fee, of course.

The Deal

Having described the king's emissaries, Don Isaac proceeds to reveal the main purpose of his letter: he needs Yehiel's diplomatic and financial assistance to take advantage of the opportunity afforded by this royal delegation to the pope, using it to undertake a secret diplomatic mission on behalf of the Portuguese Jewish community. Relying on their friendship, Abravanel was able to enlist Teixeira's help, sending him as his personal emissary to the pope—provided that his Jewish friend, Yehiel da Pisa, was willing to make the necessary financial and symbolic gestures. Anticipating the meeting with Teixeira, Abravanel offers his Jewish friend the following advice:

> He [Teixeira] will speak to the Pope. We have sought his favor, to speak to the Pope of the affairs of the Jewish communities, may the Guardian of Israel protect them, and to convince him, according to the Torah, to respond to our petitions and requests. On his honor he decided to take a vow to speak well concerning Israel. . . . If it pleases your Majesty, speak to these men with your beautiful gift of speech . . . songs in honor of the king our master [the king of Portugal]. . . . May his name endure forever, he shall rule from sea to sea and his kingdom shall be exalted. . . . And particularly to the doctor speak kind and comforting words so that he shall receive from your words grace and glory, because he is my spirit and my breath. . . . What he will ask from you, consider it as my honor. I beg you that in your goodness you assist him well.[30]

The Hebrew expression "we have sought his favor (*halinu panav*)" refers to Abravanel's verbal and financial persuasion of Teixeira before his departure. However, it seems that this was not enough: Yehiel had his own role to play. Careful to emphasize the diplomatic task at hand, Abravanel gives Yehiel practical advice on the proper behavior when meeting with Teixeira: Yehiel must sing the praises of the Portuguese monarch, impressing

Teixeira with the international acclaim for the kingdom following its conquest of Arzila and Tangier. After so celebratory and so positive a reception, the monetary gifts that Yehiel is requested to provide the Portuguese emissary will be even more effective.

This passage provides a fascinating lesson about Abravanel's ability to combine business savvy with rhetorical and political skill. With words and money, he promotes his desired goal: convincing Teixeira to conduct a secret mission on behalf of the Jewish community of Portugal. Thus, Abravanel translated his strong connections with the Jewish economic elite and the Christian nobility into political power, allowing him to intervene in Portuguese politics and diplomacy. Besides highlighting Don Isaac's social milieu, such accounts attest to his day-to-day use of rhetorical and literary knowledge as a means of promoting professional and political interests.

Exchange of Manuscripts and Gifts

The letter concludes with a description of the gifts that Abravanel has sent to Yehiel and his family. Thus, we see that besides exchanging written and oral messages through Teixeira, the families also exchanged precious goods. From another letter to Yehiel da Pisa, we learn that Don Isaac wrote to him from year to year.[31] Based on the evidence from the three extant letters, it seems that every letter Don Isaac sent was accompanied by gifts.

What did these two figures send each other? We have already seen the exchange of money: Yehiel was asked to provide Teixeira a specific sum that Don Isaac would return to him, probably through a Florentine bank with which Don Isaac worked.[32] In addition, Yehiel and Isaac would exchange Hebrew manuscripts, for the purpose of copying or expanding their personal libraries. Don Isaac writes: "A man of your great accomplishment, you requested that I, your servant, send to your Excellency the commentary on the Writings by Rabbi David Kimhi, may his memory be blessed in the world to come, and I am presenting before you *The Crown of the Elders* which I wrote, along with the commentary on Deuteronomy, which is not yet complete."[33]

Yehiel had requested the commentary on the writings by Rabbi David Kimhi (Radak, c. 1160–c. 1235), but Abravanel sent him instead two of his early works.[34] Likewise, in a letter penned in 1481, Abravanel asks about manuscripts (of Profiat Duran and Joseph Ibn Shem Tov)[35] that Yehiel has in his home, which he would like returned if "you have already copied them and no longer have use for them." In the same letter Abravanel asks if "the commentaries of Rabbi Emmanuel [of Rome] on the Pentateuch and Prophets are still in your library?"[36] The exchange of manuscripts was, it seems, an important part of Isaac Abravanel's relationship with Yehiel da Pisa. Among other things, it attests to their desire to expand their respective personal libraries, part of a larger historical and social trend of book collection that was flourishing during the Renaissance.[37] By all accounts, both libraries were quite large, investing the homes of these two members of the Jewish elite with the status of cultural centers and venues for scholars.

In 1483, two years after this letter was written, Abravanel describes his home in his commentary on the Former Prophets. Referring to his personal library, he writes: "My home is a place of congregation for sages, for there were set thrones for judgment, and from there flows, from books and from scribes, good discernment and knowledge and fear of the Lord."[38] In other words, Don Isaac and Yehiel da Pisa both consciously collected libraries, viewing them as an inseparable part of their social statuses and identities.

In a passage in the abovementioned letter of 1481, Abravanel notes that the person entrusted with bringing the requested manuscripts from Yehiel da Pisa's home was a "Doctor Gonsalo Mendes, my friend who is with you in your country."[39] The same man is mentioned elsewhere with a slightly different name, in a document dated 1477. The document is a receipt from the Florentian bankers Francesco and Bernardo Cambini listing the price of "seven volumes of the law books of Bartolo da Sassoferrato (*VII volumi di libri di legie di Bartolo*)" that Isaac Abravanel purchased through the same Gonsalo Mendes. Mendes was an occasional messenger involved in Abravanel's businesses in Tuscany, and it seems that it was he who was to pick up the manuscripts from Yehiel da Pisa's home. The sociocultural profile of Gonsalo Mendes resembles that of Teixeira: he was the son of a judge in Lisbon and was sent to study law at the University of Siena in the 1470s, funded by a royal scholarship.[40] The books Abravanel purchased through Mendes were those of the famed fourteenth-century jurist Bartolo da Sassoferato, the standard textbooks for law students at the time.[41] What did Abravanel do with these books? We do not know, but we nevertheless see that Abravanel's exchange of manuscripts with da Pisa was part of his broader commercial relations with Tuscany at the time.

To better understand the social import that the two correspondents attributed to the exchange of manuscripts, it is worth dwelling on a passage from a letter Abravanel penned in 1472. There he describes two works he has composed, his commentary on Deuteronomy and *'Ateret zeqenim*, which he sent to Yehiel:

> This book is a present sent unto my lord. Please accept my present which has been brought to you as a blessing. May it remain with you wherever my lord shall choose to dwell: study is all. So long as the earth endures, may it remember your servant the son of your maid-servant that sends his word to a distant country, because I love my master, and now, I offer you the first fruits of the soil which the Lord has given me.[42]

Abravanel discloses the social significance of the gift: his manuscript of *'Ateret zeqenim* (as well as his commentary on Deuteronomy) when added to Yehiel's library would serve as a precious symbol of the relationship between two individuals and two families. Furthermore, Abravanel emphasizes the importance of study and where it takes place—in the library. Abravanel knew that if *'Ateret zeqenim* made its way into the library of the prominent Yehiel da Pisa, then it was well on its way to being disseminated among the many scholars who visited and even lived in his home. In fact, we have testimony from a Jewish scholar who read Isaac Abravanel's work, apparently after finding it in da Pisa's library. Elijah Haim da Genazzano, a contemporary Italian kabbalist, in his essay *Igeret hamudot* (composed in about 1490) lambastes Don Isaac's views expressed in *'Ateret zeqenim*: "and now I shall go forth to battle with one sage from this generation, his name is Rabbi Isaac Abravanel of Portugal who composed the book *'Ateret zeqenim*."[43] From this we see that the presence of Abravanel's work in da Pisa's library fueled the discussions and arguments of Italian Jewish scholars in the late fifteenth century.

The Black Slave

Abravanel concludes his letter by mentioning a "very special gift" sent from Isaac's wife to Yehiel's wife:

> The woman whom the LORD appointed for Isaac your servant, even she declared: he is my brother. God brought a worthy writing and language to you, the book you have produced, to present an offering unto my Lord to strengthen your love and allegiance to him. Why should my name be absent from the doors of his house, a house where sages gather? . . . And because I am not learned I have, behold,

a young girl that has not known any man, black yet comely. She is a maidservant, well trained to work. . . . I offer her to the mistress, your wife, who is like a fruitful vine in your house. . . . I listened to her [my wife's] voice. The doctor, my master, will bring her [the slave girl] to your Excellency, because she was raised in his house until now, and she followed him as if she had been brought up with him.[44]

From archival records we know that Don Isaac's wife sent Yehiel's wife a "a black slave by the name of Biccinai from Guinea . . ., eight or nine years old, yet to be baptized."[45] The Portuguese began to explore the African coast in the 1430s and discovered the Gulf of Guinea in West Africa. Such discoveries led to the flourishing of the black slave trade in the Iberian peninsula, and from the 1440s to the 1480s, thousands of slaves were shipped to Portugal, Castile, and Aragon.[46] The gift provided by Abravanel's wife is but one example of the many black slaves brought to Portugal and the ways in which they were traded and used. While Don Isaac says the gift comes from his wife, there is no doubt that it also represented a token of Don Isaac's appreciation for Yehiel's financial assistance.

We can see how one of the goals of the letter's rhetoric was to disguise the economic relationship between the two leaders, presenting their connection as one based on good will and mutual munificence. Notably, the exchange of gifts between men pertains to the spiritual realm, whereas the exchange of gifts between women pertains to the material one. The justification for this gender-based distinction is the ability to read and write: Don Isaac writes on behalf of his wife, "I am not learned." While Don Isaac and Yehiel were certainly worldly merchants, reading and writing allowed them to elevate the character of their relationship beyond the strict bonds of commerce. As a result, they would ascribe to women the material side of their relationship—in this case, with the gift of a slave. The modern reader of the letter cannot help but be struck by the contradiction between the heroic liberation of the Jews of Arzila from slavery, on the one hand, and the sending of a black slave as a gift, on the other hand. But of course, this critique is anachronistic. Like most of his Portuguese contemporaries, Abravanel had no qualms about the African slave trade.[47]

Leadership and Rhetoric

A close reading of Abravanel's first letter to Yehiel da Pisa reveals a series of actions, models, and qualities that characterized Don Isaac's role as a Jewish leader: the intervention of the Jewish economic elite in royal politics; their profitable friendships with learned Christian nobles; a politics based on the exchange of favors between Jewish leaders in different communities; the shaping of the religious, cultural, and social mentality of the Jewish elite though epistolary writing, composition of biblical commentaries, the collection of manuscripts to stock private libraries, and study. I have tried to show in this chapter that these patterns of leadership were not unconscious. Rather, they were part of an intentionally cultivated conception of the role the Jewish elite ought to play on the stage of history, particularly during the tribulations of exile. Under divine providence, which protects Israel by scattering them throughout the Diaspora (the case of the Jews of Arzila is an example), the Jewish elites intervene in history. They conceive of this ability as a consequence of their economic power, their relationships with Christian nobles, and the sociocultural models they embody. This idea of secondary providence was manifest in their business acumen and the social and rhetorical skills they used in their dealings with the Christian aristocracy.[48] It was manifest also in the development of Jewish Hebrew rhetoric, skill in composing letters and commentaries, and the collection of Hebrew books. Rhetorical and literary talents symbolized the status of the Jewish elites—as envisioned by themselves, the members of Jewish communities, and the Christian nobility. They were also used to justify the very existence of this upper class. However, literary knowledge cannot be reduced simply to its social function: literary learning allowed Jewish elites, like Don Isaac, to develop independent self-perceptions and Weltanschauungs.

I wish to conclude my discussion by briefly comparing the Hebrew letter to Yehiel da Pisa with that discussed in the previous chapter. In Don Isaac's Portuguese letter to the Count of Faro, we see how he wields humanistic rhetoric as a sign of identity, employing literary norms to show that he, too, belongs to a humanistic noble elite. The use of eloquent Hebrew rhetoric in letters to Yehiel plays a similar role: it is a way for Don Isaac to show that he belongs to the Jewish elite. However, other than this formal parallelism, the letters could not be more different: in Don Isaac's Hebrew letter, no mention is made of classical literature or of Iberian humanistic texts. Only the Hebrew Bible, classical rabbinic writings, and Jewish medieval commentators are cited. While it is very likely that Yehiel da Pisa was well acquainted with many aspects of the humanistic trends in Florence,[49] Abravanel chooses not to include in his letter quotations from or allusions to classical or humanist works. This is to clarify, for himself and his reader, the unambiguous demarcation between his communication with Christians and his communication with Jews. While there is almost no reliable information about Don Isaac's education and learning, these two letters highlight the two education tracks that Don Isaac followed: Iberian Christian and Iberian Jewish. Just as Abravanel knew how to use his Iberian Christian literary knowledge in his social and economic dealings with Christian aristocracy, so too he knew how to use his Iberian Jewish literary knowledge in his dealings with Jewish economic elites. This careful separation between two forms of learning and discourse demonstrates Don Isaac's understanding and command of the cultural conventions of both the Jewish and the Christian milieus. Thus through his letters emerges the image of Don Isaac as a man with a dual education, operating concurrently in two separate spheres.

If we go back to the beginning of our discussion in chapter 2—the transition from Isaac Abravanel's economic documents to personal literary compositions—a very interesting tension can be discerned. The ethos of leadership propounded in these letters glorifies an aristocratic value that requires the leader to transcend his personal affairs to fulfill his sociopolitical role. Thus, in his Portuguese letter, Abravanel calls upon the Count of Faro to rise above his personal grief, and in his Hebrew letter he describes how he—as an individual—was chosen to lead a rescue mission. At the same time, this individualistic and aristocratic ethos was predicated on economic and familial organizational structures and an elitist group mentality. For example, in his Portuguese letter, Don Isaac asks the Count of Faro to overcome his sorrow to assume the responsibilities of his deceased father-in-law. Likewise, in his Hebrew letter, describing the liberation of the Jewish captives, Don Isaac makes clear that the mission was successful only due to the funds raised by the entire Jewish elite on behalf of the Jews of Arzila. This tension between the personal side of leadership and its familial collective aspects is no contradiction—on the contrary, it reveals a virtuous cycle by which the individualistic elements of leadership are directed toward strengthening the collective, while the leadership of the collective is manifested in the actions of individuals.

4 : ISAAC ABRAVANEL

PHILOSOPHER AND THEOLOGIAN

Having discussed the social and cultural context in which Isaac Abravanel's literary knowledge was forged, I wish to turn now to the more philosophical dimensions of his writing, bearing in mind the economic and social factors in the background. In a letter sent to Yehiel da Pisa in 1472, Abravanel describes his first complete work, '*Ateret zeqenim*.[1] The book was apparently written in the mid- or late 1460s, when Don Isaac was already a well-established businessman in Portugal.[2] It is, therefore, an invaluable resource for understanding Isaac Abravanel's theological, historical, and philosophical views during this period of his life.

The Philosophical Model of Maimonides and the Negative Portrayal of the Elders

As its title suggests, '*Ateret zeqenim* represents an attempt to "crown" the elders and nobles of the children of Israel described in Exodus 24:9–11, saving them from the negative depictions offered by Maimonides and by exegetes of the thirteenth and fourteenth centuries. The passage in question reads as follows: "Then Moses, and Aaron, Nadab, and Abihu, and seventy of the elders of Israel went up; and they saw the God of Israel; and there was under His feet the like of a paved work of sapphire stone, and the like of the very heaven for clearness. And upon the nobles of the children of Israel He laid not His hand; and they beheld God and did eat and drink." Abravanel's defense comes against the backdrop of medieval exegetical and philosophical discussions of the experience described.[3] The content of their sight and vision was cast in a negative light by Maimonides in his *Guide of the Perplexed*, an aspersion tightly bound up in a strictly philosophical approach, as I will show.

Chapter 5 in part 1 of *Guide of the Perplexed* opens by citing Aristotle's apology for the gradual nature of the philosophical process. Maimonides writes:

> When the chief of the philosophers began to investigate very obscure matters and to attempt a proof concerning them, he excused

himself by making a statement the meaning of which was as follows. A student of his books should not, because of the subject of these researches, ascribe to him effrontery, temerity, and an excess of haste to speak of matters of which he had no knowledge; but rather he should ascribe to him the desire and the endeavor to acquire and achieve true beliefs to the extent to which this is in the power of man.[4]

Shlomo Pines, who translated Maimonides's work into English, identified the reference here as Aristotle's *On the Heavens* (Περὶ οὐρανοῦ).[5] In the Greek original, the "chief of philosophers" claims that the philosophical desire for knowledge should not be construed as "effrontery" but on the contrary as "modesty" (αἰδοῦς). This is manifested in the philosopher's contentment with "but a little enlightenment" (μικρὰς εὐπορίας) in matters "surrounded by such unfathomable obscurities" (μεγιστὰς ἀπορίας). Maimonides identifies this quality of modesty with a slow and gradual philosophical process: the gradual formulation of reasonable hypotheses based on the philosopher's knowledge and empirical experience. He concludes his explanation as follows:

> In the same way we say that man should not hasten too much to accede to this great and sublime matter at the first try, without having made his soul undergo training in the sciences and the different kinds of knowledge, having truly improved his character, and having extinguished the desires and cravings engendered in him by his imagination. When, however, he has achieved and acquired knowledge of true and certain premises and has achieved knowledge of the rules of logic and inference and of the various ways of preserving himself from errors of the mind, he then should engage in the investigation of this subject. When doing this he should not make categoric affirmations in favor of the first opinion that occurs to him and should not, from the outset, strain and impel his thoughts toward the apprehension of the deity; he rather should feel awe [*yustaḥaa*] and refrain and hold back until he gradually elevates himself.[6]

Awe here corresponds to Aristotle's αἰδοῦς. It is interpreted as the regimen of self-perfection and study undergone by both the prophet Moses and the medieval philosopher. By refining one's moral virtues and training one's body, imagination, and intellect using ethics, logic, and the sciences, a person can arrive at various levels of perfection. The level one reaches is, of course, dependent on each individual's innate nature and, in general, the limits of human ability.[7] Regardless, it is only after a person has undertaken this regimen—and very few are truly capable of doing so—that he can approach the study of metaphysics, the study of God from a rational perspective. The imagery of "accessing God," through intellectual preparation and cultivation of moral virtues, is associated by Maimonides with the biblical account in Exodus 24, which opens as follows: "And to Moses He said: 'Come up to the LORD, you, and Aaron, Nadab, and Abihu, and seventy of the elders of Israel; and worship from afar; and Moses alone shall come near unto the Lord.'"[8] Aristotelian modesty is interpreted as the gradual path of study and virtue. Through this process a person can actualize his intellect, preparing himself to receive "an overflow overflowing from God, may He be cherished and honored, through the intermediation of the Active Intellect, toward the rational faculty in the first place and thereafter toward the imaginative faculty."[9] Using this principle, Maimonides explains the difference between Moses, on the one hand, and the elders and nobles, on the other hand. Moses is an apogee of awe and restraint—that is, of the gradual philosophical model. As Maimonides explains:

> It is in this sense that it is said, And Moses hid his face, for he was afraid to look upon God; this being an additional meaning of the verse over and above its external meaning that indicates that he hid his face because of his being afraid to look upon the light manifesting itself—and not that the deity, who is greatly exalted above every deficiency, can be apprehended by the eyes. [Moses], peace be on him, was commended for this; and God, may He be exalted, let overflow upon him so much of His bounty and goodness that it became necessary to say of him: And the figure of the Lord shall he look upon.[10]

Moses hid his face from God because he understood that God has no body or any characteristic of visible bodies. God is more akin to a transcendent sphere of being than a person, and He can be accessed only indirectly through the gradual process of intellectual exercise and cultivation of virtues, an approach reminiscent of the Idea of Good as described in book 6 of Plato's *Republic*. Through this gradual process, the prophet expands his knowledge of reality, learning to separate the domains of the world from

God. At the end, both processes meet: the actualization of the prophet's intellect encounters the gradual disassociation of any corporeality from God. Thus, the image of God seen by Moses was not an image at all. It was, rather, the absence of any image, and it represented an apprehension in which the prophet's actualized intellect conjoined with the transcendent intellect of God. Moses's intellectual actualization was manifested in his ability to distinguish between all existent things and God, a distinction that entails an analogical perspective that views God as a dimension separate from all other spheres of reality.

The modesty of Aristotle and the awe of the Maimonidean Moses emphasize that intellectual progress is limited and must be undertaken gradually. Ultimately, however, the philosopher's perspective can spread to all spheres of knowledge, including metaphysics. The elders of Israel, by contrast, were characterized by their inability to properly adhere to this gradual path. They were overly ambitious and sought to engage in forms of apprehension that may seem more immediate but ultimately lead to failure and can plunge a person into a state of dangerous confusion. This is represented, for Maimonides, by their "sight" and "vision" of God:

> The nobles of the children of Israel, on the other hand, were overhasty, strained their thoughts, and achieved apprehension, but only an imperfect one. Hence it is said of them: And they saw the God of Israel, and there was under His feet, and so on and not merely: And they saw the God of Israel. For these words are solely intended to present a criticism of their act of seeing, not to describe the manner of their seeing. Thus, they were solely blamed for the form that their apprehension took inasmuch as corporeality entered into it to some extent—this being necessitated by their overhasty rushing forward before they had reached perfection. They deserved to perish.[11]

The elders and nobles of Israel failed to adhere to the discipline of self-perfection and gradual training. They forced that which should be eased, skipping entire stages of study and preparation to directly and quickly arrive at the final station: metaphysics. The result is the complete opposite of Moses's apprehension. Whereas Moses gained mastery over both his own body and the scientific disciplines, carefully separating these from God, the nobles and elders did not. They failed to free themselves of their bodily desires, to expand their physical and cosmological knowledge, and therefore envisioned God in partially corporeal terms. In doing so, they

besmirched God's incorporeal purity, endangering themselves and ultimately warranting death. They were only saved because: "[Moses], peace
be on him, interceded for them; and they were granted a reprieve until the
time they were burnt at Taberah."[12] Maimonides's use of this midrash—
that is, his need to enlist the idea that Moses had to defend the nobles of
Israel—reflects a tension produced by the adoption of the philosophical
approach when interpreting scripture: the gap between the rationalistic
definition of God and prominent biblical figures or descriptions that sometimes fail to correspond to this ideal.

Maimonides concludes by drawing a lesson for the learned man of his
own day:

> This having happened to these men, it behooves us, all the more, as
> being inferior to them, and it behooves those who are inferior to
> us, to aim at and engage in perfecting our knowledge of preparatory
> matters and in achieving those premises that purify apprehension
> of its taint, which is error. It will then go forward to look upon the
> divine holy Presence.[13]

The learned man is one who has cultivated his moral virtues and undergone gradual training. These not only cleanse man and God of corporeality
but also help sift out those people unworthy of studying metaphysics. Politically and socially, the philosophical principle of gradual progress is almost monarchical in character: one prophet, Moses, and a small number of
worthy philosophers stand at its pinnacle. It is an approach that naturally
elicited antagonism from figures such as Don Isaac, as I will show.

Two Ideas of Jewish Elitism

'Ateret zeqenim opens with an explicit repudiation of Maimonides's claims
in The Guide of the Perplexed:

> I have heard the slander of the many, those skilled in knowledge and
> learned in sciences, the old [authorities] and the new, they who
> slander the good and righteous people, the elders of the people and
> its enforcers—those people who prophesized in the camp, who saw
> the face of the King, and saw beneath his feet the like of a paved
> work of sapphire stone. They [the exegetes] have issued evil slander
> (vayotzi'u dibatam ra'ah), saying that they cursed God in their hearts,
> and did secretly those things that were neither right nor proper, and

they erred in their sight and exchanged their glory, the glory of God with a silent idol of stone, diamonds, sapphire, and gemstones. It is a crime punishable by death to cast God in corporeal terms.[14]

Abravanel begins by alluding to the theme of slander, the crime of the "spies" in the wilderness: the words *vayotz'iu dibatam ra'ah* are a paraphrase of "And they spread the slander of the land which they had spied out unto the children of Israel, saying: 'The land, through which we have passed to spy it out, is a land that devours its inhabitants; and all the people that we saw in it are men of great stature.' . . . Those men that did bring up an evil report of the land, died by the plague before the Lord."[15] Abravanel also uses the phrase "the slander of the many," alluding to Jeremiah 20:1—where the prophet laments that he is encircled by enemies, visible and hidden alike. Abravanel thus casts himself as equally beleaguered. Using this theme, he expresses his ambivalence toward the exegetical path followed by Maimonides and later interpreters who portrayed the elders in a negative light. Seeking to separate himself from the exegetical tradition of the past, he accepts a double challenge: defending the honor of the nobles and elders, while also gaining recognition as a worthy opponent of Maimonides and his followers.

Abravanel continues, explaining the reason for his sense of kinship with the biblical nobles of Israel:

> I, Isaac, son of the prince Don Judah Abravanel, a pure Sephardic Jew, have been very zealous for the honor of the nobles of the children of Israel and I could not stand the oppression wherewith many of the older and newer . . . sages oppress them. And I said the time has come to make my own offering, to offer some balm for their mortal wounds, and some honey for their clusters of bitterness, to write upon a scroll the explanation of their apprehension [of God], that no blemishes were upon them and their knowledge was lofty— neither with strength nor with might, nor with the authority of tradition, but rather with my own spirit, and that which I have understood from the simple reading of scripture, reading the verses as they are. And I shall name this short treatise *'Ateret zeqenim*, for it shall present the crown of their glorious apprehension and rescue them from error.[16]

Abravanel intentionally blurs the lines between his own lineage and that of the nobles of Israel whom he has set out to defend. Brandishing the titles "prince" and "don," Isaac associates himself with Jewish economic court elites. In other words, he is also a noble and thus identifies with the plight of his noble forebears in Exodus. This imaginary social identification between the Jewish economic elite of his own time and the biblical nobles of Israel highlights the sociocultural themes that permeate Don Isaac's attack on the negative exegesis of the "vision of the elders," as will soon become clear.[17] At the same time, however, in identifying himself with these nobles, Abravanel develops a complex exegetical attitude toward them. The crown and glory that Abravanel wishes to bestow upon the elders through a simple reading of scripture can be achieved only through innovative exegesis, a perpetuation in some sense of the mediaeval exegetical and philosophical tradition.[18] It is these innovative readings that are meant to convince his learned readers to change their attitude toward the nobles of Israel. Thus, Abravanel linked restoring the status of the Israelite nobles to his own exegetical accomplishments as well as to the construction of his intellectual identity. Aware that such an undertaking would conflict with the model embodied by Maimonides, he adds a disclaimer:

> I was afraid because I am naked, without the clothes of wisdom. . . . I have already been cast out from study [contemplation] and become a fugitive and wanderer on the earth, now in the streets, now in the market, I go about with the merchants. . . . And the men who persecuted the nobles and leaders of the people are the heroes of old, especially . . . Maimonides. Therefore, all those who hear me will laugh at me, they shall curl their lips and shake their heads. They shall say "who is this who dares to defy renowned warriors of God, who is this who seeks to slay Moses!?"[19]

With ingenious rhetoric, Abravanel prepares his reader for the imaginary battle that is about to take place: the clash between him and Maimonides, a conflict born of Abravanel's leaving the social niche of his family (commerce) and trespassing into the domain of scholars (exegesis). If Don Isaac's authority in trade and banking was beyond dispute, his right to engage in exegesis was an entirely different story. For this reason, he had to defend his right to add his new interpretation of Exodus 24 to those already offered in the past: "therefore, I have said they [the earlier exegetes] do not [base] themselves on chains of tradition in their hands, and the gates of rejoinder to their words have yet to be shut."[20] Abravanel thus char-

acterizes biblical exegesis as an open playing field on which various interpretations compete with one another and where there is no single authority to which all must submit. This description reveals Don Isaac's polemical
intentions and his desire to confront Maimonides and other exegetes.[21]

Abravanel knew that in the eyes of learned elites, he was not fit for the
intellectual and polemical task. His place was among the economic elites,
not with scholars. In an interesting instance of self-promotion, Abravanel associates himself with the special lifestyle of the economic elite—itinerancy.
As opposed to the image of the noble that Abravanel used just a few lines
above, here he presents himself as someone who has been banished from
the paradise of Torah study. Maimonides and his interpreters are depicted
as the exact opposite of Abravanel: they disparage the nobles of Israel
based on their own aristocratic credentials; they are members of a learned
nobility who monopolize exegetical and philosophical knowledge. Abravanel's polemic against Maimonides represents a battle between two sociocultural profiles: that of the Torah scholar and philosopher and that of
the learned merchant and court Jew. The latter cannot claim professional
authority but nevertheless demands the right to participate in the discussion.

If we carefully follow Abravanel's rhetoric in this introduction, we see
that he is trying to justify his transition from political and economic activity to the realm of exegesis and philosophy by proposing an alternative to
the Maimonidean model: the learned Jewish "nobleman." As we have seen
in previous chapters, the learned noble and monarch were ideals developed
in the Portuguese literature written and cultivated by the Avis dynasty, a
theme that appears in various guises throughout Don Isaac's writings. By
writing and distributing his first work, 'Ateret zeqenim, Don Isaac sought to
define himself as a prominent intellectual figure both within his community
and outside of it. He also sought to instigate some degree of social change
within the intellectual elite, presenting a relatively new figure: the learned
merchant who feels at home in several different spheres—commerce, the
court, and Jewish exegetical literature. This new model offered by Don
Isaac is articulated through the biblical figures with whom he identifies.
Unlike Maimonides, who identified with Moses, the greatest of all prophets, Don Isaac identifies with the secondary figures of the Bible, the elders
and nobles. These, to some extent, can be said to represent the circle of the
wealthy Jewish elites to which Abravanel belonged.

The Central Philosophical Issue of 'Ateret zeqenim

As 'Ateret zeqenim opens, the dispute between Abravanel and Maimonides over the status of the nobles of Israel seems to lose some of its sharpness and centrality, making way for a seemingly different discussion about the angel mentioned in Exodus 23:20 ("See, I am sending an angel ahead of you to guard you along the way and to bring you to the place I have prepared")—in other words, a discussion of the role played by the angel in the relationship between God and Israel. The main question asked by 'Ateret zeqenim can be summarized as follows: What factors shape the fate of Israel? Is it the direct providence of God, or some natural intermediary—an angel? Abravanel believed that this subject is closely intertwined with the issue of the elders of Israel. The two accounts represent the extremities of a single literary unit that Abravanel treats as a cohesive whole (Ex. 23:20–24:18). According to Abravanel, they point to two types of relationships: the reciprocal relationship between Israel and the angel of God and the unmediated connection between Moses, the elders, and the nobles on the one hand, and God on the other hand. To defend the honor of the elders and nobles, Abravanel attempts to make sense of the dual influences exerted upon the Jewish people: that of God and that of the angel. He argues that the prophecy of Moses and the vision of the elders and nobles demonstrate the superiority of the direct providence of God over the intermediary providence of the angel. The dilemma can be summed up using a pair of terms central to Iberian literature and Christian culture during the fourteenth and (especially) fifteenth centuries: *providencia* and *fortuna*. The flagrant tension between the pagan, astrological, and Stoic element of fortuna and the Catholic belief in (and dogma of) divine providence occupied more than a few Iberian authors and philosophers during the era. Among other things, it served as a backdrop for the Iberian literary renaissance of the time—the so-called vernacular humanist movement.

For example, we can cite the vivid portrayal and personification of fortuna in the seventh canto of Dante's *Divine Comedy*—one of the sources of inspiration for the Christian Iberian writers. After Dante asks "what is this Fortune?," Virgil, his guide, responds:

> That One, whose wisdom knows infinity,
> Made all the heavens and gave each one a guide [*e diè lor chi conduce*]
> And each sphere shining shines on all the others

So light is spread with equal distribution:
For worldly splendors He decreed the same
And ordained a guide and general ministress [*general ministra e duce*]
Who would at her discretion shift the world's
Vain wealth from nation to nation, house to house,
With no chance of interference from mankind.

So while one nation rules, another falls,
According to whatever she decrees,
(Her sentence hidden like a snake in grass).

Your knowledge has no influence on her;
For she foresees, she judges, and she rules
Her kingdom as the other gods do theirs.
Her changing changes never take a rest
Necessity keeps her in constant motion,
As men come and go to take their turn with her.
And this is she so crucified and cursed . . .
But she is blest and in her bliss hears nothing
With all God's joyful first-created creatures
She turns her sphere and, blest, turns it with joy [*volve sua spera*].[22]

Many Iberian authors wrote their own works in dialogue with this notion of *fortuna*—a discrete entity that—while created by God and subject to him—is nevertheless incomprehensible and deaf to the pleas of mankind. Some authors adopted various formats of this dualistic vision. Others limited discussions of fate to questions of God's divine providence in this world.[23] Dante's description compares *fortuna* to the separate intellects that move the celestial spheres, and he even rhymes them (*chi conduce* and *general ministra e duce*). Just as the separate intellects move the heavens and thus ensure that light is evenly distributed over the world, so *fortuna* moves earthly goods from one hand to another—constantly changing the fortunes of individuals and nations; compelling them through natural, necessary movement; indifferent to human desires and wishes. As Dante says, "with all God's joyful first-created creatures she turns her sphere and, blest, turns it with joy."

Fortuna thus encapsulates the natural changes that take place in the sublunar world, motions that correspond to the motions of the heavenly spheres. Furthermore, *fortuna* is an independent entity. While she was created by God, she now moves in accordance with a predetermined, natural scheme.

This idea has some affinity to Abravanel's notion of an angel or heavenly officer, as presented at the beginning of *'Ateret zeqenim*. As I will show below, this angel is also a spiritual entity (that is, a separate intellect) created by God and appointed to rule over human fate. And although the Christian discussions of fate and providence are never referred to in *'Ateret zeqenim*, Abravanel's Portuguese letter shows that he was well acquainted with fifteenth-century Iberian literature.

For this reason, it is reasonable to cast the formal parallelism between *'Ateret zeqenim* and the Christian literary discussions of analogous issues as evidence that Abravanel's work belonged to the Jewish and Christian literary milieus.

The Astral Influence upon the Nations

To understand the relationship between this seemingly scholastic subject and Don Isaac's social profile, as well as his literary conceptions of his own role, we must delve into his views—in particular, how he envisions the different types of forces that exert their influence upon humanity: God, the stars, or an intermediary being called an angel. In the middle of the book, in chapters eleven and twelve, Abravanel sharply demarcates two types of external influence that are exerted upon human societies and religions.

Abravanel writes, "The early authorities agree, and it is the truth, that all the nations, in their lands and according to their peoples, are under the dominion of the stars."[24] In Don Isaac's view, every human (and by way of analogy, every society) is a combination of material elements molded together into a single entity with the capability of human intellect—the form of man, according to medieval Aristotelian philosophy. The combination of man's elementary components is the consequence of natural movements that, in turn, are caused by the movements of the stars. The stars move the lower elements that are responsible for those combinations that make possible the composition (in other words, the birth) of humans and other living things. Likewise, it is the movements of the stars that eventually disconnect these elements from each other and thus lead to decay and death. In the philosophical language of the era, these processes were called "generation and corruption." According to Abravanel's astrological claim—"that each particular nation has its own particular star in the heavens"—natural forces of causality are responsible, at least in part, for all human events. However, Abravanel is careful to note that human intellect is an exception. Intellect has no causal relationship with the movements of the stars and is instead controlled by those higher entities that move them: the separate intellects. Nevertheless, as far as the material and physical circumstances of humanity are concerned, humans "are dominated like animals; children, life, and livelihood are dependent on fate, for the sphere [that moves the stars] is what creates the contingency; it perpetuates this contingency for good or causes it to disappear, according to the movements and changing positions of the stars."[25]

Even though Seneca and Cicero do not make an appearance in 'Ateret zeqenim, we find there a conception similar to theirs. According to the neo-Stoic approach, addressed explicitly in Abravanel's Portuguese letter, man's circumstances and existence are at the mercy of fate—that is, the immutable causal forces of nature. In contrast, the soul (in terms of its own internal causality as well as its relationship with external factors) can be changed, provided it understands itself. In 'Ateret zeqenim, this is paralleled by the soul's ability to conjoin with the separate intellect and the cosmological order of being. Even though this chapter is more heavily dominated by astrology than Stoicism, 'Ateret zeqenim and the Portuguese letter share a similar approach: the sharp contrast between the dictates of astral determinism and the freedom of the intellect or soul. In other words, chapter 11 of 'Ateret zeqenim can be viewed as presenting a cosmological view parallel to the neo-Stoic conception of fate—a presentation that better accorded with the discourse of medieval Jewish philosophy and exegesis. What is important as far as we are concerned are the different guises in which this approach appeared—neo-Stoic in the Christian context and cosmological and astrological in the Jewish one.

God's Special Providence over the Jewish People

However, as the reader moves to chapter 12, she will find an entirely different kind of influence being discussed:

> The Creator . . . did not create each of the three worlds equally perfect; rather, it is clear that in the world of the intelligences, in the world of the spheres, and in the sublunar world, in each one, He created a unique part, much nobler and more perfect than the other parts of the world. And the supreme divine wisdom saw fit to rule it [the unique part] Himself and to bring upon it goodness and perfection through a powerful conjunction, without any intermediary.[26]

Alongside the picture of stars exerting their influences upon the physi-cal circumstances of the nations, Abravanel develops a theological and cos-mological approach: the relationship between the higher realms and the sublunar world is not blind and arbitrary. Rather, there is a direct connec-tion between the "unique part" and the ultimate cause of the cosmos—God himself. In book lambda of the *Metaphysics*, Aristotle demonstrates the necessity of a first mover for the existence of nature (by which he means a system of movements).[27] Aristotle's definition of this first mover is an intellect thinking about its own thought, the famous unmoved mover who is in a perpetual and eternal state of actuality. While he does not move, all entities at all different levels of the universe (from the stars to the sub-lunar world) yearn to emulate him and thus are impelled into movement themselves. According to the model proposed in book lambda, the relation-ship between God and the various layers of the cosmos is logical, causal, and teleological. The unmoved mover must stand at the head of the cos-mological pyramid, and the perfection of its self-thought is the model (and cause) of all natural movements.

Abravanel inherited this Aristotelian conception of God from medieval Jewish and Islamic philosophy and, in this chapter of '*Ateret zeqenim*, he uses various and sometimes even contradictory cosmological schemes to describe the relationship between God and the world. Abravanel combines Ibn Sina's model (derived from Alfarabi), which postulates an emanatory system (from God to the Active Intellect and through a series of separate intellects), with Ibn Rushd's model of a first cause (that directly acts upon the intellects and spheres).[28] This is despite the fact that Ibn Rushd was very much opposed to the Neoplatonic emanation scheme favored by Ibn Sina, which implied both hierarchy and temporality—each sphere being engendered by another, and each sphere continuing to be moved by its predecessor. Adopting this astronomical eclecticism, Abravanel maintains that God directly connects with three unique parts belonging to the three strata of the universe: separate intellects, celestial spheres, and the sub-lunar world. The bone of contention between Aristotle's Jewish and Arab interpreters, on the one hand, and Abravanel, on the other hand, is the point of contact between God and the movements of the cosmos. Ibn Sina and Alfarabi believed that there was only one point of contact: the first in-tellect. From this intellect proceed the subsequent emanations of the lower intellects and spheres. Abravanel, in contrast, thought that God has three points of contact with the universe (and in this sense his approach was closer to Ibn Rushd's): the first is the first intellect, from which proceed the other separate intellects (according to Ibn Sina); the second is the diurnal sphere that comprehends all the others (according to Ibn Rushd); and the third is the Jewish people (according to the Torah). In the realm of separate intellects and celestial spheres, the connection to God is causal and teleological (emanation, a desire to emulate God, the self-thought of the first intellect). However, the connection to the Jewish people—that is, to composed beings—is very different. Abravanel explains:

> Indeed, the world of generation and corruption, a realm that as a whole is devoid of perfection and in its parts is bereft of eternity, is turned about every day. Its leaves wither and it is brought to the grave. God performed a wonder when it came to the last complex being, the human race, possessor of all powers, and privileged it with a unique part, the nation of Israel. He perfected it . . . so that He could influence this part with perfection, through wondrous providence and without any intermediary whatsoever. The other nations, however, He subjugated to the dominion of the heavenly bodies.[29]

If in the realm of intellects and spheres the relationship between God and the intellect or sphere is one of transfer (*tsiyur*)—that is, the first intellect seeks to represent God and his thought and thus compels the first sphere into circular motion—the relationship between God and the Jewish people transcends such general, causal, and teleological connections. God's connection to Israel is through special divine providence over the history of the Jewish people. Of course, this is in contrast to the situation of other nations, whose histories are determined by the movements of astral bodies. The difference between the Jewish people and the nations is manifest in two realms: First, whereas the Jewish people have a direct connection to God, the other nations have only an indirect one—the divine influence conveyed to them is mediated by the astral bodies, the spheres, and the intellects that move them. Second, the connection of the other nations to the celestial bodies and to God is predetermined and fixed (it is based on secondary intellects imitating a first intellect). In contrast, the Jewish people do not have a fixed or naturalistic affinity to God. Their connection to him is direct and unbound by any preconditions, and God determines how the relationship will unfold. For the other nations, the relationship to the first cause is fixed and determined, and the correct response is to internalize psychologically and intellectually the laws of causality (an approach we saw in Abravanel's Portuguese letter). For Israel, however, the connection to God is supernatural: it is unfettered by natural limitations and prerequisites. This special connection cannot be forged by simply understanding the cosmological system of nature. God's relationship to the first intellect, the first sphere, and the Jewish people logically precedes the cosmos that proceeds from these three points of direct divine contact. With this argument, Abravanel developed an approach that cuts the ground out from under the feet of the elites represented by Maimonides:

> The conjunction [with God] and divine providence are not acquired through rational study and lengthy investigation, but only thanks to God's grace. This is clear because the fact that God, may He be blessed, conjoins Himself with such a vile material being as man is a fact that exceeds the boundaries of nature and is the greatest of the miracles. Therefore, study and philosophizing as a means to arrive at this goal are futile and deceitful, and intellectual study aimed at acquiring it is useless and will avail one not. Therefore, one can even find divine influx and goodness resting upon those who are not prepared to receive it, as took place at Mount Sinai.[30]

The connection between God and Israel is not the result of study or training, and it is not achieved by man learning to emulate the causality and teleology of higher worlds. It is a gift of God; it is divine grace. It is the result of God's creation of a "unique part" of humanity to which he could relate directly. It follows that the learned aristocracies—both philosophical and rabbinical—cannot claim a monopoly on the direct connection to God. They cannot define it as a relationship predicated on conditions they have set (be those rabbinic knowledge or philosophy). Thus, one can see that the theological and cosmological scheme described in 'Ateret zeqenim is in fact closely related to the polemical introduction that opens the work. For Abravanel, prophecy does not depend on the perfection of the individual. It is rather a consequence of God's a priori and special connection with the Jewish people, which manifests itself in different types of prophecy— whether the limited prophecy of the elders or the perfect prophecy of Moses. In a theological and cosmological system in which the Israelite nation is chosen and prophecy, in various degrees, is always given to the unprepared, any person (regardless of whether he belongs to a scholarly elite or is a merchant) can participate in the supposedly exclusive discussions about the relationship between God and Israel. Thus, Don Isaac's theological system as formulated in 'Ateret zeqenim is not merely scholastic: it is his passport into the world of Jewish exegesis.

It bears mentioning that the distinction between God's providence over the Jewish people in the land of Israel and the providence of the celestial bodies upon the other nations in their own countries had already been established as a trope in both Aristotelian rationalist and kabbalistic mystical circles long before Abravanel. A good example of the latter is the commentary of Nachmanides (1194–1270) on Leviticus 18:25. Nachmanides distinguishes between the nations of the world and their lands, which are controlled by the stars, and the Jewish people and the land of Israel, which are under the direct providence of God. Of the nations, Nachmanides writes that "the Glorious Name created everything, and He placed the power of the lower creatures in the higher beings, giving over each and every nation in their lands after their nations some known star or constellation, as is known from astrology."[31] This contrasts with God's special direct connection with the people and land of Israel. An example of the Aristotelian philosophical approach appears in commentary of Gersonides (1288–1344) on Deuteronomy 4 (in the "sixth lesson"): "It is clear that other nations' affairs are determined by the system of the stars whereas [the affairs of] Israel are under the special providence of God, blessed be He."[32] These two examples are but a small part of a rich literary tradition that informed Abravanel's views of fate and providence. Nonetheless, one can see that Abravanel used an existing astrological and theological approach for his own ends: to polemicize against the sociological and philosophical profile represented by Maimonides.

The Angel Michael

Toward the end of chapter 12, after adamantly distinguishing Israel from the nations, Abravanel backtracks and claims that this important distinction has been blurred with the exile. Don Isaac raises a challenge from Daniel 10–12, in which constant references are made to "Michael your prince." This implies that Israel has its own angelic patron as all other nations do. How can this be? Abravanel explains:

> The answer is as follows: Michael is not referred to as "the prince of the Kingdom of Israel" as we indeed find in the case of the Kingdom of Greece and the Kingdom of Persia [compare Daniel 10:20]. For

the providence of these princes [upon their nations] is constant and natural. Therefore, he refers to them as "the prince of such-and-such a Kingdom." However, Israel, who are not under the providence of an [angelic] prince, are not referred to as the prince of the Kingdom of Israel. For at that time they were in the Babylonian exile, and it was God's plan during those dark days that "I shall certainly hide my face from you on that day because of all the evil they have done" (Deut 31:18). And Michael, seeing that God had hidden his face from them, that they had no prince, and that the princes of the nations were inveighing against them, had mercy upon them. And he rose up to advocate on behalf of our nation, even though this was not his charge.[33]

The narrative character of the passage, with the rise of a new player in Jewish history (the angelic prince of the Kingdom of Israel), is at odds with the cosmological scheme laid out in chapters eleven and twelve. At the end of the intricate discussion in which he distinguished astrological determinism from divine providence, Abravanel was required to account for the complexities of Israel in exile. On the one hand, Israel is, at least in principle, directly connected to God—a connection that has been lost with the Jews' exile. On the other hand, because special providence has been suspended, parts of the Jewish Diaspora have been handed over to the mercies of the celestial bodies that control the foreign lands in which they reside. As a result, they need an advocate to speak on their behalf to a God who conceals his face. This is the function of the angelic prince Michael. In Abravanel's view, Michael is the first intellect. In other words, he is one of the points of contact between God and the world: "And his mercy for Israel was aroused, and he sought to tend to their well-being during the exile."[34] Abravanel presents exile as the corruption of the cosmological distinction between Israel and the other nations. It is a state of turmoil in which the astral determinism of the other nations is bound together with the special providence of Israel—now mediated by Michael.

According to this approach, the Jewish communities are subject to two sets of influence: the historical and natural influence exerted upon their Diaspora lands, and divine influence based on a connection between the Jewish people and the angel Michael. According to this model, the Jewish minority vacillates between two poles: the causality that moves the non-Jewish majority and the internal causality of the Jews (their connection to

God), with the latter partially freeing them from the dominion of the former. As I have shown in previous chapters, the tension between these two influences is a central theme in Abravanel's correspondence with Yehiel da Pisa—for example, in his account of the conquest of Arzila. This approach led Abravanel to emphasize the intermediary role played by Jewish merchants who, like Michael, compensate for diminished divine providence during exile. 'Ateret zeqenim appears to be an attempt to justify the intermediary role played by the angel Michael and the elders in guarding the distinction between Israel and the other nations. This is distinct from the scholarly elitist model, and its representatives, Moses and the philosopher. In this model, it is the philosophical apprehension and erudition of Israel's leaders that distinguish it from the other nations.

Isaac Abravanel's Historiosophy

In the concluding chapters of 'Ateret zeqenim, Abravanel describes a tripartite connection between Israel, the angel (the first intellect), and God, interpreting Exodus 23–24 in the process. The juxtaposition of the angel of Exodus 23:20 to the ascent of Moses, Aaron, Nadab, Abihu, and the elders in Exodus 24 is explained as follows: the special, direct connection between God and the Jewish people can exist only in a special place the land of Israel. The angel of Exodus 23:20 is the mediator between God and an Israel outside its land; it is the first intellect. However, this mediation endangers the Jews' belief in special providence and has the potential to lead them back toward the belief of the other nations, the astral worldview. This is why Moses, Aaron, Nadab, Abihu, and the leaders had to ascend the mountain: "in order to comprehend the lordship of God blessed is He, that he is ruler of all separate intellects and spheres."[35] In other words, before handing the people over to the angel, God wished to remind Moses and those with him that the angel who will now mediate between them is still under his control. It is God who controls all the different layers of the cosmos—as explained by Abravanel in chapters 11 and 12. Therefore, the sight of the elders and the vision of the nobles represent true encounters with the divine. This is despite the gulf between their vision and that of Moses at Sinai. Abravanel summarizes the vision experienced by the elders as follows:

> And this was the purpose of the [biblical] passage: the elders of Israel saw and understood that God Himself oversees this lower world

and the chosen people which he chose as an inheritance, He oversees the world of separate intellects and influences them with goodness and existence, and He himself moves the upper sphere, and its movement moves everything, and He is therefore the ruler and leader of all worlds.[36]

Unlike Maimonides, who starkly contrasts Moses's prophecy with the sight of the elders, Abravanel sees continuity, while acknowledging that their respective levels of apprehension were different. And unlike Maimonides, he ascribes real prophecy to the elders. The hierarchical and continuous relationship between Moses and the elders points to the special connection between God and all of the Jewish people—a connection far broader than one mediated by a single prophet standing aloof from the people. This connection is a consequence of the special relationship between God and the Jewish people. It does not depend on a specific group of intellectually gifted people who founded a nation and forged a tradition by dint of their philosophical and prophetic abilities. The nation is not the product of an intellectual elite's prophecy. Prophecy represents a series of different (and gradational) levels of understanding of the unique connection between God and Israel. There is a clear affinity between this view and that expressed by the Sage in Judah Halevi's *Kuzari*.[37] In *Kuzari*, the Jewish people are portrayed as an independent spiritual entity with a unique connection with God. It is only by virtue of this special link that prophets arise in Israel. In this sense, the existence of the prophet is predicated on the existence of a metaphysical entity (the Jewish people) and its connection with God, not the reverse. Don Isaac's attraction to Halevi's view can, once again, be understood in social terms: rather than claiming leadership status for himself on the basis of superiority in philosophy or Torah study, it was easier for a figure such as Abravanel to claim that status on the basis of strengthening the community's connection to God, which can be forged through political, economic, and literary activity.

However, in terms of the providence over the Jewish people outside of the land of Israel, we can ask the following question: if the children of Israel, in the wilderness and in exile, are not under God's special providence, what makes them any different from other nations? Abravanel's answer is as follows:

> And in terms of providence: for the [angelic] princes lead their nations and peoples according to the nature of their land, and in ac-

cordance with their history within the order of celestial constellations. Added to this are the efforts of men motivated by virtuous
causes. [In contrast] the angel appointed over Israel leads them
according to the Torah commanded by Moses—to the extent that
each one of them fulfills its commandments and judgments, statutes and rulings, so shall be his felicity, even though this is the opposite of the natural order that shifts in step with the alternating
constellations.[38]

What separates Israel in the wilderness and exile from other nations is
Israel's connection to the first intellect, as well as the rank of the first intellect in comparison to the other separate intellects (as we saw in Abravanel's
discussion of the angel Michael). The relationship between Israel and the
first intellect (or the angel of Exodus) is similar to the relationship between
the angel and God—in other words, it is a supernatural connection, a connection that logically precedes nature. This is why, unlike other nations,
that must simply acclimatize themselves to the natural order of being, Israel must adapt (by observing the divine commandments) to the relationship between God and the first intellect. This relationship, of course, is not
dictated by laws of nature but rather by God. Abravanel maintains that this
is how the children of Israel will overcome nature, escape the fates of other
nations, and ultimately gain victory—not by adapting to the natural order
as advocated by the Stoics, but rather by adapting to the religious and supernatural tripartite connection between God, the first intellect, the diurnal sphere, and Israel. Although Israel is denied a direct connection to God
in exile, the Torah and commandments (and the supernatural logic that
they express) preserve the connection that Israel once had with God and
that is now limited to the first intellect. Therefore, the children of Israel
indeed remain dependent on an intermediary, the angel who compen-
sates for their lost connection with God. However, their intermediary is
still different than those of the other nations: it is directly subordinate to
God, not to natural laws.

In some senses this approach can be understood as a rationalization of
the diverse social and literary practices of Abravanel in his dual Christian
and Jewish milieu. In a Christian context, Don Isaac advised and acted in
accordance with the natural and astral norms of the Portuguese kingdom.
This is manifested in his economic successes and his assimilation of neo-
Stoic rhetoric. In a Jewish context, however, he adopted the internal cosmic

and theological norms of the Jewish community, wielding his wealth, status, and literary and exegetical talents to protect the community, ensure its continuity, and justify his role as a leader. Thus, the variation in his style that is evident from a comparison of 'Ateret zeqenim to the Portuguese letter is a consequence of the different internal logic that prevails in each discourse and each cultural context. Nevertheless, one can easily detect the common thread running through both: the necessity of adapting to fate or providence—that is, to the relationship between higher entities and lower beings, the connection that produces historical circumstances.

Furthermore, whether Abravanel was addressing Christians or Jews, the figure of the counselor plays an important role. In his letter to the Count of Faro, Abravanel portrayed himself as an advisor, justifying this role through his literary and economic knowledge. In 'Ateret zeqenim, the angel takes on the role of advocate, mediating between God and Israel. In both cases, the individual or nation adapts to a specific cosmological or theological system through the mediation of an advisor. It is the advisor who convinces a Christian noble or a Jewish community how to adopt the logic to which they are subject (nature or the commandments). It seems that the theme and conception of a counselor are bound up in the administrative and advisory roles that Don Isaac fulfilled on behalf of the nouse of Bragança and in the court of King Afonso V.

Abravanel concludes 'Ateret zeqenim by likening the Jewish people to a celestial sphere:

> And the fourth aspect . . . [of] the nation can be compared to a sphere. For just as the sphere . . . undergoes locomotion but not changes of generation and corruption . . . so too the chosen people, all of us as one person, move in a descending and ascending locomotion. . . . For despite the intensity of exile, the glorious crown of providence has not been removed from our head. . . . It shall not be separated from its cleaving to the [separate] intellect and its cognition. . . . However, we move thus: sometimes we ascend to the most supernal heights, in terms of both physical and spiritual perfections, at other times we descend to the lowest nadir into the nations of the world.[39]

Just as the neo-Stoic conception identifies in the ebbs and tides of personal and collective fate the hand of external natural causes, factors that lie beyond our control, so Abravanel conceives of the waxing and waning fortunes of the Jews through history as a circular motion approaching and leaving the center of providence (the land of Israel)—a process that also cannot be influenced. However, there is a difference between the fate of the other nations and that of Israel. For the other nations, these changes are part of a process of the rise and fall of peoples and individuals. Their movement is analogous to Aristotelian generation and corruption. In contrast, changes in Israel's fortune resemble a different type of motion: the eternal circular motion of the stars and spheres. Thus, exile does not represent the natural corruption of the Jewish people. It is simply part of the circular motion from redemption to exile and from exile to redemption. Ultimately, shifting fortunes in both Jewish and Christian contexts are determined by a series of cosmic conditions that cannot be controlled and to which the leader must adapt himself.

Abravanel's sober mentality varied from sphere to sphere: it was manifested in a Christian context as a form of neo-Stoicism, and in a Jewish context in the guise of a specific cosmological and theological scheme. In the former, Don Isaac sought to improve his own fortunes and those of his patron. In the latter, he sought to maintain the continuity of the Jewish community by strengthening Jews' loyalty to the foundational norms of their community (the commandments, the conception of redemption, and so on) and by developing a set of external connections between them and the nobility and merchant class. In other words, Abravanel's 'Ateret zeqenim justified a model in which the leader is responsible for shaping the community's loyalty to the divine commandments and for facilitating its acclimation to divine providence. However, at the same time this leader must consolidate his power and status in the royal court and in the world of commerce and banking to properly contend with the weakened state of providence that prevails during exile—serving as a protector, a guardian angel, for his community. In a sense, one can say that in 'Ateret zeqenim Don Isaac offered a philosophical and theological conception that echoed and projected his own sociocultural profile. And in doing so, he challenged the philosophical and political model embodied by Maimonides.

5 : DON ISAAC'S FALL
FROM GRACE IN PORTUGAL

The End of King Dom Afonso V's Reign

The texts discussed until this point were composed during Don Isaac's social rise in Portugal (in both Jewish and Christian milieus) during the 1460s and early 1470s. However, the end of King Dom Afonso V's reign, as well as broader shifts in power in the Iberian peninsula, would soon bring this stage in Abravanel's life to a dramatic end. In 1474 Don Enrique IV of Castile died, throwing the delicate balance between Iberia's Christian kingdoms into turmoil.[1] Two major factions arose to fill the void. One was led by Doña Isabel, the deceased king's sister and designated heir. In 1469 Doña Isabel had been wed in secret to the heir of the throne of Aragon, Don Fernando. Against them stood the faction of Doña Juana, daughter of King Don Enrique IV of Castile through his marriage to Dom Afonso V's sister. Afonso had originally hoped that Doña Juana would marry his son, Dom João II, and thus draw the two Iberian kingdoms closer together. However, with King Enrique IV's death and the immediate coronation of Doña Isabel, Dom Afonso V made new plans and married Doña Juana himself. Thus, he hoped, he could gather around him the Castilian nobles who opposed Doña Isabel.

In 1475 and 1476, Dom Afonso V invaded Castile, hoping that the noble rebels would join his army. But the campaign was a failure, and Doña Isabel's faction was victorious on both the military and political fronts. The dynastic crisis of these years brought to the fore trends that were already evident during the foundation of the Avis dynasty: the struggle between a centralized monarchy and the nobility, as well as the recurring attempts to unite the Christian kingdoms of Iberia. Doña Isabel's ascension to the throne of Castile, which was followed by the ascension of her husband, Don Fernando, to the throne of Aragon in the mid-1470s, anticipated the union of the two kingdoms (the future Spanish Empire) and the consolidation of royal power at the expense of the nobility.

The failure of Dom Afonso V's attempt to interfere in the Castilian dynastic crisis marked his gradual move away from active rule and the transfer of royal powers to Dom João II. During his attempted invasion of Castile, Dom Afonso V had designated his son as his heir. After the Portuguese army was defeated at Toro, in March 1476, King Dom Afonso V decided that the only way to shift the balance of power was to enlist the support of King Louis XI of France. He thus decided to travel with his entourage for a personal audience with the French monarch. In August 1476, some twenty ships embarked with the king and his men from Lisbon. They passed through the straits of Gibraltar, made landfall at Perpignan, and from there traveled several months to the Marne, where the two monarchs met.[2] Lois XI refused Dom Afonso V's request for support—he was more concerned with his own political problems—and sought Dom Afonso V's political support in his own struggle with the Duke of Bourgogne. After months of travel, extensive diplomatic activity, and significant expenditures, Dom Afonso V had nothing to show for his efforts. Hope was lost, and he began to be afflicted by melancholy. In September of 1477, Dom Afonso V transferred the reins of rulership to his son Dom João II, in practice even if not formally, and for his part planned to make pilgrimage to Jerusalem. Although Dom Afonso V returned to Portugal that same year, the decline of his power and influence during these years is evident as is the concomitant rise of his son Dom João II.[3]

As was the case for other members of the Jewish economic elite, the 1470s offered Don Isaac Abravanel an important financial opportunity. Dom Afonso V's war required funding, and Abravanel obliged. In 1478 Don Isaac—along with two other Jewish merchants, Gedaliah Palaçano and Moshe Latam—lent the king the astronomical sum of 3,384,615 reais (as well as an additional 642,800 reais given to the soldiers in the form of cloth for their personal use).[4] During these years (1477–81), the plague spread through Portugal, casting a shadow on an already troubled era and compounding the wartime atmosphere and the wane of Dom Afonso V's reign. A clear echo of the grim mood appears in the opening of Isaac Abravanel's letter to Yehiel da Pisa from 1481:

> There is wrath gone out from the Lord, the plague has begun, fire is flashing up amidst the city in which I find myself, for death has come through our windows and entered our palaces, because the Lord descended upon it in fire, before the oppressing sword, before the terror of the Lord, before Him goes the plague.
>
> These past three years I have forsaken my house, I wandered with the daughters who are my daughters and the sons who are my sons,

all the children born and raised in my house. I have been a fugitive and a sojourner in the earth, as the meandering, flying swallow. We left because of the stormy wind and tempest, from rampart to rampart, from mount to hill, leaping upon the mountains, skipping upon the hills, trying to escape with our lives.[5]

There is no direct evidence of Isaac Abravanel's status and personal circumstances during these years. However, the ongoing war, Dom Afonso V's relinquishment of power, and the plagues that forced the elites to flee urban centers for the countryside must have had a negative impact on Don Isaac's day-to-day life, jarring the foundation of his political and social power.

The Death of Dom Afonso V and the Rise of Dom João II

On August 28, 1481, Dom Afonso V succumbed to the plague.[6] Dom João II officially assumed the Portuguese throne. Putting an end to his father's war by ratifying the treaty of Alcáçovas in 1479, Dom João II turned his attention to the internal affairs of his kingdom.[7] His strategy was to curtail aristocratic power to consolidate that of the crown, which had grown weak during his father's reign. At the Cortes convened in 1481 and 1482, Dom João II made changes to the nobility's oath of fealty to the crown. The previous version of the oath made the distinction between the properties received as gifts from the king—which in principle remained under the crown's ownership—and the nobles' inherited family lands, for which they enjoyed full ownership and protected rights. Dom João II imposed a new oath on his subjects that asserted the king's supreme ownership of all the kingdom's properties.[8] On the first day of the Cortes, Dom Fernando, the Duke of Bragança, got down on his knees before the new king and took the new oath on behalf of the entire nobility.[9] At the same gathering, the king pointedly made no oaths himself to the three estates, thus asserting the preeminence of royal power.[10] The king further undermined the nobility's traditional right to sit in judgment in their fiefs: before long he had forced them to allow his representatives to enter their lands and judge in their stead.

This defiant new set of polices brought Dom João II into outright conflict with the house of Bragança, whose members—due to their prestige and lands—the king regarded as one of the chief threats to his power. Dom Fernando, the Duke of Bragança, and Dom Diego, the Duke of Viseu, began to form an alliance of noblemen in an attempt to halt the king's new initiatives. Unlike his father, who had assumed the throne by virtue of his alliance with prominent nobles, Dom João II was not bound to any such agreements. He thus sought to free himself from the past, to unfetter himself from the bonds of his father's alliance with the aristocracy. Capitalizing on the air of intrigue that permeated these aristocratic circles and latching onto the convenient friendship between Dom Fernando of Bragança and Portugal's enemies, the Castilian monarchs, Dom João II had the duke arrested on May 29, 1483. He was accused of treason and disloyalty and sentenced to death.[11] On June 20, 1483, in Evora, Isaac Abravanel's patron was beheaded. The duke's family, including the Count of Faro, fled to Castile. About a year after Dom Fernando's death, the Duke of Viseu hatched a plot with other noblemen to assassinate the king. However, word of the plan was leaked to Dom João II. The duke, who was the queen's brother, was stabbed to death by Dom João II himself.[12]

In the wake of this conflict with the nobility, Dom João II turned his attention to Isaac Abravanel, who had close ties with the houses of Bragança and Viseu. On May 30, 1483, the day after Dom Fernando was apprehended, the king dispatched a messenger to arrest Don Isaac as well. A verdict issued in 1485 describes the failed attempt to arrest Don Isaac and his flight to Castile—the end of his commercial and political career in Portugal:

> After we were made aware that Dom Fernando [the Duke of Bragança], Dom Joham [the Marquis de Montemor], and their partners had conspired together to carry out the aforementioned wicked deeds and treasonous acts against us [the crown], we ordered the arrest of Dom Fernando and his associates and sent a knight to apprehend the criminal [Don Isaac]. He traveled with the knight until the city of Arraiolos. But though our knight did everything to constrain him, the criminal managed to escape, leaving our kingdom and leaving his own dwelling place (*amoorandosse delles*). After the criminal had fled the kingdom, we ordered Dom Fernando [the Duke of Bragança] be decapitated for his conspiracies, treasonous acts, and wicked plots.[13]

Don Isaac was also sentenced to death, but by fleeing to Castile, he escaped with his life. In his verdict, the judge explained the role played by Don Isaac in his patrons' plot against the king:

> And since the criminal [Isaac Abravanel] was a great servant (*muito grande servidor*) and friend to Dom Fernando [the Duke of Bra-

gança], Dom Joham [the Marquis de Montemor], and the entire house of Bragança, and since he was very rich, with many properties, and a man both exceedingly intelligent and industrious, and since he had the money that the conspirators needed to carry out their evil deeds and treasonous acts—they shared their conspiracy and treason with him. . . . And they ordered him to inform them if he planned to attend the Royal Court and to write to them about what was said about and planned against [the conspirators]. The criminal [Isaac Abravanel] accepted the task.[14]

According to the verdict, Don Isaac served as an accomplice and a spy for the noble rebels. While is difficult to ascertain the truth behind this claim, Abravanel was, without a doubt, a close friend of the house of Bragança and provided them with his banking services.

The same economic and social connections that had helped Don Isaac rise socially and economically in the court of Dom Afonso V ultimately led to his fall from grace, forcing him to flee Portugal in the first years of Dom João II's reign. The verdict also points to the exchange of letters between Don Isaac and the members of the house of Bragança. While we have no evidence of such a correspondence besides the Portuguese letter described in chapter 2, this suggests that Don Isaac conducted a steady correspondence with his patrons, even during the months of crisis precipitated by Dom João II's rise. We can only guess what historical, political, and literary information was contained in these lost letters.

As I have tried to show in the first part of this book, Don Isaac was an active participant in Dom Afonso V's alliance with the nobility (and their supporters among the commercial elites). The end of his career in Portugal, as described in the verdict, shows the extent to which his political status was at the mercy of this alliance of interests, as well as the extent to which he had entangled himself in political, economic, and cultural life in the kingdom of Portugal. Thus, we can also explain the following words from the verdict:

And so, because of the ties of friendship and familiarity (*amizade e converssaçam*) which the aforementioned Isaac Abravanel maintained with the aforementioned Duke [of Bragança], and since he fled and abandoned his residence in our kingdom in favor of residence in the kingdom of Castile, where he now resides, with no intention to return to our kingdom, despite being ordered to do so by a letter dispatched to him, even though he was assured safety in case of his return, but nevertheless has yet to do so—due to all these considerations we can only conclude that he knew of and took part in the wicked plan and treason instigated by the aforementioned duke, that he schemed and conspired against us and our royal condition, [to unravel] the good, peace, and tranquility of our kingdom. And so we order that the aforementioned Isaac Abravanel shall be executed by cruel natural death [on the gallows], . . . and all of his chattels and real estate expropriated and [returned] to the crown of our kingdom, to which they duly belong.[15]

The fact that Don Isaac had served the Bragança family (and perhaps had taken an active part in their plot against the king) was dramatically confirmed by his flight to Castile. The fact that he had fled was evidence that he was guilty—so claimed the verdict. King Dom João II executed and put to flight many members of the houses of Bragança and Viseu. With these pockets of resistance gone, he proceeded to dictate a new relationship between the crown and the aristocracy.

Thus came to an end the longest chapter in the life of Don Isaac Abravanel: forty-six years in the kingdom of Portugal. From a historical perspective, this period yielded the greatest wealth of documentary evidence about Abravanel's political, economic, and literary activities. In this part of the book, I have tried to collect all the information at our disposal to sketch the historical profile of Don Isaac Abravanel. We have seen that his origins lay in the crisis of Castilian Jewry and the foundation and rise of the Avis dynasty in Portugal at the end of the fourteenth century. Like other members of his family, he integrated himself into the commercial and banking system of the kingdom. However, unlike his family members, he cultivated literary and exegetical talents, becoming an active participant in both Jewish and Christian discourses, which imbued his commercial dealings with an air of personal and communal leadership. This all culminated in his becoming a prominent figure in the court and the community. However, when the political circumstances that had contributed to his rise shifted with Dom Afonso V's death, Abravanel was one of the first to suffer. He was forced to flee to Castile, bringing the Abravanel family's successful integration into Portugal's culture and economy in Portugal to a dramatic end.

Part Two

DON ISAAC ABRAVANEL

IN CASTILE

(1483–1492)

6 : DON ISAAC ABRAVANEL
IMMIGRATES TO CASTILE

On May 30, 1483, Abravanel was summoned to the palace of King Dom João II in Evora. En route, he learned that his patron had been arrested by the king. Instead of arriving at his audience, Abravanel fled to Castile, bringing his career in the kingdom of Portugal and the Portuguese Jewish community to an abrupt end. By fleeing he forfeited not only his status in the Portuguese kingdom but also many of the properties and much of the fortune that he and his family had amassed over the past fifty years. Nevertheless, King Dom João II did allow Abravanel's family to join him in Castile. Very little is known about Don Isaac's family life in Portugal. Only the names of his sons have reached us: Judah, born about 1460 and followed by the birth of two daughters whose names are unknown; Joseph, born in 1470; and finally Samuel, in 1473. One of Abravanel's daughters was wed to his nephew, Joseph Abravanel, who also fled to Castile in August 1484— after his patron, the Duke of Viseu, a close ally of the executed Duke of Bragança, was executed by King Dom João II himself. In the death sentence issued against Joseph Abravanel, we find the following:

> Since the accused [Joseph Abravanel] was a great servant (*servidor*) of Dom Diogo [the Duke of Viseu] and the administrator of his possessions, and since Dom Diogo held him in high esteem and trusted him, and since Dom Diogo required money to carry out his treason and hatch his plot ... he revealed his conspiracy and treason against us [the crown] to [Joseph Abravanel] ... and asked [Abravanel] to find the money ... to [help him] carry out the plot he had conceived. The accused accepted, offering to do everything in his power to produce the money. The accused began immediately to look for money. Since he was the son-in-law of Isaac Abravanel, who was found guilty of participation in the treason and plots of Dom Fernando [the Duke of Bragança], ... [Joseph] arranged to meet him [Isaac] in the city of Moura [near the Castilian border]. [Isaac] arrived there—and they both decided to give those estates

that Isaac still possessed in this kingdom to the Duke [of Viseu] to [help him] carry out the aforementioned treason and wicked plots.[1]

In the first months after his arrival in Castile in 1483, it seems that Isaac Abravanel and his family continued to make efforts to influence the political climate in Portugal so that he could return under the more favorable auspices of a new king who, unlike Dom João II, would be directly linked to the house of Bragança.

Don Isaac's firstborn, Judah, who at the time had just concluded his medical studies, depicts his father's flight from another perspective, in a poem titled "*Teluna 'al hazman*" (A Complaint against the Times). There, Judah portrays Don Isaac's arrival in Castile as a return to the roots of the Abravanel family: "And he escaped to Castile, birthplace of his parents, his ancestral home."[2]

Don Isaac did not arrive in Castile as a sojourner in an unknown land. He arrived in a familiar environment, one in which he could develop and rebuild the social status and economic prosperity he had previously enjoyed in Portugal. On the one hand, Don Isaac's crossing of this Castilian Rubicon spelled the end of the Portuguese phase of his family history, with the immigration to Lisbon precipitated by Samuel Abravanel's conversion to Christianity in 1388 and the Castilian pogroms in 1391. On the other hand, Don Isaac's immigration to Castile with his family continued the Abravanels' immigration to Portugal years earlier. It was a move made possible by the family's economic and cultural capital—that is, their mobility was a consequence of their source of income, which was not contingent upon location and thus allowed them to acclimate easily in diverse economic, national, and cultural environments. This economic continuity and the uninterrupted accumulation of wealth, cultural capital, and knowledge made immigration a far easier process. We will see this relatively fluid transition once again after the expulsion of the Abravanel family from Castile in 1492.

In Castile, Don Isaac would attain an important status within the Jewish community as well as an important position in the court of the Catholic Monarchs, Queen Doña Isabel and King Don Fernando. To illustrate how this took place, I shall focus on Abravanel's role as a scriptural exegete.

The Turn to Writing

The first documents attesting to Isaac Abravanel's activity in Castile—primarily in the first stop after his flight from Portugal, Segura de la Orden—

are literary in nature. These are Abravanel's commentaries on Joshua, Judges, and Samuel, composed in a veritable flurry of activity between October 11, 1483, and March 8, 1484. About four months after his arrival in Castile, Abravanel launched the ambitious project. The significance and purpose of this literary endeavor will occupy us in this section, beginning with Abravanel's decision to write what he did and the rationales he provided for this activity.

Commentary or Homiletics?

At the end of his commentary on Joshua, Abravanel added a colophon containing precise details about the circumstances and chronology of the commentary's composition:

> Behold I have completed that which I intended to interpret from the book of Joshua, as appeared to me when I studied with friends and those who did heed my voice—every night, I imparted knowledge. And I began [writing] this commentary on the 10th of Marcheshvan. And I completed it on the 26th of the same month in the year 5244 from Creation. And praise to God exalted who nursed me with his mercy and abundant grace allowing me to complete it: He shall gather my scattered [people] and take on my just cause and redeem me speedily, Amen.[3]

We see that Abravanel did not write his commentary in seclusion, the image one might be tempted to associate with a political "exile," but rather in the context of joint study or even a lecture with a group of scholars who would convene, according Abravanel, every night. If the account is accurate, one sees that Abravanel did not arrive in Segura de la Orden as an anonymous refugee. On the contrary, he was a well-known figure, at least within Jewish circles, and apparently a charismatic one as well. Furthermore, the collective nature of his study and exegesis shows that Don Isaac's literary project was not limited to putting pen to paper. It also had a socio-political component: it was a way for him to announce his arrival to the Jews of Castile. From Abravanel's request that God should "gather my scattered [people]"—perhaps a reference to the rest of his family, who had yet to join him in Castile—we may infer that Don Isaac was prepared to make Castile his new home, to carve out for himself a new niche within the economic and spiritual leadership of the Jewish community in a new land, in case the endeavors of the Braganças to topple the king were to fail. This ambition had an impact both on the contents of his commentary and on its unique format.

The Self-Portrait of a Court Jew

I have already discussed how, in his introduction to *'Ateret zeqenim*, Abravanel uses an autobiographical account to convey to his reader the social significance of the work. Likewise, in an introduction[4] to his commentary on the Former Prophets, apparently composed at the beginning of the project, Abravanel explains in exhaustive detail the circumstances that precipitated his flight, as well as the link between the end of his Portuguese career and his decision to write a commentary on this specific section of the Bible.

At the beginning of the introduction, Abravanel sketches the self-portrait of a Jewish nobleman: "I am the man Isaac, son of a valiant man who has done mighty deeds, his name is great in Israel, Sir Judah son of Samuel son of Joseph son of Judah of the Abravanel family, all of them were leaders of the children of Israel, from the seed of Jesse the Bethlehemite, from the house of David prince."[5] As would any Christian nobleman, Abravanel begins by presenting his pedigree, a formidable lineage stretching back five generations. He is notably reticent about the conversion of his grandfather, Samuel Abravanel, and instead focuses on drawing an analogy between the economic and political status of his house in Castile and Portugal and the religious and political status of the biblical monarchy of King David.

In the first edition of the commentary—published in Pesaro, Italy, in 1511–12, two or three years after Abravanel's death—this introduction is used as the book's title page. The words are printed in large square letters, as opposed to the less formal Rashi-script typeface used for the work itself. Even though no manuscripts from the time of Abravanel's composition have survived, we can use this title page to understand the impression that Abravanel, who was aware of the possibility that the work might be printed, wished to make upon his reader. By presenting his family's lineage at the opening of the work, he sought to highlight the social status of the author, portraying himself as a figure who should be embraced by the reader as the starting point for delving into the work itself.

Abravanel continues to describe the prelude to his dramatic flight from Portugal, the pinnacle of his career during the reign of Dom Afonso V:

> I lived peacefully in my home . . . a house full of God's blessings in the famous Lisbon, a city and a mother in the kingdom of Portugal.

The Lord commanded there the blessing in my barns and all earthly bliss. . . . I built myself houses and wide porches. My home was a meeting place for the wise, there were thrones of judgment, going out from there, through books and authors, good discernment and knowledge and fear of God. In my house and within my walls there were enduring riches and righteousness, a memorial and a name, science and greatness, as between noble men of ancient stock. I was happy in the court of the king Dom Afonso, a mighty king whose domain spread out and reached from sea to sea, prospering in whatsoever he did. . . . The Jews enjoyed relief and deliverance [during his reign]. Under his shadow I delighted to sit, and I was next to him. He leaned on my hand, and as long as he lived, I walked freely in the royal palace of Babylon.[6]

No less important than the content of this autobiographical passage is its biblical style. Abravanel describes himself by appropriating and Hebraicizing the words of Daniel 4:1, which quotes the Babylonian monarch Nebuchadnezzar: "I, Nebuchadnezzar, lived peacefully in my home, and was prosperous in my palace." Here Abravanel has split the verse in two. The first part of the verse is used to describe Abravanel's good fortunes in the Jewish community of Portugal, and the second to describe his good fortunes in the court ("the palace") of King Dom Afonso V. In the context of Daniel, the verse introduces Nebuchadnezzar's vision of the tree. This is no coincidence, and it represents a subtle and skillful rhetorical strategy. The vision of the tree augured Nebuchadnezzar's descent into madness, his exile from humanity, and his dethronement. Thus, we see that the beginning of Abravanel's account—which seems at first glance to describe the apogee of auspicious and propitious circumstances—already foreshadows the ephemeral nature of his good fortunes. As the mighty Nebuchadnezzar was driven mad and exiled from humankind, so too Abravanel would be forced to abandon his home and the palace and flee from Portugal. The symmetry between Nebuchadnezzar and Abravanel can also be applied to their failure to foresee this eventuality. Neither of them paid heed to the augurs that foretold their respective fates. Only now, after his flight from Castile, does Abravanel interpret the past retrospectively, weaving together an exegetical framework in which the events that have befallen him are imbued with religious significance. The theme dominating this narrative is the tension between divine providence and fate, as I shall show.

Abravanel's self-portrait includes a description of his own "palace." He portrays his home as a site of familial and divine blessings. However, beyond its external beauty and majesty, Abravanel's home was also a center of scholarship, analogous to the court of a king or a nobleman. The importance of his home in the Jewish community is expressed via a simile, comparing it to the Temple and to the Garden of Eden. From these all good qualities emerge: justice, beautiful writing, knowledge, fear of God, charity, and more. This grandiose description of his former home at the opening of a commentary is part of Don Isaac's debut before the Jewish elites of Castile. He casts himself as the ideal Jewish nobleman, the embodiment of the Talmudic maxim of "Torah and greatness in one person."[7]

Having described his home, Abravanel addresses his role within the court of Dom Afonso V. To describe Dom Afonso V's virtues, he co-opts the terminology of Daniel 4:1 and concludes with the language of Daniel 4:26: "Twelve months later, as he was walking on the roof of the royal palace at Babylon" (the verse that recounts the fulfillment of Nebuchadnezzar's dream, which had augured the date of his fall). In addition to drawing attention to these omens, which Abravanel had failed to notice, Abravanel describes Dom Afonso V as a monarch par excellence, endowed with political, moral, and intellectual virtues; an embodiment of the model leader promoted and cultivated by the Avis dynasty and its literature. The pinnacle of Abravanel's career in Portugal is thus presented as a result of the special relationship between a perfect Jewish leader and a perfect Christian monarch. If we recall that these descriptions appear on the book's title page, a gate that must be traversed before entering the hall, or the book itself, Abravanel's purpose becomes abundantly clear: this rhetorical display is meant to present to the Jewish elites of Castile the alluring image of a Jewish leader and courtier. Having arrived in a new environment, Abravanel took pains to emphasize his prestigious status in the Jewish community of Portugal, as well as his special connection with the king. However, the modern historian cannot help but view these two "facts" with some suspicion: Don Isaac, it seems, is tendentiously exaggerating his status in the court and in the community. As we saw above, Don Isaac was not the only prominent Jewish leader in Lisbon. Moreover, his status as a court Jew was tied primarily to the house of Bragança—not to the crown, despite his emphasis here on his personal relationship to the king.

Abravanel continues to describe the beloved king's death, casting it as another vagary of fate: "Suddenly, however, the day of affliction, punishment, and shame arrived . . . he [Dom Afonso V] fell ill . . . and in a few days death crept to his windows, the destruction in his palace. And the mother of all living took the knife to slay her son and slew him after the manner of all the earth."[8]

Don Isaac here alludes to the plague that ravaged Portugal and ended Dom Afonso V's life. His portrayal of death as "the mother of all living" (Gen. 3:20) and the death of the king as in "the manner of all the earth" (Gen. 19:31) alludes to Abravanel's Stoic conception of fate, particularly of death—ideas delineated in detail in his Portuguese letter. Dom Afonso V's sudden demise, which is likened to a binding of Isaac that ends with his slaughter by the hand of Abraham, left Don Isaac defenseless, exposed to political developments that would soon irrevocably shift the nexus of power in the kingdom. "And now my soul is poured out within me, and I am become like dust and ashes,"[9] Don Isaac writes, adopting the lament of Job (30:16–19). Like Job's, his world was turned upside down in the course of a single day.

Don Isaac's Description of His Patron's Conspiracy

In this introduction, Don Isaac provides his own version of the downfall of his patron at the hands of João II:

> His son, Dom João [II], came to the throne, a new king who did not know [the friends of his predecessor] and turned his heart to hate his ministers and to deal craftily with his servants. And he did not reveal himself to the friends of his father, the nobles and the princes of the provinces . . . his own relatives, bone of his bones and flesh of his flesh, and cunningly said to them: You shall surely die because you have all conspired against me to hand me and my kingdom to the Spanish Crown [to the Queen and King of Castile and Aragon]. And among them he arrested one of the most famous noblemen, the second most important after the king [the Duke of Bragança], who had dwelt securely with him, killing him with the sword. The remaining brothers [of the victim] fled to the mountain fearing for their own lives. . . . And the king seized all their land.[10]

Abravanel goes on to address the claim that he personally had a hand in the conspiracy against the king. Not surprisingly, he completely denies the charges:

> The king was angry with me too, although I never did any injustice . . . Only because from time immemorial and from old good times I

was an intimate friend of the persecuted noblemen and they asked for my counsel, the man, the lord of the land [the king], spoke roughly to me and attacked me with his mighty hand. He included me among the conspirators, maintaining that these men would not do anything without first revealing their secret and all their intimate thoughts to me, for my soul was bound up with theirs.[11]

If we compare these descriptions to the allegations leveled against Abravanel in the formal verdict issued against him, one can detect important similarities: both accounts address the central administrative role that Abravanel played in the house of Bragança. This was the reason he was considered fully complicit in the duke's perfidy—or, as Abravanel would have it, completely innocent. Modern historians have emphasized the political nature of King Dom João II's initiative—that is, his attempt to reshape the relationship between the crown and the nobility. They see in the opposition of the houses of Bragança and Viseu an attempt to defend personal interests, and not necessarily a concrete act of treason.[12] However, regardless of whether there truly was a conspiracy against Dom João II, it is Abravanel's view of the conflict between his patron and the crown that concerns us here. An analysis of the literary allusions pervading Don Isaac's telling of these events reveals his own stance with respect to one of the largest political crises in late fifteenth-century Portugal. Like the new pharaoh of Exodus, who forgot his father's covenant with Joseph ("Now there arose a new king over Egypt, who did not know Joseph"),[13] Dom João II violated the covenant that his father Dom Afonso V had established with the Portuguese aristocracy, particularly with the house of Bragança. Thus, Abravanel ignores, perhaps on purpose, the rationale of the king's new approach: strengthening the crown against the power of the nobles. Abravanel prefers to cast the king's behavior as wicked and as an example of a hostile fortune (*adversa fortuna*). Furthermore, he views the king's punishment of the nobility for banding together to oppose him as an act of ingratitude, a despicable recompense in light of the kindness shown to him by the nobility and the house of Abravanel. The execution of the duke, the flight of the remaining members of the house of Bragança, and the confiscation of their properties were, to Abravanel, matters of pure evil and greed—certainly not a shrewd act of realpolitik aimed at consolidating royal power. Thus, Abravanel tries to conceal the treasonous elements that pervaded the alliance between the houses of Bragança and Viseu and adopts the viewpoint of the Portuguese nobles who felt fully justified in their opposition to Dom João II's policies. He thus demonstrates his identification with the fates of the Portuguese aristocrats, an attitude notably at odds with his self-portrayal at the beginning of his introduction as an ally of the crown and King Dom Afonso V's personal advisor. Abravanel succinctly describes his fate with an allusion to Deuteronomy 1:37: "Also the Lord was angry with me for your sakes, saying, thou also shalt not go in thither." Like Moses, who was punished by God for his behavior in the affair of the twelve spies, Abravanel was punished by Dom João II for his close relationship with the house of Bragança: guilt by association. All considered, Don Isaac's defense of the conspiracy is weak at best. It is a thin veil concealing his tendentious support for the nobility's cause.

Flight as Victory

In the same attempt to rebuff accusations against him and portray himself as a defeated man forced to flee for his life, Abravanel describes his summoning by Dom João II as a battle of angelic proportions: the evil angels of the king face off against the good angel of a saving God:

> He [the monarch] sent forth a procession of evil angels [mal'akhim] to order me: Come unto me, tarry not. And I obeyed the royal order and naively went to the place indicated in the king's commandment and in his decree. And it came to pass on the way at a lodging place [where we rested] that a man came before me and said to me: Draw not nigh hither; escape and save your life![14]

The king summons Abravanel to his palace with the purpose of entrapping him, destroying him, and seizing his properties. According to Don Isaac, only divine intervention thwarted the king's plan. Abravanel thus presents himself as one worthy of special divine attention and providence. The man who warned him of the king's plans is conflated with the angel of God who saved Lot from the destruction of Sodom and Gomorrah, saying to Lot "escape and save your life."[15] Thus, Abravanel's tale of salvation further highlights his unique status and character: he is not just a leader, he is a leader graced with personal divine providence.

Abravanel continues:

> And I escaped only by the skin of my teeth. And when the sun rose upon the earth, the report was heard in pharaoh's house, and the messengers went forth in haste by the king's commandment in

which it was stated: Pursue and take him, for there is no punishment for him except for death. . . . His troops went forth in my pursuit during that night in the way that leads to the desert. The Lord being merciful, He did not suffer them to hurt me. About midnight I went out from Egypt, that is, from the kingdom of Portugal, and I arrived in the kingdom of Castile in the border city of Segura de la Orden. And he [João II] saw that he could not prevail against me and take my life.[16]

Abravanel describes his flight by drawing on vocabulary from the escapes of various biblical characters: Hagar, Lot, Jacob, and even the Exodus of the Hebrews from Egypt. Like Lot's salvation from Sodom and Gomorrah, Jacob's miraculous escape from the machinations of Laban, and the divine escape of Moses and Israel from the Egyptian army, so too the hand of providence protected Abravanel and, against all odds, helped him slip through the fingers of a powerful monarch. Thus, while Dom João II certainly succeeded in upending Abravanel's life, Abravanel's successful flight attests to the fact that God's providence watched over him at every step—a victory within defeat. The motif of conflict between the power of the king and the hand of providence defines the contours of Abravanel's account and is reminiscent of the tension between fortuna and providentia that pervaded his discussions in 'Ateret zeqenim. By returning to this tension, Abravanel justifies his decision to end his loyalty to the king and kingdom of Portugal and fall back on his historical and religious affiliation with the Jewish people.

Why Abravanel Wrote

The second part of Don Isaac's autobiographical account is constructed gradually but dramatically, as a series of addresses to others and to himself, or a series of demands for explanation. The first is addressed to King Dom João II: "By means of a letter written by me I cried out: Help, O king! . . . Shall not the judge of all the land do justly? And why have you dealt ill with your servant? . . . Make me know why you contend with me!" But despite Don Isaac's letter, the king was unmoved and was "like the deaf asp that stops its ears." The second is addressed to the King of Kings, God himself: "all my thoughts pondered what God had done to me, having done deeds unto me that ought not to be done. . . . Have I not wept for those in trouble? Why then did God harden his spirit; why did He deliver me into the hands of harsh masters?" Like Dom João II, God also remains silent, un-receptive to Abravanel's piercing accusations: "Why do You not hear me O Lord, even when I wail and cry out!"[17] The third address is introspective, an expression of self-admonishment:

> Why should you be as a man astonished? . . . Why do you cry to Him, saying "What is my trespass? What is my sin, that You have so hotly pursued after me?" God is righteous, and it is because you rebelled against His Word; it was you who made a hedge around yourself against him and you forgot the God that conceived you and gave you everything that is yours; you forgot the law of your God. You did not seek out the Lord's book. . . . And you chose the crafty tongue of a people with a strange language, and with kings and counselors of the land you did exchange vain words, [they who,] when the time of visitation comes, shall perish. You placed gold in your basket, and all the treasures of the world. And you followed the vanity of greatness, power, and majesty, and because you forgot the Lord your God, he too forgot thee.[18]

Having voiced his pain, bewilderment, and anger, it is now time for consolation. Don Isaac must now subvert the perspective of a mourner grounded on an emotional response to the blows of fate, supplanting it with a new, more honest approach: I sinned by serving as a courtier, the contrite Don Isaac admits. This mental shift provides an explanation for the departure of providence (in the form of a dip in prosperity) and even provides a solution for bringing it back: by teaching scriptural exegesis and committing it to writing. Abravanel, an innocent victim only a few lines earlier, is now culpable for his own downfall. Suddenly his deep involvement in the economic and political activities of the Portuguese nobility is revealed to be not a sign of blessing but rather the catalyst of divine wrath. This parallels the tension between the power of the king and the power of God, which he developed earlier in his account. Don Isaac's self-consolation is an attempt to cast the two foundations of his status—the royal court and the Jewish community—as irreconcilable rivals. As a result, before anything else, he must now reestablish himself by consolidating his Jewish status. He will do this within the Castilian Jewish community by delivering lessons and writing commentaries on scripture.

Concluding this autobiographical passage, Abravanel describes the transition from internalizing consolation to writing a commentary: "These evils have come upon me, because God is not within me. . . . It is good for me that I have been afflicted—that I might learn Your statutes. The law of Your mouth is better unto me than a thousand pieces of gold and silver."[19] Abravanel finally reveals the outcome of his self-consolation: his perspective of the past has changed, he has understood the message, and he has made peace with his fate. He even presents his internal consolatory discourse as evidence of his remarkable ability to rebuild himself as a leader. Indeed, this is the virtue of leaders: to know how to console themselves and to acclimate to new circumstances and conditions. After this revolution in his understanding of the flight from Portugal, providence can be seen returning and resting once again upon Abravanel—as manifested in his arrival in Segura de la Orden and his integration into the Jewish life of the city:

> The Lord our God brought before me wise and knowledgeable men, companions that heed my voice. . . . All the day, did I speak with them, and that which I had to say they heard, and they beseeched me for my opinions on the interpretation of books of the Former Prophets. . . . They encouraged me and asked me to cast forth my hand and to interpret the books of Joshua, Judges, Samuel, and Kings. . . . I chose to frequent the house of My Lord and to commit myself to a holy service (*'avodat qodesh*). . . . And I arose and performed the labor of the King—the Lord of Hosts is His name—to write a commentary on these four books.[20]

It follows that the Jewish elites of Segura de la Orden were responsible for restoring to Abravanel the mantel of leadership he had once worn. This time, however, it was not his economic or political status that stood him in good stead, but rather his ability to interpret and teach the Former Prophets. Through his lessons and charisma, Abravanel was able to rebuild for himself a status as a leader in his home of refuge. This account thus shows the social impact that Don Isaac hoped his commentary would have: just as his oral teaching accorded him status and authority in Segura de la Orden, so by committing his exegesis to writing (an endeavor prompted by the request of his Castilian audience), he could turn himself into an important leader throughout the ranks of Castile's Jewish elites.

The Abravanel at the end of this autobiographical account is the picture of a Jewish courtier who has repented and abandoned service to the crown in favor of "a holy service"—scriptural exegesis. Thus, Abravanel concludes his account of the events and thoughts that inspired him to write his commentary on Joshua, Judges, and Samuel after his flight from Portugal. It is colored throughout by the tension between God and king, court and community, capricious fortune and divine providence, showing that his commentary was an attempt to transcend fortune while at the same time gleaning insights and benefit from it—most importantly, the opportunity to start afresh.

Besides providing an explanation for Abravanel's turn to the pen, this account is positioned at the beginning of the commentary to draw the intended reader's attention to the figure of the author and thus to influence his experience, signaling how the book ought to be read. The goal is that the work will always be read in close conjunction with author's self-portrait, leading the reader to embrace him. In summary, Don Isaac responded to the terrible misfortune that befell him in Portugal by embarking on a literary project, taking the Jews of Castile by storm by introducing himself as an impressive figure and leader as well as by showcasing his imposing talents as an exegete.

7 : ISAAC ABRAVANEL'S HISTORICAL AND LITERARY APPROACH TO THE BOOKS OF THE FORMER PROPHETS

Having discussed the personal factors that motivated Abravanel to compose a commentary on the Former Prophets, I wish now to address the issue of his exegetical method.[1] Following his extensive biographical preface, Abravanel offered a summary of the interpretative assumptions lying at the basis of his commentary. This introduction is notable not only for its personal tone, its authorial self-awareness, and its clear rhetorical skill but also for its detailed discussion of the nature of the books that are the subject of his commentary. In other words, Abravanel uses this introductory section not only to answer personal questions—why he wrote this commentary, and why he chose to do so now—but also to account for the customary treatment of the Former Prophets as a discrete literary unit and to explain how these books differ from the other sections of the Hebrew Bible: the Pentateuch, the Latter Prophets, and the Writings. The answer to these classificatory and exegetical questions, of course, will shed further light on Abravanel's motives for selecting these books as the object of his first complete commentary.

A New Approach to the Bible

Abravanel opens with a seemingly innocent question:

> Our Holy Sages, may their memory be blessed, divided Holy Scripture into a primary division of three parts. They called these sections Torah, Prophets, and Writings. And it behooves us to know why they were named thus and whether there is any essential difference between one and the other.[2]

In other words, Don Isaac is asking whether the division of the canon into Torah, prophets, and writings is based on any specific criteria such as content, author, or oral versus written transmission. Abravanel ultimately casts doubt on the ability to base the tripartite division of the Bible on a clear set of criteria, but he does emphasize the importance of the tripartite hierarchy of Pentateuch, prophets, and writings. Attempting to characterize the rabbinic schema, Abravanel contrasts it with the Christian division:

> Indeed, the Christian sages divided Holy Scripture into four sections: the legal (*torii*), these are the five books of Moses; the historical (*sipurii*), Joshua, Judges, Ruth, Samuel, Kings, Chronicles, Daniel, Ezra, and Esther; the prophetic (*nevui'i*), Isaiah, Jeremiah, Lamentations, Ezekiel, the Twelve Minor Prophets, the later parts of Daniel—and Psalms as well. . . . And the wisdom (*mad'aii*) section: Job, Proverbs, Ecclesiastes, Song of Songs. And they designate these sections *legales*, *estoriales*, *propheticos*, and *sapientes*.[3]

Abravanel contrasts the medieval fourfold Christian division of the canon with the tripartite division of the Jews, the first example of many discussions of Christian exegetical literature in his commentary. His description of the Christian divisions seems to be based in part on the *Biblia Sacra* with the *Postilla* of Nicholas de Lyra (1270–1349) and the *Additiones* of Pablo de Santa Maria (1350–1435, also referred as Pablo de Burgos). The *Biblia Sacra* was usually prefaced by a text composed by Walafrid Strabo in the ninth century titled "De libris biblie canonicis et non canonicis (About the canonical and noncanonical biblical books)."[4] The text offers the same quadripartite division discussed here by Abravanel, albeit applying it to the New Testament as well—a detail that Abravanel, obviously, omitted. While Abravanel does not explicitly refer to this text here (just as he makes no mention of Jerome's introduction to the Vulgate or Nicholas de Lyra's commentary), it is very likely that these attempts to characterize biblical literature had a significant impact on Abravanel's own exegetical approach.

Having presented different schemes for organizing the books of scripture, Don Isaac proposes his own set of historical criteria:

> I have devised a different division of the Holy Scripture in accordance with the time in which they were written and compiled (*hubru*). . . . The first section is [composed] of that which was written and composed prior to Israel's entry into the land. . . . The second section contains all those books that were written while [Israel] was in the land up to the exile and the destruction of the

Temple.... The third section of the sacred books contains all those books written and composed after the Temple's destruction, after Israel's exile from its land.[5]

Before reviewing the significance of this historical division, it is worth drawing attention to the consequences such an approach has on the definition of the Former Prophets as well as Isaac Abravanel's choice to interpret them: "These four books [Joshua, Judges, Samuel, and Kings] begin their stories (*sipureihem*) with Israel's entry with Joshua into the Promised Land.... They conclude their narratives with their departure from the Land during the exile of King Zedekiah."[6] The tales of the prophets pertain to Israel's entry into the land, their settlement of it, their sins and decline, and ultimately their exile. This is an arc that parallels, in some senses, the vicissitudes of Abravanel's own life. In his autobiographical introduction, Abravanel has already likened his flight from Castile to the Exodus. It is, therefore, not unreasonable to attribute significance to the similarity between Don Isaac's arrival in Castile and the conquest of Canaan at the hands of Joshua and his armies. At the risk of speculation, one can identify the circumstances of Don Isaac's emigration as further motivation to compose a commentary on the Former Prophets. We can further add that the arc unfolding in these books—settlement, corruption, and exile—echoes not just Abravanel's own life but also the annals of his family. The members of the Abravanel family emigrated to Portugal and integrated themselves into a specific sociopolitical circle. However, spurred by shifting political circumstances, they were ultimately forced to emigrate yet again—that is, to go into exile. As we will see, Abravanel can use his commentary on the Former Prophets to retrospectively evaluate his own political and economic fortunes: it is a lens through which he can reflect upon the factors that lead to the rise and fall of leaders and nations.

Having proposed a division of scripture predicated on three historical epochs, Abravanel raises a sophisticated literary question, its answer representing an innovative approach to the exegesis of the Former Prophets: "Why were all the prophecies and words of Holy Spirit found in the Prophets and Writings, not written in the tales of the kings under whom they lived?"[7] In other words, if the division of the biblical canon is dictated by historical criteria, why do the historical books not include all the prophecies, *megillot*, and psalms composed during their respective ages? For example, why not incorporate the prophecies of Isaiah—who was active during the reigns of the last Judaean monarchs—into the book of Kings? Surely, there must be a reason why some prophetic passages (for example, the prophecies of Elijah and Elisha) were incorporated into these historical books while others were placed elsewhere? Abravanel provides an answer based on a set of literary criteria related to the characteristics common to all the accounts that appear in the Former Prophets:

> And I answer: that the prophecies, poems, and statements of wisdom that were included in the prophetic books and the books of David's Psalms, and the books of Solomon's wisdom, were not written within the books and narratives of the kings who reigned during their times for two reasons: the first reason is so as not to place a heavy burden upon the readers who would be unable to conceive the true nature of the stories if they were interspersed with lengthy prophecies, numerous poems, and the large texts on wisdom (*ha-ma'amarim hamada'iim*). Therefore, they decided to write the histories independently, as a contiguous and continuous account without interruption.
>
> The second reason is that these four books—meaning Joshua, Judges, Samuel, and Kings—were devoted in their substance and first intention to the stories and lives of the Judges and Kings. For this reason, they only included those prophecies that were directly related to the affairs of the judges, kings, and their stories. For as they were indispensable for understanding the story, it was proper and necessary to include them.[8]

In Abravanel's view, underlying the structure of the Former Prophets is the efficacy of communication with the reader. A book is not merely an anthology of sources recounting all the events that took place over a certain period of time. A book must be crafted in such a way as to be coherent to the reader. It must, therefore, adopt an organizational logic—in our case, by focusing on the stories of specific, prominent figures (Joshua, the judges, or the kings). This is Abravanel's "first reason."

Abravanel's "second reason" is based on the criteria of selection: the redactors of the Former Prophets, wishing to recount the histories of Israel's leaders from conquest to destruction, had at their disposal a variety of narratives, prophecies, poems, and wisdom texts. They were forced to choose only those texts that helped them chronicle the tales of the Israelite leaders from conquest to exile.

Abravanel continues to establish the literary criteria that delimit the Former Prophets. The first criterion is their objective:

> The first final cause (*hatakhlit*) that unites these books is to teach us benefits (*to'alot*) and useful lessons (*limudim mo'ilim*) for attaining true conceptions (*hasagot 'amitiot*), and for learning helpful virtues and moral qualities (*limud hamidot vehatekhunot*), imparted by the stories recorded in these books.
>
> The other final cause is to teach the days of old and the years of many generations. . . . Every state in its writings and every nation in its language seeks to comprehend and know the years of [their] first ancestors and the span of their years, from one generation to the next, so as to know the periods and numbers of their years. [All the more so] the children of Israel—in whom is embedded the belief in the creation of the world ex nihilo by an act of divine volition (*hidush ha'olam hakelali haretsoni*)—it was proper that they know and understand the developments of generations from the beginning of creation until the exile from Jerusalem. . . . And therefore it was necessary that they should count the years of the judges and kings and narrate what transpired, that we may know the years of the world.[9]

Abravanel identifies the Former Prophets as historical works. The tales they present are meant to cultivate and instill moral virtues in their readers, demonstrating to them the benefits of maintaining true beliefs (such as the doctrines of providence, prophecy, and miracles). Furthermore, they allow the reader to develop a sense of the historical continuity spanning generations and stretching from the creation of the world until the destruction of the First Temple. According to this approach, historical writing is both a documentation and description of events—a narrative describing the span of a people's collective life—and a literary genre that fosters ethical and religious qualities. It should be recalled that the Avis dynasty in Portugal was known for its patronage and encouragement of royal chroniclers. The most famous of these were Fernão Lopes (1385–1460) and Gomes Zurara (1410–74).[10] In chapter 3 we saw an excerpt describing the conquest of Arzila from the chronicle of Rui de Pina, who was active in the later fifteenth century. In fourteenth and fifteenth century in Castile as well, historical writing was beginning to come into its own, primarily in the form of chronicles. This was coupled with a growing interest in the works of classic Roman historians such as Livy.[11] At the same time, the influences of humanistic historical of writing in Italy had begun to make inroads into the Iberian peninsula over the course of the fifteenth century. Thus, by defining the historical intention of the Former Prophets, Abravanel was participating in a prevalent discourse in the Iberian peninsula—growing interest in historical writing. "[All the more so] was it proper that the children of Israel . . . know and understand the developments of generations," writes Abravanel, who saw in the study of a history an important means of strengthening a religious mentality.

Leonardo Bruni (1371–1444), the famous Florentine humanist who wrote historical works in the second half of the fifteenth century, characterized the writing of history as follows: "[It] requires at once a long and connected narrative, causal explanation of each particular event and the public expression of one's judgment about every issue."[12] Bruni thus directly connects the narrative of historical development with the ethical or political moral that the historian is entrusted with gleaning from it. From history books "we may learn with ease what behavior we should imitate and avoid."[13] In the preface to Livy's *History of Rome*, which Abravanel likely read, we find a similar sentiment: "What chiefly makes the study of history wholesome and profitable is this, that you behold the lessons of every kind of experience set forth as if on a conspicuous monument; from these you may choose for yourself and for your own state what to imitate, from these mark for avoidance what is shameful in the conception and shameful in the result."[14] The relationship between an account and the cultivation of moral and political virtues represents history's rhetorical dimension, an idea that Bruni learned from Cicero as well—specifically, from the second book of *De Oratore*. "The nature of the subject needs chronological arrangement," writes Cicero. However, he continues, the historian must provide an "exposition of all contributory causes, whether originating in accident, discretion or foolhardiness."[15] At the end of his commentary on 1 Kings (composed after the Spanish expulsion in 1492), Abravanel styles himself an expert on the writings of the ancient historians. Thus, when comparing the biblical King Solomon to the monarchs of classical literature, he writes: "I have not seen in the histories of the nations, the Trojans, the Greeks, and the Romans, of whose books I have seen many, an account of any other king who was as exalted, praised, and ascendant in all his deeds like King Solomon."[16] If Abravanel was indeed familiar with this literature, as I hope to demonstrate below, then his attribution of a historical and ethical purpose to the Former Prophets may have been inspired by his humanistic learning described in the previous sections of this chapter.

The historical and literary tenor of the preface grows more pronounced as Don Isaac proceeds to broach the issue of the "writer and author" of the Prophets. After citing the view mentioned in the Babylonian Talmud (Bava Batra 14b) that "Joshua wrote his own book and eight verses of the Pentateuch," Abravanel takes the liberty of disagreeing with the Sages, pursuing a very different approach:

> When I probed the verses, though, I saw that the opinion Joshua wrote his book was highly unlikely, not on account of what is said at its end, [that] Joshua died—this alone being the difficulty they [the Sages] raised in the Gemara—but rather because of [other] verses which attest to the fact that Joshua did not write them. It says regarding the setting up of the stones in the midst of the Jordan, "And they are there unto this day" (Josh. 4:9). It says, regarding the matter of circumcision, "Wherefore the name of that place was called Gilgal this day" (Josh. 5:9). . . .
>
> Now, if Joshua wrote all of this, how could he have said "unto this day" regarding them? For the writing [of them] would have followed immediately after the occurrence of these events, whereas the force of the expression "unto this day" indicates necessarily that it was written a long time after the events happened. . . . This is decisive evidence that this statement was not written until many years after Joshua's death, which proves that Joshua did not write his book.[17]

Don Isaac develops this theme further by critiquing the traditional attribution of the book of Samuel to the eponymous prophet: "The verses indicate that Samuel did not write his book in the very same way."[18] Textual sensitivity and a philological mentality are pitched here against the views expressed by the Sages of the Talmud. For this reason, some twentieth-century scholars crowned Abravanel the founder of historical Bible scholarship, and the Jewish historian Yitzhak Baer even characterized Abravanel's textual claims as demonstrating "a significant degree of criticism."[19] Regardless, Abravanel was certainly careful to defend his critical disposition toward the Sages: "Do not be amazed that I have deviated from the opinion of our sages in this matter, since even in the Gemara, they did not agree on these matters. . . . Given that our sages themselves exhibited doubts in a part of the dictum [concerning biblical authorship], it is not inadmissible for me also to choose a more plausible and satisfying approach as regards a part in accordance with the nature of the verses and their straightforward purport."[20] While Baer may have been guilty of hyperbole (as I will show below), it is abundantly clear that Don Isaac wished to study the books of the Former Prophets as books: that is, to treat them at least partially as works with human authors and clear intentions, and as altogether similar to the types of books written in his own era. Thus, Abravanel compares the authors or redactors of the Former Prophets to the chronicler and historian of his own time, a person who gathers written documents from the past and compiles them:

> What I think correct concerning this matter is that Samuel recorded the events that occurred in his time and similarly [that] Nathan the prophet recorded on his own [what happened in his time] and similarly Gad the seer on his own, each one what occurred in his time. And these writings (Ketuvim) were [eventually] gathered and compiled (*kibbetsam vehibberam yahad*) by Jeremiah the prophet, who arranged (*sidder*) the book as a whole on their basis. For if this is not so, then who gathered these texts (*ma'amarim*), which were the work of diverse agents? . . . It seems, though, that Jeremiah, when he wished to write the book of Kings, prepared the book of Samuel that precedes it, and it was he who gathered the discourses of the aforementioned prophets into a book. There is no doubt that he [then] added things to clarify the discourses as he saw fit—hence its saying, unto this day, and it was he who wrote "Before time in Israel . . . he that is now called a prophet was beforetime called a seer," and the rest of the verses which I mentioned that indicate a later date. All of these were the work of the editor (*metaken*) and assembler (*mekkabets*).[21]

According to this description, the Former Prophets were not so much written as redacted—composed through a series of intricate historical processes. The original authors wrote contemporaneous accounts of the events taking place in their own time. Subsequently, an editor or assembler collected these "primary sources" and turned them into a book by choosing what to include and what to omit. If this is true, it leads to an obvious question: Does such a process deliver a reliable and authentic account? Or perhaps, by comparing the Former Prophets to historical works and chronicles, does one essentially detract from the books' lofty, prophetic status? Don Isaac's answer to this question is decidedly ambiguous:

> There is no doubt that the prophets found written things in their time in the chronicles mentioned in Kings, which would include things from that time, written by judges or kings or other pious men from those generations and their scribes. And being scattered and dispersed the one on the one side, and the other on the other side, including matters written according to will and not according to truth, as well as extraneous matters—for this is the practice of scribes and chroniclers (*maggidei devarim*) to praise and denounce more than befits them in accordance with their love or hatred— therefore mixed into them were truth and falsehood, extraneous with necessary. For this reason, God rested his spirit upon those prophets, and commanded them to write in a book all those tales completely and truthfully, and they would gather all those writings. And the Blessed God apprised them through prophecy [how] to perfect those things, their truth, and their justice, separating between truth and falsehood, and necessary from unnecessary.[22]

While the prophet may have edited the traditions transmitted to him, he was able to preserve authenticity thanks to an act of divine intervention: God made sure that only authentic and important passages would be incorporated; anything spurious or redundant was left out. Don Isaac's comparison of the biblical author to a historian essentially places him on an exegetical tight rope: On the one hand, he has identified the biblical author as a compiler and editor of earlier traditions, a human figure responsible for creating his own book from earlier materials in the service of kings. On the other hand, unlike a typical historian, the biblical writer does not examine and evaluate documentary evidence by virtue of his human mind but rather is invested with the Holy Spirit, which guides his hand. Notably, and as pointed out by Eric Lawee,[23] Abravanel's late redactor makes an appearance only in his discussion of the Prophets. In Abravanel's treatment of the Pentateuch, no such figure is to be found.

Influences and Historical Background

A good example of historical writing during the fifteenth century in the Iberian peninsula is Fernán Pérez de Guzmán's *Generaciones y Semblanzas*, a series of biographical sketches of notable royal and noble figures from the late fourteenth to the early fifteenth century. In his "Prólogo," de Guzmán raises some critical thoughts about the historian's task, some of which bear a notable resemblance to Don Isaac's own approach. De Guzmán writes:

> It often happens that chronicles and histories that tell of mighty kings, distinguished princes, and great cities are considered suspect and uncertain, and one affords them little trust or authority. Among other things, this can be attributed to two causes: First, because among those who indulge in writing and recounting ancient stories are men with no sense of shame, and they prefer to tell extraordinary and marvelous things than true and certain facts. . . . The second shortcoming of histories is a consequence of the fact that those who write chronicles do so by order of kings and princes. Wishing to please and flatter them, and fearing to perturb them, they write more of what is commissioned of them, or of that which they believe will please [their patrons], and less of the true manner in which events transpired.[24]

From this example and the works of other contemporary historians, we see that the more historiographical writing developed in the Iberian peninsula, and the farther knowledge of ancient historical writing spread, the more historians exercised a greater degree of critical awareness in writing their own works. Abravanel's discussions of "the practice of scribes and chroniclers to praise and denounce more than befits them in accordance with their love or hatred"[25] demonstrate his ties with the growing epistemological discourse about historical writing and the issue of falsification.

Based on Abravanel's discussions of the Former Prophets and their characteristics, Baer concluded that "Abravanel was the first Jew who combined the ideas of the Renaissance with medieval Jewish learning; the first to begin looking at the heritage of the patriarchs through the prism of a historical and humanistic method."[26] Baer is referring here to the developments in scholarship and writing taking place among the Italian humanists of the fourteenth and fifteenth centuries.

Petrarch learned to imitate the classical Latin of Cicero as well as the many literary genres in which he wrote (epistolary, moral, and philosophical tracts). With his new linguistic sensitivity and skill, Petrarch drew a sharp distinction between the Latin of Cicero and the "barbaric" Latin used by his cultural rivals (the Aristotelian physicians).[27] "Tell me," asks Petraca's adversary, Jean d'Hesdin, "where do we read about Cicero's *Physics* or

Varro's *Metaphysics?*" "What a stupid question!" answers Petrarch. "This insolent barbarian delights in Greek words, but then speaks of Aristotle, who wrote these books, as if he were a Gaul [a barbarian]."[28] This linguistic and ideological distinction between classical and barbarian Latin was imparted to Petrarch's followers. The new generation of humanists went a step further: expanding their linguistic horizons to encompass Greek and Hebrew as well and broadening their historical knowledge, they began to apply the method of literary criticism to the study of religious texts. Giannozzo Manetti (1396–1459) marshaled his study of Latin, Greek, and Hebrew literature to challenge the accuracy of the traditional Latin translation of the Bible— Jerome's Vulgate—comparing it with the Septuagint and Hebrew original and proposing in its stead a new Latin translation that encompassed most of the New Testament and the Psalter. Thus, Manetti pointed to the distortions that arose from Jerome's canonical translation. In the third book of his *Against the Critics of his New Translation of the Psalter in Five Apologetic Books* (1455–59), he writes:

> Since in this third book we have decided to discuss and investigate the many significant differences and divergences of the two most famous translations of the complete Psalter [the Septuagint and the Vulgate], in order to plainly and clearly understand this matter, our discussion will proceed in a particular order. For in each serious and significant translation only three errors can exist and be discovered. For an error can occur or appear either through additions or though omissions or through unsuitable translations.[29]

The most famous example of this critical humanist bent was the 1440 treatise, penned by Lorenzo Valla (b. 1405–07, d. 1454), *De falso credite et ementita Constantini donatione*, a philological critique of the all-important Donation of Emperor Constantine. This text presents itself as an official document drafted by the early fourth-century emperor. After his conversion to Christianity and his miraculous recovery from the plague, Constantine officially grants the bishop of Rome (the pope) hegemony over the Church. Moreover, he grants the pope the lands of Italy and gives him a series of privileges. The relationship between pope, emperor, and Roman Senate is thus clearly defined. Wielding linguistic, historical, and logical analysis, Valla demonstrated that the document was apocryphal: it came from the eighth century and could not have been written by Constantine. Valla's analysis thus undermined the authority of an influential document used to define and justify papal power. Quoting a passage of the forged document, he expounds upon the Latin "barbarisms" it includes:

> *Choosing the very prince of the apostles, or his vicars to be strong advo-*
> *cates* [*esse patronos*] *for us with God....* Come back to life Lactan-
> tius, just for a moment, and shut up the gross and monstrous bray-
> ing of this ass.... Did imperial scribes in your time talk like that, or
> even imperial lackeys? Constantine chose those people not as "ad-
> vocates" [*patronos*] but to "be advocates" [*esse patronos*]. He inserted
> that *to be* [*esse*] to make a more harmonious prose rhythm. A fine
> reason to speak like a barbarian, to make your utterance go more
> prettily, as if anything pretty could be found in such coarseness.[30]

In the 1450s, Valla went on to apply his philological acumen to the New Testament as well. In the introduction to his *Annotations to the New Testament*, he partially discloses his desire to correct the text of the Vulgate while at the same time minimizing the significance of his textual criticism:

> Add to this the fact that I do not always examine the Greek words,
> but rather lay bare any ambiguities occurring in the Latin and illu-
> minate any instances when the regular practice of literal translation
> may have made things more difficult to understand. I do this to alert
> those who don't know Greek at all or who may have a shaky grasp
> of Latin about this matter, small though it may be.[31]

These examples demonstrate how the application of grammatical, rhe-torical, and historical learning derived from classical sources to religious texts was on the one hand the almost natural outcome of the early *studia humanitatis* (the study of grammar, poetry, history, rhetoric, and moral phi-losophy), but on the other hand, it was a source of great tensions in terms of the relationship to various aspects of institutional religion. Abravanel's model of a prophet redactor inspired by the Holy Spirit represents an at-tempt to contend with the tension between the new historical and literary understanding of the Former Prophets and their religious status.

However, Baer's proposed connection between Don Isaac's historical and literary approach and the critical exegetical methods of the Italian hu-manists is, admittedly, difficult to substantiate. There is no direct evidence that Abravanel was influenced by the types of discourses formulated by Manetti and Valla. We can propose a more relevant literary discourse tak-ing place in Don Isaac's Iberian milieu, a discourse that sought to define ancient literary genres and spark a renaissance in Castilian literature. An example of this trend is the letter penned by Marqués de Santillana (1398–1458) in the period 1446–49 and sent to Dom Pedro, then both Duke of Coimbra and regent. In this letter, de Santillana asks the duke: "What is this thing poetry? That we call also in the vernacular 'the gay science'—if not a fiction of useful things, covered or concealed by a very beautiful veil, woven together or separated, chanted according to a certain number, meter, and measure?"[32] From this general definition, the marquis launches into an overview of the history of poetry from biblical times to his own day, encompassing Italy, France, Catalonia, Castile, and Portugal. This important letter, which arrived in Portugal when Don Isaac was still a boy, is invaluable testimony to the interest of Iberian intellectuals in literary questions about genre, its character, and its history. We can add to such literary discussions the introductions to the chronicles of López de Ayala (1332–1407), Fernão Lopes, and Fernando del Pulgar (1436–93), as well as the discussions of Christian exegetes like Nicholas de Lyra and Pablo de Burgos—all of whom are mentioned, or at least closely paraphrased, by Abravanel in his commentaries. We can thus sketch a portrait of the literary, cultural, and religious environment that could give rise to the types of literary discussions evident in Don Isaac's commentary on the Former Prophets.

However, this picture would be incomplete without noting medieval Jewish exegetes such as Rashi, Ibn Ezra, Rashbam, Radak, Profiat Duran, and many others—who had developed a set of linguistic, grammatical, and literary skills in their study of the Bible. Presumably Abravanel did not just draw inspiration from his Christian cultural environment, and the Jewish commentators he had already studied in Portugal played an even greater role. One example of such influence is a passage penned by Rabbi Joseph Hayyun of Lisbon in the 1460s. Hayyun recounts that Abravanel sent him a question that bears a strong resemblance to the issues raised at the beginning of the latter's commentary on the Former Prophets. Hayyun writes:

> The great cedar tree, who gives heed to my words, Don Isaac Abravanel asked me . . . a single question: My petition and my request is whether Deuteronomy was from the Lord in heaven, and whether the words therein are like other words of the Torah that Moses set before the children of Israel and that from "In the Beginning" to "in the sight of all Israel"—these and those are all the words of the living God? Or perhaps Deuteronomy was composed by Moses him-

self, as someone explaining what he understood from the divine intention regarding the explication of the commandments.[33]

Thus, some twenty years before Abravanel began writing his commentary on the Former Prophets, he was already thinking about the status and nature of Deuteronomy, inquiring about its purpose as well as the status of its author: whether Moses should be viewed as a mere "copyist," relaying God's word, or "the author himself."[34] The fact that Abravanel sent his question to Hayyun indicates a teacher-student relationship. While Don Isaac never mentions Hayyun as his teacher, a study of the latter's writings demonstrates his clear influence on the former. For example, before Abravanel had done so, Hayyun introduced each commentary by explaining the general characteristics of each book. Thus, in his introduction to the Psalms, Hayyun asks the following questions: "Who wrote this book? . . . Who spoke and uttered the hymns of this book? . . . What is the manner of speech in the book [that is, is it divinely inspired]?" He further inquires into "the book's intention" and its "benefits."[35]

From this short list it appears clear that Abravanel's own discussions were informed by those of Hayyun. This exegetical method is predicated on the four Aristotelian causes (material, formal, efficient, and final), which were already guiding principles in the scholastic discussions of Christian philosophical and exegetical literature in the thirteenth century. It seems that Hayyun learned this method from none other than Rabbi Isaac Canpanton (active at the end of the fourteenth century and in the first half of the fifteenth century) head of the yeshiva of Zamora, Castile, and considered one of the chief founders of the scholastic method of Talmud study.

In his book on Isaac Abravanel, Lawee has examined the philological and historical conceptions that emerge from the introduction that we have discussed.[36] Although noting Abravanel's significant departure from his exegetical predecessors, Lawee offers as a possible backdrop the views of Radak and Duran on the origins of the traditional cantillation marks, the *qere* and *ketiv*, and the Masoretic text. For example, Duran wrote:

> And furthermore, during those seventy years of exile in Babylon, [the sacred writings] began to be overtaken by corruption and confusion, causing people to despair of them. Aware of this, Ezra the priest, righteous head of the scribes, bestirred himself, and exerted all his powers to rectify what was wrong, and thus did all the scribes who came after him. They corrected all those [biblical] books as

much as possible, such that they have been preserved for us perfectly in the number of pericopes, verses, words, letters, *matres lectionis*, and the conventions of language and other things. Therefore, they are called scribes (*sofrim*) and they composed works on this—these are the books of the Masorah. And in every passage in which they met with corruption and confusion, they inserted the *qere* and *ketiv*, being unsure [as to the correct reading given] what they found.[37]

Duran (like Radak before him) portrays a historical process of textual corruption, a process reversed by corrective efforts that resulted in the elaboration of the Masoretic text. However, he does not go to the same lengths as Abravanel. Duran's notion of editing only takes place after composition. He does not entertain the possibility that the composition itself went through editing stages: in other words, that a biblical redactor was actively involved in choosing, collecting, and editing multiple earlier sources.

Faced by this rich assortment of influences, all of which may have played their part in defining the contours of Abravanel's introduction to his commentary on Joshua, modern scholars have debated how best to characterize Abravanel's exegetical approach. Scholars like Baer deemed Abravanel a humanist. Others, such as Leo Strauss and Benzion Netanyahu, saw an essentially medieval thinker covered in a thin humanistic garb.[38] In light of the accumulated scholarship on this issue, one can view Abravanel's discussion here as representing a crossroads of sorts where different literary traditions meet: medieval Christian and Jewish biblical exegesis; Christian scholasticism; medieval Jewish philosophy; the chroniclers and historians of the fourteenth and fifteenth centuries; and the discussions of the Iberian and Italian humanists in literary criticism. Don Isaac did not make a firm choice from among these intellectual possibilities. Rather, he combined them into an integrated exegetical approach that places at its center the book, its various literary genres, its authors and editors, its different influences on the reader, and the hand of providence intervening in every stage of its "production."

Exegetical Method: Between Sephardic Iyyun and Christian Scholasticism

Besides Don Isaac's overall approach to the Former Prophets and his conception of its historical and literary background, it behooves us to characterize Abravanel's exegetical method in studying scripture, presented at the end of the introduction to his commentary on the Former Prophets:

I have seen fit to divide every book into units, but they shall not be long and large as done by Gersonides. . . . Nor shall they be short and small as done by the scholar Jerome who translated the Holy Books for the Christians. . . . I will not intend upwards or downwards but rather aim for the middle path, relating to the different matters in discussion and the different stories narrated.[39]

Unlike the classical Jewish exegetes Rashi, Ibn Ezra, and Radak, who commented on single verses and even on single words, Abravanel contends with full "units"—that is, broader literary units defined and demarcated by the principle of a single "story" or idea. This method of homiletical exegesis has major similarities with certain fourteenth- and fifteenth-century homiletical works such as those of Rabbi Nissim Gerondi (HaRan, c. 1300–c. 1376) and Rabbi Isaac Arama (c. 1420–c. 1494, author of 'Aqedat Yitshaq).[40] Interestingly, Abravanel portrays his choice as a golden mean between the methods of Gersonides and the translation and commentary of Jerome. Abravanel once again reveals his dual learning—Jewish and Christian—and demonstrates his familiarity not only with the works of Jewish commentators but also with those of Christians such as Jerome, Augustine, Nicholas de Lyra, Pablo de Burgos, and others.

Besides dividing the text into study units, as well as using a comprehensive (or homiletical) approach to relatively large literary units, Don Isaac also opens each discussion with a series of questions:

And I plan also to introduce each unit with six questions. . . . Some of them [contain] a powerful doubt (atsumot hasafeq), others can be simply untied. For the organization and delimitation of scholarly matters (devarim 'iyuniim) helps [us attain] full understanding. . . . And behold I have chosen this method of introducing the interpretation of verses with questions because I believe it to be beneficial for stirring the interest (leorer ha'inyanim); to introduce debate (lehamtsi' havikuah) and broadening study (uleharhiv hahaqira). Furthermore, the raising of questions will often lead to the deeper study (lehosif ha'iyun) of the verses and allow the discovery of meanings sweeter than honey.[41]

As stressed by many scholars, this method—raising questions, citing different opinions, and resolving doubts or questions—has its roots in the scholastic methods of disputatio practiced in the theological faculties throughout Europe since the beginning of the thirteenth century. A prominent example is the magnum opus of the famous Christian philosopher Thomas Aquinas (1225–74), the *Summa Theologica*, which opens each chapter with a series of questions. However, it seems that Abravanel did not learn this method solely from Christian sources. Hayyun, one of his teachers, also opened his discussions with a series of "doubts" and "questions." Daniel Boyarin and Yisrael Ta-Shma have described the Jewish roots of this method, which emerged to a large extent from the development of a Jewish exegetical literature starting with the Tosafists and continuing to Rabbi Isaac Canpanton.[42] On the one hand, this literature created a series of critical tools for discussing scripture and the Talmud as well as the theoretical and practical questions that these texts raise. On the other hand, Mauro Zonta documented the cultural phenomenon that he terms Hebrew scholasticism, a movement that developed in fifteenth-century Iberia among Jewish philosophers such as Joseph Albo (c. 1380–1444), Abraham Bibago (c. 1425–89), Abraham Shalom (d. 1492), Isaac Arama, and Abravanel himself.[43] This phenomenon included translating scholastic literature into Hebrew, as well as the adoption of many of its ideas and scholarly conventions. Boyarin argues that Canpanton's method of study was influenced by the scholastic hermeneutics and linguistics—albeit without pointing to any direct channels of influence. Ultimately, Abravanel drew inspiration for his exegetical method both from the so-called Sephardic Iyyun, which dominated Jewish circles in fifteenth-century Iberia and from the traditions of Christian scholasticism.

Canpanton's *Darkhei hatalmud*, an early formulation of Sephardic Iyyun, includes a clear discussion of the methodical role played by doubts and questions in the attainment of hermeneutical truth:

> Whenever you wish to study any homily or subject, . . . you must also seek out ways to raise difficulties against it, to first introduce the doubts regarding this subject or this formulation, . . . and to know . . . the difficulties that can be raised against this exegetical claim. For this leads you to arrive at the truth and to proper understanding of the matter—for he who feels disease will immediately find the cure.[44]

Doubts and questions, in other words, are the best way to identify the weaknesses of an interpretation and thus the ideal way of drawing closer to the truth.

Yoel Marciano's comprehensive doctoral dissertation on the origins of Sephardi Talmudic speculation in fifteenth-century Spain[45] points to a complex and diverse process that produced Sephardic Iyyun, beginning before Rabbi Hasdai Crescas (1340–1410 or 1411) and continuing even after the expulsion. Canpanton was not the only figure to embody Sephardic Iyyun: works such as *Halikhot 'olam* by Rabbi Yeshua Halevi (fifteenth century) were perhaps even more influential on the Jewish scholars of the Iberian peninsula before and after the expulsion. As Marciano has shown, Sephardic Iyyun represented the fusion of talmudic exegesis and specific philosophical conceptions pertaining to ultimate human perfection and cleaving to God. Duran characterized the approach as follows: "In their opinion, this show of wisdom (*hithakmut*) and this scientific investigation (*haqirah*), bring man to his ultimate felicity (*hatslahato ha'ahronah*), according him the level of the Sages in the Garden of Eden, commensurate with the level of his scientific knowledge and [talmudic] dialectics."[46] This approach aims to cultivate the intellectual abilities of the scholar in the realm of Halakhah, hand in hand with a desire to methodically encompass all aspects of rabbinic literature.

The ideal of a systematic approach fostered the search for principles that could be used to define the methods of rabbinical literature and draw the scholar closer to a holistic understanding of it. Crescas summarized the overarching logic of this system in the introduction to his *Or Adonai*:

> And because the knowledge of the Torah's commandments is the straight path that leads to this perfection. Therefore, the knowledge of the Torah, in the specific aspect in which it is achieved, should be as perfect as possible. And the perfection of knowing and comprehending them [the commandments] is in three matters: precise knowledge, easy conceptual understanding, and their memorization.[47]

As is well known, Crescas's criticism of Maimonides's *Mishneh torah* revolved around its lack of systematic method and comprehensive approach. Listing the reasons for his opposition, Crescas defined the proper speculative method developed in Castile and Aragon in the fifteenth century: "It is clear that the complete knowledge of things is when we know their causes and the matter of their subject (*homer nos'am*). And when we have imperfect knowledge of matter, we cannot be certain that we are free of error and mistakes."[48]

As explained by Crescas, the achievement of a "complete knowledge" of rabbinic literature entails an analytical understanding of its principles and formal aspects: the entire edifice of talmudic discourse can be viewed as the systematic expansion of a series of principles and axioms. Using this analytical approach, it is easier to study the Talmud as a whole and to avoid error and forgetting one's study. While Crescas's plan to write a comprehensive halakhic work never came to fruition, his aspiration certainly embodied the exegetical method that continued to develop throughout the fifteenth century. Abravanel's commentaries are heavily influenced by this exegetical approach, and like Crescas, Abravanel sought principles and rules. Likewise, Abravanel—who also sought "complete knowledge"—aspired to comprehensively review each exegetical topic not only by presenting his own approach but also by discussing the many approaches offered by his predecessors. Thus, Abravanel undertook an apologetic task. As shown by Jair Haas, Abravanel defended the Torah's perfection from as many hermeneutical perspectives as possible.[49]

Abravanel's system of questions and doubts, drawing from Sephardic Iyyun and scholasticism, tends to construct the interpretation of scripture around a central, theoretical, historical, or textual question—what he refers to as "expanding study" or "expanding discourse" (*leharhiv et hahaqirah, leharhiv dibur*).[50] Sometimes, when the question pertains to a matter of particular importance, Abravanel prefers to introduce his answer with a series of "studies (*'iyunim* or *limudim*)," "introductions (*haqdamot*)," "axioms (*shorashim*)," or "discourses (*diburim*)," exhaustively covering every aspect of the topic at hand. For example, in his commentary on 1 Samuel 8, Abravanel includes an extensive discussion of the monarchy (which I will discuss further below), which begins as follows: "and I, unlearned as I am, have prepared to comprehend the truth within this discussion with three discourses [*diburim*]."[51] This tendency to expand upon specific questions is related to the homiletical and methodical nature of Don Isaac's exegesis (Sephardic Iyyun) as well as the scholastic and literary aspects of his learning and writing.

In summary, in his introduction to his first major biblical commentary, Don Isaac discloses the full complexity of his exegesis. It is clear that these different facets of his learning contributed to his special sensitivity to texts, their processes of composition, their divisions, the ideas they impart, and the effect their authors wish to have upon the reader. As I have shown, this exegetical sensitivity is closely related to Don Isaac's social objective: rebuilding his public status in a new community. That being said, this assortment of influences and approaches did not coalesce into a single organic method. Rather, it manifested itself as an eclectic approach that involved a variety of disciplines (philosophy, history, literature, psychology, political thought, magic, astrology, and more). In the next chapter I will point to some of the salient elements of Don Isaac's interpretative eclecticism.

8 : THE FIGURE OF THE LEADER IN ABRAVANEL'S COMMENTARY ON THE FORMER PROPHETS

As I have explained, Don Isaac, an immigrant to Castile, closely identified with the biblical leaders of Israel who entered the promised land to conquer it. In his commentary, one can see time and time again how he returns to such questions as the rise of leaders and their fall, their character traits, and various aspects of the regimes of the biblical judges and kings. This political orientation can be viewed as one of the guiding principles of Don Isaac's commentary on the Former Prophets.

Joshua Mourns the Death of Moses

Don Isaac's understanding of the first two verses of Joshua can almost be called autobiographical. The verses read as follows: "Now after the death of Moses the servant of the Lord it came to pass, that the Lord spoke to Joshua the son of Nun, Moses's minister, saying, Moses my servant is dead; now therefore arise, go over this Jordan, you, and all this people, unto the land which I do give to them, even to the children of Israel."

Abravanel writes:

> Joshua was sitting between the oven and the cookstove, his head bowing down as a bulrush, laying sackcloth and ashes, grieving over the death of Moses, his master. But God, may He be blessed, informed him [by prophecy] that this was improper for two reasons. First, because Moses is the servant of God and his soul shall abide in prosperity.... Second, it is not proper to exaggerate one's mourning over the dead. As David, peace be upon him, said [2 Sam. 12:23]: "Can I bring him back again? I shall go to him, but he will not return to me." And for these two reasons, God commanded him not to sit in mourning any longer, but to rise and prepare for the crossing of the Jordan.[1]

Abravanel uses the figure of Joshua to underscore one of the most important facets of leadership. A leader must possess the strength to overcome sorrow and heartache, recover from mourning, stand up, and return to the task at hand. This idea, which we encountered in a humanistic garb in Abravanel's letter to the Count of Faro, appears once again in the opening passages of Abravanel's commentary on the Former Prophets. It is used to characterize the transfer of leadership from Moses to Joshua and to describe Joshua's preparations to fulfill his duty—the conquest of the Holy Land. Of course, Joshua is not the only figure forced to overcome adversity. Abravanel himself had had to overcome challenges: stripped of his wealth, denied his status, and forced to flee from Portugal, he had had to reestablish himself. Perhaps Don Isaac's description of Joshua represents an attempt at self-encouragement? Of course, one cannot know for sure. Regardless, in both cases—Joshua's ability to overcome his grief, and Don Isaac's recovery from the tribulations associated with his flight from Portugal—renewing one's connection with God plays an important role.

The Miracle at Gibeon and the Dispute with Gersonides

Comparing Joshua's status to that of his successors, the judges and kings, Don Isaac offers an interpretation of the word "*lefanecha*" (before you) appearing in verse 5: "There shall not any man be able to stand before you all the days of your life." According to Abravanel, the word attests to Joshua's unique qualities: "It means that only he would possess [this quality] and that none after him would possess it after his death in the days of the Judges. . . . Just like God was with Moses, who was followed by no other prophet like him, so too shall Joshua be in terms of his strength."[2] God's special providence over Joshua, from his crossing of the Jordan until his death, distinguishes him from other Israelite leaders who did not merit a sustained connection with the divine. In Don Isaac's view, this distinction is related to Joshua's special mission as well as the specific character of his eponymous book: "The special purpose of the book of Joshua is to demonstrate that all the divine goals . . . [related to the] conquest of the land were fulfilled."[3]

Joshua's special connection to God is manifested in a series of miracles performed on his behalf, most notably the stopping of the sun at Gibeon (Josh. 10). Don Isaac uses this account as an opportunity to delve into a broader discussion of the occurrence of miracles. Among other things, he attacks the naturalistic philosophical interpretation of this verse—an approach developed by Gersonides and other philosophers in the Maimonidean tradition. In a vein similar to that of his introduction to *'Ateret zeqenim*,

Don Isaac presents his approach as an attempt to defend a much-maligned passage: "It is because the passage has been made a target for all the scholars who study it; they shoot their arrows at it."[4] Once again, Abravanel rises to the task of defense: to elucidate the simple meaning of scripture and offer a more literal reading of the miracle that took place at Gibeon.

Opening his discussion of the four (Aristotelian) causes of the miracle (efficient, final, material, and formal), Abravanel asks: "What was the efficient cause of this miracle? Was it the Blessed Creator or the Active Intellect?" In the sixth essay (part 2, chapter 10) of *Milhamot Hashem*, Gersonides discusses the very same questions and concludes that "it is evident that the Active Intellect is the agent of these miracles." He notes that "as we have proven in Book 2, it is evident that the Active Intellect knows of the occurrence of these miracles and accordingly communicates this knowledge to the prophet."[5] In other words, according to Gersonides, miracles are not departures from the normal cosmological order of the superlunar world. Rather, they are the way that God's providence is made manifest— through the cosmological system and through the Active Intellect. The Active Intellect encapsulates the entirety of cosmological knowledge (the order of beings) as well the implications this order has for events taking place in the sublunar world. Because the prophet is, by definition, also a philosopher and is thus well acquainted with cosmological laws, he maintains an epistemological connection with the Active Intellect, allowing him to receive its knowledge and to use it to improve the circumstances of the children of Israel.

Gersonides, a scientist, assumed that nature obeyed a set of fixed, eternal, and teleological laws set in place by the creator. Man's ultimate purpose, and the goal of Gersonides's own intellectual endeavors, is to comprehend these natural laws. It is therefore no surprise that Gersonides, ever the rationalist, was not enamored of the idea of a miraculous suspension of the harmony and regularity of nature and, therefore, wished to reduce the degree to which nature had been violated in the biblical account. This is clear in his efforts to integrate accounts of miracles into a framework of constant natural laws—to mesh cosmic regularity with the doctrine of prophecy and the prophet's special epistemological status. According to Gersonides, miracles do not violate the cosmological order via a direct connection between God and man. Rather, they represent special instances of astral influence upon the sublunar world and of the Active Intellect upon the intellect of the prophet. In this conception, within the Active Intellect, all information about the separate intellects (that is, the movers of spheres and planets) is conceptualized and represented (*mittsayrot venirshamot*). This information is translated into influence upon the sublunar world. For this reason, Gersonides interprets the miracle in Joshua 10 as follows: "none should doubt that the [account of] the stopping of the sun for Joshua does not imply that the movement of the sun was annulled.... For the miracle of Joshua consisted in the fact that he wanted victory to be accomplished against that nation, his enemies, in an amount of time so short that none would note the setting of the sun."[6] In other words, the sun's movement continued unabated; it unfailingly followed the same eternal path it had pursued since creation. Therefore, the verse's meaning is to be understood figuratively: Joshua's victory was so swift that it was *as if* time had stood still.

In contrast to Gersonides's explanation, Abravanel presented a view of his own. Understanding it will allow us to place him within a philosophical context and in a relationship to various philosophical schools and trends. At the beginning of the "second investigation in answering of questions" about these verses, Abravanel writes:

> First, I shall say that the opinion about the existence of the Active Intellect as the Giver of Forms is a conception that the later Muslim philosophers embraced, which was followed by many philosophers from our nation. It has really been a stumbling block for the Israelites, for they believed it [the Active Intellect] to be the Giver of Forms and [believed] it to give life to our intellectual soul.... They [also] believed that it [the Active Intellect] is the bundle of life and that the reward of the souls is conjunction with it after death. From this it followed for them that they [the souls] unite in it, so that the [fate of the] righteous is akin to that of the wicked.... They believed it [the Active Intellect] to be that which exerts providence and oversees the [sublunary] world.... They believe it to rest upon the prophets, making them prophesy. From this they concluded that prophecy is something natural.... They believed that the Active Intellect effectuates all miracles, and that it is not God the Creator who effectuates them.... O my Lord, what shall I say after Israel turned the words of the Living God upside down ... affirming that God the Lord, Who is present in the words of the prophets and in the agency of the miracles, is the Active Intellect? Woe are the ears

that hear this! Of them it has been truly said: "They have belied the Lord, and said: It is not He" [Jer. 5:12]. They replaced His Glory by the last and tiniest of all separate intellects, and they said: "These are your gods O Israel, who brought you out of Egypt" [Ex. 32:4]. Be astonished, O you heavens, at this![7]

Abravanel's critique of Gersonides's position opens with a historical note: the very notion of the Active Intellect in medieval Jewish philosophy can be traced to the influence of Muslim philosophers, specifically Al-Farabi and Ibn Sina. Don Isaac was well aware of other Muslim theologians who subscribed to a more critical approach to philosophy, such as Al-Ghazali, author of *Incoherence of the Philosophers*. However, their views do not concern him here. What is noteworthy in this passage is Abravanel's use of a historical argument to refute Gersonides's position. In Abravanel's opinion, Gersonides belonged to a period in which Jewish philosophers were beholden to the philosophical influence of Ibn Sina and Al-Farabi. They went so far as to adopt and develop such concepts as the Active Intellect for the purpose of their own Jewish context, borrowing this notion directly from such philosophers.

A possible source for this historical and critical account may be Rabbi Hasdai Crescas's introduction to *Or Adonai*:

When the generations grew weak and the guardians of the ancient Oral Torah, together with its hidden mysteries and secrets, were enfeebled, the wisdom of our Sages was lost. . . . Many of the members of our nation pretended to explain visions and prophetic words by means of dreams, vain words, and the [inventions of] the gentile [philosophers] so much so that our greater sages were drawn after their words, decorating themselves with their treatises, and adorning themselves with their proofs. And at their head was the great rabbi— our teacher Rabbi Moses son of Maimon—who, with his great intellect and vast knowledge of the Talmud, as well as the breadth of his heart, understood the books of philosophers and their treatises. And they seduced him, and he was seduced, and from their frail axioms he built pillars and foundations for the secrets of the Torah in that book that he called the *Guide of the Perplexed*. And while the intention of this rabbi was proper, today rebellious slaves have risen up, and turned the words of the living God into heresy. They blemish the sacred, and with the words of that rabbi, they speak slander instead of beauty. And the root of the matter is that none until this point have contested the proofs of the Greek [Aristotle] who has darkened the eyes of Israel in our time.[8]

Crescas uses the biblical and rabbinic theme of declining generations to explain the philosophical and scientific shift in the high Jewish culture of the Middle Ages. The shift is portrayed in Crescas's rhetorical preface as a dangerous alternative to the rabbis' innate tie to the true religious substance of Judaism. Crescas, like Abravanel, defines the philosophical and scientific shift not only as a late distortion, but also as the result of the loss of authentic religious knowledge. There is no immediate way back to the authentic teachings of the past except through internal critique of the philosophies of Maimonides and his successors, especially the Greek and Arabic foundations of their systems. It is important to note that the antiphilosophical rhetoric in Crescas's introduction, as well as in Abravanel's discussion of the miracle at Gibeon, does not represent a rejection of philosophy per se. Rather, Crescas and Abravanel pursue an approach that expresses criticism of and ambivalence toward a specific form of philosophy—the medieval Judeo-Arabic synthesis. This posture became common among Jewish scholars against the backdrop of wider cultural changes taking place at the time—the challenges to Aristotelianism raised in the fourteenth and fifteenth centuries, as well as the shock that seized Iberian Jewish society in the aftermath of the pogroms of 1391 and the mass conversions that followed. In this context, the historical and critical perspective offered by Don Isaac represents an attempt to distance himself from that moment when Jewish philosophers incorporated Arabic philosophy into their thought: he wishes to consign that turning point to a specific time in the past. By doing so, Abravanel can emphasize his different historical circumstances.

In ʿAteret zeqenim (as well as in an earlier treatise, Tsurot hayesodot) Abravanel demonstrates his deep familiarity with Arabic philosophy and the different positions of its thinkers. For example, in chapter 12 of ʿAteret zeqenim—in which he tries to demonstrate the existence of a direct connection between God, the first intellect, the first sphere, and Israel and thus to prove the possibility of miracles and acts of direct divine intervention—we see how important it was for Abravanel to showcase his knowledge of the Judeo-Arabic philosophical tradition:

> And indeed, in the world of the spheres, it is also clear that there is one particular part, which is superior in perfection, and receives the

divine influx from God, may He be blessed, without any intermediary. . . . Thanks to its great excellence, [the first sphere] attains in a single motion more perfection than that which other spheres attain in their numerous motions, as has been explained in [Aristotle's] *De Caelo*. Since it is the first among the spheres in excellence and perfection, its mover is God Himself, may He be blessed, without the mediation of any separate intellect. Aristotle concurred with this [view], according to what Ibn Rushd understood from him. He [Ibn Rushd] correctly understood the intention of his [Aristotle's] words in Book Lām [book 12] of the *Metaphysics*. This is true although Ibn Sina and his followers—among them Rabbi Levi ben Gershom, in his book *Milhamot Hashem,* and Rabbi Moses ben Levi, in the tract he wrote on this topic—believed that the mover of the uppermost sphere was the First Caused [substance] and not the First Cause [God]. This is an invalid view according to the words of the head of the philosophers [Aristotle] and according to the truth itself, for nature does nothing in vain.[9]

If in his commentary on the miracle of Gibeon, Don Isaac seems intent on disassociating himself entirely from the influence of Arabic philosophy, in *'Ateret zeqenim* he shows that he is quite capable of bolstering his arguments with citations from Aristotle and Ibn Rushd. It is important, however, to be precise: in his commentary on Joshua 10, Abravanel expresses his distaste for the influence of "later Muslim philosophers"—but not all of them. Abravanel was essentially interested in establishing a solid philosophical basis for rejecting the status of the Active Intellect as the "giver of forms" and "overseer of the [sublunary] world." He wished to reject it as an entity responsible for mediating the connection between God and the world. Abravanel found this basis in the writings of Ibn Rushd, who adhered to the Aristotelian notion of God as the prime mover—that is, the notion that God moves the spheres directly. This contrasts sharply with the approach of the "later Muslim philosophers" (by which Abravanel means Al-Farabi and Ibn Sina) and their view of the crucial cosmological role played by the Active Intellect. As Abravanel explains, the first sphere in medieval cosmology moves the ones below it, or the spheres containing the planets and stars. Its movement is transmitted to the other spheres and it also physically encases them all. If God is the direct mover of the first sphere, as claimed by Ibn Rushd, then (according to Abravanel) God can suspend its movement, consequently bringing all the stars and planets, and even the sun, to a halt. This, Abravanel argues, is precisely what took place at Gibeon.

This passage from 'Ateret zeqenim proves that we should regard Don Isaac's remonstrations against the influence of Arabic philosophy with some suspicion. When Abravanel could enlist Aristotle or Ibn Rushd to serve his own philosophical and theological ends, he was happy to do so. Furthermore, he demonstrates intimate familiarity with the fine distinctions between different philosophical views, such as those of Ibn Rushd and Ibn Sina. Abravanel even pigeonholed Jewish philosophers according to different philosophical camps. While he associated Gersonides and others with Ibn Sina, he tried to place Maimonides and himself in the camp of Aristotle and Ibn Rushd.[10] In some cases, Abravanel even touts Ibn Rushd as a more authoritative interpreter of Aristotle than Gersonides was.[11] From the passages that we have cited from Abravanel's commentary on Joshua, as well as those from 'Ateret zeqenim, it is clear that Abravanel subscribed to a specific historical perspective on the evolution of Jewish philosophy and its relationship to Arabic philosophy.

However, it is important to take note of the theological significance of the Active Intellect, which Abravanel rejects as part of his exegesis on the miracle at Gibeon. In Abravanel's opinion, important subjects such as divine reward and punishment, divine providence, prophecy, and miracles were transformed by the followers of the "later Muslim philosophers" into a function of intellectual conjunction with the Active Intellect—as opposed to an unmediated connection with God. According to this approach, the most important factor in theological affairs is the relationship between man's intellect and the Active Intellect, and the means of and preparation for achieving this connection are of prime importance. In his criticism of Gersonides, Abravanel once again voices his opposition to philosophical models that place undue emphasis on a cosmological and epistemological intermediary that intervenes between God and man. The attempt to distance God from any contact with this world or intervention in it led Jewish philosophers to replace God's glory "by the last and tiniest of all separate intellects"—in other words, to replace the God of scripture with a cosmological and epistemological entity (the Active Intellect) that has been crowned" as ruler of the sublunar world. Abravanel notably appropriates Aaron's words to the children of Israel after the creation of the Golden Calf—"these are your gods O Israel"—to describe the flocking of Jewish philosophers to Ibn Sina and Al-Farabi's notion of the Active Intellect. This expresses not only religious censure but also a conception of the Active Intellect as a mere astral body. By casting God's intervention at Gibeon as a consequence of God's unmediated control over the first sphere, Abravanel follows his general tendency of drawing God closer to this world while also attempting to find a new balance between philosophy, science, and religion. Here one can see the historical gap separating Abravanel and Gersonides: Don Isaac views Judeo-Arabic philosophy as reflecting an approach that alienates God, a view that belongs to the past. In Abravanel's time, what is needed is an approach that will draw God closer.

As he continues his discussion of the Active Intellect, we find Abravanel identifying the proper balance between religion and philosophy within the works of Christian philosophers:

> And behold the Christians—the wisdom of their scholars and the understanding of their prudent men cannot be measured. . . . Born to them are men well versed . . . in the sciences of logic, physics, and metaphysics. And in all mathematical sciences they surpassed the eastern sages, and there is no end to the books they have written. Nonetheless, they never cast their hand against the Torah of Moses, the man of God and [instead] wore it as their own crown. . . . Look what they say about the essence of the soul, its immortality, prophecy, and miracles. Is there anyone among them who doubts the world was created or that miracles [can occur]? Look what they say about the essence of the soul, its immortality, prophecy, and miracles: is there anyone among them, with all their deep investigations in the sciences, who opens his mouth and shows contempt for the literal sense of the Torah?[12]

As opposed to the Arab philosophers, criticized just a few lines above, Don Isaac depicts the Christian "scholars" as intellectuals who, despite their profound knowledge of philosophy and science, do not cast any doubt on creation ex nihilo or the possibility of miracles. Abravanel admires their ability to separate religion from philosophy and science, as well as their success in finding a golden mean between the two camps. While it is unclear who Abravanel is referring to specifically, this statement represents yet another case of co-opting the views of Christian writers, a phenomenon we have seen in the previous chapter, in the case of Jerome. While Abravanel is certainly vague, we can identify in his statement a transition from the Judeo-Arabic philosophical models he inherited from the past to the Christian models he acquired as part of his Iberian literary education.

Following Yitzhak Baer, many scholars have identified in Abravanel's discussions about the tension between religion and philosophy the tenor of a specific philosophical movement—the anti-Averroists, who rose to prominence in the aftermath of the pogroms of 1391. In *The History of Jews in Christian Spain*, Baer claims: "In the fifteenth century, as in previous ages, religious Averroism existed as a historical force undermining the foundations of Jewish national and religious unity."[13] According to this approach, the opposition to the radical philosophical exegesis of scripture—voiced by Jewish philosophers such as Crescas, Abraham Bibago, Isaac Arama, Abravanel, and others—reflects an apologetic and antiphilosophical sentiment.[14] However, reading Abravanel's statements in '*Ateret zeqenim* and other works, one cannot help but notice the extent to which he admired Ibn Rushd, not to mention the extent to which he had internalized the history of Judeo-Arabic philosophy. I believe, therefore, that Abravanel's approach represents instead the adoption of a Christian discourse that does not supplant the Judeo-Arabic philosophical heritage of the Middle Ages but rather stands with it—although there is a clear historical gulf lying between them. This cultural reality, characterized by an abundance of heterogeneous literary influences (Jewish, Arab, Muslim, Christian, and classical), defines the nature of Abravanel's writings far better than Baer's oversimplistic anti-Averroistic thesis.

One can summarize Abravanel's approach to the miracle at Gibeon by citing the following passage:

I have said that the agent (*po'el*) of wonders is not the Active Intellect but rather God the Blessed alone. For it is He who created all natural things including the higher entities guiding them and he is able to change their course and cause them to deviate from their nature. The claims of Gersonides have no substance. . . . And while that influx and that message may be passed through a medium or mediums, this does not mean that we deny that He the Blessed One is the essential agent (*po'el be'etsem*) and that it is He who informs [the prophets] of all of this. As to that which [Gersonides] claimed regarding the renewal of [divine] knowledge and the innovation

of will—behold just as we can suffer it [when it comes to] the creation of the world, so too we shall suffer it [when it comes to] miraculous acts. This also does not entail a change in [divine] will, for
the Blessed God wishes for the bestowal of good, and when the natural order opposes [the bestowal of good], He will change it to the
utmost degree of perfection.[15]

The difference between Abravanel and Gersonides primarily pertains to
their respective understandings of the relationship between creation and
miracles. Both Don Isaac and Gersonides maintained that the world was
created and not preexistent. However, their respective understandings of
this notion are vastly different, with Don Isaac believing in creation ex nihilo and Gersonides in a preexistent matter that God used to create the
world. Furthermore, the idea that the world is directed toward receiving
the benefits of divine munificence proves or supports each philosopher's
thesis of creation. Gersonides maintained that there exists an internal and
inherent connection among three subjects: creation, teleology, and God's
existence. In contrast, Maimonides sought to separate the issue of God's existence from the subject of creation, essentially leaving whether the world
was preexistent or created an open question that cannot be clearly resolved
through philosophical methods. However, the main difference between
Don Isaac and Gersonides is as follows: Abravanel proposes a God who is
able to realize his intentions not only through the medium of the natural
order but also through miracles (that is, by violating the laws of nature),
while Gersonides does not see in miracles events that violate the cosmological order established at creation, nor does he see in them a fundamental deviation from the principles of nature. For Abravanel, creation is the
backdrop and explanation for miracles (miracles represent specific instances
of creation repeating itself), whereas for Gersonides, divine creation is realized only through the teleological and cosmological order of being.

How does this philosophical and theological debate color the figure of
Joshua? It was important for Abravanel to preserve as much as possible the
direct connection between God and the prophetic leader. He writes that
Joshua's "saying 'Sun, stand still over Gibeon' is not a commandment to the
sun, but rather a prayer to God that he stop the sun and suspend its movement."[16] As in 'Ateret zeqenim, the unmediated connection between God
and the prophetic leaders liberates Israel from the natural influence of the
celestial bodies. Abravanel's emphasis on the miracle of Gibeon bears some

affinity to his own experience of miracles—his successful escape from the machinations of the Portuguese monarch. However, beyond the personal aspect of Abravanel's description, the leadership of Joshua and the miracle at Gibeon represent the polar opposite of Joshua's state when he mourned Moses's death before crossing the Jordan: the magnitude of the miracle at Gibeon proves that God's providence continued even after Moses's death. That being said, the direct connection between Joshua and God, together with the former's consequential ability to free himself from the constraints of nature through the medium of prayer, "does not necessarily show his level of prophecy, but rather the needs of the hour and the merits of the recipients."[17] The miracle at Gibeon cannot erase the fact that decline ensued after Moses was succeeded by Joshua: "for [Moses's] cleaving [to God] and the level of seeing [Him face to face] was his level."[18] In some senses the miracle at Gibeon constituted the peak of Joshua's connection with God—which, however, lacked a deep knowledge of the divine. After Joshua's death, the nation deteriorates further, a situation that in many senses shapes the task and character of the next model of leadership: the biblical judge and king.

Samuel, Saul, and David

The institution of judges is introduced and summarized in Judges 2:11–18: "And the children of Israel did evil in the sight of the Lord, and served Baalim. . . . And the anger of the Lord was hot against Israel, and he delivered them into the hands of spoilers that spoiled them. . . . Nevertheless, the Lord raised up judges, which delivered them out of the hand of those that spoiled them. . . . And when the Lord raised up judges for them, the Lord was with the judge and delivered them out of the hand of their enemies all the days of the judge." Don Isaac explains these verses as follows:

> Samuel the Prophet, the author of this book. . . thought best to present before the stories of the Judges the general reason of good and evil in what happened to them and then to expose it in detail. For this reason, he said that the Lord was with Israel during the days of Joshua and their enemies fell before them by the sword and no one could stand against them. After his death, this was no more the situation, and the reason for this was neither the compulsion of the constellations nor of fortune, but the result of divine providence. During the days of Joshua, [the children of] Israel were just and

good, so they dominated other nations and God was with them. But after his death [the children of] Israel became corrupted and they began to sin before the Lord and to worship other gods. Because of this sin, they were defeated by their enemies and their defense [divine providence] was removed from over them and they were naked.[19]

According to this explanation, the judge was a leader chosen by God to contend with the waning divine providence—a situation in which the direct connection between God and Israel had been severed, allowing natural forces to take over. In this definition of the judge's task, we see a familiar motif: the tension between fortune and providence. In his discussion of the prophetess Deborah in his commentary on Judges 4, Don Isaac formulates a preliminary list of qualities that characterize a judge: "'Deborah was a prophetess and a fiery woman (*eshet lapidot*).' The fact that Scripture stated— 'a prophetess'—was to teach the perfection of her intellect and her excellent disposition[, which caused] a prophetic spirit to rest upon her. And that which is stated—'a fiery woman'—teaches that she was a woman of valor and her actions were extremely vigorous and energetic."[20] The combination of divine, intellectual, and practical virtues is the mark of the judge, "so that he may rebuke and chastise the nation as is fitting"—in other words so he or she can correct the nation's moral wrongdoings.[21]

The figures described in Judges are not portrayed with enough detail to allow Don Isaac to characterize their leadership beyond some sparse notes. By contrast, the characters of Samuel, Saul, and David, as they are presented in the book of Samuel, provide ample material for exploring the profile of a leader. For example, the miraculous birth of Samuel is used by Abravanel to emphasize a leader's virtues. Thus, from the opening verse of Samuel (1:1)—"Now there was a certain man of Ramathaim Zophim, of Mount Ephraim, and his name was Elkanah, the son of Jeroham, the son of Elihu, the son of Tohu, the son of Zuph, an Ephrathite"—Abravanel gleans information about Samuel's natural lineage: "Why did he merit prophecy? Because he was of the family of Zuphites descended from Zuph the Ephrathite, one of his early forebears. And why was he a pious God-fearing man, who kept from evil? Because this was naturally bequeathed to him by his forefathers who were all exceedingly pious men."[22] Samuel's miraculous birth compounds his formidable lineage, pointing to the special connection between God and Hannah. Don Isaac writes: "I do not think that

Hannah was naturally barren. By her temperament (*mezeg*) and build she was fit to give birth. But God the Blessed wished it to be so, and miraculously prevented her from giving birth."[23] It was not some physical defect that prevented Hannah from having children, but rather the will of God. As a result, Samuel, who was not born through natural causes, was primed and destined to save Israel from its natural decline. Abravanel interprets Samuel's name in this light:

> And it says, "and she called his name Samuel, saying, Because I have asked him (*sha'altiv*) of the Lord" [1 Sam. 1:20] [But by this] reasoning, he should have been called Saul. . . . And I think that [he was called Samuel] for one of three reasons: She may have intended by this name that God placed (*samo*) [the child] in the world. And therefore, she called him Samuel to say that God placed him. And she said "because I have asked him from the Lord" meaning: I asked him from Him and He placed him (*samo*) in my innards; or she intended by this name that Samuel is from God the Blessed and is caused by Him . . . and one can further say that Samuel [means] "his name is God" (*shemo el*) for all divine matters are called after that Holy One, Blessed is He.[24]

The voice of God—a miraculous divine creation, which Samuel hears (1 Sam. 3)—confirms the significance Abravanel ascribes to the account of Samuel's birth. Samuel, in whom divine and natural qualities were united, was called to replace Eli the high priest and his sons, whose qualities were in steep decline. Leadership is not the consequence of lineage and birthright, but rather the unique and ephemeral relationship that is forged between God and the leader with the purpose of preventing and correcting the religious and political decline of the nation.

The natural and divine elements embodied by Samuel the judge and prophet are summarized in a broad description of the qualities of a leader appearing in the tale of the three omens that Samuel relays to Saul (1 Sam. 10:2–7):

> Behold the prophet [Samuel] determined that there were three aspects [to Saul's leadership]: one related to his [Saul's] father's house and its affairs; one with the children of Israel, he being their king; and one with God the Blessed for the perfection of his soul, which is the end of all ends. And these are a natural aspect according to his

birth, a legal and political aspect related to the leadership of his people, and a divine aspect [related] to the extent [to] which he cleaves to God the Blessed. The first is related to Saul's leadership inasmuch as he is living being, the second to his being a man, the third to his being godly.[25]

Don Isaac interprets the first omen revealed to Saul ("then you shall find two men and they will say to you, The asses which you went to seek are found" [1 Sam. 10:2]) as detachment from and transcendence over the "needs of his father's house"—that is, the transition from the natural concerns of one's family to concern for the collective, or, in Abravanel's words, "for greater and more exalted things." The second sign ("Then you shall go on forward from here. . . . There three men going up to God at Bethel will meet you " [10:3]) is, according to Abravanel, a lesson to the young king, "that he should lead the children of Israel benevolently and not exploit any person nor take their possessions unjustly."[26] Finally, the third sign ("And the Spirit of the Lord will come upon you, and you shall prophesy with them" [10:6]) completes the two previous aspects of leadership in that the leader, "when he cleaves to God . . . will remove his enemies from the land of [Israel]" and at the same time "will perfect his soul and his intellect will cleave to the higher [beings]."[27] While overcoming parochial interests and proclivities and adhering to the rule of law and justice are vital qualities for a leader, they are nevertheless natural. By contrast, Don Isaac deems it important to emphasize that the charismatic leadership of a warrior and the state of cleaving to God are not natural human qualities, but rather godly ones. These distinguish the leader from the rest of the people and distinguish the Israelite leader from the leaders of other nations. Abravanel interprets the end of verse 6 ("and shall be turned into another man") in this light. He writes: "Saul departed from the bounds of humanity and entered into the bounds of divinity and spirtualty."[28] The gradation of qualities of leadership that Abravanel presents in the biblical story of the donkeys demonstrates that while he opposed a naturalistic conception of the prophet and godly leader, a notion originating in the school of Maimonides and his followers, he nevertheless maintained that God's selection of Saul was based on the latter's "natural (*tiv'iyot*) and volitional ([*retsoniyot*) dispositions" (meaning physical, political, and moral prerequisites).[29] However, unlike Maimonides, Don Isaac portrays intellectual conjunction with God as a process that requires more than just intellectual perfection. It also requires a transitory period of divine intervention that is aimed at correcting the course of natural events.

The tripartite division of nature, state, and God, used by Don Isaac to define the character traits of a leader, originates in the fourth book of Plato's *Republic*. Plato compares the tripartite structure of the polis (the ruler guardians, the auxiliaries, and the producers) to the tripartite structure of the soul (reason, spirit, and appetite). Saul, corresponding to Don Isaac's own self-portrait presented at the opening of his commentary, embodied all three types of virtues: natural, political, and divine. However, such character traits demand no small amount of effort from the leader: he constantly runs the risk of falling victim to the tension between the two facets of his character, the divine and the natural and political. A prime example of this is Saul's failure to wait for Samuel before offering a burned sacrifice (1 Sam. 13). This represents Saul's inability to withstand the pressures exerted on him by the urging of the people and the fear of the enemy. As Abravanel explains: "The meaning of Saul's [sin] is that he sinned in his small faith, casting doubt on the words of the prophet, trusting his own knowledge, and violating the commandment of God."[30] According to Abravanel, Saul's sin, which ultimately led to his losing the throne, was the result of an imbalance between his natural and political virtues and his divine ones. This explains why God refused to accept his repentance after taking pity on King Agag of Amalek (1 Sam. 15:24):

> Saul's repentance was not accepted; his sin was too grave to bear. For he sinned by little faith and little love of God. And this is because the perfection defined in man is of two species. The human perfection [which includes] those qualities that are worthy of man qua man and the divine perfection, by faith and conjunction, worthy of one of us inasmuch as he is a man of Israel. There is no doubt that Saul was perfect in the first species, the perfection in his being a man. . . . But he was deficient in the second perfection, that is, the distinction in substance and form that belongs to a man of Israel.[31]

In the autobiographical introduction to his commentary, Abravanel describes the causes that led to his downfall in Portugal: "These evils have come upon me, because God is not within me."[32] The consonance between Abravanel's interpretation of Saul's fall and his interpretation of his own fall is salient. It follows that the Jewish leader loses his strength when his special bond with God—the first cause of the cosmos—fades and deteriorates into a natural and political connection to those celestial bodies that shape the fates of all humans.

The account of David's anointment and the evil spirit that descended upon Saul (1 Sam. 16) provides Abravanel with an opportunity to elaborate upon the process by which divine providence is lost and transferred to another leader. Don Isaac views the evil spirit that filled Saul with terror as a bout of melancholy that resulted from his fall from his formerly godly state to a merely natural and human one:

> Saul, after the spirit of God had departed from him, did not remain as other men. But rather he was encircled by terrors and fell thoughts, and his imagination constantly dwelt upon his punishment and how God had torn the kingdom of Israel from him, and how his good spirit had departed from him. And from this, his blood was burned, and he was afflicted by the disease of melancholia. And the physicians have written that [one afflicted] with this disease loses his imagination and power of thought, and will be assailed by worry, and he will fear, and he will tremble, and he will erupt into despair.[33]

Saul lost his intellectual connection with God. This awakened thoughts and fantasies originating not from on high but from his own body. Specifically, it resulted from the disruption of his blood system, which causes melancholy. Melancholy is the natural mental outcome of falling from a godly condition to a natural one. (Perhaps Don Isaac also experienced melancholy after his fall from grace and arrival in Castile.). Regardless, according to ancient and medieval medical views, melancholy (which in Greek means "black humor") is a consequence of an overactive and restless soul, causing the evaporation and drying of the body's moistures, and resulting in black blood (blood that has lost much of its moisture). A soul in this condition receives increasingly larger amounts of the heavy and cloudy character of the blood and becomes muddled and depressed. Melancholy is also discussed prominently in Renaissance literature. In Don Isaac's Portuguese letter we already see how he uses words to try to heal the Count of Faro of his depression and sorrow.

In *De Vita* (On life), written in the 1480s in Florence by Marsilio Ficino (1433–99), one can find a positive view of melancholy that emphasizes the close connection between it and exceptional intellectual activity. Among other things, Ficino also discusses the idea that song can emulate with its harmony the arithmetic characteristics of the stars and thus profoundly influence the human soul. According to this approach, song can restore the influence of celestial bodies upon the soul. Thus, Ficino writes: "Hence it is no wonder at all that by means of song certain diseases, both mental and physical, can sometimes be cured or brought on."[34]

Don Isaac uses this approach to analyze David's ability to alleviate Saul's madness through his "cunning in playing" (1 Sam. 16:18): "this means that he knew the wisdom of harmony perfectly and that he was perfect not only in the practice of music but also the wisdom of it."[35] He goes on to explain that "this teaches that already the divine influence was upon David, making him 'the sweet psalmist of Israel' whose playing was sweet to God the Blessed. And therefore, his playing could heal this disease [melancholy] which, according to nature, cannot be healed without draining and changing the diseased humors which would remove the evil spirit from upon him."[36] The wisdom of playing with which David was gifted is the knowledge of combining words and sounds, allowing the player to draw down divine influx upon both himself and his audience. David's playing, the only cure to Saul's melancholy, is yet another proof that divine providence had been transferred from Saul to David. David's divine melodies provided Saul with what he had lost and what he yearned for: divine influx.

In this portrayal of David, one finds an idea dear to Don Isaac's heart: the direct connection between a leader and God—in this case, in an artistic context: this special connection is conveyed through the channel of music and song. Interestingly, Maimonides also drew a parallel between music and the onset of prophecy. However, he saw this process as taking place solely within the human soul and intellect. Music prepares the aspiring prophet by settling his mental state, "for prophecy does not rest on he who is immersed in sorrow or laziness, but rather only upon he who is happy. Therefore the 'sons of the prophet' carried before them lyre, drum, and flute and they sought prophecy."[37] Maimonides here does not posit an external astral movement of descending influx.[38] Such terminology is foreign to Maimonides but is commonly found in the writings of Ibn Ezra and Gersonides, who had stronger proclivities toward astrological speculation.

Exploring the other virtues ascribed to David ("[he is] a mighty valiant man, and a man of war, and prudent in speech, and a comely person, and the Lord is with him" [1 Sam. 16:18]), Don Isaac sees proof of David's exceptional qualities: he is a musician, but not like "other musicians and players who are perfected in their imaginative power but weak in their temperament. For [David was also] a valiant man and a man of war."[39] David was a warrior, but different in that "a man immersed in the stratagems of war [usually] does not trouble his time with song and music." Furthermore, David was a learned man, unlike "most musicians and poets who are perfected in their imaginative power but lack true intellect." He was also good-looking, yet not a "pursuer of women."[40] In other words, it was important for Abravanel to portray David as the consummate leader, a man gifted not just with many virtues (beauty, bravery, morality, imagination, and intellect) but also those that are generally not found in a single person—a combination that would normally lead to insurmountable psychological tensions. In David, however, all virtues existed together in harmony. In this sense, David differed from Saul, who was incapable of maintaining such a wide spectrum of qualities. Saul could not overcome the tension between them, and he was also not gifted in the first place with such a wide array of talents.

To conclude our discussion of Abravanel's conception of leadership, I would like to note that he consistently emphasizes the resting of divine providence upon the leader and how this goes hand in hand with the leader's ability to act upon the world through the medium of his diverse talents (physical, political, artistic, scientific, and religious). An example of this trend is Abravanel's comparison of two versions of the same hymn (2 Sam. 22 and Psalms 18). According to Don Isaac, the version of the hymn in Samuel was composed by David "in his youth, when he was [immersed] in troubles. And he includes references to all misfortunes so that every time the Holy One, Blessed is He, saved him from some misfortune, he could sing this song."[41] Miraculous salvation goes hand in hand with its glorification in the form of a psalm, each one complementing the other. By contrast, "the book of Psalms was written by David, peace be upon him, at the end of his days, to guide the individual in his prayer," a guide for the supplicant "when misfortune and distress befall him, as befell David himself."[42] Abravanel further adds a religious and astrological explanation for the transformation of the young David's psalms into prayers that can be recited by every Jew: "for these words have wondrous qualities for drawing down divine influx upon him who prays with them, benefitting him in particular ways according to the power of each psalm."[43] The hymns, in other words, are both a poetic thanksgiving for the special connection between God and the young David and, at the same time, tools that can, if used correctly, cause divine influx to descend upon any supplicant who employs them. If we follow the example of David and his psalms, Abravanel's exemplary

leader is not only someone who merits providence by virtue of his character and actions, but also someone who publicly glorifies this unique connection with God through the medium of speech and music, committing
these to writing and sharing them with the public. The power of a leader
cannot be separated from its implementation and publicization. We can
extend this understanding to Don Isaac's literary activity. His commentary
on the Former Prophets was not some supplementary side project, some
appendix to his primary activities in commerce and politics, but rather an
essential expression and communication of his virtues as a leader.

9 : DON ISAAC'S REPUBLICANISM

Traditionalist or Innovator?

As we already saw in Abravanel's *'Ateret zeqenim*, as well as in his description of the miracle at Gibeon, his desire to emphasize the direct connection between God and Israel (or, more specifically, Israel's leaders) led him to eschew interpretations of scripture informed by a philosophical and naturalistic bent, in favor of more traditional ideas about divine providence. In one of the many articles that marked the five hundredth anniversary of Don Isaac Abravanel's birth, Leo Strauss dubbed Abravanel a "traditionalist," describing him as "unphilosophic" and "to some extent even anti-philosophic."[1] Strauss even held him responsible for bringing to an end Maimonides's philosophical enterprise—the attempt to identify the Torah's legal code with Plato's ideal republic. Similarly, other scholars saw Abravanel's rejection of the rationalist project as regressive—a return to the conservative and traditionalist approach of Rabbi Judah Halevi as expressed in his *Kuzari*.[2]

This prevailing scholarly portrayal of Abravanel as a conservative or traditionalist thinker is challenged by his commentary on an important passage in 1 Samuel 8. Here, Abravanel employs terminology and concepts that originated from the renewed interest of humanists in Renaissance Italy in the idea and history of republican regimes. In many senses, Abravanel's commentary on these verses is one of the first republican texts ever written by a Jew in the Middle Ages or even the early modern era.

Scholars like Strauss and Benzion Netanyahu offered various solutions to account for this discrepancy between Don Isaac's overarching conservatism and the innovative approach evinced in his discussions of monarchies and republics.[3] However, they, rarely took note of an important fact: philosophical rationalism and humanistic political philosophy were two separate intellectual constructions that emerged from two different eras. Compared to the former, Don Isaac was conservative, but compared to the latter he was a Jewish innovator. In other words, what seems at first glance like a contradiction between two irreconcilable views can be understood as a transition from one period to the next.

As I hope to show in this chapter, reading Abravanel as an eclectic thinker is a preferable approach. Don Isaac's ambivalence toward Maimonides and his followers was integrated into his adoption of humanistic ideas during a period of complex and gradual cultural and historical transition—a time when the philosophy of the Middle Ages was beginning to give way to the philosophical innovations of early modern humanism.

The Request to Appoint a King in Medieval Exegesis

Abravanel's commentary on the elders' request to appoint an Israelite king is an excellent example of the "homiletical" and perhaps even scholastic character of his biblical exegesis—that is, the use of a theme within the biblical text as the basis for a broad methodical discussion of a topic. The request for a king in 1 Samuel emerges against the backdrop of the wicked behavior of Samuel's sons, Joel and Aviah, as well as the recurring crises that took place under the regime of the judges, as described at length at the end of Judges and the beginning of 1 Samuel. The elders essentially wished to replace the existing system with a monarchical regime:

> Then all the elders of Israel gathered themselves together and came to Samuel to Ramah. And they said to him, Behold, you are old, and your sons walk not in your ways: now make us a king to judge us like all the nations. But the thing displeased Samuel, when they said, "Give us a king to judge us." And Samuel prayed unto the Lord. And the Lord said to Samuel, Hearken to the voice of the people in all that they say to you: for they have not rejected you, but they have rejected me, that I should not reign over them (1 Sam. 8:4–7).

Commenting on this turning point in the biblical narrative, that dramatic moment when the Hebrews and their culture entered into a new monarchical era, Abravanel raises a seemingly simple question: "Why was the Lord angry and why was Samuel displeased that Israel asked for a king if it is one of the commandments in the Pentateuch?"[4] The commandment to which Abravanel is referring appears in Deuteronomy (17:14–15):

> When you come to the land which the Lord your God is giving you, and possess it and dwell in it, and say, "I will set a king over me like all the nations that are around me," you shall surely set a king over you whom the Lord your God chooses; one from among your brethren you shall set as king over you; you may not set a foreigner over you, who is not your brother.

Abravanel's discussion goes far beyond an attempt to resolve the textual difficulty that arises from a comparison of Deuteronomy to Samuel. Instead, he offers a broad theoretical discussion that evaluates the monarchical revolution in ancient Israel and its repercussions.

Abravanel begins his discussion with a long review of the various approaches—from the Talmud to the views of the medieval Jewish and Christian exegetes—to Samuel's and God's initial rejection of the people's request. Here, once again, we see the imprint of Don Isaac's dual Christian and Jewish learning. As he explains, some sages in the Sifrei (sect. 156) and the Babylonian Talmud[5] explained that the people desired a king to facilitate their worship of idols. Others claimed that it was the timing of the elders that was at fault. Responding to these views, Abravanel writes laconically that "this is a very unlikely view" and "it does not seem correct to me."[6]

This kind of rebuttal is characteristic of Don Isaac's method. He often quotes talmudic and midrashic texts but seldom uses them as a basis for his views, preferring to engage with the approaches of medieval exegetes and philosophers.

Abravanel cites another explanation that is taken from the homilies of Rabbi Nissim Gerondi. There, R. Nissim Gerondi distinguishes between the "law of the king" (mishpat hamelekh; that is, sociopolitical law, which is intended to regulate the polity and is not necessarily subject to "true, and just law" [mishpat tsodeq amiti]) and the law of the Torah ([mishpat hatorah], which is dedicated to true justice "endowing our nation with divine influx").[7] According to R. Nissim Gerondi, the elders sinned by asking for a king because "they believed that for political order to be enhanced, adjudication should issue from the crown and not from judges, and therefore they said [to Samuel] 'you have grown old and can no longer judge.'"[8] In other words, the elders inverted the proper hierarchy between the law of the Torah and the law of the king and blurred the boundaries between them. While Don Isaac believed it was important to distinguish between the law of the Torah and the law of the king, he ultimately rejected R. Nissim Gerondi's explanation of 1 Samuel 8.

The explanation that Abravanel prefers and presents at length ultimately derives from the Latin supercommentary penned by the Jewish converso Pablo de Santa Maria (or de Burgos originally Solomon Halevi) on the commentary of Nicholas de Lyra on 1 Samuel 8. In this important commentary, Pablo offers his own explanation for the sin of the elders. We have already discussed how the introductions of Jerome and Nicholas de Lira influenced Abravanel's introduction to his own commentary. This long discussion of an interpretation offered by Pablo shows that it is quite likely that Abravanel was well versed in the writing of these Christian exegetes. He may even have possessed manuscripts containing the works of Jerome, Augustine, Thomas Aquinas, de Lyra, Pablo, and others. The interpretations of this passage offered by de Lyra and Pablo are predicated on the Aristotelian distinction between a constitutional monarchy and an absolute monarchy, "in which the king may do anything at his own discretion."[9] Abravanel offers a translated and abridged version of the Latin original and asserts that the sin of the elders was as follows: instead of asking for the ideal type of monarch "who is subject to the laws of the Torah and the commandments," they asked for a dangerous tyrant "who is not subject to any law (*dat*)."[10] In the Latin, this is expressed as a distinction between full or absolute power (*potesta plena absoluta*), which places the king above the law, and limited power (*potesta limitata*). As Abravanel well understood, drawing a distinction between a tyrant and a king is ultimately meant to justify a benevolent monarchical regime by distinguishing it from absolutism and despotism. It should further be noted that Pablo's solution represents an attempt to correct the view of de Lyra. The latter understood the elders' request as a deterioration from the Kingdom of Heaven to a kingdom of flesh and blood: "If the rule of a King is excellent, it follows that [the rule of] God as an immediate King is even better, since God is better than man."[11]

Abravanel's review of his exegetical predecessors demonstrates well his combined study of Christian and Jewish sources, as well as the overall support for a monarchical regime expressed by exegetes of both faiths. In some sense, we can say that the monarchical revolution was so ingrained in the consciousnesses of these exegetes that they ironically understood Samuel's opposition as justification for the monarchy, instead of a repudiation of it. Abraham Melamed and others have shown that while most Jewish thinkers in the Middle Ages accepted a positive view of the monarchy, there were some who expressed their reservations or rejected the idea of a monarchy outright.[12] As we will see below, this is even more applicable to Christian thinkers. These dissenting voices are not mentioned in Abravanel's overview: he wished to present a unified picture of the Jewish and Christian exegetical consensus before offering his own approach.

Don Isaac Against the Monarchy

In contrast to the clear promonarchical bent of Abravanel's exegetical predecessors (as he portrays them), he presents an antimonarchical conception that he divides into three discourses (*dibburim*). The first addresses
the question whether "the king is necessary for the political community
(*baqibuts hamedini*)."[13] At the beginning of his discussion, Abravanel
harshly criticizes the prevailing view that draws a parallel between the reign
of a human king over his country and the reign of the heart over the body
and God over the cosmos. An example of such an organic and theological justification for the monarchy can be found in Aquinas's *De Regimine
Principium*:

> Again, those things are best which are most natural, for in every
> case nature operates for the best; and in nature government is al-
> ways by one. Among the multitude of the body's members there is
> one part which moves all the others, namely, the heart; and among
> the parts of the soul there is one force, namely the reason, which
> chiefly rules; also, there is one king of the bees, and in the whole
> universe one God is the Maker and Ruler of all.[14]

As opposed to this conception, which was shared by many thinkers in
the Middle Ages, Don Isaac draws attention to the possibility of another
kind of political regime:

> For indeed their thought that a king is required and necessary is
> false. For it is not impossible that a nation should have many leaders
> who convene, unite, and reach a consensus and can thus govern and
> administer justice. And why can they not have terms of office, from
> one year to the next—or for a shorter or longer duration? When the
> turn of other judges and officers (*shoftim ve-shotrim*) comes to re-
> place them, they will investigate the abuses of trust committed by
> their predecessors. . . . Finally, why cannot their powers be limited
> and determined by laws or norms? Reason suggests that [in a dispute]
> between the one and the many, the many should be heeded. For it
> is more likely that one man will willfully sin with the kingship . . .
> than that many men will do so when they take counsel together.[15]

Abravanel proposes the republic as an alternative to the monarchy, thus
earning himself the designation as the first republican in the history of Jew-

ish political thought. As demonstrated by Melamed,[16] we can find praises of republican government in the writings of one of Abravanel's contemporaries, Yohanan Alemanno (1434–1505), who showered lavish praise on the republicanism of Florence:

> Seven precious virtues wander among all the people of this land. The first is the great extent to which leadership is in the hands of its people from the least to the greatest. Because of this, all the fathers teach their sons and youths from their early days all the ways of government, of the state, magnanimous acts and virtues. Because they are all royalty, each rules as king over the people by turn when his time come, according to his luck, he rules his peers when the lot falls on his name. This is the reason that if you ask them you will find them all wise, understanding and knowledgeable in laws customary in each country for each people, so they will know how to judge when their turn comes to lead their people as a flock. This is not done where there are great leaders and kings, and the people do not expect to become officials since they are musicians and artisans.[17]

Alemanno lived from 1488 until 1494 in Florence, where he enjoyed the patronage of the da Pisa family. He describes here the rotation of government positions in the Florentine republic—though, if we compare his words here to what we regard as historical reality, he may have been guilty of exaggerated idealization. During the fifteenth century, the government of Florence was essentially an oligarchy composed of a group of families headed by the house of Medici—in other words, it was not exactly the egalitarian republic portrayed by Alemanno in his *Shir hama'alot leshlomo* (The Song of Solomon's Ascents). Despite the gap between image and reality, it is clear that Alemanno, like Abravanel, was well aware of the ethical and political benefits of republican government, the reason for its superiority over monarchies. Even if Abravanel was not, as scholars first thought, the only medieval thinker to express republican views, his approach was nevertheless exceptional in the history of Jewish political thought. It is therefore important for us to search for the antecedents of his approach.

The Historical and Intellectual Backdrop for the Revival of the Republican Model

Renewed interest in the republican model and it's political and philosophical underpinnings was the outcome of a complex series of processes taking place in medieval and early modern Italy. One important factor was the political, economic, and cultural rise of the cities of northern and central Italy between the twelfth and fifteenth centuries. These developments created a concrete basis for comparisons of contemporary political reality with the ancient Roman past.[18] Another factor was the gradual consolidation of autonomous rule in the Italian cities, a process that took place parallel to—and that fostered—their growing prosperity. This autonomy was characterized by a specific form of government: the commune, an amalgam of republican, aristocratic, and monarchical components (prominent examples include Florence and Venice).[19] This political entity was to some extent in tension with the authority of the Holy Roman Emperor, on the one hand, and the pope, on the other hand. A third element driving the republican model was the gradual development of neoclassicist and humanistic culture among the urban elites of various Italian cities, alongside other aspects of medieval culture.

As we have seen in the first part of this book, humanistic culture allowed these elites to style their own works after the literary genres of classical Latin literature (for example, poetry, plays, orations, and epistolary writing) as well as to imitate and develop classical notions of morality and statecraft (including republican ones), using these ideas of the past to answer questions posed by urban life in the present. Humanist culture, in which interest in republican conceptions thrived, looked in the classical descriptions of political and urban life for models that could address the contemporary questions and concerns of the urban elites in northern and central Italy. Through their scholarship, the humanists turned classical Latin texts, originating in the context of the political and public life of ancient Rome, into a lens through which to evaluate the new political and social reality that had emerged. These classical works allowed the urban elites to better understand their relatively new circumstances and environment and, above all, provided models—such as the republic—to organize and justify their political rule.

One of the first mature expressions of humanist republicanism is Leonardo Bruni's famous 1404 panegyric to the city of Florence, *Laudatio Florentinae Urbis*.[20] As I hope to show, there are some important affinities between Abravanel's discussion of 1 Samuel 8 and Bruni's speech. However, before comparing them, I would like to begin by noting that Bruni—unlike Petrarch, whom we discussed in the first part of this book—was a new type of humanist. From 1398 until 1400, Bruni studied Greek under the tutelage of the Byzantine scholar Manuel Chrysoloras (c. 1355–1415). Bruni also enjoyed the patronage of the humanist and statesman Coluccio Salutati (1331–1406). He thus learned to translate ancient Greek texts into the classical Latin of Cicero. Later, he produced important translations of the works of Aristotle, Plato, Plutarch, Homer, Xenophon, and others.

Bruni's *Laudatio* of Florence is an imitation and adaptation of another speech: the panegyric to Athens composed by the Greek writer Aelius Aristides (117–181) in 155. We see here an excellent example of the use of classical portrayal of cities and states in antiquity to understand the urban and political realities of Florence at the beginning of the fifteenth century. In his speech, Bruni follows in Aristides's footsteps: beginning with a description of the city's external characteristics, following this with a discussion of the virtues of the city's inhabitants (virtues they inherited from its Roman founders), and concluding with a portrayal of Florence's republican regime. This regime, Bruni asserts, both reflects Florence's supremacy over other cities and states and explains it. In the last part of the speech, we find a description of a nonmonarchical regime that closely resembles the description of government by many leaders referred to by Abravanel:

> Indeed, the magistracies [*magistratus*] were created to carry out justice; they have been empowered to punish criminals and especially to ensure that there is no one in Florence who stands above the law. . . . In many ways care has been taken that these upholders of the law to whom great power has been entrusted do not come to imagine that, instead of the custodianship of the citizens [*custodiam civicum*], a tyrannical post has been given to them. . . . First of all, the chief magistracy that is commonly viewed as possessing the sovereignty of the state is controlled by a system of checks and balances. Hence there are nine magistrates instead of one, and their term is for two months, not for one year. This method of governing has been devised so that the Florentine state may be well governed, since a majority will correct any errors in judgment, and the short terms of office will curb any possible insolence.[21]

The rule of law and preservation of civil liberties are identified here with a regime of citizen officials who serve for short terms. The plurality of positions and the quick turnover of office holders is intentional: it strengthens oversight over the government; empowers the rule of law; and diminishes, as much as possible, the threat of tyranny. Without a doubt, this is the model that Abravanel envisioned when he mentions "terms of office" and "many leaders who convene, unite, and reach a consensus."

Abravanel did not need to read Bruni's speech to familiarize himself with the republican theory used by the latter to justify Florence's regime. As we saw above, Don Isaac maintained commercial and religious ties with both Jews and Christians in Tuscany for many years. Therefore, he was doubtless well aware of the government in Florence and of the comparisons drawn by humanists such as Bruni between it and classical republican theories.

A Historical Comparison of Systems of Governance

Having discussed the theoretical possibility of a political organization predicated on the rule of the many, as opposed to that of a single monarch, Abravanel moves on to an empirical discussion—that is, a comparison between monarchical states and republican ones.

Abravanel's portrayal of monarchies is decidedly negative: "Look at their abominations and their idols; every man of them does that which is right in his own eyes, and the land was filled with violence. Who will tell him what to do?"[22] Here, Don Isaac is essentially referring to those monarchies in which he lived—specifically, Portugal. The personal dimension of his scathing critique is encapsulated in the words, "Who will tell him what to do?" The same words appear in Don Isaac's autobiographical introduction to his commentary, when he describes his powerlessness against the accusations levelled against him by Dom João II. This was the moment when Abravanel experienced firsthand the consequences of an absolute monarch's power, the moment when he realized how truly arbitrary it could become. As many modern scholars, including Aviezer Ravitzky,[23] have pointed out, Don Isaac's personal experience of being targeted by a king gave rise to his hyperbolic descriptions of the absolute and capricious nature of royal power. As opposed to a monarchy, which inevitably devolves into tyranny and despotism, Abravanel praises the Italian republics. He writes:

> Today we have seen many lands under the leadership of judges and governors chosen for three months at a time, and God the king is with them. Theirs is an elected government with limits; they rule the nation with a firm hand and lead it in wars [and] none can stand [against] them. . . . And if one of them sins in some matter, others will, before long, replace him. And he who has sinned will

receive his proper punishment such that [others] will not willfully sin again.[24]

The emphasis on election, limited terms of office, curbing political power through law (*besidur mugbal*), and the oversight and the corrective influence of political rotation shows that Abravanel was well versed in the practice and theory of republican government in his time: the same points appear in Bruni's description of the Florentine government. It bears noting that Abravanel renders the Latin term *magistratus*, the term used by Bruni as "judges and governors" (*shoftim umoshlim*). The use of the word "judges" alludes to Abravanel's preference for the rule of the biblical judges over the monarchy founded in 1 Samuel 8. Furthermore, as noted by Ravitzky, it seems that the basic Aristotelian distinction between constitutional monarchy and tyranny—a notion accepted by most political philosophers in the Middle Ages—has been co-opted here to present a binary of monarchy versus republic: only a republic can have a government that is bound to the rule of law.[25] Monarchies always devolve into "absolute power (*hayekholet hamuhlat*)."[26] This important shift in the conception of the relationship between law and governance has its source in the historical and cultural changes overtaking urban life during this era, as we saw earlier in the example of Bruni.

This change is expressed later in Abravanel's portrayal of the historical transition from the Roman Republic to the Roman Empire:

> Have you not known? Have you not heard?—of the fourth terrible beast, the evil Rome that ruled the entire world by force and it devoured the whole earth, crushed it underfoot, and broke it to pieces. And it was governed by many excellent consuls. But afterwards it was ruled by an emperor alone; it was then that it lost its freedom.
>
> And even today, the Kingdom of Venice, she that was great among the nations, and princess among the provinces, and the Kingdom of Florence is a glory to all lands, and the kingdoms of Genoa . . . Lucca, Siena, and Bologna, and many other states have no king, but are led by elected leaders for set terms and for set periods as I have mentioned. And they are upright states; there is nothing crooked or perverse in them.[27]

Scholars have debated how best to understand this passage, a passage so exceptional and unprecedented in medieval Jewish literature. Yitzhak Baer saw it as clear proof of Don Isaac's humanism, writing that "the humanist is an avowed republican."[28] However, Leo Strauss maintained that Abravanel's antimonarchism reveals his theocratic inclinations—an approach he inherited from Christian exegetes such as Jerome, de Lyra, and Pablo de Santa Maria.[29] Ravitzky has contributed to the discussion by comparing Abravanel's discussion to that of Aquinas in his *De regimine principum*.[30] In book 1, chapter 5, the Christian theologian expressed the following antimonarchical sentiments:

> For sometimes those who desire to be ruled by a king fall victim instead to the savagery of tyrants, and a great many rulers have exerted tyrannical sway under the pretext of royal dignity. Clear examples of this appear in the case of the Roman commonwealth. For the kings were expelled by the Roman people when they could no longer bear the burden of their rule, or, rather, of their tyranny. They then instituted for themselves consuls and other magistrates by whom they commenced to be ruled and guided. . . . However, the Romans became exhausted by the continual quarrels which eventually grew into civil wars, and the liberty which they had so striven to attain was then snatched from their hands by those civil wars, and they began to be under the power of the emperors. . . . Some of these emperors faithfully pursued the common good, as kings should, and the Roman commonwealth was increased and preserved by their efforts. Most of them, however, were tyrants to their subjects and weak and ineffective in the face of their enemies, and these brought the Roman commonwealth to naught. A similar process occurred in the case of the people of the Hebrews. At first, while they were ruled by judges they were plundered on all sides by their enemies, for each man did only what was good in his own eyes. Then, at their own request, kings were divinely given to them; but because of the wickedness of the kings they fell away from the worship of the one God and finally were led away into captivity.[31]

While Aquinas's words can be construed as pro-republican, this should not be exaggerated: he is ultimately supporting a form of constitutional monarchy. That being said, this passage was used by the philosopher Tolomeo da Lucca (1236–1327) to develop a political philosophy that supported republican government. Did Don Isaac, many years later, develop a similar line of thought? We have no way of knowing, but if we compare the end of our excerpt from Aquinas about the "people of the Hebrews" to the statement of Abravanel about the supremacy of the rule of the biblical judges, it does not seem implausible.

It is also important to note two components of Abravanel's approach: a preference for Rome's republican era over that of the empire and the identification of the Italian republics of the late Middle Ages (for example, Florence and Venice) with the ancient Roman Republic. These two elements constitute integral parts of Bruni's humanistic justification of Florence's government. One of the reasons for Florence's superiority over other states, Bruni explains, is its historical origins—that is, its establishment during the republican period of Roman history:

> Accordingly, this very noble Roman colony was established at the very moment when the dominion of the Roman people flourished greatly.... Moreover, the Caesars, the Antonines, the Tiberiuses, the Neros—those plagues and destroyers of the Roman Republic—had not yet deprived the people of their liberty.[32]

In Bruni's view, Florence's birth during this era bequeathed to its people the qualities and virtues of the ancient Romans—especially the regime of the republic and the Roman notion of liberty. In his later book, *History of the Florentine People* (1419), Bruni further explains how Florence's liberation from the rule of the Holy Roman Empire after the death of Frederick II in 1250 restored Florence to its original historical and political state: liberty and republicanism.[33] According to this historical narrative, the relationship between the ancient Roman Republic and the regime of Florence represents the continuity of the Roman people and their virtues—especially their overcoming of the empire and its destructive influences. Of course, for Bruni this was more than just a historical and political comparison between Florence and ancient Rome. It was also a new literary, rhetorical, and philosophical justification of Florence's government, even if in reality Florence was far from being a true republic.

Against the backdrop of Bruni's concept of the historical continuity of the republican model, it is easy to see why Abravanel naturally associated the Italian republics with the Roman Republic. Furthermore, we can better understand the sharp distinction he draws between the Roman Republic and the Roman Empire and see in it further evidence of his acquaintance with the humanistic justification of the Florentine regime. In our previous discussion of Don Isaac's correspondence with Yehiel da Pisa, we saw that

Abravanel maintained commercial and literary ties with Tuscany: he copied Hebrew books sent to him by Yehiel and even purchased Christian works himself. Thus, while we may lack any direct evidence of Abravanel's exposure to Bruni's writings—or to those of any other Italians, for that matter—the affinities between their respective formulations, as well as Abravanel's many years of commercial ties with Tuscany, suggest that he was well acquainted with the Italian republics and their new republican ideology. It should be further noted that in his commentary on Deuteronomy (completed in 1496), Don Isaac reiterates his main points about the superiority of republics over monarchies, suggesting that he deemed this an important subject.

Having established the theoretical feasibility of a republican government and having shown the superiority of classical and medieval republics—as borne out by historical and empirical evidence—Abravanel concludes his discussion of the necessity of a king by offering the following fascinating statement:

> It is thus apparent that the king is a necessity neither for the people nor for the political community—nor for bringing unity, continuity, and absolute power. Therefore, I believe that originally kings were not elected by the people but were rather imposed by force, and whoever was stronger prevailed (*kol de'alim gevar*) as it says: "Let us go up against Judah, and vex it, and let us make a breach there for us, and set a king in the midst of it, even the son of Tabeal" (Is. 7:6). And even then, they [the kings] were only appointed as functionaries—to serve and to lead the collective—but they became lords, and when God gave to them the world and its fullness and all of its inhabitants, then this leprosy spread, so that it became accepted that one man would arise, reign over his people, and lead them like donkeys.[34]

If kings are not a natural or necessary part of human society, then monarchies are produced by revolutions and violent coups. As Abravanel puts it, "whoever was stronger prevailed." If we take into account the fact that the monarchical revolution is described in 1 Samuel 8 as resulting from a request of the people, then we can see in Abravanel's harsh words about the rise of kings the signs of an acute historical and literary sensitivity. Don Isaac understood that the account presented in Samuel did not include all

the events that must have led to the transition to monarchy. The calm presentation belies a more violent process.

We have seen that throughout his discussions of the monarchy, Abravanel takes pains to portray the king as a potential tyrant. This tendency has
a clear historical backdrop: the gradual centralization of royal power in
Portugal, Castile, and Aragon and its consequences for the nobility, the
Cortes, and other components of medieval governance. Dom João II (like
the Catholic Monarchs) represents a prominent example of the tendency
toward centralization that had already begun to emerge at the beginning of
the Avis dynasty's rise to power in Portugal. As we have described in previous chapters, the rise of King Dom João II led to an all-out assault against
the most prominent members of the Portuguese aristocracy—a struggle
that led to the execution of Don Isaac's patron and forced him to flee for his
life. Thus, the tyrannical picture of kings painted by Abravanel in his commentary in some sense echoes the political developments of the fifteenth
century (primarily those that led to the rise of Dom João II). This being the
case, Abravanel's support for the republican model should be understood
as support for the rule of the aristocracy, an advocacy for the aristocratic
and democratic components of medieval monarchy that checked royal
power. James Hankins has shown that the republican model portrayed and
praised by Bruni represented rhetorical and tendentious support for the
specific type of oligarchy that governed Florence.[35] In some senses, the aristocratic background that informs Don Isaac's critique of the monarchy corresponds to the collective elitist regime that ruled Florence—a regime that
he clearly preferred. Nevertheless, we cannot downplay the great novelty
of Abravanel's republican views, nor can we ignore their significant impact
on Jewish political discourse at the dawn of the modern era.

Theocracy

Abravanel did not limit himself to an abstract and general opposition to
monarchy. He wished to demonstrate that, for the chosen people as well,
monarchy is not a theological necessity. Referring to the second chapter of
the Talmudic tractate Sanhedrin, Don Isaac lists the three common justifications for rule by a king: (1) "for the purpose of war, to save the nation
from its enemies"; (2) "to dictate their laws and establish the regulations for
the sake of a political community"—that is, to legislate laws beyond those
stipulated by the Torah; and (3) "to administer punishments not dictated

by the law when the time demands and which are facilitated by absolute power"—in other words, to punish people for political reasons and not because they have violated the laws of Torah.[36]

Abravanel makes the following seemingly simple point: "it is apparent that these three notions are all attributed to God the blessed, as He performs these [functions] toward the nation of Israel. Therefore, He is their king and no one else."[37] In Don Isaac's view, the idea that a king is necessary for the Jewish people requires one to assume that God's covenant with the nation of Israel—expressed through the divine providence that attended Moses, Joshua, and other judges, as well as in the laws transmitted at Sinai and enforced by Israelite judges and courts—was insufficient. According to this logic, a king is needed to fill this gap. However, Abravanel argues, this supplemental factor comes at the expense of the covenantal regime of God, which attributes to God the role of legislator and savior and draws a stark distinction between the divine source of law and military success, and the person chosen to serve in a military or a judicial position. Strauss was the first to identify the Christian antecedents of Abravanel's outspoken support of a covenantal regime. If we turn to de Lyra's commentary on 1 Samuel 8, we find an emphasis on the superiority of a theocratic regime—or, as he puts it, a regime in which "God is the immediate king of this people (*rex immediatus illius populi*)." In this context, de Lyra is careful to define Moses, Joshua, and the judges as "deputies but not kings (*vicarii et non reges*)."[38]

Abravanel added a further argument that clearly sums up the idea that a monarchy is antithetical to a covenantal regime or theocracy:

> For that which we have seen of them [the kings of Israel and Judah] empirically (*banisayon*), is that they rebelled against the light, and led the hearts of Israel astray, as was apparent in the case of Jeroboam ben Nabat and those who followed him—they caused Israel to sin and led to them [the children of Israel] being exiled from their land.[39]

Did Abravanel take this idea—of the link between the sins of the kings and the exile—from the text of Aquinas that we cited above? This is Ravitzky's view. However, it is not impossible that Don Isaac developed the idea from his own reading of Kings or some other source. In any case, using the motif of the king as a figure who corrupts the morals and religious virtues of the people, Abravanel suggests that the monarchical turn in Jewish history produced a hybrid government—that is, a government predicated upon a theological and political contradiction, a government that was paradoxically theocratic and monarchical at the same time. This contradiction led to the decline of the kingdoms of Israel and Judah and ultimately to exile.

As mentioned above, Strauss understood Abravanel's clear distinction between covenantal rule and monarchy as a repudiation of the philosophical and political project initiated by Maimonides. Even if we do not accept Strauss's negative judgment of this move, we can identify in the tension that Abravanel creates between covenant and monarchy a parallel to the Christian distinction between what Augustine called *civitas Dei* (the city of God, a polity in which there is no political hierarchy among men) and the *civitas terrena* (the earthly city, in which intrapersonal hierarchies and norms prevail to impose some kind of order upon humans and regulate the shifting circumstances of their lives). Abravanel's critique of the monarchy also vaguely implies a new kind of alliance between covenantal and republican rule, the former identified by him as the regime of the judges prior to the monarchical revolution of 1 Samuel. This new alliance is predicated on the following analogy: just as the covenant between God and Israel leaves the position of legislator and ruler empty—in the sense, these positions can be seized only through devastating acts of violence—so too republican government leaves legislative and executive positions empty. In other words, republican governments clearly distinguish between political authority and power and the individual: an individual cannot take possession of a political position, as he always remains a temporary officeholder. This implies that both covenantal and republican regimes implement the same basic principle—that political rule transcends human individuals. Objecting to the establishment of the monarchical regime described in 1 Samuel 8 that eventually forced Israel into exile and influenced by Christian exegetes, Abravanel turns to the theocratic model of the judges, associating it with the ancient (and modern) republics of Italy. Thus, he couples a retreat from the philosophical and theological justification of monarchy with a new theocratic and republican synthesis.

Monarchy as a Sin

In conclusion, I would like to focus on a point made by Strauss regarding another affinity between the Christian exegesis of de Lyra and that of Abravanel. Most Jewish exegetes and halakhists—chief among them Maimonides (*Hilkhot melakhim vemilkhomteihem*, chap. 1, sect. 1)—understood Deuteronomy 17:15 ("you shall surely set a king over you whom the Lord your

God chooses") as a positive commandment to appoint a monarch. However, Abravanel took a different position, asserting "that asking [for a king] is not a commandment but only a permission, the result of the evil inclination."[40] Justifying his position, he writes:

> It is similar to the passage of: "When you go forth to war against your enemies, and the Lord your God has delivered them into your hands, etc. And you see among the captives a beautiful woman, and have a desire for her, etc." [Deut 21:10–11]. It is not a commandment that he must desire her, that he must take her and must have intercourse with her in her impurity—it is rather [the granting of] permission in relation to the evil inclination. The commandment [is mentioned only] after that first act of intercourse: "Then you shall bring her home to your house" [Deut 21:12].[41]

In his commentary on 1 Samuel 8, de Lyra writes:

> Concerning the appointment of a King, insofar as the people are concerned, it was not a specific authorization to do so (*concession proprie dicta*), but rather a permission (*sed magis permissio*), just as the divorcing of a wife was conceded due to the hardness of man's heart (*ad duritiam cordis eorum*), as stated in Deuteronomy 24.[42]

De Lyra's comparison between the establishment of the monarchy and the act of divorce shows that, in his view, the monarchy is based in sin, not divine fiat. A man must refrain from seizing power just as he must stop himself from taking a wife and divorcing her. After the evil has already been done, the sin can be contained; it can be regulated by a series of laws. This position led de Lyra to justify the rule of monarchs as a necessary evil in the face of unfortunate circumstances brought on by sin. The same exegetical argument is used by Abravanel to reject monarchy altogether. Strauss, Netanyahu, and others entertained the notion that Abravanel adopted the view of Augustine: that the rule of one man over another is rooted in sin. In their opinion, this led to a negative turn in Jewish political thought. Abravanel may also have been influenced by classical rabbinical sources that formulated the principle "the Torah spoke only against the evil inclination" in regard to the laws of the captive woman (BT Qiddushin 21b) to cope with undesirable circumstances that nevertheless could be incorporated into a halakhic framework. Regardless, Don Isaac's emphasis on the evil inclination points to his special sensitivity to the historical and dangerous aspects of monarchical government. It seems that for him a more harmonistic approach that combined the rule of a king with the rule of law and religion—an approach that dominated mainstream Jewish political thought in the Middle Ages—was no longer a possibility.

Abravanel's understanding of the episode in 1 Samuel 8 is multifaceted, and as I have tried to show, it is reminiscent of many sources, Jewish and Christian alike. The antimonarchical position that arises from Abravanel's writings drew the attention of modern scholars who sought to examine, from different perspectives, whether these views could be connected in some way to the advent of modernity. That is, could Abravanel be seen as the first modern Jewish political philosopher? The question is legitimate, but it has a tendency to ignore the complexity of a discussion comprised of many strata of political thought—Jewish, Christian, Islamic, and classical. Besides the novelty of antimonarchism and republicanism, it is worth noting another literary aspect of this passage. Operating within a specific historical and autobiographical background, Don Isaac sought to combine and organize the different layers of political thought. This included sources ranging from Aristotle to the talmudic sages, Augustine, and the Jewish and Christian commentaries of the Middle Ages, not to mention a comparison between monarchies and republics in his own period and in the past. Abravanel thus contributed a broad literary and historical perspective to discussions of monarchical rule, as well as integrating Jewish particularity into the major trends of classical and Christian history and literature.

The novelty in Don Isaac's approach lies in his attempt to combine Jewish political history with the political history of Europe, a history defined by the transitions from republic to empire and from empire to Christian monarchies and republics. To develop this historical and literary perspective, Abravanel availed himself of sources from different times and religions. The outcome proved surprising to modern historians. They identified clashing influences, such as republicanism sitting alongside patristic writings. This sense of contradiction and confusion can be understood as a sign of Abravanel's era: a period of transition and flux, a time when the different layers of philosophy and history (the present, the near past, and the distant past) resided alongside each other without any clear scheme or overarching organizational system. Therefore, we should not be surprised to find conceptual inconsistencies, nor should we try to subsume one aspect of Abravanel's philosophy in favor of another.

10 : SUCCESS AT THE COURTS OF THE CATHOLIC MONARCHS

Don Isaac and the Mendoza family

In our discussion of Abravanel's commentary on the Former Prophets, we underscored the important role played by political questions. Therefore, it is no surprise that politics played a part in Abravanel's public life as well. Upon his arrival in his Castile, he quickly returned to political and economic activity—this time, in the court of the so-called Catholic Monarchs, Queen Doña Isabel and King Fernando.

Soon after his arrival in Castile in 1483, Don Isaac began tax farming on behalf of Cardinal Don Pedro Gonzalez Mendoza (1428–95). Extant documents show that Don Isaac continued to work as a tax farmer for the cardinal for some time. Presumably due to his success in these endeavors, he was appointed chief accountant of the Duke of Infantando, Don Iñigo Lopez de Mendoza (1438–1500). Furthermore, we know that Abravanel loaned 1.5 million *maravedi*[1] to the Crown to help fund its war against Granada. Don Isaac's nephew, Joseph Abravanel, is also mentioned in documents from the second half of the 1480s, in which he is described as a successful tax farmer, and in the early 1490s, Joseph Abravanel was appointed chief tax collector of Plasencia.[2] We do not need to delve into the intricacies of the Abravanel family's commercial dealings to conclude that, within just a few years, they managed to successfully transfer their capital and businesses from Portugal to Castile and to re-create for themselves the same socioeconomic status that they had enjoyed for fifty years in Portugal.

Documents attesting to the economic activities of Don Isaac and his family members not only reveal the successful transfer of their business ventures, they also provide important political and cultural information. As he had done in Portugal, Abravanel forged a relationship with a prominent noble family with close ties to the court—in Castile, that family was the house of Mendoza.[3] Capitalizing upon his relationship with this noble house, not to mention his relationship with the local Jewish elites, he managed also to forge connections with the Crown. He served the Mendozas by managing their assets, and he served Queen Doña Isabel and King Fernando by assisting them in the consolidation of their reign and their efforts to complete the Reconquista of Granada.

The story of the house of Mendoza is that of the rise of a group of Castilian nobles in the royal court from the second half of the fourteenth century and throughout the fifteenth. During this time, they reached the pinnacle of their political and cultural influence. As explained in part I, Doña Isabel assumed the throne of Castile in 1474. She was immediately forced to face the resistance of certain noble houses that were supported by King Dom Afonso V of Portugal. During this conflict against enemies within and abroad, the support of the house of Mendoza played an invaluable role in securing Doña Isabel's victory. In exchange for that support, the house of Mendoza received new noble titles—for example, Don Pedro Gonzalez de Mendoza was appointed cardinal of Spain and went on to receive further prestigious Church appointments; likewise, Don Iñigo Mendoza was accorded the title of duke of Infantando. As mentioned above, both Don Gonzalez and Don Iñigo were Don Isaac's patrons in the 1480s and early 1490s. Abravanel thus found patrons who resembled those he had had in Portugal, and it is not impossible that the houses of Mendoza and Bragança enjoyed ties that facilitated Abravanel's new relationship.

Like the house of Bragança in Portugal, the house of Mendoza played a pivotal role in the periodic royal crises that beset Castile in the late fourteenth and early fifteenth centuries. However, unlike the house of Bragança, the house of Mendoza produced a series of renowned writers: the historian and chronicler Pero López de Ayala; the famous biographer of the Castilian monarchs and noblemen, Fernán Pérez de Guzmán (c. 1377– c. 1460); and the important humanist poet, the Marqués de Santillana, to name just a few examples. De Santillana's humanist library was one of the first and largest of its kind in the Iberian peninsula.[4] It included classical Latin and Greek works translated into Castilian and Italian, the works of Italian humanists such as Leonardo Bruni, the works of French and Italian poets, patristic works, chronicles, histories, and more. Cardinal Mendoza, the marquis's son, was notable for his Castilian translation of part of Homer's *Iliad*—a translation based on the Latin translations of Bruni and Pier Candido Decembrio (1399–1477).[5] Furthermore, beginning in the late 1470s, the cardinal, the Duke of Infantado, and other members of the house of Mendoza were generous patrons of the Castilian arts and Castile's new architecture, which acclimated Italian and Flemish trends.

As financial advisor to the cardinal and the duke, Abravanel certainly assimilated more than a bit of the literary and artistic environment that pervaded their homes and palaces. Furthermore, as we have seen above in our analysis of Abravanel's commentary on the Former Prophets, there were some affinities between the literary, historical, and political interests of Don Isaac and those of the Mendoza family. For this reason, we can see in Abravanel's service to the Mendozas a measure of continuity, complementing his previous participations in Portuguese court culture and further exposing him to the literary and artistic innovations of the fifteenth century.

The Causes of the Spanish Expulsion

However, this continuity could not efface the major changes taking place in Castile between 1483 and 1492, the year of the expulsion. Just as tensions and power shifts in the relationship between the Portuguese Crown and the nobility led to Abravanel's fall from grace and forced him into exile, so too the recurring crises within the Castilian court from the end of the fourteenth century to the rise of the Catholic Monarchs impacted the Jewish communities. As we saw in part 1, the pogroms of 1391 prompted the mass conversion of many Jews in Castile and Aragon (including Don Isaac's grandfather). These conversions led to the so-called converso problem— or more precisely, the question of the New Christians. A combination of the royal succession crises and the social and religious crisis precipitated by the phenomenon of the New Christians would ultimately lead to the expulsion of the Jews. Modern historians have argued how best to evaluate the relative importance of the various factors that contributed to and shaped the expulsion policy. This is not the place to weigh in on this debate, but it is important to describe the primary events that influenced the decision of the Catholic Monarchs to lend their support to this policy.[6]

When Don Isaac Abravanel arrived in Castile in 1483, Queen Doña Isabel and her husband, Don Fernando, had been in power since 1474 and 1479, respectively. As we saw in part 1, Doña Isabel's accession to the throne precipitated a foreign war with Portugal and a civil war at home with the supporters of the royal claimant, Princess Doña Juana. By 1479 Doña Isabel and Don Fernando had emerged victorious. In 1478, they had responded positively to the appeals of some elements in the Church that sought papal permission to establish a national inquisition in Spain—that is, a court entrusted with investigating heresy among the New Christians. This attempt to solve the converso problem was combined with a series of political decisions meant to defend the New Christians from the harmful influence of the Jews. Among other things, these included measures that expelled Jews from certain regions or sequestered them into separate neighborhoods. Thus, for example, the Cortes reached the following decision in 1480:

> Since from continued conversation and common life of Jews and Moors with Christians great damage and unpleasantness is caused, ... we order and command all the Jews and Moors of all the cities, towns and places in our kingdoms ... that their quarters be separated from those of the Christians, and not be in common.[7]

In 1483, the year of Don Isaac's flight to Castile, the Jews of Andalusia were expelled by order of the Inquisition and with the agreement of the Catholic Monarchs. In the same year, Tomas de Torquemada (1420–98) was appointed grand inquisitor over all the lands of the Catholic Monarchs, and with him at the helm, the Inquisition expanded its activities and reached greater prominence. Trials and executions were frequent. Given the anti-Jewish and anticonverso propaganda that flourished at the behest of the Inquisition in the 1480s—a point emphasized by Yitzhak Baer and Haim Beinart—it is not difficult to detect the general trend that ultimately led to the expulsion of the Jews.

However, the pernicious influence of the Inquisition and the New Christian problem aside, for many years, some degree of continuity in the relationship between the Crown and nobility and the Jews could still be discerned. In many cases, the Catholic Monarchs defended the Jews against attacks of the people or the Church. Likewise, they usually upheld the privileges of the Jewish communities and were happy to avail themselves of Jewish tax farmers such as Abraham Seneor and his father-in-law, Rabbi Meir Melamed. Don Isaac's successes further demonstrate this trend: the Catholic Monarchs balanced their support for the establishment of the Inquisition by adhering to the traditional conservative policies toward the Jewish communities in the Iberian peninsula.

But with the war in Granada, the scales were tipped. Just a few years after their victories over the king of Portugal and his Castilian allies, Doña Isabel and Don Fernando capitalized upon a border incident with Granada to launch an all-out war against the last bastion of Islamic rule in the Iberian peninsula. In a persistent struggle that lasted almost ten years (1482–91) and required the extensive mobilization of the kingdom's technology, wealth, and armies, the Catholic Monarchs conquered Granada. The Reconquista was finally complete. On January 2, 1492, they led a victory procession in the streets of Granada. It seems that the conquest of Granada quickly disrupted the delicate balance that had prevailed between the traditionalist policies of the Crown and the innovative policies of the Inquisition led by Torquemada. Ultimately, the latter emerged victorious. In late March, three months after the conquest of Granada, this prompted the formulation and signature of the expulsion edict. It was carried out between April 29–May 1 and the end of July in the same year.

Was Don Isaac Blind to the Danger on the Horizon?

In his biography of Don Isaac, Benzion Netanyahu expressed some doubts regarding Don Isaac's ability to properly evaluate the danger posed by processes that had begun to take place with the crowning of the Catholic Monarchs. Netanyahu writes:

> That a Jewish leader should have offered his services, particularly at such a time and place to rulers who were then openly forging a most dangerous weapon to be directed against his brethren—brethren by origin, if no longer by religion—must certainly appear extremely strange, to say the least, to a present-day reader.[8]

Netanyahu was quick to compare Don Isaac's blindness—and the blindness of Iberian Jewry as a whole—to that of the Jews of Germany on the eve of Adolf Hitler's rise to power. He concludes that though Abravanel's path brought him into the circles of the Castilian nobility and the court of the Catholic Monarchs, he "did not read the signs of the time."[9] In other words, from the historian's retrospective point of view, Don Isaac failed to read the situation with prescience and failed to anticipate that the expulsion was imminent. However, it may be more accurate to view the course of Don Isaac's life in Castile in the 1480s as expressive of the two opposing facets of royal policy toward the Jews. After all, he was well aware that his own success and that of his family could help preserve the traditional policies of the Crown and the nobility vis-à-vis the Jews.

Did Abravanel fail to properly read the political reality of Castile, as asserted by Netanyahu? Or did he perhaps rely on the balance between the new anti-Jewish policies and the more traditional positive ones, a balance that was shockingly and unexpectedly disrupted? Historians have no way of knowing for sure: most of Don Isaac's literary references to the Catholic Monarchs and the processes that precipitated the expulsion were penned retrospectively and with the benefit of hindsight. As we saw in our discussion of his commentary on the Former Prophets, Abravanel was sensitive to political developments and conceptions in both past and present. His time spent serving the house of Mendoza and frequenting the court of the Catholic Monarchs certainly reinforced this trend. However, the tragic end of the Jewish presence in the Iberian peninsula upended the central element of his identity, his belonging to the economic and political elite of Iberian Jewry. Don Isaac regarded himself as the consummate representative of an ancient Iberian Jewish heritage—a heritage that the expulsion abruptly cut short. The network of social and cultural identities that we described above in this book was threatened with complete disintegration by the expulsion, a tragedy that befell Don Isaac when he was fifty-five years old. From this perspective, we can perhaps understand why Abravanel was reluctant to relinquish a communal and familial history that tied him to the Iberian peninsula, not to mention his properties and his economic position. However, this traditional approach to Jewish existence in the Iberian peninsula is not necessarily evidence that Abravanel was unaware of the dangers and shifting fortunes taking place in the 1480s. It should also be taken into account that Don Isaac was a new immigrant in Castile at the time. He was engaged in establishing his new status, and this may have skewed his view of the political reality taking shape around him.

The Expulsion Decree and Exile

The expulsion decree was the extreme, albeit logical, outcome of the policies that had led to the establishment of the Inquisition and the intensification of its activities throughout the 1480s. The expulsion edict presented the situation as follows:

> You know well, or ought to know, that because we were informed that in our realms there were some bad Christians who Judaized and apostatized from our holy Catholic faith, whereof the chief cause was the communication between the Christians and the Jews; in the Cortes which we convened in the city of Toledo in the past year of one thousand four hundred and eighty years, we ordained that the said Jews should be set apart in all the cities, boroughs, and places of our realms and juderias dominions and to give them Jewish quarters and separate places where they might dwell, hoping that with this separation [the matter] would be corrected, and in addition we

took care and gave an order whereby inquiries should be made in our said realms and dominions, which, as you know, has been done for more than twelve years and is being done, and by it many offenders have been revealed, as it is known and as we are informed, by the Inquisitors and many other religious persons, both churchmen and laity. Thereby is established and made manifest the great damage to the Christians which has resulted and results from the participation, conversation, communication which they have held and do hold with the Jews, of whom it is proved that they always attempt by whatever ways and means they can to subvert and detract faithful Christians from our holy Catholic faith . . . and so that there may be no place for further offense against our holy faith, both in those whom until now God has chosen to preserve, and in those who have stumbled, fallen into sin, and removed themselves from Holy mother Church, which because of the weakness of our human character and the diabolical cunning and subterfuge which constantly makes war against us, could easily happen unless the principal reason for it is not removed, which is to expel the said Jews from our Kingdoms, for when a crime is committed by someone in some society or corporation it is right that such society or corporation should be dissolved and eliminated, and that the few should be punished because of the many and the ones because of the others.[10]

According to this political and religious outlook, there was only one way to protect New Christians from the harmful influence of their erstwhile brethren: the Jews had to be expelled from the kingdom. This was the justification marshaled by the edict to support the major political innovation that a general expulsion constituted in the history of the Iberian peninsula. Jews had certainly been expelled from other parts of Christian Europe— England in 1290, and France and Provence during the fourteenth and fifteenth centuries. The uniqueness of the expulsions from Castile and Aragon was, first of all, a matter of scale: over the course of three months, tens of thousands of Jews were forced to choose between conversion or the abandonment of their homeland. Previous expulsions had been applied to far smaller communities: with the exception of England, there had never been a general expulsion of an entire country's Jewish residents. Likewise, previous expulsions had never been applied to a Jewish Diaspora with roots as ancient and established as those of the Jewish communities in Castile and Aragon. These communities could boast unbroken historical continuity throughout a vast geographical area and had been integrated into most branches of the region's economic and cultural life. Another prominent novelty of the Spanish expulsion was, of course, its close association with the Inquisition, as noted above. The apprehension, questioning, and torturing of New Christians and their separation from Jews gave rise to the idea of a general expulsion. However, after the expulsion was carried out, the Inquisition did not rest. On the contrary, the entire Spanish empire, Portugal, and other Christian kingdoms and republics (in Italy and France) were subjected afterward to the authority of the Inquisition—that is, to the investigation and policing of Christian populations, new and old.

Given the profound shift in the relations between Crown, Church, nobility, and laity, the Jews were left with few possibilities for averting the harsh decree. Many historians have pointed to the time that elapsed between the signing of the edict (March 31, 1492, in Granada) and its first publication (April 29 and May 1) arguing that this delay is evidence of the attempts of Jewish courtiers to dissuade the Crown from carrying out the decree. However, most accounts describing such activity—including that of Don Isaac—are not supported by any official royal document and should therefore be treated partly as literary responses to the expulsion after the fact and regarded with a healthy amount of suspicion. Most extant documents pertain to the liquidation of Jewish loans and properties, conversions to Christianity, and the departure of Jews from the territories of Castile and Aragon.

The most geographically accessible location for Don Isaac and his family to make a new home was, of course, Portugal. However, due to the death sentences issued against Don Isaac and Don Joseph, this was not a realistic possibility. There were three other destinations available to the Sephardic exiles: North Africa (mainly for the Jews of Granada), Italy, and the Ottoman Empire. Don Isaac and his family embarked from Valencia for Italy, apparently in July 1492. They managed beforehand to liquidate most of their loans. The Catholic Monarchs even made a special exception on Don Isaac's behalf, allowing him to take with him "1,000 gold ducats and jewelry."[11]

Unlike the two most prominent Jewish courtiers of the time, Abraham Seneor and Meir Melamed, who converted to Christianity along with their families, the members of the Abravanel family—like most of the Jewish exiles—accepted the edict. However, unlike many others, the Abravanels had wealth at their disposal and were thus able to pay for the voyage to Italy and present themselves as attractive refugees to the Italian rulers.

As the Abravanel family departed for exile, we can see how the changes and crises of the Iberian peninsula led to a series of conversions, pogroms, and migrations, eventually unraveling the ancient and powerful connection that tied the Abravanel family to the Iberian peninsula. The period 1483–92, the years Abravanel spent in Castile, was bracketed by harsh political experiences: before it, the rise of João II to the throne of Portugal, and after it, the new set of policies instituted by the Catholic Monarchs and the Inquisition against the Jews in Castile and Aragon. It should therefore come as no surprise that Don Isaac's exegetical activity during these years was preoccupied with questions of leadership, politics, and government. As we will see in the next part of this book, the new circumstances created by the expulsion for the Sephardic Jewish Diaspora necessitated a literary and theological response—one that differed from those provided in the 1480s.

Part Three

DON ISAAC ABRAVANEL
IN ITALY
$$\left(1492-1508\right)$$

11 : ABRAVANEL'S ARRIVAL
IN NAPLES

*Integration of the Sephardic Exiles into the Jewish Communities
of the Italian Peninsula: Challenges and Issues*

In the last days of July 1492, Don Isaac and his family departed from the
Iberian peninsula. They arrived in the city and kingdom of Naples in late
September (on the 22nd, it seems), just a month after King Ferrante (1424–
94) granted the first Sephardic exiles permission to enter. This episode is
described by the Jewish chronicler Elijah Capsali:

> And from the children of Israel expelled from their dwellings in
> Aragon, Catalonia, and Valencia they went over the pass and took
> lodging among us [see Is. 10:29] and arrived on the first day of the
> month of Elul 5252 [August 24, 1492] on the shores of Naples,
> Italy. . . . And in advance of the ships' arrival, the Jews sent an emis-
> sary to implore the king to receive them. At that time, a wise and
> powerful man ruled Naples, and God was with him, and his name
> was King Fernando. . . . And while his name did resemble that of
> the oppressor King Fernando of Spain, it was not because of any
> similarities between them. . . . Thus were the ways of the King of
> Naples higher than the ways of the King of Spain. . . . And when the
> righteous King heard that the Jews had arrived to dwell in his land,
> his heart was glad and his honor did rejoice. And he said: "Come o
> ye blessed ones of the Lord!" And the Jews came, and they became
> a large community.[1]

In contrast to Caspali's optimistic portrayal, we find a bleaker picture in
the account of Solomon Ibn Verga:

> Ships from the Sephardic Diaspora arrived in the province of Italy.
> And there also, the famine was heavy, and in the ships the plague
> was mighty as well, and the poor knew not what to do, and, in the
> end, they disembarked. But the men of the towns would not allow
> them to enter. And they went to the province of Genoa, and there

too there was a famine in the land, but there [at least] they allowed them to enter the city. And the children could not bear it, and they would go to houses of idol worship [churches], converting [to Christianity] in exchange for a morsel of bread.[2]

With the exception of Rome, Naples boasted the largest Jewish community in Italy.[3] It was, therefore, capable of receiving relatively large numbers of Spanish exiles. However, as demonstrated by modern historians, few Spanish Jews ended up settling in Italy, as most of the Jewish communities there were too small to handle the massive influx of exiles.[4] It did not help that the peninsula became the nexus of a European war shortly after the expulsion, adding further challenges to the absorption of Jews—as we will explain in chapters 15–17. Nevertheless, Naples was without a doubt an important way station for many wealthy Sephardic Jews and an important stage in their immigration to and settlement in Italy and the Ottoman Empire.

Naples: A Jewish Political and Cultural Center for the Abravanel Family

It is estimated that the Jews residing in Naples in the late fifteenth century— split up among various *giudecche* (Jewish quarters)—constituted approximately 5 percent of the total population. In this kingdom, the Jews enjoyed the legal status of servants of the royal chamber (*servi camerae regis*) and benefited from the rights such a status entailed. When Naples was conquered by Alfonso V of Aragon in 1442, he founded a dynasty that would rule over Naples and southern Italy up until the crisis of 1494. The reigns of Alfonso V (1442–58) and his illegitimate son, Ferrante (1458–94), were characterized by cultural and economic prosperity. Many Jews participated in Naples' good fortunes, and some even left central and northern Italy in the second half of the fifteenth century to settle there. The most famous of the Neapolitan Jews was the scholar and doctor Rabbi Judah Messer Leon (active in the second half of the fifteenth century), who established a yeshiva in Naples that was attended by many students.[5] In addition, in the 1480s Jewish printers—including Joseph and Azriel Gunzhauser and Joshua Soncino, as well as the latter's nephews Gershom and Solomon— made their homes in Naples.[6] From the late 1480s until 1494, the kingdom was an important center of the early Jewish printing trade. With the establishment of the Aragonese dynasty by Alfonso, Naples also attracted many scholars and humanists such as Lorenzo Valla, Giannozzo Manetti, and most notably Giovanni Pontanto (1426–1504), who served as King Ferrante's secretary.[7] All in all, Naples was a hub of rich and diverse cultural activity.

Abravanel was quick to enter in King Ferrante's service, rising again to his previous status as an important Jewish courtier and leader. He describes his quick reestablishment in a commentary on the Haggadah, *Zevah pesah*: "With the noise of mighty waters, we arrived in the Kingdom of Naples; we were accepted peacefully. . . . For God took pity on me there and my possessions increased in the land. He made for me a hand and a name like the holy people in that land, a merchant, conducting his business peacefully and agreeably."[8] Don Isaac's description of his return to commercial activity attests to his skill at adapting to new environments. It goes without saying that quick integration into a completely new economic and social order was a privilege of the wealthy. Accounts from this period tell of a plague that broke out in the city, including in the Jewish neighborhoods, in 1493. Many Neapolitan and Sephardic Jews succumbed to the disease, and it seems that the city was abandoned.[9]

Except for Don Isaac's own accounts, we lack any sources that document the nature of his commercial activity or his status in the court during these years.[10] In 1494, King Alfonso II, who ruled Naples from 1494 to 1495, confirmed that "Jude Abramanel [Abravanel] son of Don Isaac Abramanel [Abravanel] who, as he himself explained, resides in this city, Naples, with the aforementioned father, his wife, and his whole family, in conformity with the privileges granted by His Royal Majesty to the Jews of this Kingdom" should be granted the same rights as those afforded to native Jewish residents of Naples.[11] This document, which mentions Abravanel as "father of the right-holder," confirms that Don Isaac and his family members had successfully integrated themselves into the economic and social sphere of the royal court. A review of the small number of financial documents that mention the Abravanel family yields a similar picture: the family made inroads into the salt, grain, and oil trade in the kingdom's southern regions.[12] That said, until the military crisis of 1494, we lack any clear picture of how Don Isaac and his family acclimated in the Neapolitan kingdom. It is notable that Don Isaac's name does not appear in the few documents that have reached us: only his oldest son and other family members are mentioned.

Did Don Isaac, who was fifty-five years old when he arrived in Naples, remove himself from day-to-day business activities, handing over these responsibilities to his sons and sons-in-law? We have no way to know for sure. His turn to intensive writing, shortly after his arrival in Naples, may suggest that he was less involved in political and commercial activity during these years. However, even if he was less active in economic life, his conception and model of leadership, as described in the previous two parts of this book, remained intact. On the one hand, his commercial, political, and banking activities allowed him and his family to assume important positions in the royal court and the Jewish community. On the other hand, his homiletical and literary activity was aimed at diffusing his image as a leader and scholar.

After his arrival in Naples, Abravanel returned to his commentary on the Former Prophets, moving on to the books of Kings. He also wrote *Rosh amanah* and two other works, *Tsedeq 'Olamim* and *Yemot 'Olam*, which it seems were never completed and have not survived. Don Isaac's arrival in Naples and his turn to writing are reminiscent of his activities after his arrival in Castile. This time, however, a number of factors—old age, the military crisis of 1494, and his forced itinerancy—prevented him from consolidating a new status as a financier, merchant, or community leader. As a result, during the last period of his life (1492–1508), Don Isaac was first and foremost a writer, and it was during these years that he composed the vast majority of his monumental exegetical oeuvre. In what follows, I will try to characterize the main components of this new flurry of literary activity.

Rabbi Meir Arama's Letter about Abravanel's Plagiarism

In 1857, an important document pertaining to Abravanel's work as a writer was published in the Hebrew periodical *Hamagid* by Haim Pollack. The document in question was a letter written by the son of Rabbi Isaac Arama, Rabbi Meir Arama. It was copied by hand by Rabbi Tam Ibn Yahya on the back of the title page of the first edition of Isaac Arama's commentary on the Pentateuch, *'Aqedat Yitshak* (1547). Rabbi Meir Arama explains in the letter that he "found his [father's] stolen words in the books of Rabbi Don Isaac Abravanel."[13]

In her book on Rabbi Isaac Arama, Sara Heller-Wilensky examines the claims made in this letter and summarizes its purpose as follows: "Rabbi Meir Arama hoped that copyists would copy the words of his letter and use them to preface all future editions of *'Aqedat Yitshak*."[14] In other words, he was trying to defend his father's "copyright" and reputation and disabuse readers of the notion that it was Don Isaac who was the real author of any parallel passages. Or, in the poetic language of Rabbi Meir Arama, "Perhaps they will think the latter to be the former, and they will judge him a thief in their eyes, and instead of being the offended party he will be considered among them the offender."[15] Besides indicating that plagiarism did indeed take place, a fact that has been examined and confirmed by scholars such as Heller-Wilensky[16] and Shaul Regev,[17] the letter provides important details about the relationship between Abravanel and Rabbi Isaac Arama:

> It once happened that God led a man to our house—a man with power and Torah. . . . He had grown up on high mountains, like the mountains of God, with kings and counselors of the land. . . . His name was Don Isaac Abravanilia [sic], he fixed times to study my Torah [that is, the teachings of Isaac Arama] and he had intercourse with me, naturally and unnaturally. He drank my wine and the bread that was my right, and he ate, and was filled, and grew fat. . . . And it came to pass in those days, that his heart grew haughty [as if he were] a lord, to have built for him houses, floors, and open spaces, taken from the choicest of my buildings, and to bring sacrifices and burned offerings from the sheep of my flock. He made many books and composed works to be heard outside in the streets and the markets . . . and he called them "new" . . . but the words were ancient; from the words of the elderly they were copied. Indeed, they are stamped like a seal upon my right hand, and all who see them will recognize them that they are [my] children with no blemish whatsoever. . . . And this [man] came to me in my tent, and fathered through me, [offspring] in the image of my likeness. He entered my space, he searched [my body], and he found all that was good. . . . He kissed me and stripped me of my jewelry and my ornaments and adorned himself with my finery, with the earring that was in my ear and the golden necklace that was upon my neck. . . . He coveted the image of my likeness and fashioned it with a graving tool and declared its name Ben oni [son of my own might]. . . . And had that nobleman said in his many treatises "these are the words of the master, and I have come only to add unto them" . . . then there would be no guilt. . . . To the contrary, blessing would rest upon him for having publicized and spread the wisdom of his elders.[18]

Rabbi Meir Arama, speaking here as his father, portrays Abravanel's plagiarism as an act of rape and deceit. Abravanel, whose fame presumably preceded him, was a welcome guest in Rabbi Isaac Arama's home in Naples from 1492 to 1495. According to this letter, Don Isaac's many encounters with Rabbi Isaac Arama, in the aftermath of the expulsion, led him to realize that Arama was a prominent Jewish scholar, and he was willing to learn from him and his writings. We know that during this period Abravanel occupied himself with several literary projects—he completed his commentary on Kings and his work *Rosh amanah*, to name two examples. Abravanel did not compose his commentaries in isolation. For example, David Ben-Zazon has drawn attention to the collective nature of Abravanel's commentary on the *Guide of the Perplexed*—a work that was based on his shared study with other scholars.[19] Likewise, in various places in his commentary on the Former Prophets, Abravanel mentions the scholars who "heed my voice"[20]: he says it was they who pushed him to commit his words to writing. Rabbi Meir Arama's letter casts the collective context of Abravanel's commentary in a different and more problematic light. Don Isaac created his works by collecting and studying a diverse set of sources, but he did not always cite others by name—even when he copied entire passages from them verbatim. At the same time, portraying Abravanel's works written after the expulsion as the "image" of Rabbi Isaac Arama's likeness is certainly an exaggeration. The dozens of books written by Abravanel during this period were not copied in toto from the works of Rabbi Isaac Arama—even if sometimes they incorporated pages copied from *'Aqedat Yitshak*. Rabbi Meir Arama's letter not only levels the accusation of plagiarism, but it also showcases Abravanel's curiosity and his insatiable desire to publish, a tendency we have discussed above and will discuss further below. Abravanel's anthologizing, study, and sometimes even plagiarism allowed him to write books that were extensive in scope. Few other works can compare to them.

Another negative portrayal of the character of Abravanel's leadership, as well as the quality of his works, appears in the writings of Rabbi David Messer Leon (c. 1470–1526), son of Rabbi Judah Messer Leon (c. 1425–98). The latter was head of the yeshiva in Naples and the most prominent intellectual figure in the Jewish community in the years before the arrival of the Spanish exiles. In 1886, the famed scholar and bibliographer Moritz Steinschneider published Rabbi David Messer Leon's searing attacks on Abravanel, which appear in his work, *'Ein haqoreh*, written around 1508.[21] Messer Leon openly mocks Don Isaac for his imperious arrogance: "He would almost have made himself Messiah with all his self-aggrandizement about his Davidic lineage . . . something which was not boasted by even our holy Rabbi

[Rabbi Judah the Prince, author of the Mishnah].... Indeed, his name is Isaac (*Yitshak*) for it is fitting to laugh at him (*le-tsaḥeq mimenu*).[22]

Like Rabbi Meir Arama, Messer Leon was also an outspoken critic of Abravanel's exegetical projects, and he too accused Abravanel of plagiarism: "He is a fool, for who appointed him to interpret [the *Guide of the Perplexed*] like this? For he has been nothing but a merchant all his days, and occasionally he will expound upon explanations (*peshatim*) which he has stolen [from others]."[23] One of the harshest of Messer Leon's attacks on Abravanel reveals that the criticism has a socioeconomic context:

> Don Isaac Abravanel, helpless as he is, often praises himself. And that wretched man has no distinction and no honor in the fundamentals of philosophy. And so, he lauds himself at the expense of exegetes who are far greater than us. This is the manner of his folly—to boast of that which he does not have. For everything I have seen of his in his commentary on this book [the *Guide of the Perplexed*] is nothing but vanity, grasping of wind, foolish [misunderstanding] of the master's principles, due to his facile understanding of philosophy.... Who gave him the confidence to argue against the master [Maimonides]?... And he thought that by doing so he could conceal his shame and his shortcomings, by immersing himself in the wisdom of the master all day, conjuring up [new] works using stolen works, the robbery of a poor man in his house.... And for the sake of the master's honor I will pursue him ... I will uncover his robe before the eyes of the leaders—that which he interpreted ... and though it is stolen, I will reveal to my comrades his wickedness.[24]

The Don Isaac whom we saw in Rabbi Meir Arama's accusations—a literary collector and a plagiarizer—appears here as well. Furthermore, it is clear that Messer Leon considered Abravanel an interloper in the realms of exegesis and philosophy. In his view, Don Isaac "has been nothing but a merchant all his days" and thus was incapable of interpreting Maimonides without resorting to literary theft. We therefore see again the tension between two elite classes of Jews, rabbis and merchants, mentioned in part 1 in our discussion of Abravanel's attacks of the Maimonidean model of leadership. The arrival of the Abravanels in Naples was not welcomed by all Jewish leaders, and it endangered the local Jews as well as the more veteran Sephardic leaders.

12 : COMMENTARY ON KINGS AS A
RESPONSE TO THE EXPULSION

Don Isaac attaches great significance to the completion of his commentary on the Former Prophets in the immediate aftermath of the expulsion, a notion that echoes throughout his commentary on Kings and features prominently in the book's autobiographical introduction. Interpreting Kings allowed Abravanel to reflect upon the history of the Jews in Spain (a history that had come to a tragic end with the expulsion) and compare it to the events described in the biblical accounts: the decline of the ancient states of Judah and Israel, the Temple's destruction, and the nation's exile. This comparison emerges in the first lines of the introduction, which begin with the presentation of Abravanel's pedigree. Don Isaac introduces himself as "Isaac son of my lord, the great leader Judah Abravanel . . . from a nation scattered and separated, of the exiled community of Jerusalem which was in Sepharad"[1]—in other words, he is a leader of a community dually exiled, expelled from both the land of Israel and the Iberian peninsula. Thus, Abravanel's leadership does not pertain only to a specific Jewish Diaspora within a single state (the kingdom of Naples), but rather to the entire Sephardic Diaspora, characterized not just by its geography but chiefly by a shared past.

Let us look at Don Isaac's personal introduction to his commentary on Kings. It seems that this introduction was written soon after his arrival in Naples, a few months after the expulsion. The introduction can help us understand how the collective memory of this trauma was formulated and how Don Isaac personally responded to it.

Two Narratives: The Wanderings of the Author
and the Spanish Expulsion

Don Isaac opens his commentary with details of his autobiography. It consists of two stories, the first containing the second. Abravanel integrates the narrative of expulsion into the narrative of his literary accomplishments—specifically, the belated completion of his commentary on the Former Prophets. The first half of this work (on the books of Joshua, Judges, and

Samuel) was completed in Castile in the years 1483–84, the second half was finished in September 1493, on Italian soil. In other words, the communal trauma of expulsion is incorporated into the personal framework of a leader's life and works. Abravanel writes:

> That which befell me during [the writing] of my commentary on the books of Joshua, Judges, Samuel, and Kings is the opposite of that which happened to Hiel of Bethel who built Jericho. He laid its foundation with Abiram his firstborn, and with his youngest son Segub he set up its gates. And I made an oath to the Lord in the earlier days which were better than these today, when I was complacent in the Kingdom of Portugal, my homeland, to interpret these four books, seeing that few had interpreted them, and because the burden of the king and princes were woven and laden upon my neck I could not do it. Until the hand of the Lord struck at me, and the King of Portugal considered me his enemy.... And I escaped the sword of the oppressor only by fleeing to Castile. And when I arrived there like a stranger in the land, like a traveler who turns aside to tarry for a night, I taught from the book of the Lord to pay my debts, and I wrote commentary on the first three books [of the Prophets].[2]

Abravanel compares the process of writing his commentary on the Former Prophets to the life of Hiel of Bethel, whose fate is described in 1 Kings 16:34: "In his days, Hiel of Bethel built Jericho. He laid its foundation with Abiram his firstborn, and with his youngest son Segub he set up its gates, according to the word of the Lord, which He had spoken through Joshua the son of Nun." Hiel violated Joshua's prohibition—that no one of the children of Israel was to rebuild the city of Jericho (Josh. 6:26). Hiel ignored the curse and paid for it dearly: all of his children, from his firstborn to his youngest son, died over the course of the construction.

Abravanel uses this story to present his exegetical project (which began with his flight from Portugal and ended with the expulsion from Spain) as similarly pervaded by catastrophe and tragedy. However, he inverts the order of the verse—the firstborn dying first and the youngest son dying last: for Abravanel, the beginning of his commentary was marked by personal loss and the end by the general expulsion of the Jews from Castile and Aragon. The theme at the center of this analogy is the idea of divine intervention. In both cases, God intervened in the course of natural events because prohibitions had been violated and oaths broken: Hiel transgressed the prohibition of rebuilding Jericho and doomed his sons to death, while Abravanel failed to uphold his oath to complete his commentary on the Former Prophets, which led to his flight from Portugal and later to his expulsion, with the rest of Iberian Jewry, from Castile and Aragon. It was only after all these upheavals that Abravanel completed the commentary.

Courtier or Exegete?

Don Isaac goes on to recount his successes in the court of the Catholic Monarchs between 1484 and 1492. His account is marked by an ambivalent mixture of self-denigration and self-aggrandization:

> And when I wished to begin writing the commentary on the book of Kings, I was called to the house of the king—he is the king of Spain, supreme over the kings of the world, he is the ruler of Castile, Aragon, Catalonia, Sicily, and the other islands. And I arrived in the court of the king and queen (*hamelekh vehashegal*) and I was close to them for many days. And the Lord made me favorable in their eyes and in the eyes of the nobles who sat the first in the kingdom. And I busied myself with their service for eight years. . . . Therefore, the Torah became slack. . . . And for the service of the kings of the nations who are not from the children of Israel, I abandoned my heritage, the kingdoms of Judah and Israel and their stories.[3]

Abravanel's return to political and economic life after a period of intensive writing (1483–84) is presented here as a radical shift, likened to a move from the courts of the kings of Judah and Israel to the court of the Catholic Monarchs. Abandoning exegesis in favor of an economic career in the royal court is depicted in ambivalent terms. Don Isaac's description of how he was called to serve the Catholic Monarchs is used to further signal his distinguished status. That being said, this success is portrayed as a distraction from Torah study, temporarily suspending his exegetical project. He alludes to this idea by paraphrasing a verse from Habakkuk (1:4): "So the Torah becomes slack and justice never prevails. The wicked surround the righteous—therefore judgment comes forth perverted."

However, before we delve into a discussion of Don Isaac's mixed feelings on this subject, it is important to note that the close ties between Abravanel and the Catholic Monarchs, as they are presented here, are not entirely supported by the evidence found in other documents that have reached us. It seems that after the expulsion, Abravanel had no qualms about tweaking the details of his autobiography—describing the financial services he provided for the house of Mendoza as if his were the most prominent position in the royal court. To style himself a leader, it was important for Abravanel that he be remembered as the only court Jew to serve the Catholic Monarchs. For this reason, he concealed the full extent of his Jewish and Christian environment: he makes no mention of the house of Mendoza or of other Jewish courtiers, such as Abraham Seneor and Meir Melamed.[4]

Feeling guilty for having relinquished his exegetical project, Abravanel retrospectively dismisses his political achievements as insignificant. He draws attention to the contradiction between his economic activity in the court of the Catholic Monarchs and his primary task as a religious and political leader, writing commentaries on scripture. However, as we have seen in descriptions of Abravanel's life in Naples, this negative portrayal of success in the courts of the Catholic Monarchs, coupled with regret for his having abandoned exegesis, does not express any true intention to repudiate his august status as a court Jew. The depiction of Abravanel's life in Castile should therefore be understood as a retrospective literary dramatization— it is a narrative of a court Jew's dual loyalty to the kingdom of Castile and the Jewish community. In any event, the trauma of the expulsion prompted Don Isaac to paint his rise in the court not as a success story but rather as folly, the abandonment of his exegetical duties. It is almost a story of betrayal.

The Publication of the Expulsion Edict and Don Isaac's Confrontation with the Catholic Monarchs

Abravanel goes on to describe the circumstances by which the Catholic Monarchs reached the decision to sign the edict that would expel the Jews of Castile and Aragon:

> In his ninth year, the year of the scattering of Israel, the King of Spain conquered the entire State of Granada and the great city of Granada—full of people, princess among states. And due to his feeling of power and his haughty heart, his spirit was renewed and he offended, imputing this his power unto his god. And Esau [the king] said in his heart, "How shall I appease my god who girds me with strength to wage war? How shall I welcome my creator who

gave this city into my hands, if not by gathering under his wings the nation that walks in darkness, the scattered sheep of Israel, to return this rebellious daughter to his religion and faith or to cast them out to another land."[5]

Like many contemporaneous Jewish chroniclers,[6] Abravanel links the expulsion to the conquest of Granada, offering a religious and psychological explanation for the connection between these two events. The completion of the Reconquista symbolized the victory of the unificatory policy pursued by Aragon and Castile and headed by the Catholic Monarchs ever since 1474.[7] To summarize the sense of power that seized the two monarchs, Abravanel presents the psychological profile of a king succumbing to the sin of hubris. He portrays the policy of religious uniformity pursued by the Catholic Monarchs as a thanksgiving sacrifice—Fernando offered up the Jews of his kingdom to his god, converting them to Christianity or exiling them from his kingdom.[8] Abravanel thus personified the factors that led to the expulsion, gathering them together under the political and religious image of a single man, the king. He ignored the argumentation offered by the expulsion edict itself—which was, as I have explained, predicated on the idea that the Jews constituted a pernicious influence on their converted brethren. Don Isaac preferred to portray the expulsion edict as an attempt to convert the Jews by force, or a decree for which a Jew is obligated to die by martyrdom. Thus, Abravanel presented the goal of the Catholic Monarchs (the conversion of Spanish Jews)— in contrast to that of the Jewish leadership, whose goal was to preserve the religious loyalty of the entire community. The formidable challenge that the policy of religious uniformity posed to the Jewish leadership is expressed here as a battle between two leaders: Abravanel and King Fernando.

> When I was there in the court of the king, I wearied myself by crying out until my throat was dry. I spoke to the king twice even thrice, with my very mouth I begged him: "Save O king [Don Fernando]! Why should you do this to your servants? Ask for many gifts and bribes of gold and silver, everything that belongs to every man of the House of Israel he shall give on behalf of his land." I called upon my friends, they who had audiences with the king, to ask on my people's behalf. And the nobles took counsel to speak to the king with all their might, to annul the decrees of anger and wrath, his plot that he had plotted against the Jews to annihilate them. [But] like

the deaf cobra he stopped his ears and would not be swayed by anything. And the queen stood at his right to lead him astray. With her persuasive words, she caused him to carry out his action from beginning to end.[9]

As I noted in chapter 10, until the edict was officially published, there were still opportunities to push for its cancellation or postponement. During this period, the edict's existence was kept a deep secret, known only to select members of the church and court. Abravanel claims here that he met three times with the Catholic Monarchs during this period, attempting to have the edict dismissed.

We know that King Don Fernando and Queen Doña Isabel signed the edict on March 31, 1492, in Granada. It was published only on April 29 in Aragon and May 1 in Castile. Scholars have been unable to find any evidence that Abravanel was in Granada during April.[10] Likewise, Christian sources mention no meetings between Abravanel and the Catholic Monarchs. It is therefore possible that Abravanel exaggerated the role he played in the Jewish efforts to avert the expulsion. Once again, he seeks to present himself as the sole representative of his nation during this dark hour.

Don Isaac's narrative appears in the literature written by the Sephardic exiles and those around them. In these texts the tale functions as a symbolic myth, meant to glorify the greatness of Don Isaac Abravanel, who is cast as the leader of Spanish Jewry. Thus, Rabbi Solomon Ibn Verga copied Abravanel's account into his 1550 book, *Shevet Yehuda*.[11] Likewise, in his book, *Seder eliyahu zuta*, Elijah Capsali discusses Abravanel's audiences with the Catholic Monarchs (though he adds that Abraham Seneor and other Jewish leaders met with the monarchs as well).[12] At the same time, it should be noted that the expulsion also produced Christian legends. One of the most famous of these revolves around the figure of Grand Inquisitor Tomas de Torquemada:

Tomas de Torquemeda . . . was a very erudite man, with much influence on the Catholic Monarchs, such that he was one the principal causes of the expulsion of the Jews from Spain. When after much deliberation, the Monarchs had already resolved to send the Jews away from their kingdom, they began again to waver in their decision due to the huge sum of money offered to them by the Jews, if they would not expel them. When the good father and zealous devotee of God discovered this, and considered how much evil would result from the commerce of Jews with Christians, he took under his mantle a crucifix of our Lord (*imaginem Cruxifix Domini nostri*), and boldly presented himself before the Catholic Monarchs, and among other things, he declared the following: Judas once sold the Son of God for thirty dinars, and your Majesties intend now to sell Him a second time for thirty thousands. Here is He whom you have sold! As he said this, he held up the crucifix before their eyes. Terrified, the Monarchs decided not to rescind their former decision to expel the Jews, and instead proceeded with its execution.[13]

Even a superficial comparison of the Christian legend to Don Isaac's account demonstrates their similarity: both stories feature a prominent character who stands up to the Catholic Monarchs with the goal of influencing royal policy—whether to pursue the new policy of expulsion or preserve the status quo.

Regardless, this portrayal of Abravanel's face-to-face audiences with Don Fernando and Doña Isabel represents the climax of his attempts to personify the causes that would lead to the expulsion. One can see in this act of personification—which is applied to both the exiles (Don Isaac) and the architects of the expulsion (the Catholic Monarchs)—a self-coronation of sorts. Abravanel crowns himself over the Jewish exiles, giving himself a title analogous to those earned by Don Fernando and Doña Isabel (the Catholic Monarchs) by virtue of the Reconquista and their new religious policies. Describing how he sought to persuade Don Fernando to revoke the expulsion edict, Abravanel lists the tools he had at his disposal: rhetoric, the wealth of the Jewish elites, and the mutual dependence of the Jewish leaders and the Christian nobility. But against these powers of persuasion stood the will of a satanic queen. According to Abravanel, it was her resolve to see the expulsion carried out that ultimately tipped the scales. In other words, Abravanel placed the blame for his failed negotiations with the king squarely on Doña Isabel's shoulders. This accusation marked the beginning of a Jewish historiographical tradition in which it is Doña Isabel who is held chiefly responsible for the expulsion.[14] It should be noted that Abravanel makes no mention of the roles played by the Church and the Inquisition in creating the conditions necessary for the expulsion—unlike the modern historiographical perspective, which regards these as major factors that led to the expulsion edict.

The tale of a window of opportunity before the publication and imple-

mentation of the expulsion edict was used by Abravanel as a tool for molding his own sociopolitical image. He uses this story to distinguish himself
from other members of Jewish society—those who knew nothing of the
expulsion edict—and thus elevates himself to the status of Spanish Jewish
society's exclusive representative to the Catholic Monarchs. By describing
his relationships and unmediated contact with the Spanish monarchs, he
was not attempting to project to his readers the idea of failure. Rather, he
wished to create the impression of a powerful and distinguished leader
who negotiates with kings and queens and who can continue to tend to the
needs of the Sephardic exiles in the future.

Farewell to Spain, Exile, and the Work of Memory

Abravanel goes on to describe the shock that seized the Jews of Spain upon
the edict's publication:

> And when the people heard these evil tidings, they mourned. And
> in every place where the king's command and decree arrived, there
> was great mourning among the Jews, and they trembled greatly, the
> anguish of a mother giving birth to her first child. Ever since the day
> that Judah was exiled from its land, there was nothing like it upon
> the land of the gentiles.[15]

To portray the shock of Castilian and Aragonese Jews upon learning of
the expulsion edict, Abravanel strings together a series of biblical verses.
The first verse is, "And when the people heard these evil tidings, they
mourned: and no man did put on him his ornaments" (Ex. 33:4). The "evil
tidings" (*hadavar hazeh*) referred to by Abravanel are, of course, the contents of the expulsion edict. In the context of the verse, however, the reference is to the evil tidings delivered to the children of Israel in the wilderness: that no member of the generation responsible for forging the golden
calf would be allowed to enter the promised land. The second verse used by
Abravanel is, "And in every province, wherever the king's commandment
(*dvar hamelekh*) and his decree arrived, there was great mourning among the
Jews, and fasting, and weeping, and wailing; and many lay in sackcloth and
ashes" (Est. 4:3). The phrase "dvar hamelekh" is used by Abravanel to refer
to the expulsion edict. In the book of Esther, it refers to King Ahasuerus's
order "to destroy, to kill, and to cause to perish, all Jews, both young and
old, little children and women, in one day" (Est. 3:13). The third verse used
by Abravanel is, "And Isaac trembled greatly, and said, Who? where is he

that took venison, and brought it me, and I have eaten of all before you came, and have blessed him? Indeed, and he shall be blessed" (Gen. 27:33). Here Abravanel links the trembling of the Jews of Spain, inspired by a fear of an uncertain future, to Isaac's trembling when he realized that Jacob had stolen Esau's blessing. Later in the passage, Abravanel further compares the Jewish response to the expulsion with the mourning of the Jews over the exile to Babylon: "For I have heard a voice as of a woman in travail, and the anguish as of her that brings forth her first child, the voice of the daughter of Zion, that bewails herself, that spreads her hands, saying, Woe is me now! for my soul is wearied because of murderers" (Jer. 4:31) and "And the king of Babylon smote them and slew them at Riblah in the land of Hamath. So Judah was exiled from their land." (2 Kings 25:21). By weaving these biblical allusions into his narrative, Abravanel seeks to etch the memory of the expulsion into the minds of his readers as tantamount to a third destruction of the Temple, this time taking place on gentile ground. He thus perpetuates an ancient medieval trope of using the memory of the Temple's destruction to create a framework in which to organize later events within Jewish historical consciousness and historiography.[16]

Like most Jewish chroniclers of the expulsion, Don Isaac goes on to present a grim picture of the departure for exile:

> And with no strength, 300,000 people of the nation to which I belong walked by foot. Both young and old, little children and women, in one day from all the provinces of the king—and whither the wind was to go, they went. And their King went out before them; the Lord was at their head. One did say, I am the Lord's and others write on their hands "[this belongs] to the Lord."... And many terrible travails befell them, robbery, destruction, hunger, and plague.... And God overtook them with the plague and they were a horror to all the kingdoms of the earth until they were swept away utterly by terrors and they remained but a few of many.[17]

With grave descriptions, Abravanel portrays the suffering and deaths of the exiles. Ultimately, however, his purpose is to instill within the survivors the notion that they are a chosen elite bearing an exalted religious tradition: they are representatives of the entire Iberian Jewish community. This is implied by Abravanel's imagery of a "remnant" which is based on the verse in Jeremiah (42:2): "And they said to Jeremiah the prophet, let, we beseech you, our supplication be accepted before you, and pray for us unto the Lord your God, even for all this remnant; (for we are left but a few of many, as your eyes do behold us.)" The departure for exile is presented as the renewal of the covenant between the exiles (who declare their loyalty to God) and God. Though God has punished them, he proceeds before them and guides them.

At the end of the introduction, Abravanel describes how he was exiled with the rest of Spanish Jewry, explaining at the same time how he chose to contend with his new circumstances upon his arrival in Naples:

> I too chose their way, the way of a ship in the midst of the sea, and I, in the midst of the exile, came with my entire house . . . to here, the great city of Naples. . . . And I said to myself that I would pay my vows, to interpret the book of Kings, that which I had not done until this point, also because it is time to act on behalf of the Lord, in memory of the destruction of our Temple and its glory, and the exiles that have befallen our nation as written in this book. . . . If Hiel of Bethel laid the foundations of Jericho with his firstborn, and set up its gates with his youngest son, then I am the man—see my affliction!—with the younger [the lesser] of exiles and the expulsions that have befallen me, my personal exile from the Kingdom of Portugal, I laid the foundations and began to interpret these four books. And the firstborn of exiles, the greatest of them, that is the bitter and swift exile . . . when we were expelled from our settlements in Spain . . . with this I set up the gates of this commentary and completed it.[18]

Describing himself before the publication of the expulsion, Abravanel emphasized the social gap between him, the Jewish courtier, and the rest of Castilian and Aragonese Jewry. Now, however, at this pivotal moment in his narrative when the expulsion was carried out, it was most important for him to present himself as a figure who nobly relinquished his distinguished status out of a sense of loyalty and belonging to the entirety of the Sephardic "nation." By accepting the shared fate of his community and by disseminating this story, Don Isaac acquired for himself the image of an eminent leader of the exiles.[19] The literature of the Sephardic exiles adopted this image—that of a Jewish courtier who accepted for himself the fate of his brethren—wholeheartedly.[20] In fact, Sephardic Jewry has preserved and cultivated this narrative until the present day. However, without diminishing the significance of Don Isaac's departure for exile, the historian must nevertheless address Abravanel's choice not to mention other prominent figures of Spanish Jewry who also were forced to leave the Iberian peninsula. Among those who arrived in Naples along with the Abravanels were Rabbi Isaac Arama, Rabbi Joseph Yaavetz, Rabbi Judah Hayyat, and David ben Shlomo Ibn Yahya.[21] This omission sheds light on another important dimension of Don Isaac's narrative: it is not a chronicle—that is, an attempt to describe what happened and to whom. Instead, it was a way of transferring leadership from one place to the next and of establishing his reputation in Naples. Therefore, the two images of Don Isaac—the one a Jewish courtier and defender of his people before the Catholic Monarchs; the other a leader who departs for exile with the rest of his brethren—were forged with the aim of gaining the respect and admiration of the Sephardic exiles. And in this, Abravanel succeeded.

In his account of his arrival in Naples, Abravanel mentions more than once his oath to interpret the books of the Former Prophets. Using the motif of the oath, Abravanel links the expulsion to his own failure to complete his commentary and to the feeling of guilt this entailed. Thus, the incomplete commentary becomes a symbol for the detachment of the exiles from God and religion, as well as a symbol of the critical need to renew this connection. Writing a commentary in the aftermath of the expulsion is intended to give author and reader alike a feeling that the severed bond between God and his people is being restored.

In addition to the corrective significance imputed to his commentary, Don Isaac portrays it as an act of thanksgiving for his salvation. However, as a survivor with a debt to his God, Abravanel did not consider himself bound by only a personal debt. He believed that his main debt was communal: he felt the need to shape the communal consciousness of the survivors of the expulsion, especially their religious and historical mind-set. Therefore, at the very beginning of his commentary, Abravanel establishes the connection between the biblical exile and the destruction of the two Temples and the expulsion of Spanish Jewry. As he says: "[I shall] interpret the book of Kings . . . because it is a time to act on behalf of the Lord, in memory of the destruction of our Temple and its glory, and the exiles that have befallen our nation as written in this book."[22] The commentary on Kings, which includes descriptions of the destruction, is a means of inculcating into the Sephardic émigré the historical consciousness of exile, allowing him to understand his circumstances after the expulsion in light of the conditions created by the destruction of the Temple from antiquity to the present day.

Abravanel concludes his autobiographical introduction by elaborating upon the analogy drawn between himself and Hiel of Bethel. Just as Hiel rebuilt the ruins of a city, paying for it with the lives of his two children, so Abravanel builds his commentary upon the ruins of his demolished personal and political status, as well as the ruins of Spanish Jewry as a whole. The commentary on the Former Prophets is thus meant to replace what he had watched collapse before his eyes: his personal power and prestige as well as the ancient glory of Iberian Jewry. In Abravanel's view, his exegetical act corrects the harm wrought by exile. Exegesis protects and perpetuates a glorious past: both that of the exiles and that of Abravanel himself. It can be argued that this narrative of how the commentary came to be is presented in the form of an introduction to identify the fates of the exiles with Abravanel's autobiography. The reader thus enters the commentary by fully identifying with Abravanel's image as well as with the history of the first Temple's destruction. This introductory rhetoric casts the commentary on Kings as a tool—the means by which the exiles can once again find their place in the canon of Jewish history and at the same time receive a new leader.

A careful reading of this introduction shows that Don Isaac was well equipped to respond to the expulsion immediately after his arrival in Naples. While his answer is sophisticated, it can be summarized as relying on two fundamental principles. The first is to nominate himself as a leader of the exiles by producing and disseminating a number of images: his audiences with the Catholic Monarchs, his departure for exile with the other members of his community, and his turn to the study and interpretation of scripture immediately after his arrival in Naples. The second principle is to renew the consciousness of Jewish exile among Iberian Jews by comparing the expulsion to the destruction of the Temple with the goal of instilling in them a conception of dual exile. Iberian Jews are part of the entirety of Jewish history. But at the same time, they are unique exiles with a shared past—a past that can help them reorganize themselves into new communities in their new Diaspora lands.

13 : SOLOMON

THE IDEAL KING

The Primary Theme of Kings

Having described how Don Isaac linked the composition of his commentary to the expulsion of himself and his coreligionists from Spain, I wish now to delve into the content of the work, showing how Don Isaac integrated his own conception of leadership into his exegetical treatment of Kings. As we learn from the commentary's first pages, the main themes addressed in Kings are the history of the Israelite monarchy (consisting of two periods: unity and schism) as well as the behavior of its individual kings, the relationship between this behavior and the decline of the kingdom, and the eventual exile of Judah and Israel. Abravanel summarizes the book's purpose as follows:

> There is no doubt that the custom in Israel was, as is today the case among the nations, to commit to writing all matters pertaining to the kings and their actions. And these books were called chronicles (*divrei hayamim*). . . . And among these narratives and accounts (*hasipurim vehahagadot*) were necessary words and extraneous ones. . . . And they included words written according to will—as is the practice of authors who relate stories to praise or impugn more than is proper, in accordance with their own love and hate. And behold, when the Holy One Blessed is He commanded the prophet to write the accounts of the kings in a book, the purpose of the recounting was not for the sake of the story as is the case in a chronicle. Rather, it was to make known the branching of generations, and the lineages of the kings one from the other, and to inform us of their righteousness or wickedness, [to teach us] their actions for which they received reward or punishment. And all of this was in accordance with the prophetic truth and divine revelation (*hitva'adaut haelohii*).[1]

In this passage, Abravanel compares Kings and Chronicles to medieval chronicles. His purpose in doing so is to define the unique literary character of Kings: it is a historical record written from a theological vantage point, and its accounts revolve around the themes of divine reward and punishment. It goes without saying that these are the subjects that occupy Don Isaac throughout his commentary. According to Don Isaac, if a chronicle is primarily aimed at a description and justification of a given king's reign, then the book of Kings has a different purpose. It focuses on the relationship between kings and God and explores the influence of this relationship upon the historical fortunes of the kings' subjects—primarily inasmuch as their behavior gradually led to the conditions of exile.

The expulsion of the Jews, as portrayed in Don Isaac's autobiographical introduction to his commentary, was the political and religious decision of a haughty king who viewed his might and victory in Granada as a sign of personal divine favor and providence. Against this notion of a special, personal connection to God—the claim Abravanel imputes to the Catholic Monarchs in response to their political and military successes—Don Isaac offers a commentary on Kings that revolves around the relationship between the biblical kings and God, as well as the transition of Judah and Israel from a powerful and unified kingdom under the reign of Solomon to one plagued by division, decline, and ultimately destruction and exile. To counter the power of the Catholic Monarchs, who were responsible for expelling Don Isaac and his coreligionists from their homelands, Don Isaac extols the might of King Solomon. This may be why Abravanel devoted half of his commentary to a description and discussion of various aspects of King Solomon's kingdom.

The Anointment of King Solomon and the Measures Taken to Secure His Reign

The account of Solomon's coronation appears in the first chapter of Kings, which describes how Solomon was anointed by Zadok the priest and Nathan the prophet. Abravanel develops this biblical account into an expansive discussion that compares the anointing of kings to that of high priests. As Don Isaac mentions more than once, "in anointing . . . two final causes are united. The one is that the anointed person is special and distinguished. The second is that he is prepared to receive divine inspiration—for both are necessary for the High Priest who must consult the Urim and Thummin and for the king upon whom the sacred spirit of God should rest."[2] In other words, anointing is the "sign of divine chosenness," and its purpose is "to draw attention to the fact that he (and his children) have been given the kingship just as the priesthood was given to Aaron and his sons after him, an eternal covenant of priesthood. Therefore, the anointing of kings was compared to the anointing of priests to inform us that the kings are eternal in their reigns just as the priests are eternal in their priesthood."[3] Interestingly, Abravanel notes "that the anointing oil was concocted only once—in the time of Moses."[4] He explains the reason for this as follows: "it was the divine will that this oil should be eternal, and that it would miraculously never be depleted as time passed, so that it would also be used in the future to anoint the kings in the age of the Messiah—indicating the eternity of the Torah."[5] From his detailed discussion of Solomon's anointing, the impression which Abravanel wished to transmit to his readers is clear: he sought to paint the picture of a monarchy that is predicated on a unique connection to God, the support of prophets and priests, the downflow of divine influence, the guarantee of eternity, and many additional signs of stability.

In his commentary on chapters 2 and 3 of Kings, Abravanel focuses on various aspects of Solomon's succession of David. He elaborates at length on David's last will and testament to his son and explains: "For the practice of elders to deliver their will before their deaths was always the custom of the holy ancestors. . . . And I believe that the reason for this . . . is because before one's death one finds oneself clear in intellect and bright in insight."[6] Thus, it is during this unique moment, when the intellect is on the verge of departure from its body, that the ailing king's true knowledge is transmitted to his heir. This transmission, which involves God, is what constructs the profile of the new king. Thus, for example, Don Isaac interprets David's statement "I go the way of all the earth: be you strong therefore, and show yourself a man" (Kings 2:2) as follows:

The first is his statement "I go the way of all the earth"—in doing so he wished to comfort Solomon his son, to speak to his heart, that he should not mourn excessively over his death. . . . That Solomon should not say that his pain and sorrow are not for his father but rather for himself—that he remain isolated with no support, due to [his father's death]. To refute this [notion, David] said to him "and show yourself a man," meaning until now you were a soft youth. Now you must strengthen yourself and be a complete man. You do not need my guidance and you certainly have another help that is far greater than me. . . . And that is the divine assistance which is attained and achieved through the Torah and commandments.[7]

In his characteristically neo-Stoic tone, Don Isaac turns Solomon's final farewell to his father into a formative moment in which the new king must overcome his natural dependence on his father and reveal the true source of authority, "the divine assistance which is attained and achieved through the Torah and commandments." This emotional moment, when Solomon inherits his father's crown, may be understood as a message to the Sephardic Jewish reader: he too is expected to overcome hardship and death and rediscover "the divine assistance" that, according to Don Isaac, is the source of continuity for every Jew.

Furthermore, Don Isaac describes at length the contents of David's last will and testament. David imparts to Solomon the importance of securing his reign and keeping it safe from the machinations of his internal enemies such as Joab and Shimei:

> Our master, David, did not command Solomon to kill Joab and Shimei . . . and he did not give his young, soft son, the designated heir, dangerous advice to execute military men at the very beginning of his reign. Rather he wished to relate to Solomon what Joab and Shimei had done to him so that he would be cautious with them and not give them positions of power in his house lest they overcome him.[8]

Don Isaac also addresses the need of the new king to treat his subjects benevolently—not "to treat them as a king does his servant, but rather as brothers and equals."[9] Abravanel defends Solomon's marriage to pharaoh's daughter and attributes it to similar considerations. It was necessary for Solomon to secure and consolidate his reign: "After mentioning that Solomon removed all those who would curb his power within his kingdom, that is his domestic enemies, the [narrator] mentions that he took a further measure to perpetuate and establish his reign—making peace with and marrying the daughter of Pharaoh, King of Egypt, who was a great king residing in close proximity to him. And he did this so that he could be at peace with [Pharaoh] and forge with him a relationship of great love."[10]

The Wisdom of Solomon and Philosophy

In his discussion of Solomon's succession and the manner in which he secured his reign, Abravanel does not limit himself to reflection on the king's anointing, the politics of containing domestic enemies, and diplomatic relations with the neighboring kingdoms. Rather, he extends the discussion to include an interpretation of Solomon's prophetic dream and the result-ing gift of wisdom, casting these as necessary prerequisites for his illustri-ous reign: "Scripture states that Solomon was assisted in the preparation and establishment of his reign by divine providence and supernal prophetic influence and by the perfection of wisdom bestowed upon him."[11]

With these words, Don Isaac introduces a discussion spanning more than twenty pages, which describes the nature and role of Solomon's wis-dom. The opening chapters of Kings—which seem to tell the story of a con-voluted and controversial transfer of power from a dying king to his unpre-pared heir—are developed by Abravanel into a miraculous final preparation for Solomon's successful reign. Abravanel's discussion of Solomon's wisdom demonstrates Solomon's superiority over other kings. Furthermore, the discussion is used by Don Isaac to articulate his own views about the con-nection between knowledge and political power.

In the first section, which is dedicated to a discussion of the unique character of Solomon's wisdom, Don Isaac distinguishes between wisdom (hokhmah) and the studies of philosophers. To be more precise, he portrays wisdom as the mirror image of science and philosophy, casting the former as the solution to all the limitations and problems of the latter. Abravanel thus further develops his polemic against the Maimonidean model of the philosopher prophet, while also explaining Solomon's superiority over all other wise men of antiquity.

Basing himself on Maimonides's model of the philosopher's gradated progress, which we discussed in part 1, Don Isaac lists five shortcomings of science's inductive method. He identifies the general problem as a con-sequence of man's need to rely on inductive reasoning:

> Because man's intellect is tied to his body and is the actuality of a natural body with organs, the intelligibles (muskalot) reach him through the senses and imagination, so much so that Aristotle stated that nothing is [contained] in the intellect that was not first in the senses. And he states that it is the intellect which extracts the intel-ligibles—that is, the universal forms (tsurot hakolelot), abstracted from individual forms attained via the senses and made present in the imagination.[12]

The inductive method extracts the "universal form"—the general defi-nition of a given entity—and the other three Aristotelian causes (the final cause, the efficient cause, and the material cause) from sense experience and from the imagination, which can preserve and retrieve the sensual impressions of objects. At the same time, induction activates the potential intellect of the philosopher. As he is a creature composed of body and soul, man can activate his intellect only by processing information attained through the senses. However, the inductive method requires work (the first deficiency) and time (the second deficiency). Moreover, the inductive method aspires to invert the natural sequence of human perception and does so only with great difficulty: "Those things which are lower and baser in their nature and existence are more easily attained by us. [By contrast, those matters] which are more precious and sublime in their existence and nature are more hidden from us" (the third deficiency).[13] In other words, science and philosophy aspire to understand natural and metaphysical entities that lie beyond humans' immediate sense experience. The fourth deficiency, according to Abravanel, is "the limit of our intellect in apprehending the causes of things in their entirety. . . . Meaning, that the ultimate forms cannot be apprehended by human intellect, for humans apprehend from the senses and the imagination."[14] Abravanel reviews the four Aristotelian causes, in each case explaining that because human intellect depends on the senses, "[man] cannot naturally apprehend the nature of anything but those accidents which are revealed to his senses."[15] While Abravanel does not deny the ability of the human intellect to understand the causes of nature, he notes its limitations: "Although the reality of the substantial forms can, to a certain extent, reach the intellect through special accidents, they are not apprehended in their substance and immediately."[16] Human apprehension of the causes, therefore, remains partial and indirect. The fifth and final deficiency of human intellect is "that errors and mistakes befall human apprehension; as it is attained through the senses, it will encounter the truth not in a deductive fashion but rather by accident and to a limited extent."[17] The human intellect is always dependent on the particular context of sense perception. As a result, it remains bound to the lack of certainty that follows from induction based on specific instances: "And because his method of attaining intellect is from effect to cause, and often one thing will be the effect of two different and even opposite causes, the human intellect will conclude, in error, that only one is the cause."[18]

According to Abravanel, philosophy and science seek to invert the normal sequence of human perception, in which sense perception precedes intellect. They seek, through an inductive method, to reach the cause from the effect. As Abravanel puts it, "Human intellection is the opposite of nature and reality. For the immaterial entities, which are more existent in their nature (*yoter nimtza'im betiv'eihem*), are less existent in our intellect, whereas the material things which are less existent in nature, . . . are more existent in our intellect."[19] It is the tension between the natural hierarchy (from pure intellect to matter) and the human sequence of perception (from matter to intellect) that philosophy—through its gradual, inductive method—seeks to overcome. But it cannot erase this rift entirely, and therefore the philosophical and scientific project is inherently limited and plagued by the deficiencies enumerated by Abravanel.

Unlike human wisdom, which is constructed through a gradual process, the wisdom of Solomon understands the causal structure of nature, immediately and miraculously. It requires no induction. As Abravanel explains:

Indeed, the second way, from the cause to the effect and from the prior to the latter, is the intellection of separate intellects who see the King's face. For they are simple intellects separate from matter, and because of the influence of the Blessed God, they apprehend things as they are in reality. I mean that they apprehend effects from their more prior and sublime causes. Not that they know prior causes *before* effects in a chronological sense (*qedimah zmanit*), but rather *before* in a natural [hierarchical] sense. For indeed in one moment, they will see the causes of things and their effects together.[20]

Induction seeks the path to first causes through effects, those impressions that man encounters first in his life (that is, through sense impressions). In contrast, the second way—the wisdom of Solomon—immediately transports the one who possesses it to the end of inductive reasoning and even further, beyond its limitations and uncertainties. He who possesses the wisdom of Solomon "sees the king's face," reaching the same level as the separate intellects that, with one glance, can perceive the entire chain of causation that creates the world. This panoramic perception of the causal structure of the world encompasses the entire cosmos, and it is the goal that philosophers and men of inductive science aspire to reach. This is the mark of Solomonic wisdom's superiority. As Don Isaac puts it, "Solomon became wise through the second path, the miraculous path, and in this regard, he was superior to all other wise men before him and after him."[21]

The Practical Character of King Solomon's Wisdom

Solomon's knowledge was distinct from philosophy not only in quality and nature. Later in his discussion, Abravanel explains that the main difference between these two types of knowledge are related to their respective practical and utilitarian horizons. Because Solomon did not need to invest large amounts of time and energy acquiring knowledge, and because the perfection of his perception alleviated the need for second-guessing or doubting, his task was very different from that of a philosopher or scientist. Solomon did not need to concern himself with the question of how one recognizes the causality operating within the world. His chief concern was how to harness and take advantage of the laws of causality.

Abravanel notes the practical application of Solomon's wisdom in a number of disciplines. The first is medicine:

> Solomon's knowledge included the uses (*to'alot*) of all sublunar entities and their properties. . . . I mean their contraries and their opposites, their similarities, the ways in which they change, their relative hierarchies, and their organization within the totality of the sublunar world—nothing was withheld from the king. And therefore, he wrote a book of remedies [including] all those things that are naturally related to human health.[22]

The second discipline was astrology: "Because Solomon arrived at certainty within that science [astrology] . . . and attained certainty about the nature of the forces [of the stars] inasmuch as they move matters in the sublunar world. And in the practical art, he did as he willed and flourished."[23]

The third discipline was metaphysics:

> Solomon attained [understanding] of the existence of the separate [intellects] and the certainty of what they are—as much as is [humanly] possible. . . . And his knowledge reached the level of knowing their meaning and their forces and their governance over sublunar [beings]. . . . And about the science of the separate [intellects], Solomon composed many songs. . . . For it was the practice of the ancients to discuss divine matters [metaphysics] through song. And it appears that he composed the majority of his songs [in reference to] the supernal [angelic] princes, each one receiving [its own song], in accordance with its providence over each nation. . . . And he com-

posed the book Song of Songs in reference to the divine providence over the Assembly of Israel.[24]

Just as Solomon's knowledge of nature was realized in his mastery of medicine, and just as his perfect knowledge of astronomy was realized in his harnessing of astrology, so too his metaphysical knowledge about the essence and powers of the heavenly entities was transformed from speculative knowledge into practical utilization of "the paths and means and preparations that are needed to bring down the influx of each prince of the separate [intellects]."[25] Thus, on three levels of reality (the sublunar world, the stars, and the separate intellects), Solomon's perfect and miraculous knowledge allowed him to harness natural and supernatural causality practically and effectively—or more specifically, politically—to improve the fortunes of both his subjects and other nations. Abravanel notes that "[people] would come from the nations to hear [Solomon's] wisdom and they would bring him tribute that he should teach them how these nations should serve their gods, that is the princes up high, in such a way as to draw down [divine] influence upon their lands."[26]

It is interesting to compare Abravanel's discussion here with that of the humanist Marsilio Ficino in the third book of his *De Vita*, published in 1489—just few years before the expulsion. In book 3, chapter 21, which is dedicated to "the power of words and songs for capturing celestial benefits (De virtute verborum atque cantus ad beneficium coelest captandum)," Ficino portrays the natural magic in songs similar to those of Solomon:

> But remember that song is a most powerful imitator of all things. It imitates the intentions and passions of the soul as well as words; it represents also people's physical gestures, motions, and actions as well as their characters, and imitates all these and acts them out so forcibly that it immediately provokes both the singer and the audience to imitate and act out the same things. By the same power, when it imitates the celestials, it also wonderfully arouses our spirit upwards to the celestial influence and the celestial influence downwards to our spirit.[27]

The magic of song, according to Ficino, channels natural forces (on different levels of the cosmos) through the use of imitation—the use of language to represent and replicate. The magic of song is meant to create a continuity and a similarity between the qualities of the natural power, their representation within the soul of the singer, and their influence upon the souls of the audience. It is difficult to say whether Don Isaac was directly acquainted with Ficino's ideas. Regardless, there was no lack of intermediaries who could have transmitted the ideas of the former to the latter. To name two examples, Abravanel's son Judah, was in direct or indirect contact with the Ficinio's circle, and Yohanan Alemanno, whose patrons were the da Pisa family and who was in direct contact with Pico della Mirandola and Ficino's circle. Without reaching any definitive conclusions about Ficino's influence on Don Isaac, we can nevertheless say with confidence that the idea of natural magic—understood as the science of connections and relationships between different beings—was commonly discussed in the Italian peninsula at that time.[28]

In light of the practical character of Solomon's wisdom, it is no surprise that Don Isaac moves on to discuss the political and economic elements of his wisdom—disciplines that in more traditional medieval hierarchies are placed far lower than metaphysical pursuits. In the introduction to his discussion of the governance of the individual, the household, and the state, Don Isaac inverts the relative importance of practice versus speculation:

> For it is rare that one perfect in theoretical intellect (*sekhel 'iyuni*), should attain perfection in matters of practical intellect. For those who are involved in theory cannot involve themselves in matters of practice and governing. . . . Indeed, because his wisdom was miraculous, Solomon was perfect in both theory and practice on the highest possible level. And this was true both in terms of governance over oneself . . . that is the science of ethics, as well a person's governance over the members of his household . . . which is the knowledge of governing a home [economy], or the governance of a state or kingdom according to justice and law and proper arrangement which is knowledge of how to govern a state.[29]

A regular philosopher has little time to dedicate to practical issues: he must devote himself entirely to the tedious and laborious process of attaining metaphysical knowledge. Solomon, by contrast, was spared the challenges that generally block the path of those who seek perfect knowledge in metaphysics. He was thus left entirely free to delve into issues of ethics, economics, and politics. The superiority of Solomon's knowledge lies precisely in its application—not in the theoretical question of "what" but rather in the technical question of "how." This idea is particularly salient in

the way Abravanel emphasizes Solomon's economic activity, distinguishing him in this regard from other kings:

> Most of his governance in matters of state pertained to the inven-
> tion of new and innovative ways of generating wealth and amassing
> large amounts of money without exacting it from his people and
> his properties through taxation or theft—as is done by tyrannical
> kings who seek to grow wealthy. But [Solomon] would send ships
> to Ophir for gold and to Tarshish for large amounts of merchandise,
> and the amount of gold in [his] house was so great, that he made
> two hundred suits of armor and three hundred shields.[30]

Solomon's reign was characterized by the application of economic
know-how, as opposed to the use of force against his subjects or neighbors.
With the latter—for example, Tarshish and Ophir—he conducted commercial dealings. Unlike tyrannical monarchs who steal wealth from citi-
zens and enemies alike, Solomon turned himself into a positive economic
agent of development and growth. He initiated international trade with his
neighbors and based the power of his country on the profit he made from
his economic activities—not by lording himself over his subjects: "Without sword or spear he would rule all the kingdoms of the world, and all
the nations would bring him tribute and serve him all the days of his life."[31]
In this model, amassing wealth through economic activity obviates the
need to resort to violence or war. The wealth of the king contributes to the
wealth of his subjects, as well as to the wealth of neighboring states. Thus
violence, instead of being an effective means of growing wealthy, is construed as an obstacle that prevents the development of fruitful and lucra-
tive commercial relations. This approach bears a resemblance to that espoused by Don Isaac's father, Judah Abravanel, in the latter's letter to King
Dom Afonso V. There, Judah tells the king to adopt certain economic initiatives to deal with the devaluation of Portugal's currency at the time. According to this view, royal intervention in the economy and commerce expands
the king's treasury and thus helps revalue his currency. The foundation of
the king's power, then, is the economic welfare of his subjects.

King Solomon: Between Prophet and Philosopher

Having discussed Solomon's perfect knowledge of the Torah's simple meaning as well as its deeper esoteric layers, Abravanel now attempts to contex-
tualize Solomon's status vis-à-vis two other scholarly and religious types:

the prophet and the philosopher. We have already pointed to the difference between a philosopher, whose apprehension develops gradually and slowly, and Solomon, who attained wisdom in a flash of prophetic enlightenment. Abravanel uses this contrast to reiterate his opposition to the identification between prophecy and the cultivation and improvement of one's intellect. Don Isaac emphasizes the superiority of Solomon's wisdom, which derives from a divine source and is meant to be directed toward a practical task. As Don Isaac puts it: "Science is not a necessary preparation leading to prophecy. . . . For science is one of God's kindnesses and gifts to the prophets in accordance with what is required by their mission."[32] Science is not a preparation to receive prophecy, nor is it a necessary result of it. Rather, it is the sum total of information needed by the prophet to carry out his specific mission.

From the all-encompassing breadth of Solomon's wisdom and its economic and political character, Abravanel is able to learn what distinguishes the king from the great prophets, such as Moses and Isaiah: "While we can admit that the prophets had wisdom in relationship to their level of prophecy, this should not be understood to apply to the knowledge in which Solomon was perfect—meaning his knowledge in governing his home and his state, all of which was far from the dealings of prophecy."[33] The breadth of Solomon's wisdom is actually indicative of the inferiority of his knowledge compared to that of the greatest prophets. Their knowledge did not require such breadth because they dealt primarily with only the most sublime things, "those things that are unique to Him the Blessed, and the manner of His providence over his creations and especially the Israelite nation."[34] Thus, while Solomon's intellectual prowess outstripped that of the philosopher—his knowledge was true and certain, effective and practical— compared to other prophets, the practical and political horizons of his wisdom ranked him among the lowest of them.

Solomon stands between the figures of the philosopher and the prophet. He is most similar to the figure of the magus, who is featured in the literature composed in the circle of Ficino and by Giovanni Pico de Mirandola (1463–94).[35] In the 1460s, Ficino translated a collection of Hermetic texts from Greek into Latin. The Hermetic texts are a series of theological and magical texts attributed to the mythical Egyptian figure Hermes Trismegistus, who was considered the founder of the *Prisca theologia* (the first theology), a body of esoteric knowledge transmitted by Orpheus and Pythagoras to Plato. Ficino's Latin translation was widely disseminated in Europe and was printed as early as 1473. Another work that influenced the members of Ficino's circle was a work on magic and alchemy, *Picatrix*—written originally in Arabic but translated into Hebrew as well. Using these sources, Ficino and Pico developed their theory of the natural magical, which Pico summarized as follows: "Magic is the practical part of natural science; (*magia est pars practica scientaie naturalis*)," "what man the magus makes through art, nature made naturally in making Man (*quod Magus homo facit per artem, facit natura naturaliter faciendo hominem*);" "to operate magic is nothing other than to marry the world (*maritare mundum*)."[36] This "marriage" is effected "through the union and actuation of those things that exist seminally and separated in nature."[37] In other words, magic, in the view of Pico, is knowledge of the natural links between different entities and different levels of reality.

The popularity of natural magic was not limited to the Florentine milieu (where Ficino's circle was active). It was also much loved by the humanist Lodovico Lazzarelli (1447–1500), who lived in Naples in the late 1480s and early 1490s. Lazzarelli translated Hermetic texts and wrote a treatise of his own on Hermetic magic. In one of these works, he compares Hermes to a biblical prophet and tried to adumbrate a conception of kingship that he hoped to recommend to King Ferrante of Naples. Was this magic-infused environment the catalyst for Don Isaac's understanding of Solomon's practical wisdom? The following words of Don Isaac would seem to suggest that was the case:

> And indeed, Joseph son of Gurion [Josephus] in his Book of Antiquities which he wrote for the Romans, recounts the extreme greatness of Solomon's wisdom—for he knew the matters of demons and their actions and the oaths to be used to adjure them. And [Josephus] attests that when Titus conquered Jerusalem he saw that one of the Romans had been possessed by a demon and he was performing strange and bewildering actions. And one priest came, his name was Eleazar, and he praised himself that he knew the wisdom of Solomon as it pertained to demons. And he called the demon through the possessed person's ear, and on the priest's hand was a signet ring. And immediately the demon departed from the Roman's body and he regained his health and strength. However, the priest said to Titus, "if you wish, I will force the demon to enter another body." And so Titus, wishing to test him, told him to put the demon

in the body of another one of his men. And the priest adjured the demon to enter that man's body. And they looked for the man and found him with his eyes blinking, and his legs stumbling, with spittle on his beard, and with no ability to speak. And Titus knew that the lips of priest held wisdom—the great wisdom of Solomon which never was among kings and which will never be again.[38]

Abravanel was familiar with the Latin translations of Josephus and has quoted here (with no small amount of paraphrasing) a passage that appears in the eighth book of *Antiquities of the Jews*.[39] This quote is not only indicative of Abravanel's learning. The specific situation being described here is worthy of note: the superiority of Solomon's wisdom, which is expressed in its practical and magical effectiveness, was not the exclusive ability of the king but was rather transmitted, at least in part, to the priesthood. Thus, Eleazar the priest, right before the destruction of the Temple and the fall of Jerusalem, could still implement this superior wisdom by exorcizing and adjuring demons. This paradoxical state of affairs—the juxtaposition of political and military weakness with religious and spiritual superiority— strongly alludes to the situation of the Jewish exiles in the aftermath of the expulsion. On the one hand, they had experienced firsthand the debilitating consequences of political frailty. On the other hand, they continued to cling to their sense of religious superiority. Thus, Abravanel's emphasis on the practical and magical superiority of Solomon's wisdom vis-à-vis that of gentiles not only catered to the tastes of Italian humanism. It was also a rhetorical tool for buttressing notions of religious superiority among the Sephardic exiles.

14 : THE TEMPLE
CONSTRUCTION, GLORY, DESTRUCTION

The Court of King Solomon and His Administration

Having discussed the different forms of wisdom and thereby drawn a distinction between Solomon and other kings—as well as between Solomon and other scholars—Abravanel goes on to underscore the power and majesty of Solomon's kingdom and court. To this end, he enlists his own experience from his time spent in the courts of Dom Afonso V in Portugal and the Catholic Monarchs in Castile. Thus, for example, Abravanel describes the three scribes of King Solomon (according to 1 Kings 4:2–3) as follows: "One was a scribe of law and rulings (*hamishpat vehadinim*); the other was a scribe of the king's taxes, finances, and holdings; and the third was a scribe of chronicles and the king's documents."[1] Likewise, Don Isaac understands the figure "Zabud the son of Nathan the principal officer, and the king's friend" (1 Kings 4:5) through the prism of an institution from his own time—the king's "favorites":

> For this was the practice of the kings to have a man sitting beside them at all times, one who could entertain them and eat with them, giving them joy and speaking to their hearts, someone with whom the kings could safely confide the deepest secrets of their hearts. Even today this is the practice among the kings of France, and in their language, they call this "companion" a *mignon*.[2]

In a similar vein, explaining Solomon's "twelve officers over all Israel who provided provisions for the king and his household" (1 Kings 4:7), Abravanel describes the services rendered by royal clerks—especially their care for and understanding of the danger of inflation and the royal deficit:

> So that the land in which [the king dwells] not be burdened by [the king's] upkeep, and in order to avoid the inflation of food prices, and so that nothing would be lacking to anyone who needed it, . . . Solomon wisely organized [a system of] officials [from the twelve tribes] throughout the land. And they were responsible for buying

food with the king's money. . . . And every official would support [the king] during his appointed month of the year, so that the king would never lack anything . . . [yet] without causing inflation.[3]

Don Isaac also describes the power of Solomon's military, noting the number of horses at his disposal—a fact that Don Isaac viewed in a positive light, despite its being a violation of the prohibition in Deuteronomy that forbids the king to amass many horses:

And indeed, this number of horses is immense. And I have never heard among the kings of the [gentile] nations, and I have never seen in the chronicles of any of their ancient monarchs, that there was ever a king under the sun who had . . . 40,000 horses during peace time for no other purpose except honor and glory. . . . And I believe that Solomon did not decide to increase the number of horses and cavalrymen out of hubris. . . . Rather, [he adopted] wise counsel [and his purpose was] that the kings around him would fear him, submit to him, and offer him tribute.[4]

The Jewish Temple and Christian Cathedrals

By comparing at the beginning of the commentary the details of Solomon's kingdom to kingdoms of Abravanel's time—in terms of the royal court, systems of administration, the economy, and the military—Abravanel laid the ground for a more dramatic analogy aimed at establishing the superiority of Judaism over other religions in the minds of his readers. Abravanel compared the Temple (its construction is described in detail in 1 Kings 6–8) to Christian churches, especially the Gothic cathedrals that dominated the skylines of European cities during his era. Abravanel's discussion of the Temple is particularly lengthy, covering dozens of pages. He doubtless considered it one of the climaxes of his commentary and one of its greatest innovations. As described by Ram Ben-Shalom, one reason for Don Isaac's particular interest in the Temple was related to its size in comparison to that of cathedrals—edifices quite familiar to the Spanish exiles, both from their homeland of Castile and Aragon and from their new Diaspora in Naples.[5] Abravanel writes at the end of his discussion:

And I have seen men of our nation and men of the nations of the world, they that understand among the people, who have thought that Solomon's building only contained those chambers (*batim*) mentioned in Scripture ... and have, for this reason, ruled and stated that the building [the Temple] was small in stature, for it had so few chambers, and more than these can be found in every city and every state of the land of Edom in their houses of prayer. And this [thought] occurred to them because they were drawn after the simple meaning of Scripture as if there existed in the Temple only those rooms mentioned in the text.[6]

Abravanel is referring here to the idea—prevalent among Christians as well as certain elements among the Jewish elites—that contemporary churches, and especially cathedrals, were far larger than the ancient Jewish temple in Jerusalem. This comparison was used to highlight the inferiority of Judaism vis-à-vis the glory and power of Christianity, a power given concrete expression in Gothic architecture. The denigration associated with the expulsion drove Abravanel to invert this comparison, touting the Temple as a source of pride and an example of Jewish superiority. For example, discussing the verse, "And for the house, he [Solomon] made windows of narrow lights" (1 Kings 6:4), Abravanel writes:

It seems that Solomon commanded that windows of glass be installed in the Temple so that light would enter but without anyone detecting [its source]. ... And they are called in the vernacular "vidrieras." And today also, it is the practice to install them in the walls of houses [of worship].[7]

Abravanel is referring here to the stained-glass windows of cathedrals (and perhaps other buildings, including some large synagogues), essentially superimposing this Gothic style onto the description of the Temple as it appears in Kings. Another similarity between the Temple and cathedrals is height: "And Josephus wrote that the Temple was like a tall tower with its apex in the sky."[8] Furthermore:

But the clear truth is that on top of the inner sanctum (*devir*), the outer sanctum (*heikhal*), and the courtyard (*ulam*) stood floors (*aliyot*), one atop the other. ... And the height of the Holy Temple, from floor to roof—meaning, [from the floor] to the first ceiling— was 30 cubits. And the height from this [first ceiling] upward [to the uppermost ceiling] was 90 cubits, the height of all three of the floors above the Temple. Therefore, the total height of the Temple, including all its floors, was 120 cubits.[9]

Later, Abravanel invokes the image of Abimelech's "tower of might" (from Judges 9:51), to convey the idea that height was one of the main principles of Solomon's construction scheme.[10] Unlike the "tabernacle built by Moses . . . for the needs of the hour," Solomon built the Temple as a "permanent sanctuary for all eternity."[11] This is why the dimensions of the tabernacle were doubled and sometimes even tripled in Solomon's Temple. Thus Solomon's blueprints, as understood by Abravanel, seem to imitate and even exceed the dimensions of the cathedrals in his era.

Another way in which Abravanel portrays the Temple as superior to the churches of his era is by drawing attention to the amount of gold Solomon used in its construction. Basing himself on Rashi and other exegetes, Abravanel calculates the total amount and value of gold needed to plate the inner and outer sanctums: "And this demonstrates that the gold used to plate the inner sanctum and the outer sanctum . . . was 1,800 talents . . . 22,140,000 ducats of pure gold according to the weight used in Italy."[12] But Abravanel does not end by citing this astronomical number. He goes on to elaborate upon the "glorious craftsmanship . . . used to smelt the gold," comparing it to the practices of "men today who know how to smelt gold and use it to write with as if it were ink."[13] These fantastical descriptions of the liquid gold used to plate the Temple are meant to create the impression of a truly immense sum. But "wonder not about this extreme amount of gold, for King David (peace be upon him) provided 3,000 talents of gold and 7,000 talents of silver to plate the chambers, . . . and all of this shows that [the matter] was from God."[14] Abravanel explicitly links the amount of gold used to build the Temple, and the great fortune at David's disposal, to religious ascendancy. Don Isaac thus adopted the Christian notion that economic power, expressed through the construction of eminent cathedrals, goes hand in hand with the superiority of the Christian faith. However, he inverted the association, using his discussion of the Temple to demonstrate that it is actually Judaism that is the supreme religion—not Christianity.

The Significance of the Date of the Temple's Construction

In addition to discussing the Temple's physical and architectural characteristics, Abravanel addresses the religious significance and symbolism expressed in the biblical narrative that describes its construction. The first allusion discussed by Abravanel is the date of the Temple's construction, 480 years after the Exodus. The fact that this number has a secret meaning is suggested by its recurrence twice in the history of the Jewish people:

When the children of Israel left Egypt, they built the tabernacle. From then until the construction of the Temple by the hand of Solomon, 480 years elapsed. Likewise, 480 years after that, the House of God was built yet again by Zerubbabel.[15]

The repetition of this number throughout the history of all three sanctuaries is no mere coincidence. Rather, it embodies a broader historical lesson that Abravanel explains as follows:

And just as the sanctuary built by Solomon . . . in terms of its sanctity and in terms of Solomon's perfection . . . was nevertheless certainly inestimably lower in sanctity and godliness in comparison to the tabernacle built by Moses . . . and by the same value was the construction of the Second Temple by Zerubbabel lower in sanctity and conjunction with God and the divine spirit [in comparison to] the building constructed by Solomon. . . . And the [relationship] between the three of them [the sanctuaries of Moses, Solomon, and Zerubbabel] was [characterized by] a perceptible decline in spirituality, sanctity, and godliness, a similar amount with each decline. It is as if during the time of the Second Temple, the children of Israel were extremely old and well along in years, and from that point forward, their vitality came to an end. . . . Until a spirit from upon high shall awaken us. . . . This is as Ezekiel mentioned at the end of his book: Mount Zion will be rebuilt and the fallen tabernacle of David reestablished, and the great house of the Lord will be upon high, and the glory of the latter house will be greater than that of the first.[16]

The repetition of the number 480 alludes to a cyclical process of gradual decline that continued up until the destruction of the Second Temple. But it also demonstrates the reverse cyclical process that will lead to a miraculous and messianic rise in power, from utter desolation to undisputed ascendancy—the end of exile and the building of the final Temple. In other words, the history of the Jewish people moves in a circular motion: it proceeds from Temple to destruction, and from destruction to Temple.

Allegorical Exegesis or Religious Exegesis?

Abravanel's second discussion of the allusions contained in the construction narrative revolves around the question of whether "the labor of the divine tabernacle and the construction of the Holy Temple which was constructed according to the same form . . . are a symbol, allegory, or allusion (*remez umashal vehe'arah*) to other scientific and divine matters. Or [perhaps] none of these are alluded to and these things were simply done and intended for themselves alone or for honor and glory."[17] Abravanel is raising here the issue of whether it is appropriate to apply allegorical exegesis to the high-resolution description of the Temple's dimensions and vessels as presented in the book of Kings. His discussion seems to begin by acknowledging, in principle, the validity of allegorical exegesis. He summarizes the contents of this exegetical tradition by citing Josephus, the Talmud and Midrash, Maimonides, Gersonides, and "the Christian sages," emphasizing the cosmological and metaphysical messages they find embedded in the text. After these summaries, Abravanel reaches two conclusions of his own. First, "it is not proper that we seek an allusion or moral in every one of the individual things mentioned in the account of the tabernacle and the construction of the Solomon's sanctuary."[18] Second, "I deem it improbable that the matter to which this edifice would allude would be a detail of the sciences, of those things that can be obtained through speculation and inquiry. For the Blessed One did not need to allude through His tabernacle and Temple to matters that are known to and attained by learned men."[19] Thus, on the one hand, Abravanel wishes to minimize the use of allegorical exegesis in his reading of the construction narrative, while on the other hand, he wishes to shift the use of allegory—to the extent that it should be used—from cosmology and metaphysics to something more sublime and unique, "that it should instill within us belief in the law of the Torah and that which can be achieved through its commandments so that the allusion and parable should be a guide to a person regarding what he should do."[20] The structure of the Temple should not be understood as a microcosm of the structure of the world, as the philosophical and metaphysical approaches would have it. Rather, it points to the requisite knowledge for proper religious behavior.

We will cite some examples. Abravanel describes the cherubs at length, dealing both with their physical dimensions and with the allegorical message their features convey. Abravanel cites Maimonides's interpretation, according to which the cherubs allude to the existence of the separate intellects. Abravanel adopts this interpretation in part but embellishes it in two respects: First, he notes that the cherubs of Solomon, unlike the cherubs of Moses, drew down divine influence not only to the Torah but also to the place in which the Temple is situated. And second, the two cherubs are "in the form of two small children . . . one a male, the other a female, alluding [to the fact] that every man and woman from the children of Israel should from their childhood spend their days, constantly [studying] God's Torah. . . . And by virtue of the Torah they learn in their youth, they will spread their wings above and cleave to the heavens."[21] The cherubs thus point to the transition from the nomadism of the tabernacle to God's permanent presence in the Temple. However, it is important for Don Isaac to teach his reader a lesson that can be applied in a state of itinerancy (such as exile): by studying the Torah and the commandments, man and woman alike can become Temple cherubs upon whom divine influence can rest.

Perhaps sympathetic to the harsh conditions undergone by the Spanish exiles, Abravanel is careful to distinguish between ideal religious behavior and its reward. Abravanel interprets the symbolism of the curtain (*parokhet*) and the wall (*kotel*), the barriers that demarcate the outer and inner sanctum, as an allusion to the fact that "the divine Torah should be observed by a person sincerely and not in order to receive a reward."[22] However, immediately after laying out this strict distinction between religious behavior and its recompense, Don Isaac interprets the meanings of the three vessels in the outer sanctum (the table, the candelabra, and the altar) as alluding to the three types of reward a person receives for sincere observance of the Torah and its commandments: "the table . . . and the shewbread . . . allude [to the fact that] that a righteous person will never be abandoned and will never lack bread, and that his wealth and honor will not come to him through happenstance, according to the dictates of nature, but rather [will be determined] by divine providence."[23] Likewise, "the candelabra alludes to the second type of reward which is a necessary consequence of observing the Torah—that is, the reward of the soul—wisdom and science."[24] Abravanel is not referring to just any type of science: he has in mind wisdom that a Jew ought to adopt—"the true wisdom which . . . agrees with the principles of the Torah."[25] Finally, Abravanel explains that "the incense altar alludes to the third type of reward that emanates from the Torah . . . and that is the eternal endurance of the soul after a person's death."[26] Thus, the Temple alludes to the fact that a Jew who adheres to his religion merits that his body, intellect, and soul will be conjoined, each one in turn, with God and is also granted a resilience that appears to be compensation for (or perhaps as a protection against) the harsh and denigrating experience of expulsion.

The Historical Cycle: Rise and Fall

Don Isaac concludes his long discussion of the Temple with a statement that is surprising in its simplicity:

> All of this . . . is to say that everything done by the nation of Edom in Rome, the capital of their faith, as well in other states, that which they made in their houses of prayer, is considered as void and naught when compared to the three structures [the tabernacle and two Temples] built as sanctuaries to the Lord. And all of these are but a drop in the sea in comparison to the house of the Lord that will be built in the future with the coming of our Messiah, may he appear speedily.[27]

This raises the question: Did Don Isaac really spill so much ink to strengthen his readers' feelings of religious superiority? Perhaps the gap between the sheer length of his discussion, which encompasses a wide array of sources and ideas, and the seemingly simple conclusion it provides can be explained by going back to Abravanel's autobiographical introduction to his commentary on Kings. There, he declares the goals he wishes to achieve by writing his commentary—namely, "to commemorate the destruction of our Temple and its glory, and the exiles that have befallen our nation."[28] Facing the destruction of Spanish Jewry, Don Isaac offers an account of the Temple's beauty and grandeur. In contrast to the abandoned home of the Spanish exile, the Christian churches appeared to be at the height of their power and glory. Nevertheless, the exegete can disinter the Temple's long-lost greatness and represent it within the imagination of the exiles as a tangible and beneficial religious alternative to Christianity. We can thus understand the breadth of Don Isaac's discussions as an attempt to give his reader an important experience: to spend as much time as possible in the Temple by delving into the details of its dimensions and construction. It is a literary tour, reestablishing for the reader the messianic link between the Temple's ancient glory and the future glory of a temple still to come. Thus, the Spanish Jewish exile is given a religious edifice of his own and can see in the destruction of his community a way station on the path to a messianic redemption.

But we cannot truly understand Don Isaac's rhetoric without discussing the destruction of the Temple, the second act in the narrative of the Temple's construction. Don Isaac proposes two ways of understanding the destruction of the Temple and the exile that followed it: the first is to attribute it to the religious failings of the children of Israel, a consequence of their refusal to observe the Torah and its commandments; and the second is to see in it a natural process of decay and decline. In the middle of a discussion dedicated to glorifying the Temple, Abravanel suddenly slips into a sobering commentary on God's words to Solomon in 1 King 6:11–13: "And the word of the Lord came to Solomon, saying, concerning this house which you are building, if you will walk in my statutes, and execute my judgments, and keep all my commandments to walk in them; then will I perform my word with you, which I spoke unto David your father: And I will dwell among the children of Israel, and will not forsake my people Israel." Abravanel writes: "For Solomon was very powerful to construct the Temple as a wondrous structure. . . . Therefore, God warned him and said: the house which you are building, think not O Solomon that it will remain standing forever."[29] Even though the Temple far outshone any Christian church, its grandiose dimensions were no guarantee of its eternity. Eternity is not a consequence of power expressed through architectural feats. Rather, it depends on proper religious behavior—which is difficult, and perhaps impossible, to maintain for a long period of time. This is why Don Isaac sees in God's mention of the condition for the building's endurance ("if you will walk in my statutes") an allusion to its destruction, an event described at the very end of Kings.

The decline in the Israelites' religious behavior is coupled with a natural explanation for the destruction. In his commentary on 1 Kings 11, which recounts Solomon's penchant for gentile women and pagan gods, Don Isaac explicitly addresses the natural process that chipped away at Solomon's historically unprecedented economic, political, and religious prosperity, attributing that process to the onset of ethical and religious weakness in Solomon's final years. According to Abravanel, "All these perfections [wisdom, might, and wealth] were possessed by Solomon in his adolescence and youth. But look again and you will see that in his old age, they were all taken from him."[30] The leader's conjunction with God, as related in the narrative of Solomon, is a natural process of empowerment and attainment of wondrous achievements. But it is balanced by decline in one's old age, the consequence of negative natural influences (desire, women, idolatry, and so on). Abravanel summarizes the account of Solomon as follows: "Let not the wise man glory in his wisdom [Jer. 9:22]. . . . This was all said about King Solomon. . . . And [God] said to him that he should not have gloried and thought that these belonged to him, since the only glory comes from cleaving to the divine, drawing down and bringing perfection."[31] According to Abravanel, the perfection evident in the tale of Solomon and the Temple's construction points to Solomon's unique connection with God and the Jewish religious superiority that follows from it. But conjunction with God is a temporary state, and it wanes with the natural powers of every leader, as we will see below.

Iberian Jewry: Fall and Rise

The natural cyclical process of a physical body's growing strength, followed by debilitating weakness, is used by Abravanel as a framework to explain the historical decline embodied in destruction and exile—as well as the resurgence and renaissance that should follow it. It is thus no surprise to find at the end of Abravanel's commentary on Kings, which describes the destruction of the First Temple, an elaboration upon this historical conception:

> Behold we have learned from the histories of this book (*sipurei sefer hazeh*), that the children of Judah and Israel were all exiled because of their wicked actions. . . . But indeed, not all were exiled at once, but rather at separate times. And just as the decay of natural, vital, and psychic powers begins with the limbs farthest away from the heart and then proceeds to those closest to it, and last to decay is the power of the heart, so too the first [to be exiled] of the children of Israel were those in the Transjordan, who like the limbs are farthest away from the heart. And after them were Samaria and its cities which were closer to the heart, and finally Jerusalem and the house of the Lord—the source of life and strength—were destroyed.[32]

The exile of Israel and Judah is the result of religious erosion, caused by the gradual and natural diminution of the nation's spiritual power. The construction of the Temple constituted the peak of the nation's historical development, but it was also the beginning of the end. This process of gradual decay and decomposition is portrayed by Don Isaac as a process by which the most vital components for the nation's existence (Judah, Jerusalem, and the Temple) are gradually distilled from the rest. This central element of the nation, described as the heart of the national body, will ultimately become the nucleus of a new, glorious development—the Jewish Diaspora in the Iberian peninsula:

> And you should know that kings and magnates of the rulers of the gentiles had already come with the king of Babylon to Jerusalem

and led the Jews to their lands, and among them was Pyrrhus who was the king of Sepharad. Indeed the great Hercules who was from Greece traveled throughout the world to conquer lands with his heroism and his wisdom which was great, and [he came] to the Western land, and after so many heroic acts in the conquest of lands he came with many ships and a great army to Sepharad and settled there, and ruled throughout the land of Sepharad. And because he longed for his native land, he went to the land of Italy and from there to the land of Greece, and he was one of the magnates who went to destroy the great city of Troy for the third time. And when Hercules left Sepharad he bestowed his kingdom upon the son of his sister who was called Hispan [Hispanus], and on whose name the whole land of Sepharad is called in the vernacular, Hispania. And this Hispan had but one daughter, whom Pyrrhus, who was also a Greek magnate, took as wife, and he was present at the destruction of the First Temple, and brought from Jerusalem members of the tribes of Judah, Benjamin, and Simon, and Levites and Cohenites, many persons who willingly came with him.[33]

Without delving into the details of this foundational myth, which has already been discussed by scholars such as Yitzhak Baer, Haim Beinart, and Ram Ben-Shalom,[34] it is important for our purposes to discuss the direct connection Don Isaac makes between the destruction of the First Temple and the common foundation of the kingdom of Spain and the Iberian Jewish community: the end of the kingdom of Judah is the beginning of the glorious Spanish Diaspora. Basing himself on Castilian chronicles from the periods of King Don Alfonso el Sabio (the wise; 1221–84) and other sources (including the writings of Isidorus Hispalensis [c. 556–636]),[35] Abravanel links the destruction of the First Temple to the fall of Troy, the beginning of one of Rome's founding legends. Thus, Abravanel linked the emigration of Jews to the West with the rise of the kingdoms of Western Europe. One should not see in Abravanel's account an attempt to offer an accurate historical picture. Rather, it represents the internalization of literary and mythical traditions meant to antedate the arrival of the Jews in Spain from the destruction of the Second Temple to the destruction of the first. As noted by scholars, taking such a narrative to heart would have some clear utilitarian benefits: it would mean that the Jews had arrived in Spain long before Jesus's crucifixion and were thus absolved of any guilt for his death, that the

Jews had had a hand in the founding of the Spanish kingdom, and that the community as a whole could boast a pure and noble bloodline. However, most importantly for the logic of Abravanel's historiographical perspective, the Jews who were exiled to Spain did not return to Zion and did not participate in the construction of the Second Temple:

> And the Jews settled in the kingdom of Spain from then until today, and they spread out to all the cities. . . . And they did not return to Jerusalem at the time of the Second Temple, for they said that that remembrance (*peqidah*) was not a complete redemption. . . . Therefore, they will not return until when the Lord will return again the captivity of Zion, and the children will return to their border from Assyria, Cush, and the islands of the sea.[36]

In Abravanel's view, the refusal of Spanish Jews to return to Jerusalem during the Second Temple era suggests that the expulsion of Spanish Jewry is an event belonging to a messianic age, a time in which God scatters the most ancient and glorious of communities to lay the ground for the true redemption. According to Abravanel at the end of his commentary, the Second Temple era "was not a complete redemption but rather a temporary and frail remembrance [by God]. . . . And it demonstrates that even today we still remain in the first exile, until He [God] gathers the scattered people of Israel and brings it to its land and rebuilds its city."[37]

Here the historical cycle draws to a close. Just as decline from the peak of power, embodied in Solomon's kingdom, to the lowest point of the First Temple's destruction gave rise to the Spanish Diaspora, so too the declining powers of the Spanish Diaspora—a process of decline that ended in the tragedy of the expulsion—will soon lead to complete redemption. The Sephardic exiles are heirs to a long and glorious history, tied directly to the kingdoms of David and Solomon. The exile and dispersion of this unique elite marks the beginning of their messianic return of to their historical roots, Jerusalem and the Temple.

The idea of the Spanish expulsion as a messianic or premessianic age is a centerpiece of a series of books written by Abravanel some years after his commentary on Kings. What is important for our purposes is that, immediately after the expulsion, Don Isaac proposed a theological and historical model that could create for the exiles a self-image as an elite, with a distinguished and ancient past and a task of historic and messianic proportions.

The tale of the founding of Spain at the end of Kings is thus not the story of a great community that is no more, but rather a call on the Sephardic exiles to preserve their shared historical background in their new communities, creating a new Sephardic network in the Mediterranean Diaspora and later in northern Europe and the New World. In light of this literary, religious, and political project, we can now better understand the title Don Isaac gives himself at the beginning of his commentary: "Says Isaac son of my master, the great officer in Israel, Don Judah Abravanel, from the stock of Jesse the Bethlehemite, from the seed of David, prince and commander of people, from a nation scattered and separated, the exile of Jerusalem which is in Spain."[38] In other words, Don Isaac was not content to merely reestablish the community of Sephardic exiles through his literary, historical, and theological oeuvre. He also offered himself up as their leader.

15 : THE MILITARY CRISIS IN ITALY AT THE END OF THE FIFTEENTH CENTURY

About a year after he completed his commentary on Kings—"at the end of the month of Marcheshvan, the year 'the sound of rejoicing and salvation' (1494)"[1]—Don Isaac completed his next work, *Rosh amanah*. Its apparent purpose was to defend Maimonides's thirteen principles of faith from the criticisms leveled against them by later Jewish philosophers, such as Rabbi Hasdai Crescas and Rabbi Joseph Albo. This work embodies the same Jewish apologetic approach that we have seen in other works by Abravanel. In the introduction, Don Isaac expresses his concern for the wavering religious faith of the Sephardic exiles: "I was astounded to see my nation, the dear children of Zion, impoverished in their knowledge of the fundamentals of the Lord's Torah and the principles of belief in the God of the Hebrews, belief therein being necessary for they who are the good and the upright."[2] Abravanel's intricate defense of the Maimonidean principles of faith, like his commentary on Kings, offers an ideological framework that can preserve Judaism during an age of expulsions and flight, when sturdy communities and organized institutions are desiderata.

Before long, Don Isaac's ambitious project to restore and rebuild Spanish Jewry in a new land fell prey to the great crisis that convulsed the Italian peninsula between 1494 and 1559. However, before describing these events, it is important to recall that this was the third major crisis that upended Abravanel's life. After the falling out between the nobility and crown with the rise of João II to the throne of Portugal, and after the succession crisis of Castile that gave rise to an alliance between the Catholic Monarchs and the Inquisition (the ultimate cause of the Spanish expulsion in 1492), Abravanel found himself thrust at the end of his life into the midst of an international political and military crisis taking place on Italian soil and continuing for more than fifty years.

The Collapse of the Italian Equilibrium

The Italian humanist historian Francesco Guicciardini (1483–1540) opens his famous work *Storia d'Italia* with a description of the balance of power that had prevailed in Italy during the second half of the fifteenth century. In 1454, after a long period of warfare, the Italian states reached a state of equilibrium enshrined in the Treaty of Lodi. However, this peace did not achieve the much wished-for stability between the five great states of Italy: Venice, Florence, Milan, Rome, and Naples. The wars of the first half of the century gave way to a diplomacy of suspicion, which produced a number of local military scuffles. Guicciardini summarizes this fragile balance as follows: "Full of emulation and jealousy among themselves, they did not cease to assiduously observe what the others were doing, each of them reciprocally aborting all the plans whereby any of the others might become more powerful and renowned. This did not result in rendering the peace less stable; on the contrary, it aroused greater vigilance in all of them to carefully stamp out any sparks which might be the cause of a new conflagration."[3]

One example of the tensions that characterized the second half of the fifteenth century was the alliance forged between Duke Ludovico Sforza (1452–1508), the governor of Milan, and the French kings Louis XI (1461–83) and Charles VIII (1483–98). Together they hoped to oppose the house of Aragon, the dynasty ruling Naples at the time. In the first half of the century, the French house of Anjou and the house of Aragon had fought over control of the southern Italian kingdom. After many years of war, Alfonso V of Aragon finally emerged victorious in 1442. The alliance between France and Milan was based on the former's claim to the throne of Naples and southern Italy. It exemplifies the practice, common to Italian states during the era, of enlisting the intervention of larger foreign states in their local politics. It was this policy that would lead to the collapse of the delicate balance of power in Italy. Thus, the two reasons for the outbreak of war at the end of the century were the unremitting tension between the Italian states and the use of foreign intervention to settle intra-Italian disputes.[4]

Another explanation is the shrinking of the elite classes heading the Italian states to a limited aristocracy that enjoyed exclusive rights. These elitist regimes conflicted with the explicit interests of large swaths of Italian society whose members believed that they deserved to play a more active role in public life. As a result, the loyalty of Italian subjects to their leaders began to unravel, leading to rebellions and, at the end of the century, the over-throw of several monarchs and rulers: the house of Medici in Florence, King Afonso in Naples, and Sforza in Milan. Thus, a variety of factors, domestic and foreign alike, laid the groundwork for the outbreak of war as the century drew to a close. Italy became a battleground between three great European powers—France, Castile and Aragon, and the Holy Roman Empire—and a stage for numerous domestic revolutions within the Italian states.

The French Invasion and Its Consequences

In 1494, King Charles VIII of France—at the behest of the house of Sforza in Milan, the Venetian Republic, and Pope Alexander IV—invaded the Italian peninsula.[5] One of the king's objectives was to conquer Naples and wrest control of the kingdom from the Aragonese monarchs—especially Alfonso II, who had assumed the throne of Naples after the death of his father, Ferrante, in 1494. For Charles VIII this was merely a means to an end: the French king wished to use the war as a stepping-stone for launching a crusade against the Ottoman Empire, which had risen from the ashes of Byzantium and had grown into a formidable threat close to home. When Charles VIII reached Rome, Alfonso II abdicated the throne in favor his son Ferrandino. On January 21, 1495, Alfonso fled to Sicily. Abravanel, it seems, followed the king into exile.[6] On February 22, Charles VIII entered Naples. A few weeks earlier, on January 17 and 18, chaos broke out in the city. Opponents of the king launched attacks against those Jews and New Christians who had chosen to remain in Naples instead of fleeing with Ferrandino, and all the city's Jewish quarters were exposed to pogroms.[7] This was the third time Abravanel lost all of his property, not to mention some of his writings and books. The combination of the French invasion and the outbreak of major pogroms in the Jewish neighborhoods destroyed any chance of reestablishing Spanish Jewry on the basis of settlement and acclimation in the kingdom of Naples.

On March 31, the Holy League was forged—an alliance between the pope, the Catholic Monarchs, and the Holy Roman Emperor Maximilian von Habsburg (1459–1519), as well as the Italian states of Venice and Milan. Its purpose was to oppose the French invasion of Italy. By mid-May, King Ferrandino had launched an offensive against the French forces in Calabria. He was assisted by Spanish troops commanded by Gonzalvo de Cordoba, el Gran Capitán (1453–1515). The general had been dispatched by King Don

Fernando of Aragon. Historians believe that Abravanel had made Gonzalvo's acquaintance back in Spain. In 1495, they met again, apparently in Messina, Sicily, while el Gran Capitán was en route to Calabria. Abravanel's nephew Don Joseph Abravanel would meet Gonzalvo later in Messina in 1501. More importantly, Don Isaac's son Judah Abravanel would eventually become his personal physician in Naples—serving in this position from 1503 to 1507.[8]

By the end of May, Charles VIII had withdrawn from Naples. Alfonso relinquished the Neapolitan crown and retired to a monastery in Palermo—this was after his son Ferrandino, informed him that he had no intention of returning the crown to him after the French were expelled from the city. When Ferrandino returned to Naples on July 7, 1495, he was met with opposition and numerous challenges—the beginning of the end of the Aragonese dynasty in South Italy. Ferrandino passed away on October 7, 1496. This only sped up the decline of the dynasty, which would finally come to an end in 1501. In 1503, el Gran Capitán annexed the kingdom of Naples to Aragon and Castile. Abravanel, who had left Naples along with Alfonso II, had no interest in returning to Naples during such turbulent times. Thus ended Don Isaac's service to the house of Aragon.[9]

Don Isaac in Corfu and Monopoli

In the midst of these dramatic historical circumstances, Abravanel resolved to embark from Sicily for Corfu, an island under Venetian hegemony, as a way station on his way to Salonika.[10] The decision to move with his family to territories under Ottoman control was shared by many exiles who left Naples after the litany of crises precipitated by the French invasion.[11] As early as 1493, Abravanel had sent his third son, Samuel, to Salonika to study in the yeshiva of Rabbi Joseph Fassi.[12] When Abravanel arrived in Corfu in the summer of 1495, he acclimated quickly to the local Jewish community, which was now home to more than a few Spanish exiles. In the introduction to his commentary on Deuteronomy, part of which was composed in Corfu, Abravanel recounts: "I entered a ship in the heart of the ocean, and by God's grace, I came to the Island of Corfu and settled there."[13] In Corfu, Don Isaac would reunite with prominent Iberian-Jewish figures, including David Ibn Yahya from Lisbon and Eliezer al-Tansi from Castile, whom he had met in 1492. Like him, they had lived in Naples for some time after the expulsion. Both men held Don Isaac in high esteem, as we learn from a letter penned by Saul Hakohen in 1507.[14] In this account, Hakohen attests to Abravanel's status and prestige among certain circles of Jewish exiles—perhaps indicating the success of Abravanel's literary and homilet-ical "propaganda," which we analyzed in our discussion of his commentary on Kings.

The Sephardic émigrés in Corfu, like the Jewish community as whole, participated in the Venetian sea trade. They lived on the border between Venice and the Ottoman Empire and viewed firsthand the conflict between these two great powers. As described by Abravanel shortly after his arrival in Corfu (or shortly after his departure), the Sephardic exiles seemed more invested in survival than in their Judaism:

> After seeing men of virtue begging at the gates of cities, abandon-ing life in the hereafter, chasing after temporary life like rebellious slaves—and all their days they are diligent about their money and the profits which they desire—. . . with dice and games, with jest and light-headedness they run about. And towards God, the begin-ning of his path and the giving of his Torah, no man looks even in a dream.[15]

With the war raging in Italy, and the atmosphere of desperation and de-spair that descended upon the Sephardic exiles who were forced to flee from Naples, Abravanel threw himself into his exegetical activity with re-doubled vigor. Between his arrival in Corfu in the summer of 1495 and his final home in Venice in 1503, Abravanel completed an impressive list of commentaries and treatises: *Zevah pesah* (a commentary on the Hagga-dah), *Nahalat avot* (a commentary on *Pirkei avot*), *Ma'ayanei hayeshu'ah* (a commentary on Daniel), *Yeshu'ot meshiho* (a commentary on the mes-sianic Aggadot in the Talmud and midrash), *yeshu'ah* (a commentary on the messianic prophecies in the Bible), *Shamayim hadashim* (a philosoph-ical treatise on the creation of the world), a commentary on Isaiah, a com-mentary on the Twelve Minor Prophets, and *Mif'alot elohim*. It is impor-tant to note, however, that in Corfu, Don Isaac only began this ambitious list of literary projects. The majority of these works were completed in the city of Monopoli, an important port between Bari and Brindisi on Italy's Adriatic coast, where Abravanel moved in 1496. After settling in Monopoli, Abravanel abandoned his plan to travel to Salonika or the Ottoman Empire. Furthermore, his decision to settle down in Monopoli, only recently con-quered by the Venetians, demonstrated some measure of faith in the Vene-tian Republic and a desire to tie his fate to its. If after the French invasion of Naples and the fall of the Aragonese dynasty, Don Isaac gave up on the idea of making a home for himself in Naples, perhaps we can see in his decisions to leave Corfu and return to the Italian peninsula the gradual integration of his family into the culture, economy, and society of Italy in the late fifteenth century.[16]

In the introductions to his commentaries, Don Isaac recounts his travels, as well as the events that took place during this period and prompted him to write. For example, in the introduction to his commentary on Deuteronomy he writes:

> I came to the island of Corfu. . . . And the Lord made it happen that that which I had written on this book came to me [meaning he found the manuscript of his commentary on Deuteronomy, a project he had begun many years earlier]. . . . And my soul reveled, and joy seized it and kissed it. And [my soul] said: I will add to its greatness and its glory as follows.[17]

It seems that when he fled from Naples, Abravanel had been forced to abandon the bulk of his library and most of his writings. When he arrived in Corfu, he found in the possession of one of the exiles a manuscript of the commentary he had begun to write in Portugal—the incomplete commentary on Deuteronomy that he had sent as a gift to Yehiel de Pisa in 1472. This unlikely and serendipitous find prompted him, so he recounts, to complete the commentary almost twenty years after he had begun writing it.

In other autobiographical introductions, Don Isaac describes his bitter feelings about his old age, his sense of isolation, and his misfortune following the expulsion from Spain and the wars in Italy:

> For I have become too old to be a man. My strength has left me. . . . And the light of my eyes is also not with me. . . . My heart is dizzy, evil and bitter, and though long ago . . . I was a man of life with many deeds, I have now been deprived of all grace. And I, where have I come? To a nation whose tongue I know not, and whose speech I have not within me.[18]

Such radical fluctuations in temperament—from utter despair to sudden bursts of energy and hope—characterize the many works composed by Abravanel during this period, all of which sought to console, appease, and reanimate the broken body and soul of the Sephardic exile.[19]

16 : A DEFENSE OF JUDAISM IN THE MIDST OF THE STORM

While Don Isaac certainly suffered from unfortunate circumstances, it is important not to be misled by the air of despair that pervades the texts quoted at the end of chapter 15. The Italian crisis elicited a very strong literary response from Don Isaac, one that produced many commentaries and treatises. Perhaps the sheer scope of Abravanel's literary endeavors was intended to match the size of the challenge he envisioned before him. Perhaps it was a consequence of his distance during these years from large Jewish population centers. Perhaps he was driven to write by the perceived needs of the hour. Or perhaps it was an internal or personal need, an attempt to connect himself to a Jewish community that had been scattered across the Mediterranean. Of course, we cannot say for sure. In this chapter and the following one, we will try to characterize two major types of responses that arise from Abravanel's imposing literary oeuvre composed in the wake of the expulsion, the first being psychological and cosmological and the second being messianic—always bearing in mind that focusing on these two trends hardly exhausts the wide range of topics discussed by Abravanel in the many commentaries and works he composed between 1495 and 1502.

The Printing of Rosh amanah, Zevah pesah, and Nahalat avot

We will begin with a trilogy of works that Abravanel composed during the start of the war in Italy and continuing after he moved from Sicily to Corfu: *Rosh amanah* (The pinnacle of Amanah [faith], 1494), *Zevah pesah* (Paschal sacrifice, 1496), and *Nahalat avot* (Heritage of the fathers, 1496). He completed the trilogy after his arrival in Monopoli. If we disregard the short respite during which Don Isaac devoted his time to completing his commentary on Deuteronomy—having discovered his old draft of the work, to his great surprise and elation—these three works can be said to have been written consecutively. It is therefore no surprise to find all three together in a single volume (the first printed book to contain Abravanel's writings) that was published in Istanbul in 1505 by the printing house of David and Samuel Nahmias.[1]

Each work in the volume is introduced with its own title page, which contains a poem by Judah Abravanel, surrounded by a subtle frame composed of animals and tree branches. As shown by scholars of the early Hebrew printing press, such as Adri Offenberg and Abraham Yaari,[2] this frame was brought from the printing house of Eliezer Alantansi, in which the Nahmias brothers had apparently worked before the expulsion. Scholars have surmised that the Nahmias brothers joined the Abravanel family on their voyage from Valencia to Naples in 1492. Can we can conclude from the ties between Alantansi, the Nahmias brothers, Don Isaac, and Judah Abravanel that the composition, production, and printing of the volume was a joint endeavor? We have no way of knowing for sure, but the correlation between the order in which the works were written and their organization within the single volume—as well as the short time that elapsed between the composition of the works and their preparation for printing—all suggest that the author, printers, and their assistants planned the project together.

It should be noted that the Nahmias brothers printed the halakhic compendium *Arba'ah turim* in 1493, and in 1505 they printed a Pentateuch that included *Haftarot*, megillot, and the commentaries of Rashi, Radak, and Abraham Ibn Ezra.[3] Thus, after publishing the *Arba'ah turim*, which covers most areas of practical halakhic observance, the Nahmias brothers went on to publish two other works (the Pentateuch and the writings of Abravanel) that serve as auxiliaries to services in the synagogue and rituals at home (the reading of the Pentateuch and megillot, the recitation of the Haggadah, and the study of *Pirkei Avot*). If this program of publication was a consideration shared by the author and printers, the volume should be understood as a collection of commentaries on ritual texts—the Haggadah and *Pirkei avot*, the latter traditionally read in Sephardic synagogues on the sabbaths between Passover and Pentecost. These are prefaced by *Rosh amanah*, which contains a short overview of the fundamental principles of the Jewish faith.

Rosh amanah

The logic used to organize the works included in the 1505 edition suggests that, before delving into commentaries focusing on Jewish ritual, Don Isaac wished to ensure that his Jewish contemporaries were still interested in Jewish rituals at all—a pressing concern in the aftermath of the expulsion. At least, this seems to be the intended purpose Abravanel's defense of Maimonides's thirteen principles. In practice, Don Isaac moved the discussion away from the theoretical question of whether or not Judaism has dogmas or principles and toward a discourse that was more heavily colored by social and practical concerns. Instead of viewing Maimonides's principles as the cornerstone of the Jewish faith, Don Isaac proposed a more relativistic and social approach. This is demonstrated, for example, in the following paragraph in the sixth chapter of the treatise:

> Those principles and foundations put forth by Maimonides are not merely principles of faith or religion. Rather, [Maimonides] intended them to be principles of Judaism such that he who believed in them would be included in that "Israel" about which the Mishna said, "All of Israel have a share in the world to come. . . . Even if one knows nothing else of the Torah, belief in these principles is sufficient to acquire spiritual perfection."[4]

In chapter 11, Don Isaac proceeds with his argument and explains the cumulative psychological impact of the principles, making recourse to an analogy drawn from Aristotelian physics. He explains how every natural entity is a combination of matter and form. If its conditions—*hakhanot* ("preparations" or "dispositions"), in the terminology of the Middle Ages— undergo change, its form may change as well. Like objects in nature, the Jews are also a combination of form and matter. And like natural entities, they too may change their form (that is, their faith) if external conditions shift dramatically, as happened after the expulsion:

> Beliefs are actualized in a man's heart and soul in the same way in which natural forms are actualized and fixed in their subject. Natural generation necessarily depends upon prior preparation . . . relevant to the form that is being actualized. There is an analogy to this. For water to receive the form of air it must be heated and must expand. In this way its matter is prepared for receiving the form of air.[5]

There is thus no difference between the form taken on by a natural entity like water and the religious form of a human being: both are contingent on prior causes and conditions that may elicit a change in form. In times of crisis, it is vital to be cognizant of the conditions that preserve the religious form of the Jewish individual:

> Thus, knowledge and study, the pursuit of experience and its investigation, and the use of the senses with respect to those things which

bring one to belief, are the dispositions and propaedeutic (*hakha-not vehaqadamot*) which bring a person to faith. There is no doubt that seeking these dispositions is a matter of will and choice and that they can be acquired over time. After these dispositions, however, which the soul acquires over time, are acquired, the form of the belief which follows from them is fixed in the heart and soul of the man.[6]

The adoption of a religious belief is the product of a process that combines free will and necessity. A person can freely accumulate knowledge and experience, creating within herself or himself the necessary dispositions—what today we might call a psychological and cognitive foundation—for accepting religious faith. Seymour Feldman has shown that Abravanel's emphasis on free choice during the preliminary stage before the acceptance of the principles is intended to repudiate the deterministic views of Rabbi Hasdai Crescas.[7] For his part, Crescas ascribed no role to free will when it came to the acceptance of religious principles.[8] Don Isaac emphasizes that while preliminary acquaintance with religion is a relatively free process, acceptance itself "happens suddenly with no choice and no will."[9] The moment one's soul has internalized a critical mass of knowledge and experience about a certain belief, the belief is accepted—naturally and necessarily. Here we see the reason for Abravanel's interest in Maimonides's principles of faith. Abravanel's chief concern was not a technical or scholastic question about whether Judaism could be predicated on a limited number of principles. Rather, he was interested in determining the critical mass of knowledge necessary to leave an imprint on a Jew and ensure that she or he would remain within the framework of Jewish faith, community, and history. How is the Jewish form to be reimprinted upon the Spanish Jewish exiles during a time of radical historical flux? This is the question Abravanel sets out to answer. It is thus no surprise that Don Isaac's discussion of Maimonides's thirteen principles is situated at the very beginning of the first printed volume of Abravanel's writings. The discussion, which revolves around the question of the minimal ideological conditions necessary to ensure the continuity of the Jewish social and religious framework, was viewed by the printers—and perhaps also by Abravanel—as a preface that offered the foundations for the more in-depth treatment of Judaism that we will discuss presently.

Zevah pesah

In *Zevah pesah*, Abravanel takes the next step, going beyond the bare minimum of knowledge required to remain a Jew; offering an expansive, indepth discussion; and painting a cosmological and psychological scene around the story of Passover—with the goal of impressing the Sephardic exile and having her or him once again embrace Jewish history. To this end, Abravanel is careful even in his introduction to focus his reader's attention on the crises, expulsions, and exiles undergone by Don Isaac himself, allowing the reader to identify closely with him and his experiences. The narrative is meticulously crafted. The course of the author's life is portrayed as a cyclical tale of ebbs and flows, ending in a nadir. That is a crisis that, on the one hand, includes the Passover of 1496, celebrated with the specter of the French invasion and the destruction of the Jewish community in Naples, and, on the other hand, is infused with deep nostalgia for a lost home, Iberia:

> For I have heard those who say, behold the day comes, the festival of festivals, the Passover of God, when He freed prisoners from house of bondage. Behold it is His time, a time of love. And now my soul is poured out upon me. I find trouble and sorrow, and my soul is desolate and silent. I remember the days of old. They are my festivals and the joy of my Passover, when the secret of God was upon my tent, when my wife and children were like olive plants around my table, my boys [sitting] around it.[10]

Don Isaac wrote the commentary as the festival approached. According to his own account, he completed it the day before, on "the fourteenth, the eve of Passover [5]556 [April 7, 1496]."[11] The juxtaposition of the approaching Passover with the historical circumstances in which Abravanel finds himself yields the greatest of ironies: the difficult and all-encompassing trials experienced by the Jews at the end of the fifteenth century stand in stark contrast to the religious memory of the Exodus. The dissonance is a painful one. Abravanel goes into further detail and contrasts the upcoming holiday to the glorious celebrations he had once experienced in Portugal and Castile. Through this comparison, he projects his own image as an émigré torn between past and present, even going so far as to vividly describe his own emotions, mental crisis, and depression. His nostalgia for his once glorious past stands in for the yearnings, nostalgia, and longing of Sephardic Jews collectively, and it is meant to strengthen their identification with the emotional drama of their leader.

In the preface that discusses exile, expulsion, melancholy, and longing, the commentary is presented as comfort for Abravanel in his personal despair and for the Sephardic Jewish community in its national despair:

> I have said: it is time to act for the Lord, to interpret the tales and wise words of Passover, to comprehend the meaning of exile and its causes, and the ways of redemption and its wonders, including passages and homilies with honorable explanations. . . . I call this treatise "*Zevah pesah*" [Ex. 12:27] for it is my sacrifice to the Lord from my broken spirit, a blessing of thanksgiving from those who wander the wilderness [see Berakhot 54b].[12]

Abravanel's commentary on the Passover Haggadah is presented as fulfilling a mission, "a time to act for the Lord." He offers his readers the perspective they so dearly missed during times of crisis and their struggles to contend with the challenges posed by the cruel tides of history. The name of the commentary, *Zevah pesah*, further projects the shift in perspective that it hopes to instigate among Sephardic Jews in response to their exile. The allusion to Exodus in the commentary's title transports the reader back to the first Passover sacrifice, that offered by the children of Israel in Egypt to their God "who passed over the houses of the children of Israel in Egypt, when He smote the Egyptians, and delivered our houses" (Ex. 12:27). The commentary on the Haggadah reminds the reader, like the biblical ritual of offering the paschal lamb, to appreciate the miraculous survival of the Jewish people over the course of many exiles, in spite of the great travails they have undergone. Employing the expression a "broken spirit," Abravanel evokes the prayer with which the exile beseeches his God, on his own behalf and on behalf of all his exiled brethren. Finally, comparing the exiles who wander from land to land with "those who wander the wilderness"— a scenario discussed in BT Berakhot and that obligates one to make the *Hagomel* blessing after arriving back in civilization—Don Isaac defines his commentary as a thanksgiving blessing to God for allowing him and his brethren to survive so many exiles. The transition from a victim oppressed and haunted by tragedy to a survivor who thanks the Lord for his salvation is precisely the psychological shift—the consolation—that *Zevah pesah* is meant to effect in the minds of the community of Sephardic exiles.[13]

Disrupting the Astrological Order

It is within the commentary itself that the psychological shift alluded to in the work's autobiographical introduction and title takes place. Without detracting from the importance of the wide range of topics covered by the work, it can be argued that the work is primarily structured around the motif of God disrupting and altering the astrological order. This motif has two primary implications: (1) the inversion of the astrological and historical order by an act of divine intervention and (2) the impressive and compelling expression of God's personal providence over Israel.

The motif appears a number of times throughout the commentary, but it is most fully expressed toward the end of the *Maggid* section of the Haggadah. This section of the Haggadah contains a discussion of the meaning of the paschal sacrifice, whose reading is accompanied by the ritual presentation of the seder plate with a substitute of the paschal sacrifice. As alluded to by its title, the interpretation of the paschal sacrifice on the basis of the idea of a disrupted astrological order constitutes the heart and soul of the commentary as a whole. In its perspective, the Passover and Exodus become an impressive astrological scene. If in *Rosh amanah* renewed faith in the principles of Judaism transforms the reader from a skeptical exile into a reinvigorated Jew, in *Zevah pesah* the insertion of the astrological drama into the heart and center of the Exodus narrative and the Passover ritual is meant to prompt the defamed Sephardic refugee to change his perspective on his own fate.

The state of the children of Israel in Egypt before the astrological order was disrupted is characterized by Abravanel as follows:

> It is the sign of Aries which rules Egypt and influences it. And therefore, the Egyptians would worship it and venerate its form [the lamb]. And while the children of Israel were also led astray by the worship of Aries . . . they never abandoned the service of the Lord, but rather thought that they would receive good things from that zodiac sign.[14]

According to the astrological worldview, which we encountered previously in Don Isaac's *'Ateret zeqenim*, every nation is subject to the influence of a specific sign of the zodiac. Shaul Regev has shown that even though astrology "was a practical and common science in Renaissance Italy, Abravanel naturally preferred to situate and study this new doctrine through the writings of his Jewish brethren, Ibn Ezra and [Abraham] Bar Hiyya, as opposed to the writings of gentiles."[15] During the fifteenth century, the Iberian peninsula hosted its fair share of astrological speculation, which attracted the interest of Jews and Christians alike—Enrique de Villena, Rabbi Abraham Bibago, and Rabbi Isaac Arama are just a few examples. Abravanel notes that "the sign of Aries is the firstborn, the greatest of the twelve zodiac signs in power and ability. And in the month of Nissan it is at the zenith of its power."[16] It thus comes as no surprise that Egypt was the greatest world power at the time. According to the same logic, the sign of Aries, the firstborn of signs, also rules over firstborn children. In the astrological and historical context of Egypt's political ascendancy, the children of Israel (who immigrated to Egypt) produced a cultural and religious hybrid: they incorporated astrological components into their Hebrew religion, hoping to avail themselves of the source of Egyptian power in addition to the power of the God of Israel. This state of affairs can be understood as a thinly veiled reference to the circumstances of the Sephardic émigrés in Abravanel's own time. They too are tempted to adopt the purported source of Castile and Aragon's greatness: the Christian faith.

Against this dangerous temptation, an obstacle to redemption, Don Isaac presents Moses as the leader sent by God to the children of Israel with the goal of disabusing them of their admiration of the source of Egyptian power, Aries: "Through His covenant, and through their cries, the Blessed Lord defeated the causes that prevented their redemption, namely, their evil deeds. . . . Therefore he sent before them a man, Moses his servant, to first entrench within them the true faith and law."[17] Due to Moses's leadership, the children of Israel returned to "the completeness of faith and cleaving to the Lord." Now the process of the Exodus could begin. In Don Isaac's view, this process has two components (one human and the other divine), each complementing the other. The first process involved God "eclipsing" or "striking" Aries.[18] By disrupting and realigning the astral order, Aries is subjected to the supreme authority of the divine will, and its astral influence is reversed from positive to negative. As Abravanel explains:

> And behold the Lord separated the land of Goshen upon which His nation dwelt. Indeed, because the supernal constellations required the enslavement [of Israel] to the Egyptians in Egypt, none other than the Holy One Blessed is He needed to command the heavenly hosts and to annul the power of Aries on that night. And being that

[Aries] ruled over the firstborns of Egypt, the plague of the first-borns proceeded from it according to its normal influence.[19]

The second parallel process is the liberation of the children of Israel from the influence of Aries. This liberation required the performance of a ritual that completes the astrological upheaval begun by the divinely precipitated eclipse. This was accomplished through a psychological shift in which the veneration of the zodiac sign and its power was supplanted by faith in God's special providence over the children Israel:

> And behold, according to the natural order, the firstborns of Israel were also included in this plague. . . . Therefore, in order to save Israel from that plague, the Blessed Lord commanded that . . . "every man shall take for himself a lamb, according to the house of his father, a lamb for a household" for [the lamb] resembles and is influenced by the sign of Aries, and they should slaughter it . . . so that they would admit through their actions that the sign of Aries had been eclipsed [or struck]. . . . For the action was a sign unto them . . . that they no longer believed in the sign of Aries as in earlier times, and that they were leaving Egypt by the gracious hand of their God [who had] annulled Aries's power.[20]

According to this model, God eclipses the zodiac sign Aries to free the children of Israel from its influence. For their part, the children of Israel needed to slaughter the earthly manifestation of Aries, the lamb, to rid themselves of their own belief in astrology. Thus, the children of Israel emulated the divine actions by performing a ritual that lay the ground for a profound psychological shift. The two facets of freedom (objective and subjective) thus complement each other, coming together in the cosmological and psychological drama by which the Children of Israel were freed from their Egyptian bondage. This drama, which constitutes the heart and soul of Don Isaac's commentary, is meant to impress the Sephardic exile but also to effect within her or him a shift in perspective, paralleling the process undergone by the children of Israel during the Exodus. In this exegetical approach, the ritual of the Paschal Lamb is turned into a psychological victory that the Sephardic reader gains by his refusal to submit to the historical powers of European kingdoms and his renewed attachment to the cosmological and historical conceptions of Judaism. This psychological victory is obviously only partial. It exists only in the mental representation of the historical and cosmological significance of Passover and fails to manifest itself within concrete historical reality. Nevertheless, the exiles' adherence to the historical and theological framework of their Judaism makes possible the continuity of their community. And perhaps this adherence has importance beyond its concrete historical existence—if we accept, as Don Isaac suggests, that the Spanish expulsion is a prelude to the redemption, similar to the Exodus: "and if you say that the supernal constellations prevent and withhold your redemption and salvation, know and see that the heavens are unto the Lord and whither He wishes He will turn them, for He will realign the supernal constellations, and He will annul natural causes as He wishes."[21]

Should historical shifts like the expulsion and the military crisis in Italy be seen as similar cases of divine disruption of the astrological order, astral convulsions that will ultimately lead to the redemption of Sephardic exiles and the Jewish people as a whole? Regardless, in *Zevah pesah*, we see the same rhetorical thread that runs through *Rosh amanah*—persuasion of the skeptical exile. Here, however, this idea has been expanded to encompass a broad and overarching cosmological and historical worldview.

Nahalat avot

In the city of Monopoli in late June 1496, about three months after completing *Zevah pesah*, Don Isaac completed his monumental commentary on *Pirkei avot*, *Nahalat avot*, a work that takes up almost two-thirds of the 1505 volume. In his preface to the work, Abravanel explains that the commentary was written at the behest of his third son, Samuel (1473–1551), who asked his father to commit to writing the homilies he had heard from him in the past. That being said, *Nahalat avot* is also a sequel to *Zevah pesah* in the sense that it, too, is a commentary on a canonical text with important liturgical use in the context of the synagogue. Furthermore, by choosing to comment on *Pirkei avot*, Don Isaac was perpetuating a traditional Iberian Jewish genre that had been employed for centuries by great figures like Maimonides, Rabbi Jonah Gerondi, Rabbi Bahya ben Asher, Rabbi Menahem Meiri, Rabbi Simeon Ben Zemah Duran, Rabbi Shem Tov ibn Shem Tov, Rabbi Joseph Hayyun (Don Isaac's teacher), and many others. The renewal of this tradition in the aftermath of the Spanish expulsion was perhaps viewed by Abravanel as a way of demonstrating cultural continuity.[22]

Don Isaac opens the book with a preface framed as a letter to Samuel, who at the time lived in the Ottoman city of Salonika, far from Monopoli:

You surely asked me to interpret for you the book of precious *mish-nayot* and of pure sayings. . . . For the words that you heard from my mouth were sweet to you, they were upright and good interpretations. . . . And you said: will words that are spoken by mouth, that fly about in the wind, [conveyed] by travelers, be established in much-observant hearts and attentive ears? . . . Let my father arise and write them down as a memorial in a book.[23]

Don Isaac uses the geographic distance between himself and his son, as well as the chronological gap between the period before the expulsion and the period after it, to convey the importance of continuity—despite the dispersion of Sephardic Jewry and the challenges posed by the expulsion and the wars in Italy. To this end, Don Isaac describes his son's love for the homilies that his father had delivered on *Pirkei avot* before the expulsion, as well as his son's fear that his father's teachings would be forgotten. This is Abravanel's rhetorical way of justifying the composition of the commentary to his readers. Samuel's request that his father preserve his words in writing is used at the beginning of the book to exemplify the proper attitude a Sephardic exile ought to cultivate toward Jewish exegetical tradition, especially the glorious tradition of Iberian Jewry.

The Length of Exile and the Chain of Tradition

Later in the introduction, Don Isaac returns to the issue of the historical continuity of Torah study. This time, however, he focuses on the chain of tradition that stretches back to Rabbi Judah the Prince, redactor of the Mishnah, and before him all the way back to Moses at Sinai. According to Abravanel, based on the opening mishnayot of *Pirkei avot*, the chain of tradition is comprised of four groups (*kitot*) that came one after the other: the elders (*zeqenim*), the prophets (*nevi'im*), the men of the Great Assembly (*anshei kneset hagedolah*), and the sages of the Mishnah. Each group—or period in Jewish history—consists of, according to Abravanel's calculations, "twelve generations or twelve receivers, as if the divine wisdom always wished this to be the number, corresponding to the [twelve] tribes of Israel."[24] After identifying this cyclical dimension of Jewish history, Don Isaac adds an important note:

Know and understand that the Holy One Blessed is He gazes and observes until the end of generations. He saw that the exile was very long and that the farther generations were from the first source, the first spring, the weaker they grew. . . . And therefore, Divine Providence was wise to periodically create a great person who would be like a torch to spread light to the generations after him, as if the duration of time was a long and very dark road, and light shone from one part of the road to the next by candles and torches created to illuminate the road by day and by night.[25]

The exile is full of exemplary figures who take pains to preserve the framework of Judaism even under the harshest and most challenging of circumstances. Without a doubt, Don Isaac thought of himself in such terms, especially when it came to facing the challenges of the expulsion. He saw himself as a "candle" to light the way for generations to come. Therefore, he developed an extensive apologetical argument that spans his commentary on *Pirkei avot*, articulated through the device of a gradual and systematic exegesis on the tractate.

According to Abravanel's harmonistic understanding of the tractate's progressive structure, an understanding that he endeavors to demonstrate throughout his commentary, the first chapter of *Pirkei avot* is dedicated to "pillars"—that is, the principles of Judaism (the centrality of Torah, serving God, and performing good deeds). The second chapter discusses the ways by "which a person can act to achieve perfection."[26] The third chapter discusses "ways to distance oneself from sin."[27] The fourth chapter defines human perfection in the context of the Messiah, the final judgment, and the resurrection of the dead. And finally, the fifth chapter—which, according to Abravanel and most others, is the true end of the tractate—discusses the methods by which a person will arrive "at the purpose of his creation and the perfection of the sublunar world which was created on his behalf."[28] Without exaggerating the extent to which Abravanel was systematic in this regard, we can see a thread running throughout the commentary: beginning with the pillars of Judaism, through the means of attaining perfection and avoiding sin, and concluding with the cosmological goal of Jewish existence. The apologetics—or religious defense of Judaism—offered by Abravanel throughout the commentary presents the wider cosmological significance of proper Jewish behavior in a period when it seems to have had little influence on historical reality. In our discussion below we will demonstrate the nature of Abravanel's apologetics by exploring one of the climaxes of *Nahalat avot*—the commentary on Rabbi Akiva's three aphorisms, "beloved is man in that he was created in the image [of God]," "beloved is Israel in that they were called children of the omnipresent," and "everything is foreseen, but the right [of choice] is granted" (*Pirkei avot* 3:14–15).

Isaac Abravanel and Pico della Mirandola on Human Dignity

Don Isaac opens his long discussion of Rabbi Akiva's three aphorisms by musing about the proper attitude to adopt when the framework of Jewish existence faces the threat of disintegration and collapse:

> Rabbi Akiva answered . . . that the truest way a person can extricate himself from sin . . . is by observing safeguards and by making safeguards to his safeguards, and that the reflection (*hahistaqlut*) that is needed to [achieve] this end does not involve disparaging humanity's material components. . . . Rather, when he reflects upon three other ideas, he will recognize the preciousness of his [cosmological] degree and the ascendancy of his stage within reality.[29]

Don Isaac praises Rabbi Akiva for not treating humanity with a negative attitude and not "disparaging the material of man, [regarding] it as inferior from beginning to end."[30] Rather, Rabbi Akiva treats humanity as very positive, praising "the preciousness of his [cosmological] degree (*yoqer ma'alato*)." This is intended for a conservative purpose—to preserve the normative framework of Judaism. Despite the talmudic and midrashic context cited and emphasized by Abravanel, it is hard not to link the terminology of *yoqer ma'alato* to the humanistic discourse of the fourteenth and fifteenth centuries regarding the dignity of man (*dignitas hominis*)—meaning man's cosmological position as a free being.[31] It is especially difficult not to see in Don Isaac's words an echo of the humanistic mental shift that treats humanity as something that overall is positive, rejecting the negative antihuman discourse that constituted a central trend within medieval philosophy. To name just one example, in the 1190s Pope Innocent III authored a treatise *De miseria condicionis humane* (On contempt for the world or on the misery of the human condition).[32] The positive attitude toward man was regarded by modern scholars in the nineteenth and early twentieth centuries as a characteristic feature of the ideology of humanistic circles in Italy, distinguishing them from the philosophers and theologians of the Middle Ages. While scholarship in the second half of the twentieth century began to identify problems with this simplistic distinction, it is nevertheless important to put Abravanel's words about human dignity within

the context of a literary milieu close to him chronologically and themati-
cally. Conversely, it is also important to reiterate that when Abravanel discusses the creation of man in God's image, he does not disclose his humanistic influences. Explicitly at least, he discusses these ideas solely within
the context of medieval Jewish sources. Nevertheless, we know from Abravanel's Portuguese letter and various discussions in his commentary on the
Former Prophets that he was acquainted with Christian literature, both
from his own era and from earlier periods, and that he had no qualms about
using the contents and ideas of such works for various purposes.

Moreover, in the early sixteenth century, Don Isaac's oldest son, Judah
Abravanel (Leone Ebreo), composed a book titled *Dialoghi d'Amore* (*Dialogues of Love*), whose third section contained an extensive discussion of
Plato's *Symposium*. The discussion bears clear affinities to those taking place
in the Neoplatonic circle of Marsilio Ficino, who translated the *Symposium*
and wrote a commentary on it. In Judah Abravanel's dialogue, Aristoph-
anes's discussion of humanity's formerly androgynous state leads Philo
(one of the two speakers in Judah's dialogue) to assert that "the fable comes
from a tradition that was referred by an author more ancient than the
Greeks, that is, the sacred history of Moses concerning the creation of the
first human parents, Adam and Eve."[33] Later, Philo explains the connection
between Plato and scripture: "He did not tell this as a fable with such specific details, but he declared the substance of the fable in a succinct way;
and it was from him that Plato took his fable, amplifying and adorning it
after the manner of Greek oratory, thus creating a disordered and confused
version of the Hebrew material."[34] Judah Abravanel's explanation of similarities between scripture and the works of Plato can be traced back to an
ancient myth given new prominence by his father, Don Isaac, in the latter's
1504 commentary on Jeremiah: "and after the destruction, Jeremiah traveled to Egypt and lived there for many years without prophecy. And the
master [apparently Ibn Falaquera] and the Greek sages [the Church fathers,
such as Augustine] attest that Plato spoke with him there."[35] Moshe Idel
and Abraham Melamed have argued that the fondness for Plato evinced
by Don Isaac and his son Judah derived both from the identification of
certain affinities between the views of Plato and the views of the Torah
(an approach shared by many Jewish thinkers at the time) and from their
internalization of Christian and humanistic Neoplatonism.[36] If Plato and
the Christian Neoplatonists were actually drawing their ideas from scripture, as the myth of Jeremiah and Plato's meeting would suggest, then

there would be no reason not to adopt contemporary Neoplatonic Christian ideas.

Does this explain the lack of explicit references to Neoplatonist and humanist philosophers in Don Isaac's writings? It is difficult to say for sure, but regardless, Don Isaac was certainly familiar with the humanist and Neoplatonic discourses taking place around him in Italy. For this reason, it is important to compare his approach to those of Christian thinkers such as Giovanni Pico della Mirandola.

Pico della Mirandola's speech, *Oratio de Hominis Dignitate*, written in 1486, is perhaps more expressive of the shift in the approach to humanity that took place in the humanistic literature of the fourteenth and fifteenth centuries than it is of anything else. That being said, it should be borne in mind that the speech develops existing literary motifs and conceptions expressed and written by Francesco Petrarch, Coluccio Salutati, Giannozzo Manetti, Ficino, and others.[37]

The oration opens by addressing humanity in overtly positive terms, describing it as nothing short of wondrous:

> Most venerable fathers, I have read in the records of the Arabians that Abdul the Saracen, on being asked what thing on, so to speak, the world's stage, he viewed as most greatly worthy of wonder, answered that he viewed nothing more wonderful than man. And Mercury's, "a great wonder [*magnum miraculum*], Asclepius, is man!" agrees with that opinion.[38]

Pico goes on to define in what sense man is a "great wonder":

> Accordingly, now that all things had been completed, as Moses and Timaeus testify, He [God] lastly considered creating man. But there was nothing in the archetypes from which He could mold a new sprout, nor anything in His storehouses which He could bestow as a heritage upon a new son, nor was there an empty judiciary seat where this contemplator of the universe could sit. . . . Finally, the best of workmen [God] decided that that to which nothing of its very own could be given should be, in composite fashion, whatsoever had belonged individually to each and every thing.[39]

The wonder of man is thus a consequence of his indeterminacy. "At man's birth, the Father placed in him every sort of seed and sprouts of every kind of life," Pico writes in summary.[40] Within man inhere all the forms of existence, from inanimate objects to divine beings, and man chooses his place in the cosmos by choosing to adopt or cultivate one of these forms. Speaking through the mouth of God, Pico emphasizes the importance of human freedom in the dynamic process by which a person defines his place within the cosmos:

> A limited nature in other creatures is confined within the laws written down by us. In conformity with thy free judgment [*pro tuo arbitrio*], in whose hands I have placed thee, thou art confined by no bounds; and thou wilt fix limits of nature for thyself. I have placed thee at the center of the world, that from there thou mayest more conveniently look around and see whatsoever is in the world. Neither heavenly nor earthly, neither mortal nor immortal have We made thee. Thou, like a judge appointed for being honorable, art the molder and maker of thyself; thou mayest sculpt thyself into whatever shape thou dost prefer. Thou canst grow downward into the lower natures which are brutes. Thou canst again grow upward from thy soul's reason into the higher natures which are divine.[41]

Abravanel's Opposition to the Maimonidean Understanding of the Image of God

Don Isaac's discussion of the image of God, the theme expressed by Rabbi Akiva's statement "beloved is man in that he was created in the image," bolsters the connection to the Neoplatonic discourse regarding humanity. At the beginning of his commentary on Rabbi Akiva's statement, Abravanel summarizes the Maimonidean understanding of God's image, an issue raised in the first chapter of the *Guide of the Perplexed*. In Don Isaac's understanding, the meaning of God's image in Maimonides's approach is an analogy between an incorporeal God who is devoid of sensuality, on the one hand, and human intellect, which performs intellection without resorting to the use of the body or senses, on the other hand. Maimonides writes:

> That which was meant in the scriptural dictum, *let us make man in our image*, was the specific form, which is intellectual apprehension, not the shape and configuration. . . . Now man possesses as his proprium something in him that is very strange as it is not found in anything else that exists under the sphere of the moon, namely, intellectual apprehension. In the exercise of this, no sense, no part

of the body, none of the extremities are used; and therefore, this apprehension was likened unto the apprehension of the deity, which does not require an instrument, although in reality it is not like the latter apprehension, but only appears so to the first stirrings of opinion.[42]

In Maimonides's view, man and God share nothing, and man cannot reflect God in any way whatsoever. The similarity between man and God suggested by the biblical text is an expression of the fact that a person can negate herself by exercising her intellect, meaning she can suppress her psychobiological nature and act on a purely intellectual plane. Don Isaac summarizes Maimonides's approach as follows: "the divine and human are equal in terms of their negation."[43] This is the meaning of being created in God's image—not that divine and human intellect bear any similarity. "In reality," man and God could not be more different.

This analogical interpretation of man's creation in the image of the divine entirely removes from the word "image" (*tselem*) any visual or physical connotation, and certainly any suggestion that man can share God's qualities or reflect them in any way. Thus, for Maimonides, the phrase "God's image" refers to the form of a human—that is, her or his intellect, the species-constituting difference that distinguishes humans from animals. It does not, however, suggest a true affinity between God and man.

In contrast to this view, which widens the gap between God and man and thus emphasizes man's inferiority as a physical being, Abravanel develops another approach. As he explains, God could not create the world without conceiving some spiritual model of the universe that contained the vital components of creation—perfections (*shelemuyot*), in Abravanel's terminology—or the inanimate objects, vegetative beings, living beings, and intellect. This being the case, God encompasses "a conceptualization [*tsiyur*] and a universal order that acts, brings into being, and creates."[44] The word "tsiyur" refers to an intellectual representation or spiritual archetype of the world, a notion reminiscent of Plato's Ideas. The created world is in fact the emanation of divine representation, which actualizes and breaks apart its individual components. As Abravanel explains: "In the Blessed Creator all these perfections were present without distinction, ordering, or hierarchy. . . . They were in simple unity. . . . For within Him the Blessed One, all things are completely one. And these perfections are not within him as particulars and are not limited as is the case for existent beings."[45]

Besides God, there is only one creature who contains all these components (or perfections) of the divine representation of the world: man. In
this sense man is created in God's image, meaning man reflects the spiritual
model encapsulated by the creator's all-encompassing knowledge. As Abravanel puts it, "and because there are no [other] created beings in whom all
perfections are combined in the fashion of the divine representation, save
the human species, therefore, it is stated of [man that he was created] in
God's image, for within his form are present all the perfections which are
present in the supernal conceptualization of the Blessed One when he influences his creatures."[46] Thus, man is a microcosm, a "model of the entire
world."

Abravanel continues:

> Within [man] is contained the intellectual power to recognize and
> perceive the reality of things and their substance, separated from
> their accidents and individual cases.... And this faculty is in the
> form of the highest world of [separate] intellects, for their actions
> are done with constant scientific intellectualizing (*haskala mada'it*).
> And within [man] is contained the vital capacity of movement and
> sensation which resembles the world of spheres which move un-
> ceasingly. And within [man] is also found the natural power of
> nourishment and generation and all aspects of the body and its
> decay, and this is like the sublunar world which is generated and
> corrupted.[47]

In contrast to Maimonides's interpretation of God's image, Abravanel
offers an interesting series of images and reflections: God, the creator, contains the spiritual representation of the created beings; and the world is a
realization of the components of God's own representation and their new
organization and is, in its totality, a reflection of the divine, primordial
model. In other words, man is a microcosm and thus reflects God's archetype of the world.

Abravanel concludes by writing: "Thus you see that man is the likeness
of the Holy One Blessed is He and His image in that he is impressed with
the archetypes and actions used by God to create the world in wondrous
fashion. And just as the Holy One Blessed is He rules His creatures, so too
He endowed man with the [characteristic] of being in his image, inasmuch
as mankind rules over the sublunar world."[48] It is the fact that man is funda-
mentally similar to God—and not just in a negative sense, as Maimonides

would have it—that allows him to rule the sublunar world. This is also the explanation for the miracles wrought by the prophets of Israel: the creative powers of divine archetype can be exercised by humans as well. Thus, opposing the Maimonidean view—which, according to Abravanel, denies the existence of any features common to God and man and limits human dignity to intellect alone, at the expense of all other features—Abravanel presents here an approach in which man, in all of his faculties and characteristics, reflects the divine. If we combine this approach with the declaration that opens Abravanel's discussion of the "preciousness of [man's cosmological] degree," it is difficult not to see in this departure from the Maimonidean approach a manifestation of the shift toward a positive view of humanity that, as we have mentioned, was among the touchstones of humanism.

Children of the Omnipresent

Abravanel goes on to explain Rabbi Akiva's statement, "beloved is Israel in that they were called children of the Omnipresent." Abravanel's approach seeks to grapple with the contradiction between "the image of God," a term applied to humanity as a whole, and the special status of "children of the Omnipresent (*bnei hamaqom*)," a designation limited to the Jewish people. To this end, Abravanel once again raises a theme that we have encountered previously: the idea that the difference between Israel and the nations is predicated on the distinction—and tension—between *providentia* and *fortuna*. As we discussed above, Abravanel believed each nation to be subject to the influence of a specific astral body that determines its fate and bears responsibility for its successes and failures. The Jewish people, in contrast, is not subjected to the influence of any astral body but enjoys the unmediated providence of God. The status of "children" used to describe Israel's relationship with God reflects the Jewish people's unique ability to most completely realize and actualize the divine image that is part of man. Jews do so by living their lives in accordance with the Torah and its commandments, thus cleaving to God and drawing down divine influence and providence. In this part of Abravanel's discussion, the extremely competitive consciousness of the Sephardic exile clearly comes to the fore. He is torn between a Christian environment, with its history and the cosmological system that drives it, and a broken Jewish milieu, with its own unique but traumatic history, driven by its own hidden theological mechanisms.

Freedom and Foreknowledge

This long exegetical section of *Nahalat avot* concludes with a discussion of Rabbi Akiva's paradoxical statement, "everything is foreseen, but the right [of choice] is granted." Abravanel interprets the statement according to the tension, or antimony, between God's complete and all-encompassing knowledge and human freedom. To solve the tension, he turns to the archetype we have seen previously:

> Behold if so, the Blessed Lord can apprehend man's body and soul without material vessels. . . . Indeed . . . individual things come into being through the medium of time, which is an accident that derives from movement. And we can say that the Blessed One's knowledge is not acquired from things subject to time, for [His knowledge] precedes their existence and is their cause. As to the third doubt, that the One who knows will be completed by the knowledge and thus be increased [and] become multiple: . . . Behold, because God's knowledge, will, and conceptions are what give existence to things and are not acquired from them, it does not follow that the more sublime would be completed by the less sublime, that His knowledge would derive from something other than Himself. And He does not gain his substance from others. And the many pieces of knowledge unite within Him, in accordance with His unified archetype and ordered will.[49]

Abravanel explains that, regardless of any changes taking place among humanity or in the sublunar world in general, God has no need to update his knowledge. This is because God's relationship with the world is not an external one that can be measured by time or in relationship to changes taking place in the world. Rather, it is an internal knowledge that issues from God, from the creator's primordial and generative representation, into the world. Thus, the spiritual model of the world that is present within the creator is not just the world's distilled essence but also encompasses all of its actualizations within creation: the first cause comprehends both itself (the divine archetype) and the entire reality that is created by it. The divine model of the world is thus turned into a picture of the entire span of human history. Abravanel borrows turns of phrase from Crescas's *Or Adonai* such as "by knowing Himself and by representing His [own] will, which is He Himself, beings acquire reality outside of Him" and "it is not conceivable that [God] would activate them [all existent things] and not know [them]."[50] According to Crescas (and Abravanel), the causality that is manifest in the creation of the world requires that the infinite totality of individual entities be included within God's knowledge of himself.

That being said, God's panoramic perspective of history does not exempt men and women from participating in the drama of free will:

> Even though the human intellect was preceded by its cause—that which created it and that which bound it to a body—its intellectual activity and its [ability] to choose between different options (*devarim efshariyim*) is by virtue of itself. And the intellect is not forced or compelled to apprehend or choose one way or another, neither by their characters nor by their material properties, nor by constellations in the heavens, nor by the divine knowledge which does not compel the nature of what is possible. The activity of the intellect qua intellect is utterly free in its actions. However, when it comes to sins, it is the volitional appetitive faculty that is active.[51]

As discussed by Feldman, when it comes to free will, Don Isaac opposes Crescas's deterministic approach "that [actions] are possible in their essence but are obligated by their causes."[52] In contrast to this view, which is formulated in *Or Adonai*,[53] Abravanel wonders: "can blindness to causes be called possibility?"[54] This expression appears almost word for word in Isaac Arama's *'Aqedat Yitshak*.[55] Like Isaac Arama, Rabbi Joseph Albo, and other Jewish thinkers, Abravanel could not accept a view that would limit man's freedom to myopic ignorance of the causes behind his actions. Don Isaac was interested in a positive notion of freedom. As stated in the excerpt above, a human being, consisting of intellect and body, is subject to two types of causality that correspond to his or her dual nature: the one intellectual and the other natural, material, and imaginational. A person can give in to his or her desires and impulses or reintroduce, through decisions and actions, the superiority of the intellect over other components of his or her humanity. There is no divine, astrological, or human cause that forces a person to act in a specific way. This is due to the simple reason that humans' complex nature exposes them to different types of drives and influences that require them to arbitrate and create their own set of priorities. By choosing between different drives and organizing them into a hierarchy, each person shapes his or her true character. Similar descriptions can be found in Pico's *Oratio De Hominis Dignitate*: "If the seeds of sensation, he will grow into [a] brute. If rational, he will come out a heavenly animal."[56]

This idea creates an interesting tension. On the one hand, the world is reflected within God with no time line and in a panoramic, harmonious fashion. On the other hand, insofar as human existence is concerned, the order of the world—meaning the order and arrangement of the essential constituents of the universe—presents a dilemma, in which human freedom is entrusted with constantly ordering the human and nonhuman environment for good or for evil. Humans can adhere to the divine hierarchy or, conversely, adopt an invalid set of priorities. Thus, that which exists within God as a tranquil and comprehensive image of the world becomes within man or woman the tempestuous drama of freedom. Humans have the power either to corrupt the divine image within themselves and the world or to confirm it, reproduce it, and thus complete creation. This human drama serves the consistent apologetic agenda of Abravanel that is evident throughout his commentary. The Jew, having overcome the tribulations of the expulsion and the temptation to convert to Christianity, and by remaining loyal to a proper Jewish lifestyle, realizes his freedom and thus causes divine influence to once again rest upon the Jewish people.

Abravanel summarizes this dual apologetics of freedom and Judaism by invoking a talmudic passage:

> The celestial bodies act upon the sublunar world . . . and they move the elements, combining them or dissolving them, preparing them with different dispositions. . . . And, according to this, every man's actions are compelled according to the hour of his birth. . . . [But] the constellations do not indicate the observance of commandments or the committing of transgressions whatsoever, for such [actions] are chosen by man. . . . The constellations provide the disposition and the human intellect, through its free will, gives them finality and perfection. . . . The Sages stated . . . "He who is born under Mars will be a shedder of blood, a butcher, a mohel, or a bloodletter" [see Sabbath 156a] This teaches that the person [born under Mars] will not necessarily be a shedder of the blood of innocents but rather that the constellation will create some disposition in his temperament (*mezeg*). And a person has the power to use his intellect to change this evil indication or disposition and to use it to do something that causes no harm . . . to be a butcher, or to help

heal bodies by bloodletting, or to add a spiritual advantage by being a mohel. . . . And all of this indicates that the human soul can change the stars and annul the disposition that proceeds from them by changing the temperament and disposition to its opposite, to the good.[57]

The Jewish person faces a dilemma. She faces a choice between the influence of astrological forces (the forces of history) and "intellect," which is identified with the supreme good of man. History does not force a person to act in a specific way. One who is born during the rule of Mars can grow up to take on a variety of different blood-related tasks. He has the power to direct his circumstances one way or another, for good or for evil. And while he cannot change his circumstances entirely, he has the freedom to organize them as he sees fit: either to correspond with the divine order or in a temporary, invalid manner. Abravanel uses talmudic statements and philosophical debates revolving around human freedom versus (natural or divine) determinism to cultivate in his readers a notion of freedom. However, this apologetics of human freedom is aimed, first and foremost, at providing a new and appealing justification for Judaism.

If we recall that *Nahalat avot* is part of a broader literary project that includes two other works (*Zevah pesah* and *Rosh amanah*), we can perhaps detect in Abravanel's defense of Maimonides's thirteen principles, his commentary on the rituals of the Passover sacrifice, and his praise of human freedom a unified and consistent literary theme: the attempt to convince the Jewish exiles from Castile and Aragon that they can overcome the destructive repercussions of the expulsion and exilic existence in general. Cleaving to Judaism is, in Abravanel's view, the way to invert or uproot the oppression of expulsion. However, liberating oneself from the awe of Christian states and their historical power, a liberation that Abravanel seeks to effect through all three of his works, can come to fruition only through the rhetorical efforts of a leader. The leader, skilled in writing and oration, must draw his community back to its original freedom. In this sense, we can see Abravanel's three works—as well as their printing by his acquaintances and friends—as part of a broader effort to reorganize and reestablish the exiles in their new Diaspora lands.

The apologetic vein that we have described posed a challenge to scholars of Abravanel: What is the dominant theme in Abravanel's literary oeuvre? Is it his conservative leanings or his relatively innovative philosophical means of expression? In my opinion, one should not seek to privilege one aspect over the other. As I have tried to show here, Abravanel drew inspiration from the discourse of his era with respect to persuasive oration, astrology, freedom, and a new understanding of the human condition. At the same time, his primary goal was to preserve the ideological and social framework of the medieval Jewish community. This goal is manifested in his attempt to draw a clear cosmological and historical distinction between the nation of Israel and the gentile peoples, as well as by his showing a clear preference for medieval Jewish literary frameworks over the new humanistic literary genres with which he was also familiar (neoclassical orations, dialogues, literary and historical prose, and more). The result of this innovative apologetics is the integration of many new ideas into medieval Jewish frameworks. When placed within the contexts of a war-torn Italy, exacerbating the already dire circumstances of the Sephardic exileswho had arrived in Naples, Don Isaac's literary projects seem to represent a complex endeavor, a mixture of old and new. It is an attempt to convince his readers that a Jewish existence is still possible and to inculcate within them the notion that they have a personal responsibility in the unfolding historical and religious process.

17 : MESSIANISM

Abravanel's Messianic Writings: A Scholarly Dilemma

Immediately after completing *Nahalat avot*, Abravanel moved onto his next work, a commentary on the book of Daniel titled *Ma'ayanei hayesh'uah*. He completed the work in Monopoli in January 1497, as he writes in the colophon: "On the first day of the month of Tevet the year 'for the crown (*nezer*) of his god is upon his head' [Num. 6:7; the numerical value of nezer *is 257*] in the sixth millennium."[1] In the same colophon, Don Isaac summarizes the general purpose of the book: "in this precious book that I have composed, my intended goal, the purpose of my words, and all my desire is to strengthen weak hands and to give might to stumbling knees." Until recently, scholars understood the work as a messianic commentary, the first part of a trilogy of Abravanel's messianic works that were written consecutively during the years 1496–98: *Ma'ayanei hayeshu'ah* (Wells of salvation), *Yeshu'ot meshiho* (Salvation of his messiah), and *Mashmi'ah yesh'uah* (Announcer of salvation). Scholars sought to find the catalyst for this outburst of messianic creativity. Yitzhak Baer's view on this issue is well known: at the end of his groundbreaking article about Don Isaac Abravanel, he writes:

> As far as the history of exile is concerned, [Abravanel's] science of natural development was abandoned. The erstwhile humanist was turned back into a populistic preacher, a calculator of ends who made assertions about the various stages of the redemption process. . . . [He no longer] interprets historical reality and the traumatic experiences of the expulsion from Spain, as well as the general expulsions of the late Middle Ages, in terms of cause and effect. [His explanations] have returned to the embrace of myth, an embrace from which Abravanel had [in the past] begun to redeem Jewish history.[2]

According to Baer, if Don Isaac was the precursor of a modern historicist approach in his commentary on the Former Prophets, the expulsion drove him back into the "embrace of myth," populistic homiletics, and a nonrational, nonnaturalistic perspective on history.

In his important book on Abravanel, Benzion Netanyahu goes so far as to present Abravanel as "the father of the messianic movements of the sixteenth and seventeenth century."[3] Netanyahu certainly does not intend the statement as a compliment. He holds Abravanel responsible for the Jewish people's tragic mistake, blaming him for providing a misguided answer to the distress of his people in the aftermath of the expulsion. The messianic turn of Don Isaac and that of many Jewish thinkers after him, when placed in the context of the expulsion of Jews from Western Europe, constitutes for Netanyahu the explanation for the historical, cultural, and political backwardness of the Jews in the early modern period. As he asserts emphatically in the introduction to his book, "The three hundred years between the end of the Middle Ages and the French Revolution saw, as far as the Jewish people is concerned, not an emergence from the Middle Ages, but rather an intensification of their unfavorable aspects."[4] Not limiting himself to generic accusations, Netanyahu contrasts Abravanel to his Christian contemporaries: "Both Savonarola[5] and Abravanel opened new historical lines. Savonarola was the forerunner of the great movement of the Reformation which stirred Europe during the sixteenth and seventeenth centuries. Abravanel was the forerunner of the messianic movement which stirred and agitated Jewry during the same period."[6] If the Reformation led to impressive historical successes precisely because it emphasized the moral and tangible aspects of Christianity over and above apocalypticism, in Judaism the opposite occurred: apocalypticism overtook the tangible, practical, and real. Netanyahu explains:

> Abravanel's messianic theory reflects the tragedy of the Jewish messianic movements, and to a large extent the tragedy of the Jews in the Middle Ages. It was a tragedy of a people that built imaginary towers that breathed an atmosphere of dreams and not of reality. The worst aspect of that tragedy lay in the fact that while the nation's soul floated between clouds in the heavens, its beaten body was being dragged on the ground bleeding from a hundred wounds. There was no bridging the abyss between the ideal and the reality.[7]

In *Messianism in Medieval Jewish Thought*, Dov Schwartz analyzes Abravanel's messianic conceptions and concludes that "Abravanel's messianic endeavor dealt a fatal blow to the naturalistic idea [of messianism] and marginalized it altogether."[8] Following in the footsteps of Leo Strauss and Netanyahu, Schwartz sees in Abravanel a philosopher who "defeat[ed] medieval rationalism in the version of Maimonides and his disciples, who had supported the naturalistic messianic idea."[9] According to the model used by Schwartz throughout his book, Maimonides represented the climax of a complex historical process in which Jewish thinkers disabused themselves of apocalyptic notions of the redemption in favor of more rationalistic or naturalistic approaches. Schwartz summarizes the messianic vision of such approaches as follows: "In the days of the messiah, the people of Israel will attain independence and the whole world will adhere to the intellectual ideal [perfection of intellect attained via religion, philosophy, and science]."[10] Thus, the return of Abravanel and his contemporaries to more apocalyptic models is interpreted by Schwartz in a negative light. He views it as the end of the philosophical religious projects of the previous era: "the Middle Ages, then, ended with the victory of apocalyptic messianism in its moderate version."[11]

Abravanel is thus accused by prominent scholars of a double crime: he relinquished the naturalistic, rationalistic understanding of messianism cultivated over the course of the Middle Ages and revived apocalyptic ideas of redemption that distanced Jews from modern realism. As shown by Schwartz, Abravanel's return to the embrace of apocalypticism represents a return in some senses to the ideas of Saadia Gaon as expressed in his *Book of Doctrines and Beliefs* (chapters 7 and 8), an account that preceded medieval attempts of Jewish philosophers, chief among them Maimonides, to refine elements of Jewish messianism or neutralize them. Netanyahu and Schwartz have shown how Abravanel's apocalyptic approach was not merely the product of his personal preferences. The political circumstances of his era, which undermined the status of Iberian Jewry, as well as other historical shifts all had a part to play. In a book dedicated to messianism among the Jewish exiles from Spain and Portugal, Isaiah Tishby describes and analyzes various expressions of the rise of apocalyptic trends during this era. He offers the following historical explanation for the phenomenon:

> The generation of the expulsion, as well as the generations immediately before it and immediately after it, beginning with the pogroms of 1391 and ending with the movements of Hareuveni and Molkho (and their offshoots) until c. 1540, were possessed by powerful messianic foment which left its mark on external reality and which found expression in fevered efforts to hasten the redemption.... The historical phenomena, bound up in the decrees and expulsions

discussed, produced two types of responses: (1) explicit declarations that interpreted [contemporary] events as the birth pangs of the Messiah and the coming of the redemption; (2) kabbalistic works primarily dedicated to expounding upon religious secrets that had been brought down from upon high, including prognostications about the future to come.[12]

According to Tishby's historical narrative, the messianic writing of Abravanel is a prominent example of the "strong messianic tensions that were perpetuated and even exacerbated until the general expulsion of 1492 and afterwards."[13] In his famous *The Messianic Idea in Judaism*, Gershom Scholem casts the messianic and apocalyptic tensions expressed during the expulsion era—and the dashing of messianic expectations—as the backdrop for the rise and proliferation of Lurianic Kabbalah. In this comprehensive narrative, Scholem maintains that Abravanel's messianic writings—which Scholem refers to as "the most important codifications of the Messianic idea in later Judaism"[14]—belong to a transitional era in which messianic expectations were committed to writing but within old theological and philosophical paradigms and without producing "new religious concepts and principles."[15] This is attested to by Abravanel's extensive recourse to *Megilat hamegaleh*, penned by Abraham Bar Hiyya in the first half of the twelfth century. Abravanel was particularly indebted to the fourth section of the work, which explicitly discusses Daniel's visions, and the fifth section, which proposes an elaborate astrological understanding of Jewish history.

In *Messianic Mystics*, Moshe Idel challenged what he refers to as "traumatic-historic" interpretations of messianism, the views that regard moments of historical crisis as explanations for the renaissance of messianic activity. Idel has shown that the widely accepted association between the expulsion from Spain and kabbalistic and messianic thought is, in most cases, unfounded. For this reason, Idel has called on scholars to relinquish the approach that views diverse messianic phenomena as variations on a single theme and to adopt a more pluralistic approach that ascribes greater importance to particularistic aspects of a given messianic ideology, such as the experiences of individual thinkers, the geographic and cultural environment, and the syncretic character of messianic conceptions.[16]

In some senses, one can see an application of this pluralistic approach in Eric Lawee's analysis of Abravanel's messianic work, *Yeshu'ot meshiho*. Without downplaying the influence of historical context (the expulsion and Jewish and Christian polemics), Lawee shows that Abravanel's work not only answered contemporary needs but also offered a wide array of exegetical approaches to the messianic passages scattered throughout the Talmud (literary, comparative, theological, and allegorical), as well as to the various interpretations given to them over the course of the Middle Ages (the critical assessment of different exegetical approaches). Therefore, Lawee proposes that Abravanel's claim to innovation in his messianic exegesis should be taken seriously.[17]

Adding to the perspectives I have already mentioned, I deem it important not to lose sight of the specific context in which Abravanel wrote his messianic works. For example, if we look at *Ma'ayanei hayeshu'ah*, we find a sequel to Abravanel's previous (nonmessianic) literary projects. As shown by Joseph Hacker, the public reading of the book of Daniel was an accepted practice in Sephardic synagogues after ninth of Av.[18] In the introduction to his *Tanhumot ha'el* (Consolations of God, 1578), Rabbi Isaac Ibn Aroyo wrote that he would "adduce parts of the book of Daniel during the weeks between the weekly portions of *Vaethanan* to *Shoftim*."[19] Abravanel's commentary on the book of Daniel thus represents the next installment in a series of works dedicated to explicating Jewish liturgical and ritual texts. On the eve of Passover 1496, Abravanel completed his commentary on the Haggadah. Just a few weeks later he completed his commentary on *Pirkei avot*, which was traditionally read during the period between Passover and Pentecost. After these two works, he moved on to his commentary on the book of Daniel, which was connected to the fast of ninth of Av. We thus see a correspondence between the progress of the Jewish calendar and the series of commentaries that Abravanel composed in 1496 and 1497. In the same article, Hacker points to the widespread phenomenon among sages of the Sephardic Diaspora to deliver lectures and homilies during specific weeks of the year on the five megillot, the book of Job, Proverbs, Daniel, and *Pirkei avot*, "thus generating an exegetical project encompassing scores of commentaries on these works and others during the sixteenth and seventeenth centuries, written by scholars in the various centers of the Empire."[20] Abravanel's commentaries on *Pirkei avot* and Daniel thus belong to the beginning of this wave of exegetical activity among the exiles from Spain and their descendants.

Without detracting from the weight of the questions raised by Baer, Scholem, Netanyahu, and Schwartz, in the following discussion I will offer an interpretation of *Ma'ayanei hayeshu'ah* that is more heavily based on the approaches articulated by Idel and Lawee, attempting to pin down the literary, philosophical, and rhetorical frameworks in which the book was composed. To underscore the literary activity at work in *Ma'ayanei hayeshu'ah*, I will avoid discussing here the question of the work's sources.

The Choice of Daniel

Don Isaac explains at some length why he chose the book of Daniel as the object of a messianic commentary. In the introduction to *Ma'ayanei hayesh'ua*, which is composed as a sort of broad historical fresco, Abravanel begins by painting the picture of the people of Israel's exile as one that lies between Edom and Ishmael, between Christendom and the Islamic world. Afterward he describes the glory of Iberian Jewry and its ultimate decline, and finally he explains why he chose Daniel and a messianic exegetical approach:

> I looked at these books in the Writings, and I raised my eyes and I saw Daniel, a man greatly beloved, speaking marvelous things that bring forth his fruit and leaf in its season. And the Spirit of the Lord shines in him; before he was formed in the belly, he was anointed to preach good tidings unto the meek, and He created a vessel for his handiwork to proclaim liberty to the captives, and the opening of the prison to them that are bound.[21]

Don Isaac does not present the book of Daniel as a work most fitted to his exegetical intentions. Rather, he describes it as a prophecy of the hour, with contents that possess him and seize his attention against his will. Abravanel sees in Daniel a fruit that has ripened before his very eyes: in his own lifetime, the visions concealed in the book are coming true, revealing the secret of the expulsion from Spain. The connection between "speaking marvelous things" and "bringing forth the fruit in its season" suggests that in the era of the expulsion, the miraculous visions of Daniel have proven their own prophetic value. It is thus a propitious time to begin interpreting the book. The pressing historical relevance of Daniel is thus used as a justification for choosing to explicate the book. However, it is also a rhetorical tool used to turn Daniel's visions into a source of consolation for the Spanish exiles. The commentary presents its readers with the impressive imagery of Daniel's visions, using them as a framework particularly well suited to the realities of the late fifteenth century, comforting the readers, and healing their pain.

All these elements—the canonical book of Daniel, the military crisis in

Italy, an author and leader exiled from his land, and a readership scattered and oppressed by the expulsion—join together to create a context in which we can understand Don Isaac's messianic writing. If we adopt this approach, we see that the historical circumstances not only prepared the ground for the reading of Daniel, but also for Don Isaac, leader and author, to address his audience. As he writes at the end of his preface:

> I, Isaac, arose. . . . I stand to intercede for His people during its dark night, and to awaken it from its slumber of exile—like a man who awakes from his sleep. . . . And I composed this commentary on Daniel because he among the prophets truly heralds good fortune and announces salvation, and at the threshold of exegesis on his visions, I have chosen to stand. And because when the nation of God suffers, its heart grows hot, and the nation thirsts there for water, and their souls fail from thirst.[22]

Like the image of a leader who is a candle in the darkness of exile, a figure we encountered above in *Nahalat avot*, Don Isaac here defines his relationship with his readers as that of a leader who has appeared and detected, before anyone else, the link between historical circumstances and Daniel's visions. As a leader, Abravanel stirs and inspires his readers, relaying good tidings to them. The author awakes and awakens his readers along with him.

Commentary as Refuge

The relationship between Don Isaac and his readers can be further understood from the imagery of thirst in the commentary: the identification of the exiles' spiritual needs that the author must meet. The name of the book, *Ma'ayanei hayesh'ua*, and its structure are closely related to the idea that it provides for the spiritual needs of its readers and author. "Now this is the name by which it will be called," Don Isaac explains, "it is *Ma'ayanei hayeshu'ah* [wells of salvation], and they are twelve wells of water for the cursed, and seventy palm trees for chapters."[23] The title of the commentary and its division into twelve wells (parts) and seventy palms (chapters) are designed to present the commentary as an oasis in the desert of history—that is, a source of relief in the midst of the desolation of the late fifteenth century.

Abravanel based the structure of the book on Exodus 15:27 ("Then they came to Elim, where there were twelve wells of water and seventy palm trees; so they camped there by the waters"), comparing the historical environment of the exiles to that of the generation in the wilderness. His commentary is the oasis: readers may use its chapters to slake their spiritual thirst. Through immersion in the wonderous literary environment of *Ma'ayanei hayeshu'ah*, the readers are meant to find solace for the tempests in their souls, for the suffering that, like thirst and hunger, chews away at their historical and religious consciousness. As Abravanel writes in his elegant prose: "Therefore the poor and destitute seek water, and the word of God cannot be heard when they are wasted with hunger and devoured by pestilence. To you O people I call 'Ho! Everyone who thirsts, come to the waters and all who seek God should tarry here and learn to consume their feed—grains of the heavens, treasured fruit . . . and its smell is fragrant and he will drink and forget his poverty."[24]

Don Isaac and the Prohibition on Calculating the End

The water that the commentary provides its readers is the water of life, water that refreshes and excites messianic faith and calculations of the date of the end of days. Abravanel was well aware of the negative attitude expressed in classical rabbinic literature toward those who attempted to determine when the redemption would arrive. He even provides a long list of those who erred in their calculations, including "Rabbi Saadia Gaon, Rashi and Rabbi Abraham son of Rabbi Hiyya, Nachmanides, and other sages who each one, in his own time, sought to find delightful words in this matter, and despaired."[25] However, Abravanel could also rely on the words of praise expressed by Abraham Bar Hiyya about attempts to calculate the redemption in the introduction to his *Megilat hamegaleh*:

> Anything with its primary basis in the Torah, and which stores good for Israel in this exile, or strengthens their hearts in faith, or contributes to their confidence and hope—it is good for a person to study and to give his heart, to search through its hidden secrets, and to reveal its treasures. . . . And you will find that the matter of the End, which we yearn for, and to which our eyes are peeled, holds all of these good qualities.[26]

To defend his decision to engage in this line of inquiry, Don Isaac draws a distinction between "those who calculate ends (*mehashevei qitzin*)"—that is, "self-proclaimed sages who calculate the courses of the heavenly bodies and their constellations and conclude when the redemption will take place"—and those who "study and understand the End through the words of prophets and those who spoke with the Holy Spirit."[27] According to Abravanel, it is the first type of prognosticator who is being censured by the Babylonian Talmud in Sanhedrin 97b. By contrast, the second group—composed of philosophers and exegetes, including Saadia Gaon, Rashi, Abraham Bar Hiyya, and Nachmanides—is not ignoble at all. Abravanel explains the drive behind messianic speculation by referring to the words of Aristotle that we discussed in the first part of this book:

> And this inquiry, with all the danger it entails, is doubtless a precious one. And for this reason, it is proper to expand the inquiry.... Behold you see in the treatise of the philosopher [Aristotle] in his book of the heavens and earth [De Caelo], that when he wanted to study why the wandering stars that are close to the first sphere have many movements while those that are far from it have few movements ... he apologized for delving into these hidden scientific inquiries (derushim) and he said that we should not attribute to him presumptuousness. ... And he admitted that he did not have true knowledge ... and that he should be praised for the little he had achieved of these pearls [of astronomical knowledge], given their difficulty and depth. For while a man cannot achieve complete knowledge of this matter through natural means, it is man's essence and therefore it is proper for him to study these with all his ability. And if he does not arrive at a syllogistic proof (mofet), he will nevertheless have acquired some knowledge, and he can hope that they who come after him will clarify and supplement [the results of] his own study.... And if the philosopher said such things about the study of matters that held no relevance for him, [how much more so] for the hearts of men whose foundations are in the dust, whose honor and glory is consumed by the sword, as is our [plight]—what else can they do but to seek out the word of God, [to determine] when He will come, when He will see fit to give their souls rest and to reprieve them from their toil?[28]

Messianic speculation is compared to scientific study. The same natural drive to uncover the truth that impels the scientist to study the heavens and propose theories about the movements of the stars compels the exegete to study the descriptions of redemption recorded in the Prophets and Writings and propose dates for the arrival of the redemption. Abravanel further emphasizes that if scientific research satisfies the philosopher's curiosity to know about the distant heavens, then study of the redemption and calculation of the end answer a far more pressing need: the desire of Jewish exiles to know when they will be relieved of suffering.

To further defend this messianic approach, Abravanel raises yet again the link between the canonical text and historical circumstances, but this time from a different perspective. Don Isaac uses the verse from Daniel 12:4, in which the angel says to the prophet: "But you, O Daniel, shut up the words, and seal the book, until the time of the end: many shall run to and fro, and knowledge shall be increased." In other words, Daniel is told to hide within his book the date of the end of days "until the time of the end." Abravanel explains that "God concealed [matters] . . . in this exile, unlike the exile in Egypt and Babylon. And this is due to [the present exile's] length, lest the hearts of the exiles despair [upon learning] of its [great] duration."[29] Daniel thus conceals the secret of the exile—the secret of its long duration. It is a secret that eludes all who read and study the book, and it becomes evident only when the historical circumstances are ripe and the eschaton grows near. When the time arrives, the words of the angel "will clarify and illuminate themselves, and if during exile they were shrouded in darkness, in the time or redemption they will be clear and illuminated."[30]

Furthermore, drawing inspiration from the Zohar (1:117b), Abravanel asserts that the words of the angel "will be purified and tried in the kiln of the tremendous suffering that will be during that time."[31] Don Isaac combines these historical justifications with a psychological and social one: whoever studies the secret of the end during an era when the historical circumstances are ripe will not only succeed in uncovering its secrets, but the very act of unraveling the secret will yield extremely beneficial psychological and social results. Abravanel designates authentic prognosticators of the end with a title taken from the previous verse in Daniel: "they that turn many to righteousness." He explains that "because they will strengthen the nation of God with their faith and add great hope and trust in the grace of the honorable God, they will be able to bear the pain of exile with the knowledge that salvation is imminent."[32] Thus Don Isaac's response to the talmudic prohibition against eschatological prognostication combines historical explanations with psychological ones, as encapsulated in the following words: "In my opinion, the time of redemption is at hand, and we today are at the end of exile . . . and therefore it is a time to act for God, by writing this treatise, to bring good tidings, and to pronounce salvation. Yet I do not decree that that which this treatise states is absolutely true."[33] In this last sentence, Abravanel disavows any claim to absolute knowledge: the messianic message of *Ma'ayanei hayesh'ua* is by no means a certain one. That being said, it is a message that is much needed in light of the historical circumstances.

The Visions and Dreams of Daniel

We have thus far argued that Don Isaac's messianic exegesis was a consequence of his own assessment of the fundamental historical changes taking place in the late fifteenth century and his belief in the positive social implications of renewing hope in the Messiah's imminent arrival. However, to fully understand the correspondence between Daniel's hidden message and the historical situation, we must take into account another element of the commentary, the prophetic status of Daniel's visions. According to Abravanel, the messianic contents of Daniel are esoteric and obscure because of the specific prophetic mode in which they were expressed: that of dreams and visions.

Based on the Maimonidean understanding of prophecy, Abravanel distinguishes between three grades of prophecy: the first "is the grade of our master Moses. . . . This is when the divine influence rests [directly] upon the prophet's intellect . . . and he sees explicit things . . . with no parable and no riddles of image or form."[34] In other words, the highest level of prophecy is characterized by the prophet's clear intellect, "without the imaginative faculty and its impressions having any influence or rendering [the prophetic] message in physical form."[35]

In the second level of prophecy, the divine influence first rests upon the "prophet's intellect and then passes through the imaginative faculty." Abravanel explains the process by which divine influence extends to the imagination: "When the influence rests upon the prophet's intellect . . . he will not feel its reception, because of the depth of the intelligible message and the deficiency of the one apprehending it. . . . For this reason it extends . . . to the imaginative faculty engraving therein forms and images."[36] The extension of divine influence to the prophet's imagination in the guise of pictures and images reflects the prophet's inability to bear and receive the divine message as is. In the transition from intellect to imagination, the contents of the prophecy are veiled, requiring the prophet (and the reader of his prophecies) to decipher the images through interpretation—in other words, to recover the lost, cryptic content embedded within it.

In the third and lowest stage of prophecy, divine influence descends even further and rests upon "the external senses." This causes the prophet to experience prophecy not on the level of imagination but rather "through his sense perception alone, such that the prophet sees with his eyes and hears with his ears divine sense experiences (*hamuhashim ha'elohiyim*) which do not exist in the physical world."[37] In summary, Abravanel asserts that the prophecies of Daniel are of the second and third stage: in other words, they are figurative prophecies that conceal their intellectual content. The true content of Daniel's prophecy has remained opaque until the generation of the expulsion, and in this time—in light of a new, oppressive reality—the truth suddenly appears before Abravanel's very eyes.

The Secret of Daniel's Visions

What is the secret of Daniel's visions and dreams, and what is their purpose? This is the question raised by Abravanel: "And why did the Holy One Blessed is He see fit to convey prophetic sights and visions to Daniel, telling him the meaning of these kingdoms and their actions, when prophecy had ceased and when he was in the land of the Chaldeans?"[38] Based on the third chapter of *Megilat hamegaleh*, as well as the eighth chapter of Saadia Gaon's *Book of Doctrines and Beliefs*, Abravanel answers by referring specifically to the vision of four kingdoms:

> And just as before their entry into the land, the Blessed Lord roused their foe Balaam against them as well as [giving prophecy to] Moses ... to anticipate and announce their fortunes and misfortunes, so too, when they left the Land for exile, the Holy One Blessed is He deemed it proper to testify before them all the future exiles and hardships that would befall them so that they would not think that they had been abandoned to happenstance ... to tell them of their exiles and hardships in the four kingdoms so it would be known and publicized that everything was from Divine Providence.[39]

In other words, we must see the visions and dreams of Daniel (chief among them, the vision of four kingdoms) as different representations of the history of exile. At the beginning of Israel's long exile, God's influence rested upon Daniel (and King Nebuchadnezzar) in the form of prophetic dreams in which a condensed, cryptic, and imagined history of exile and redemption was conveyed. However, the visual nature of the prophecies is ambivalent: On the one hand, it vaguely adumbrates the history of the exile during the era of the four kingdoms, showing how their rise and fall is part of a comprehensive divine plan. On the other hand, it conceals the details of this future history—the length of exile, its darkest hours, and the precise identity of each of the four kingdoms. Abravanel has an explanation for this balance between concealment and revelation. According to him, in this instance, God acted like a doctor tending to a patient about to experience a difficult disease:

> And we find yet another purpose, and that is the pronouncement of punishments in law systems is in one sense beneficial and in the other sense harmful. In terms of its benefit: man's heart is evil from his youth, and it is his nature to be drawn after sin . . . and because man is predisposed toward sin, the lawmakers had to designate penalties in order to instill fear. . . . But there is damage wrought by pronouncing punishments—for those who know that their punishment will arrive in the future, will continue to sin. . . . And they will despair of [doing] good, so much so that the Torah commanded that when one besieges a city to fight against it, that one must proclaim an offer of peace to it. And if [the enemy] refused to make peace, one besieges the city, but does not surround it on all sides, but rather leaves one side open for flight, so that the men of the city will not lose hope entirely—for when they despair, they will fight with great vigor and commit heinous evils. . . . And the Blessed God seeing the benefit of pronouncing punishments on the one hand, and its harm on the other, took a middle path. And this was to pronounce punishments in the souls of the sinners and to inform them that He would recant and take pity on them if they would return to Him. . . . And when the Holy One Blessed is He decided to inform His people of the great hardships that were destined to befall the nation, He decided to tell them also—so that they would not despair—that they would still bear fruit in their old age. Thus, their hearts could endure, and their hands gain strength to bear their exiles and their hardships. And this is the [practice of the] best of doctors who will say to the patient, "you are about to undergo a difficult bout of [sickness] with terrifying symptoms—but fear not, for it will be followed by relief and healing."[40]

Abravanel explains the psychological and social logic of the balance between the punishment of exile and the expectation for redemption. At the beginning of exile, the Jews could not bear the tribulations of exile as a divine punishment without having "one side open for flight." In other words, they needed a faithful portrayal of the end of exile, a description of the ultimate redemption. Daniel is thus the divine cure for exile. The book was written in the early days of exile to anticipate the long history to come, but primarily to help the Jewish people overcome the difficulties of exile by establishing a historical consciousness predicated on the dual principles of exile and redemption. The outline of the history of exile presented in Daniel's visions retrospectively demonstrates their own prophetic nature and thus reinforces the likelihood of a redemption. The historical consciousness based on exile and redemption is a cyclical one. The crises of the present confirm the prophecies and promises of redemption recorded in scripture. In his biography of Abravanel, Netanyahu saw in this vicious cycle an attempt to flee from historical and political reality. However, without denying this component of Abravanel's message, we can see in this consciousness the cultural ability to integrate changing historical events into a theological and political framework, a means of allowing Jewish collective existence to continue unabated.

Historical Exegesis or Anti-Christian Polemic?

Don Isaac's commentary on Daniel is primarily focused on the exegesis of Daniel's visions. He tries to turn each vision, and every detail within each vision, into a realistic historical narrative. Thus, for example, Don Isaac interprets the fourth beast's "teeth of iron" (Dan. 7:19) as follows:

> And behold, [Daniel] portrayed the advisors [Roman consuls] as teeth because teeth are individual body parts and yet they consume food for the benefit of the entire body. . . . Thus were the consuls of Rome: Scipio, Cicero, Quintus Fabius Maximus, Marcus Antonius, and Pompeus. . . . For they were distinguished men in Rome but not kings. Rather they were servants of the general good, and they would conquer lands and cut up the rebellious and difficult nations, grinding them up and bringing them under Roman rule.[41]

Abravanel's attempt to understand the hidden meaning of the fourth beast's iron teeth is not only used to identify the creature as a symbol of the Roman Republic and Empire—which, according to Abravanel, includes the empire's breakup into Christianity and Islam. Most scholars have understood Abravanel's main goal as an attempt to refute Christian claims that Christendom, which rose from the ashes of the Roman Empire, is none other than the kingdom of the Messiah. While this motivation certainly holds true, it is worth drawing attention to the literary element of Abravanel's efforts as well. As Don Isaac explains, his commentary is designed to find a correspondence between "all the details of the images" and real historical events and details: "for it is impossible that they do not attest to real subjects [when their] lesson is understood."[42] More than Don Isaac sought to contend with Christian apologetics, he wished to create—using his historical exegesis of Daniel's vision—a realistic impression upon his reader. Seeing how time and time again, the details of Daniel's visions and dreams correspond to details of world history, the reader is convinced, retrospectively, that the book of Daniel is a prophetic work.

Calculating the Date of the Redemption

Abravanel's integration of messianic exegesis with the concrete history of the fifteenth century is exemplified by his interpretation of the words of the angel about the length of exile and the date of the advent of the redemption: "And from the time that the daily sacrifice is taken away, and the abomination of desolation is set up, there shall be one thousand two hundred and ninety days (*yamim*)." (Dan. 12:11) Abravanel calculates these 1,290 days as follows:

> And without a doubt the angel sought ways to hide the matter, and therefore I think that when he said yamim he did not mean real days and not even years. Rather the [word] yamim is to be included as part of the count, for the numerological value of yamim with its two *mems* and two *yuds* is 100. And then the total sum, when [the] value [of the word] yamim is added, is 1390—from the time when the daily sacrifice was discontinued until the "abhorrence" was established in Constantinople, and this was when [the city] was conquered by the Persian Turks. And because this was the first sign of the redemption and the beginning of vengeance, therefore, the angel mentioned it first. And this number is precise—with no doubt whatsoever. For the Second Temple was destroyed in the year 3828 and three years earlier the daily sacrifice was discontinued . . . that is, 3824 years after creation. 1390 years after this, Constantinople was conquered.[43]

Turning the word "days," mentioned by the angel, into years and further using numerology to add 100 to the sum explicitly enumerated by the angel are just some of exegetical and esoteric techniques employed by Abravanel to calculate the date of the redemption. The influence of Bar Hiyya and Saadia Gaon is patent. The dual implication of the word "yamim" clearly shows that Don Isaac's exegetical goal was to link the verse to world events taking place in his lifetime, which could be accepted by his readers as "first heralds of the redemption."[44] In the fall of Constantinople to the Ottomans in 1453, Don Isaac saw the beginnings of a new world order, presaging the advent of the next age. David Ruderman has shown the prevalence of messianic expectations and calculations in response to the fall of Constantinople, for Jews and Christians alike.[45] It was part of a broader trend of messianic stirrings in the fifteenth century and part of the general Jewish and Christian proclivity for astrological calculations and prognostications.

After the fall of Constantinople, the Ottoman Empire proceeded to spread its power across the Balkans, conquering cities and islands from the Venetians. The growing strength of the Ottoman Empire and its steady march toward Western Europe stirred trepidation in the Christian world and fueled plans for new crusades, so that—while an intra-European war continued to be waged upon Italian soil—war broke out between Venice and the Ottoman Empire. In Don Isaac's messianic perspective, the wars in Italy and in the Greek-speaking regions of Europe were the first signs of a broad struggle between Christendom and the Ottoman Empire—a struggle, in other words, between Edom and Ishmael. Based on Daniel's visions of the four kingdoms (which Don Isaac identifies as Babylon, Persia, Greece, and Rome), Abravanel concluded that Islam and Christianity are in fact two offshoots of the Roman Empire. The struggle between these two powers will lead to the collapse of the fourth kingdom and the establishment of the fifth kingdom of the Messiah. Thus, by making calculations based on the words of the angel, Abravanel manages to link the great cataclysms of the late fifteenth century to the messianic visions of Daniel.

Interpreting the words of the verse "Blessed is he who waits, and comes to the one thousand three hundred and thirty-five days," (Dan. 12:12) Abravanel describes the period that will elapse between the conquest of Constantinople and the coming of the Messiah:

> "Blessed is he." . . . This indicates that, after the capture of Constantinople, the troubles in Israel will increase. . . . And they will be driven out from the gentile nations. . . . Until 1435 years after the destruction of the Second Temple, which is fifty years after the capture

of Constantinople [1503 CE]—then unto the Jews will be light and joy. Therefore when [the verse] stated, "Blessed is he who waits," this means that fortunate is the one who has the strength to bear the sorrows of exile and withstand the test of the Lord and does not leave the religion and reaches the year 1435—for then the end of sorrows will be at hand, and then, perhaps, the King Messiah will appear, or Rome will be destroyed, or vengeance will be exacted from the nations.[46]

In Abravanel's view, the period between 1453 and 1503 CE was one of trials. It was a time of international crisis, as we have seen, but also a period of expulsions and the exhaustion of the Jews' tribulations. Those who withstand the historical test will merit seeing the next age, the age of Israel's redemption and the exacting of vengeance against their oppressors. Later in the commentary, Don Isaac singles out some further dates, suggesting a more complex process—thus, 1503 is only the beginning of salvation, 1534 is the year of redemption, and 1575 is the year of the resurrection of the dead.[47] Regardless, we can see the second role played by the calculations: they tie Daniel's visions not only to the recent past (the conquest of Constantinople, the expulsion from Castile and Aragon, the crisis in Italy, and the struggle between Venice and the Ottoman Empire) but also to the near future. Don Isaac concluded *Ma'ayanei hayeshu'ah* in January 1497, while the oppression and trials of expulsion were still at their severest. According to Abravanel, however, salvation would be at hand a mere six years in the future. Intervening between the recent past and near future is the present, the difficult day-to-day life of the Sephardic émigré, the intended audience for Don Isaac's messianic rhetoric. Thus—and as indicated by the focus on the phrase "blessed is he who waits" (Dan. 12:12)—we can see in Don Isaac's messianic writing and homiletics an attempt to replace the uncertainty of the present with fervent expectation for cataclysmic changes on the horizon. When the reader enters the psychological state of messianic expectation, it is clear (at least in Don Isaac's view) that his connection to the religious and social framework of Judaism will grow stronger. This is the apologetic effect Don Isaac hopes to elicit through his messianic exegesis.

Historical Revolution, Messianic Revolution

Toward the end of the book, Don Isaac launches into a long astrological discussion aimed at further supporting his calculations. As discussed by

Julius Guttmann, this chapter (which Abravanel calls "The Gate of Heaven") is based entirely on the fifth chapter of *Megilat hamegaleh*.[48] The thrust of the discussion is as follows: the second half of the fifteenth century is a unique historical period in world history. At mid-century, the constellation that ruled during the exodus returned, an event referred to by Don Isaac as "the great conjunction (*mahberet*) within Pisces."[49] Describing the influence that this great convergence had on the Jewish people during the exodus, Don Isaac emphasizes its revolutionary influence on history:

> Since the effect of the great conjunction is to bring the nation and the subject that receives its influence from one extreme to the other. . . . Therefore, its action will not fall on the average nation . . . but rather will fall by necessity on the most debased nation, enslaved in a land that is not theirs, in order that the constellation bring it to the zenith of the highest rank. Since the people of Israel were in this extreme of debasement and defect, in being slaves to the Egyptians, what was not true of any other nation, therefore the emanation of this great conjunction fell on it to elevate it to the uppermost degree of human perfection.[50]

While Don Isaac is not interested in grounding his messianic claims solely on astrological determinism, he sees in the recurrence of the great conjunction the same event that took place during the exodus: the cosmological conditions that allow for a radical historical shift from one extreme to the other. He continues:

> From creation until now, Saturn and Jupiter conjoined in Pisces only twice: first, in the year 2365 during the sojourn of Israel in Egypt three years prior to the birth of Moses. . . . Now around the year 5224 [1464] from the creation. . . . Since the two conjunctions are equal—both being in the grand conjunction of the constellation of Pisces—it is necessary that the second corresponds completely to the one during the exodus from Egypt. Therefore, it is necessary that just as the first conjunction exerted its influence upon Israel and caused them to emerge from slavery to freedom, from bondage to redemption, . . . so too this second Israelite conjunction will herald prophecy and redemption for the community of Israel. There is no doubt that the time of the birth of the man of God, the Messiah, has already come. . . . According to the methods

of the astrologers, the new conjunction will by necessity renew the actions of the first which was active during the exodus, with great and wondrous changes in the nation, transitioning them from one extreme to the other.[51]

Messianic and astrological exegesis both tie the great events taking place in the second half of the fifteenth century with the promises of redemption. They portray the experience of expulsion as a reflection of the negative aspects of the historical revolution taking place, an experience that will soon change when the positive side of the process (the messianic side) becomes evident. Netanyahu concluded his book on Abravanel with the adamant claim that "Abravanel's enormous power of logical thinking was devoted to prove the most illogical of all things."[52] The accusation that Don Isaac tried to paint the experience of the expulsion in decidedly messianic colors fails, however, to take into account two important factors. First, Abravanel did not concentrate all of his literary and leadership efforts on messianic solutions. Rather, he saw in messianism yet another avenue for his postexpulsion Jewish apologetics. Second, in the context of a mass expulsion and the establishment of new Spanish Jewish communities, addressing the question of the historical and theological horizons of the exiles was inevitable. In other words, Abravanel's messianism was bound up in a social process of constructing new communities in new locations and under new historical circumstances.

The Messianic Trilogy and Other Aspects of Abravanel's Life and Works

In Monopoli, Abravanel wrote his second messianic work, *Yeshu'ot meshiho*,[53] as a sequel to *Ma'ayanei hayeshu'ah*. He completed it on December 16, 1497. The work is dedicated to the exegesis of *Pirqei derabi Eliezer*, chapter 29, as well as of messianic Aggadot throughout the Talmud. The setting for *Yeshu'ot meshiho* is the Iberian Christian apologetic literature of the fifteenth century composed in the aftermath of the pogroms and mass conversions of 1391 and aimed at exerting further theological pressure on the Jews of Castile and Aragon to convert to Christianity. Don Isaac inveighs against the talmudic and midrashic exegesis of the Jewish converso Jeronimo de Santa Fe, formerly Joshua al-Lorqui, who is commonly known in Hebrew literature by the disparaging epithet *hamegadef*—an acronym of his Spanish name and the Hebrew word for "blasphemer." Jeronimo wrote

the book *Ad Convicendum Perfidiam Judaeorum*, which translated into Hebrew as *Sefer hapoqrim*. The work was used as an important source text
in the Christian-Jewish disputations organized by the Church in Tortosa
and San Mateo in 1413 and 1414. Abravanel's recurring discussions of the
Christian exegesis of rabbinic Aggadot points to the apologetic character
of *Yeshu'ot meshiho*, which, like his previous books, was written with the
purpose of protecting and preserving the Judaism of the Sephardic exiles.

On February 26, 1498, about three months after finishing *Yeshu'ot meshiho*, Abravanel completed his third messianic commentary, *Mashmi'a
yeshu'ah*.[54] This was the final part of a messianic trilogy that he describes as
follows: "these three works consist of about eight quires, and I have titled
the entire collection *Migdol yeshu'ot*."[55] *Mashmi'ah yeshu'ah* is a commentary
on the Bible's messianic prophecies. Its goal, like that of *Yeshu'ot meshiho*, is
to refute messianic Christian apologetics. In the introduction to the book,
Abravanel explains that his commentary is a solution to and a cure for the
external and internal forces that threaten to shatter the messianic consciousness of the Sephardic exiles. He thus proves his mettle as a leader
who is capable of defending his nation against the pressures of Christianity
and who is worthy of taking over after the failures of the former leadership
of the Iberian Jewish community. Abravanel was particularly opposed to
the messianic approaches espoused by Rabbi Joseph Albo and Rabbi Isaac
Arama (the spiritual successors of Rabbi Hasdai Crescas), who did not
accept the coming of the Messiah and the resurrection of the dead as fundamental principles of the Jewish religion. Abravanel's commentary on the
messianic prophecies of the Bible thus concludes an extensive exegetical
work that expounds upon most of the messianic literature in the Bible and,
at the same time, helps complete the historical portrayal of the crises of the
fifteenth century as an expression of the messianic era.

Is Don Isaac's impressive messianic trilogy evidence that he had fallen
under the spell of messianism, as claimed by Netanyahu and Baer? To answer this question, it is worth bearing in mind that during the years 1496–
1503, when Don Isaac lived in Monopoli, the already dire circumstances of
the Jews deteriorated even further in a number of respects. In 1497 King
Manuel I of Portugal—adopting and even surpassing the policies of the
Catholic Monarchs—converted the Jews of his kingdom by force. Likewise, after years of war, the Catholic Monarchs finally defeated the French
forces in Italy and annexed the kingdom of Naples to their empire. At the
same time, the tensions between the Ottoman Empire and the Venetian

Republic erupted into a war that would last for three years (1499–1502). While Venice ultimately won the war, it lost much of its political and economic strength as a result. It was under the cloud of these major changes that Don Isaac conceived the idea that a radical messianic shift in the fortunes of the Jewish people was at hand.

However, as the year Don Isaac had proposed as the date of the "beginning of the redemption" (1503)[56] drew closer, he seemed to be more occupied by his efforts to expand and complete his more standard exegetical works and less like a man eagerly awaiting a radical messianic upheaval on the horizon. David Ben-Zazon has identified in one manuscript of Abravanel's commentary on the *Guide of the Perplexed* an important testimony, written by the author himself, in which he explains how he worked on expanding this commentary during his time in Monopoli in 1496 (that is, at the same time he was writing *Ma'ayanei hayesh'uah*). "I reviewed this chapter [part 1, chapter 50] with light study," writes Abravanel, referring to the light (that is, small) commentary that he wrote on the *Guide of Perplexed* before the expulsion, during his years in Portugal and Castile and Aragon. He continues: "And afterwards . . . I studied it in Monopoli in the year 1496, and I found matters that I would not have supposed when I wrote [the first version of the commentary]. Therefore [I composed] an independent commentary on this chapter."[57] In other words, at the same time that Abravanel was working on his messianic commentary on Daniel, he was also editing his commentary on the *Guide of the Perplexed*, expanding it from a "light study" to an extensive commentary. In the years after he completed his messianic trilogy, Abravanel went on to write two cosmological and theological works about the principle of creation ex nihilothat can be viewed as the direct sequel to his commentary on the *Guide of the Perplexed*: these were *Shamayim hadashim* (completed on April 7, 1498) and *Mif'alot elohim* (1501). The notion of creation ex nihilo is the ultimate theoretical basis for asserting divine intervention in the course of history, and many scholars have pointed to the underlying logic shared by both messianism and creation ex nihilo.

Abravanel continued to write further commentaries on the Prophets. In 1498, he completed his commentary on Isaiah, a book with more than a few messianic segments, and a few years later he wrote a commentary on the Twelve Minor Prophets. We also know that at this time, Abravanel developed a friendly relationship with Gonzalo de Cordoba—the general of the Spanish army in Italy who from 1495 until 1503 resided in Barletta, a port city near Monopoli. Various documents place Don Isaac and his son Judah in Barletta in 1501. Gonzalo and his army were stationed there for two years, and it can be assumed that Don Isaac and Judah met Gonzalo several times during this period. These few details do not suggest any radical shifts in Abravanel's life or that his life began to be defined by a deep personal loyalty to the messianic content presented in his commentaries. Even though the year that he had designated as the date of redemption was close at hand, we do not see any messianic changes in his personality or political and spiritual behavior.

In 1503, the political and military situation in the Italian peninsula became clearer. Gonzalo finally bested King Louis XII at the Battle of Cerignola, paving the way for the annexation of the kingdom of Naples. Some months later, he was appointed King Ferdinand's viceroy in Naples. The war between the Venetian Republic and the Ottoman Empire ended in 1502 with the signing of a peace treaty, leaving Venice with most of its islands and strategic port cities for maritime trade between the East and the West.

With the victory of the Spanish Empire and the Venetian Republic, the Abravanel family found itself split into two branches: the members who returned to Naples and those who settled in Venice. Thus, for example, we know that Judah Abravanel served as Gonzalvo's personal physician in Naples from 1503 to 1507. Afterward, his younger brother Samuel joined him, eventually becoming a great patron of the Jewish community in Naples. In contrast, their middle brother, Joseph, settled in Venice with his father in 1503.

18 : THE LAST YEARS IN VENICE (1503–1508)

Don Isaac's Settlement in Venice and His
Return to Political and Commercial Life

"And from there he traveled with his second son, Don Joseph Abravanel (may the Rock keep him and give him life) . . . and both went to the city of Venice, a great city to God."[1] This sentence is taken from the biography of Don Isaac penned by Barukh Forti (Hezqeto) in 1551. The use of the expression, "may the Rock keep him and give him life," along with other passages in the biography, indicates that Forti was acquainted with Don Joseph, the son of Don Isaac Abravanel. It appears that it was he who told Forti of Don Isaac's move to Venice. Why, however, did Don Isaac and Don Joseph move to Venice when they did? Later in the biography, Forti provides one explanation:

> It was his intention to affect a compromise between the Doges of Venice and the current King of Portugal in matters pertaining to the spice trade. And when the Doges and advisors, the judges of the land, saw the vast knowledge that was in his heart . . . they admitted him into the inner circles of their counsel, and revealed to him all their hidden secrets, and his word was precious in their eyes, in the manner of a man who seeks the word of God.[2]

If we rely on Forti's account, which was probably based on accounts relayed by Don Joseph, we can conclude that in 1503—the same year that Don Isaac designated as "the beginning of salvation"[3]—he returned to his political and commercial activities, moving to Venice for this purpose. It seems that he wished to offer his services to the Venetian Republic, to mediate between Venice and Portugal in issues related to maritime trade. Before explaining the nature of Don Isaac's role as an intermediary, it is worth reiterating that his return to political and economic activity, as well as to his literary activity, suggests that Don Isaac had a complex relationship with his own messianic calculations.

The backdrop to Don Isaac's role as a mediator was the 1498 discovery of a new sea route to India by the Portuguese explorer Vasco de Gama (c. 1460–1524). Following Portugal's discovery of Africa's west coast and the Cape of Good Hope during the fifteenth century, de Gama succeeded in traveling around Africa and arriving at the port city of Calcutta on the southwestern coast of India. The discovery of this new sea route radically changed the relations between Europe and the East: traders no longer had to sail from India to Arabia, traverse the Arabian peninsula and Egypt by land, and then embark from there for Venice. The discovery of a direct sea route to India, one that did not pass through the Mediterranean, jeopardized the foundation of Venice's commercial power, which was predicated on its control of the sea routes between Europe and Egypt. After the discoveries of da Gama and Christopher Columbus, the bulk of Europe's commerce and trade shifted gradually from the Mediterranean Sea to the Atlantic Ocean. While the Venetians sought to enlist the assistance of the Mamluk Sultan in Egypt in blocking the Portuguese sea route to India, they ultimately failed.[4]

It is against this backdrop of the emerging competition between Venice and Portugal over trade with India and the Orient that Don Isaac offered his services. Forti describes Don Isaac's meeting with the Venetian Republic's Council of Ten (Consiglio dei Dieci) as admission into the republic's inner circle, making him a party to their inner secrets. While Forti's descriptions may be hyperbolic, the meeting certainly attests to Don Isaac's importance and status, and furthermore, it situates him at one of the most important crossroads of world economic history in the late fifteenth and early sixteenth centuries.

According to the official summary of the meeting, which has been preserved in Venice's archives, Don Isaac proposed that "he would send his nephew to Portugal to submit there a solution of his own concerning these affairs [the spice trade]." According to the same document, the Council of Ten responded to Don Isaac's proposal as follows: "When he returns, we shall listen to everything he proposes, and after due consideration and evaluation of all, we shall not deviate from the terms of the agreement as we deem reasonable and appropriate. If the agreement will really be ratified, he [Abravanel may] rest assured that the gratitude of our State will not pass over him."[5]

The implication is clear: Don Isaac shared with the Venetian Republic an interest in the success of his nephew's diplomatic mission. However, by all accounts, the mission did not go well. King Manuel I of Portugal, having discovered a new and cheaper route to India, saw no reason to reach any trade agreements with Venice. Thus, to the best of our knowledge, ended Don Isaac's political and commercial career.

To understand the wider context of this mission, two additional factors should be taken into account. As Benjamin Ravid has shown, the Venetian Republic had a hostile attitude toward Jewish bankers and merchants during this era.[6] Only a small group of Jews were allowed into the city during the day to conduct their business, and even they were not allowed to reside there permanently. Instead, they were forced to live inland, in the nearby city of Mestre. In the year that Don Isaac and his son arrived in Venice, a small group of Jewish bankers were given permission to live in the city for a limited period of ten years. In granting this approval and enlisting Don Isaac's diplomatic assistance, we can see a shift in Venice's policy and attitudes toward the Jews. This would gradually lead to the establishment of the city's famous Jewish ghetto in 1516.

The Captive Grandson in Portugal

Another factor to be considered was that during the expulsion in 1492, Don Judah's son, Isaac (who was then a baby), had been sent to Portugal. He did not join the dangerous voyage with the rest of his family to Italy for fear that the Catholic Monarchs would seize him and baptize him by force. Around the time of Don Isaac's move to Venice, Judah Abravanel composed a poem entitled "Teluna 'al hazman" ("A Complaint against the Times"), in which he describes the fate of his son, Isaac:

> When the children of Sepharad were driven out
> The king ordered a trap to be devised for me:
> So that I should not take flight and escape through the gorge
> He ordered my only son to be taken—the one who had drunk my milk
> To force him to follow the king's religion.
> But a good man, one trusted by me, revealed this plan to me.
> As if he were a thing I had stolen
> I sent the child, with his wet nurse, in the deep of the night.[7]

Before explaining what happened to his son, Judah mentions his father's flight from King Dom João II of Portugal in 1483. He then relates his son's fate:

> And when he [the king] learned of my son's coming to his kingdom
> And that I was about to flee to my father's house in Italy,

He imprisoned the boy and held him, and ordered
Him never to return whence he had been exiled.
And after the death of that king there came to power a witless one—
A fanatic in his religion, a hollow man.
He persecuted the community of Jacob and enforced
Conversion on them, the children of my noble people.
Many of them took their own lives rather than
Break the laws of He Who gives us succor.
And my son, the apple of my eye, was still held, and even his name [Isaac]
Taken from the rock whence I was hewn, was changed.
He is now twelve and to this day I have not seen him.
Thus, I am punished for my covetousness and error.[8]

The baby Isaac was thus used as a pawn by the king of Portugal to exact vengeance upon the Abravanel family, especially Don Isaac. The child was taken from his guardians and baptized. In 1497, Dom Manuel forced all the Jews of his kingdom to convert to Christianity, and Judah Abravanel despaired of ever seeing his son again. Perhaps the diplomatic services that Don Isaac rendered on behalf of Venice were an attempt to rescue his grandson? We cannot say for sure, but it is not unreasonable to speculate that the journey of Don Isaac's nephew to Portugal had some connection to the bitter fate of the twelve-year-old Isaac.

However, beyond the family tragedy and a father's deep longing for his lost son, all expressed in the poem, it is important to draw attention to one further point: the fate of the exiles who were scattered among Portugal, Italy, and the Ottoman Empire became entangled in the relations between the sea powers—Venice, Castile and Aragon, and Portugal. Don Isaac's activity during his many years in Portugal and Castile was in the eyes of the officers of the Venetian Republic a source of invaluable knowledge, and they had every interest in taking advantage of it. Over the course of the sixteenth and seventeenth centuries we see many Jewish conversos of Iberian origin serving as agents and intermediaries in the trade networks of naval powers and empires.

Don Isaac Completes His Literary Oeuvre

Abravanel's literary accomplishments, from his arrival in Venice until his death in 1508, include a series of commentaries on the Latter Prophets (Jeremiah and Ezekiel) as well as a commentary on the Pentateuch (Genesis, Exodus, Leviticus, Numbers). Moreover, Abravanel worked on completing a full commentary on Maimonides's *Guide of the Perplexed*, though only a partial commentary on the work has reached us. As shown by David Ben-Zazon, based on his examination of the various manuscripts of the commentary, Abravanel delivered lessons on the *Guide* throughout his life, writing partial commentaries in Portugal, Castile, and Italy.[9] Moreover, he wrote in a 1507 letter to Saul Hakohen that "indeed it is true that recently I resolved in my heart to interpret this book,"[10] meaning that he planned to write a comprehensive commentary on the entire work. However, it appears that he never completed the task. As one copyist of the commentary put it, "And this copyist [Rabbi Leon Malki] has it from tradition that the commentator (his memory for a blessing) was called up by the heavenly academy before he could complete this precious book."[11] Without delving into the contents of these commentaries, we can surmise that Don Isaac hoped to bequeath the following literary legacy to the generation to come: (1) a full commentary on the Pentateuch and Prophets; (2) a collection of commentaries and treatises revolving around the *Guide of the Perplexed* and other works of Maimonides; (3) a messianic trilogy; and (4) a series of commentaries on Maimonides's thirteen principles of faith, the Passover Haggadah, and *Pirkei avot* (all of which were printed in Istanbul in 1505, as we have discussed).

This ambitious exegetical enterprise was aimed at leaving a deep impact on biblical exegesis, Maimonidean philosophy, and Jewish apologetics in the aftermath of the expulsion. Besides this vast corpus, we should note some works that were either lost or never completed: *Mahaze Shadai* (a treatise on prophecy), *Tzedek 'olamim* (a treatise on theodicy), and *Yemot 'olam* (a history of the Jewish people from Adam to the expulsion). In the aforementioned letter to Hakohen, Abravanel lists all the commentaries and works he had written up to that point. He refers to his commentary on the Pentateuch as "the first of Zion and highest in degree" because "all my thoughts and knowledge are contained therein."[12] Let us therefore end our review of Don Isaac's exegetical career with a discussion of his commentary on Genesis.

The Commentary on Genesis and the Technological and Political Development of Mankind

Yitzhak Baer was the first scholar to note the social critique that emerges from Don Isaac's exegesis in his commentary on the stories relating to the dawn of humanity at the beginning of the book of Genesis.[13] Here we will expand on Baer's insight and compare Don Isaac's critique to his own so-cial status and commercial activities.

There seems to be an interesting contradiction between Don Isaac's ac-tions and words. Adam's state before the fall is described in Genesis 2:5–7:

> And every plant of the field before it was in the earth, and every herb of the field before it grew: for the Lord God had not caused it to rain upon the earth, and there was not a man to till the ground. But there went up a mist from the earth, and watered the whole face of the ground. And the Lord God formed man of the dust of the ground, and breathed into his nostrils the breath of life; and man became a living soul.

Abravanel explains the passage as follows:

> The overall intention of this long passage is to inform us that God created man in His intelligible image so that he would endeavor to complete his soul by knowing his creator, apprehending His actions, and likening himself to Him. . . . And for the organization of [man's] life, God also formed everything necessary for [man-kind's] existence. . . And all of this was by natural existence, so that we would have no need for labor, work, or human arts (mela'kha enoshit), but rather that all of [humanity's] needs would be available and found before him always, so that he need not trouble himself with tending to the needs of his body and concern himself only with the perfection of his soul. . . . And for this reason, [God] com-manded [man] that he suffice with the natural things created to meet his needs, and not be drawn after luxuries (motarot) which require the activities of the arts and conventions (devarim mefur-samim). And thus, his intellect would not be turned toward the ef-forts to satisfy the needs of the body which is the opposite of spiritual perfection—[humanity's] ultimate end.[14]

With respect to the state of humanity in the Garden of Eden, these de-scriptions do not seem to contain any major innovation that goes beyond the well-known ideas espoused by Maimonides in Guide of the Perplexed in chapter 2 of part 1:

> Accordingly when man was in his most perfect and excellent state, in accordance with his inborn disposition and possessed of his in-

tellectual cognitions—because of which it is said of him: Thou hast made him but little lower than Elohim [Ps. 8:6]—he had no faculty that was engaged in any way in the consideration of generally accepted things, and he did not apprehend them. So among these generally accepted things even that which is most manifestly bad, namely, uncovering the genitals, was not bad according to him, and he did not apprehend that it was bad. However, when he disobeyed and inclined toward his desires of the imagination and the pleasures of his corporeal senses—inasmuch as it is said: that the tree was good for food and that it was a delight to the eyes [Gen. 3:6]—he was punished by being deprived of that intellectual apprehension. He therefore disobeyed the commandment that was imposed upon him on account of his intellect and, becoming endowed with the faculty of apprehending generally accepted things, he became absorbed in judging things to be bad or fine.[15]

What attracted Baer's attention was not Don Isaac's description of Adam diverting his attention from intellectual objects of inquiry to imaginary ones, but rather the contrast Don Isaac draws throughout the commentary between the perfection of the soul through knowledge of the creator and the care for man's and woman's biological life beyond their natural needs. When men and women exceed their natural needs, they are forced to divert their intellect from contemplation to the imaginary representations involved in the world of arts and in the desires that sustain them. Thus, men and women develop a social, economic, and technological existence, feeding an ever-expanding world of objects and images that Abravanel refers to as "luxuries."

Human composite nature—a body and a soul—requires humans to live in a society and to develop a system of social representations that allow this society to function. However, this distances humanity from the truth. "It was not possible for a human according to his perfection to be alone in the world without a society and state," Abravanel explains, "for by himself, he would be unable to gather and tend to his food. . . . And the result of this was that in their being part of a society, [humans] needed, in accordance with practical intellect, [the notions of] good and evil. It is this which brought the Tree of Knowledge and the Tree of Good and Evil to the world."[16] In other words, Abravanel interprets the fall of Adam, the murder of Abel, the flood, and the Tower of Babel as part of humankind's gradual deviation from nature and truth and the development of a new reality based on desires, economics, political regimes, and the social imagery that correspond to these phenomena—all of which continued to multiply.

Thus, for example, discussing the sin at the Tower of Babel, Don Isaac writes:

> And behold in the early days of the generation of the Dispersion, all of the human race was influenced and led by the Blessed One in all their matters, with no intermediary, be it for good or for evil. . . . And within them was instilled pure, natural behavior, with no striving after luxuries and imaginary arts. And along with this, they had a single language: the language that the Holy One Blessed is He had taught Adam. But when they journeyed away from He who preceded the world, and strayed from the natural behavior, pursuing arts that withhold perfection, building a city and a tower—the Lord came down to see their actions. For until that point, it was He who had truly led them with His providence. And He said: "since these [people] were not content to be a single nation and a single language, and this they begin to do, to engage in imaginary arts, I will hide my face from them and [cease] to lead them, entrusting them [instead] to the celestial officers."[17]

The generation that attempted to build the Tower of Babel separated humanity from "the natural order," plunging it into a world of "arts" and "artificiality," "with no end": "for when it comes to arts, they add [new] ideas all day and all night."[18] By satisfying its needs through the practical arts, humanity disrupts the balance between human needs and what is naturally accessible. It opens up the possibility of luxuries—that is, a world of products that correspond not to natural needs but rather to imaginary ones. Furthermore, man's and woman's transitions into a world of labor and imagined needs, the cornerstone of the city and the social and political relations within it, are a deviation not just from nature but also from God's direct providence. From this point forward, there are distinct nations, their histories and fates guided by astral bodies instead of by God.

Influences: Seneca, the Cynics, Josephus, and Augustine

Baer was the first to compare Abravanel's critique of luxuries to the ninetieth letter of Seneca to Lucilius. In doing so, Baer sought to demonstrate that Don Isaac's interest was not only historical, to describe humanity's intellectual deterioration in the earliest stages of its history. According to Baer, Don Isaac wished also to deliver social and moral criticism, the likes of which arise clearly from the following words of Seneca:

> Houses, shelter, creature comforts, food, and all that has now be-come the source of vast trouble, were ready at hand, free to all, and obtainable for trifling pains . . . it is we that have made all those things valuable, we that have made them admired, we that have caused them to be sought for by extensive and manifold devices. Nature suffices for what she demands. Luxury has turned her back upon nature, each day she expands herself, in all the ages she has been gathering strength and by her wit promoting the vices. At first, luxury began to lust for what nature regarded as superfluous, then for that which was contrary to nature; and finally, she made the soul a bondsman to the body, and bade it be an utter slave to the body's lusts (*illius deservire libidini iussit*). All these crafts by which the city is patrolled—or shall I say kept in uproar—are but engaged in the body's business; time was when all things were offered to the body as to a slave, but now they are made ready for it as for a master.[19]

In this letter, Seneca draws a stark distinction between philosophy and the march of human progress and technology. In Seneca's view, philosophy is not part of the technological and social evolution of mankind. Unlike these developments, philosophy teaches "that nature has laid upon us no stern and difficult law . . . that we can have everything that is indispens-able to our use, provided only that we are content with what the earth has placed on its surface."[20] The rationality of technological and social develop-ment is not equivalent to the reason of philosophy. The former is enslaved while the latter is, in Seneca's words, the "right reason (*recta ratio*)."[21] Against enslaved, aimless, and endless rationalism, Seneca proposes the principle: "follow nature (*sequere naturam*)"[22]—that is, follow the internal and natural end of human rationality. In the first part of this book, we noted that Abravanel was versed in the writings of Seneca. It seems that his em-phasis in Genesis on concepts like the arts (*melakhot*), luxuries, and the natural order (*haminhag hativ'i*) is part of the admiration felt by his con-temporaries toward Seneca.

In an article published in German a year after that of Baer,[23] Isaak Heine-mann offered a corrective to Baer's approach and proposed that Abravanel's commentary on the first chapters of Genesis was influenced not only by

Seneca but also by the views of the Greek Cynics, an approach he encountered through the medium of Latin literature: "Instead of the unique original sin in the Bible, Abravanel develops the idea of a repeated fall of humanity away from nature; i.e. he inserts the biblical narrative of the origin in the cynic scheme of the *diastrophe* [decline or decadence]."[24] According to Heinemann, Abravanel combined Maimonides's understanding of the sin of Adam with ideas drawn from the Cynics and developed a pessimistic view of humanity's deviation from nature—that is, the process by which humanity distanced itself from nature, supplanting it with the artificial.

The comparisons suggested by Baer and Heinemann have contributed much to our understanding of the literary context in which Abravanel's commentary on Genesis was composed. However, as Leo Strauss argued, this perspective is not enough. We must also compare Abravanel's social critique to the writings of Flavius Josephus and Augustine, authors much loved by Don Isaac. Both authors—the one a Jew and the other a Christian—associate the founding of the city, the political community, and the human economy with the sin of Adam as well as with negatively portrayed biblical figures such as Cain. At the beginning of his *Jewish Antiquities*, Josephus writes:

> After long travels Cain settled with his wife in a place called Nais, where he made his abode and children were born to him. His punishment, however, far from being taken as a warning, only served to increase his vice. He indulged in every bodily pleasure, even if it entailed outraging his companions; he increased his substance with wealth amassed by rapine and violence; he incited to luxury and pillage all whom he met, and became their instructor in wicked practices. He put an end to that simplicity in which men lived before by the invention of weights and measures: the guileless and generous existence which they had enjoyed in ignorance of these things he converted into a life of craftiness. He was the first to fix boundaries of land and to build a city, fortifying it with walls and constraining his clan to congregate in one place. This city he called Anocha after his eldest son Anoch.[25]

In his book, *City of God* (*De Civitate Dei*), Augustine proposed an even closer and more radical link between the sin of Adam and the gulf between the City of God and the Earthly City. In Augustine's view, the original sin opened up for mankind a negative horizon of self-sufficiency—or, to be more precise, independent meeting of needs, supplanting human reliance on God and nature. The first city built by Cain after the murder of his brother Abel symbolizes for Augustine the implementation of Adam's sin and the indomitable independence of humanity that views itself as an end unto itself. As Augustine puts it, "By striving after more, man is diminished; when he takes delight in his own self-sufficiency, he falls away from the One who truly suffices him."[26] Sin opens a divide between the realm of the divine and the realm of the human, the latter of which develops its own independent internal logic.

As opposed to the lack of boundaries and the power that characterizes the Earthly City, the City of God is identified by Augustine with the murdered Abel and the patriarch Abraham. The City of God is not part of the world of earthly cities; rather, it is the destination of the believer on his path back toward obedience to God. Or as the church father said: "The first founder of the earthly city [*terrenae civitatis conditor*], then, was a fratricide [*fratricida*]; for overcome by envy [*invidentia victus*], he slew his brother, who was a citizen of the Eternal City and a pilgrim on this earth [*civem civitatis aeternae in hac terra peregrinantem*]."[27] Abel represents for Augustine the image of a believer, a citizen of the City of God who resides in this world and in the Earthly City as a foreigner on a journey—or, more accurately, on a pilgrimage to God.

Abravanel did not accept the sharp Augustinian dichotomy between the City of God and the Earthly City and instead expressed the distinction as follows: "And because in the generation of the dispersion, there were good and righteous men, Noah, Shem, Eber, and Abraham . . . and they clung to their pure practices and natural sufficiency, immersing themselves in the study of the divine wisdom, . . . therefore, the providence of the Blessed Lord did not depart from them, and the Lord set apart for Himself a righteous man, Abraham, and his offspring after him, to be a chosen people among the nations."[28] As opposed to other nations that distanced themselves from God and nature, one group, Israel, continued to preserve a natural order and the unmediated connection with God. Does this mean that Israel is obliged to adopt the Augustinian model of a pilgrim, or the model of the Stoics and Cynics—who aspire to free themselves from dependence and imaginary needs? Don Isaac answers as follows:

And you cannot ask: if these arts of luxuries and the political order of the city were evil in the eyes of the Lord, why did He not forbid them to Israel afterwards? For the answer to this has been explained. For when the Blessed One saw that Adam and all of his offspring were immersed in the desire for the arts of luxuries, and were steeped in them, he did not forbid them to His people. For he foresaw and beheld that they would not remove these [vices] from themselves, for even Israel is flesh. Rather he enjoined the children of Israel to treat those artificial things with just hands and a suitable path.[29]

The nation of Israel thus does not represent a radical alternative to the course of human history, but rather the reduction and limitation of its most negative elements by relying upon the nation's unique connection with God.

Theory and Practice

Baer and Strauss correctly traced the influence of the Church fathers and Seneca upon Don Isaac's views. However, it is also important to note that Abravanel spent his entire life working in commerce, tax farming, and money lending. In other words, his career was heavily tied to the very luxuries that he so sharply condemns in his commentary on Genesis. Furthermore, at the same time he was criticizing human luxuries, it seems that Don Isaac was serving as a mediator between two states, Venice and Portugal, regarding commercial relations. Did he detect no contradiction or hypocrisy in the dissonance between his words and his behavior? It seems that Don Isaac's ambivalent attitude toward his own craft was not necessarily an attempt to categorically reject human crafts, but rather his observation from a distance—a more objective perspective that allowed him to best contend with the various facets of his own profession. If we add to this picture Abravanel's many references in his commentary on Genesis to the Kuzari, as well as his adoption of Judah Halevi's notion of Jewish chosenness, we can perhaps offer a more harmonious interpretation of the relationship between Abravanel's commercial activities and his critical remarks about human states and economies.

In Abravanel's opinion, the division of humanity into different peoples was a consequence of technological and political developments, a complex process involving human invention, deviation from God and nature, and the formation of national groups:

God made it happen that they would not all agree with a single will regarding the language they would use to refer to the new things that they had invented. Therefore, one family would refer to any crafted thing by a certain name, one that was different from the term used by another family. And when the innovated conventional words, which were different in each family, were combined with the first language they had [all once] shared, their languages were muddled and increased and they began to differ in accordance with their distinct conventions.[30]

Anything created by human hands needed a name. However, because the names of artificial inventions, unlike natural objects, required a group of speakers to reach a consensus, the words used to describe humanity's technical inventions hastened the process of division that underlies social and technological development, generating separate languages and distinct national groups. The differences between these groups caused them to be scattered across the globe. However, Abravanel explains that "the true knowledge and sanctified language" were preserved "by Abraham alone. . . . And therefore Abraham alone was like the perfection of the fruit of the human species as a whole, whereas other humans were like a shell, as the rabbi mentioned to the King of the Khazars [in Kuzari 1:95]."[31] Did the model of Israel as the nucleus or core of a humanity scattered in every direction resonate with the circumstances of Don Isaac and his fellow Spanish exiles? Don Isaac—a merchant, courtier, and community leader—witnessed a world convulsed by major changes, including those related to the expansion of the Iberian kingdoms and the dispersion of the Sephardic Jewish community. Does the image of Israel as a nucleus whose members remains loyal to the natural and divine origins of humanity not also represent a way of dealing with the phenomena of dispersion and expulsion? Amid a humanity undergoing great changes and unprecedented expansion (the discovery of the Americas and the discovery of the sea route to India), the idea of Israel as a defensive group that withstands these changes by virtue of its religious and cultural ethos had the power to console the Sephardic exiles, alleviate their fears, and enable them to cope with the present. We will never know what Don Isaac's true attitude was to his calculations of the redemption, but it is clear that he never explicitly disavowed his messianic outlook and expectations. Regardless, we can perhaps identify in the model we have described a different approach, one primarily focused on shaping the Sephardic émigrés' collective elitist consciousness against the backdrop of the rise of new empires.

It is worth noting that Don Isaac's son Judah (Leone Ebreo), author of

Dialoghi d'Amore, interpreted the story of Adam's fall and its consequences on the history of Israel and the world in similar fashion. Particularly prominent in his writings is the cyclical approach that views the story of humanity an almost inevitable process by which primordial unity deteriorates and falls into separation and disintegration. At the same time, however, this allows for the blooming of powers latent in each one of its different components, ultimately leading back to unity:

> This, Sophia, is the allegorical wisdom that the true history from Moses signifies: the union of the male and female in man, their establishment in Paradise, the command laid on them, their division, their sin through the deceit of the serpent, the punishment of all three, the possibility of a remedy, the engendering of evil and imperfect offspring, and finally of the perfect one who succeeded the first two; all these things (following the allegorical meaning) the first man really suffered in his body and they signify the life and works of every man, his ultimate happiness, the demands of his corporeal nature, and the consequences of excessive sin together with its punishment and the possibility of eventual salvation.[32]

Is Judah Abravanel offering a more optimistic picture of the march of human progress than that portrayed by his father? This issue has been the subject of debate among scholars.[33] Regardless, Don Isaac and his son Judah share a historical, natural, and divine conception of humanity's development that one can correct or refine from within, ultimately leading to a messianic eschaton (Don Isaac) or a return to a lost unity (Judah Abravanel). Perhaps this can explain why Don Isaac did not adopt the lifestyle of a messianic preacher, remaining a merchant and community leader throughout his life.

The Commentary on the Guide of the Perplexed and the Question of Don Isaac's Conservatism

Baer greatly admired the social criticism that Abravanel voiced in his commentary on Genesis. However, Strauss viewed it as a retreat from the tradition of Jewish political philosophy in a Maimonidean key. Don Isaac had succumbed, Strauss argued, to the Christian antirationalist approach to political problems. Benzion Netanyahu found an echo of Abravanel's conservative or even reactionary approach in a letter written by Abravanel and sent to Hakohen regarding his exegesis of Maimonides's writings. Abravanel begins with a mea culpa: "My sins I recount today, during the turbulence of my youth, I pursued the study of the natural and divine sciences. And after the days of evil were upon me, and I grew too old to be a man, I thought to myself: Why grow wise from the books of the Greeks and the children of Gentiles? . . . And I therefore dedicated myself to the study of the Pentateuch."[34]

The epistle and the long commentary on the *Guide of the Perplexed*, which it seems Abravanel edited and expanded in the same year, support the claim that Don Isaac was a conservative. Indeed, his commentary on the *Guide of the Perplexed* is, as this exegetical tradition goes, a conservative one. He strives to harmonize the views of Maimonides with the beliefs he regarded as traditional theological foundations of the Torah. Don Isaac opposed any interpretations that sought hints and secrets—in other words, readings focused on drawing attention to the tension between the *Guide*'s revealed layer, which ostensibly supports the basic tenets of biblical theology, and its esoteric layer, which incorporates radical philosophical positions. As Abravanel writes: "It is incumbent upon us to praise the author of the *Guide* for his justice, for reestablishing the fallen Torah in three matters . . . regarding creation ex nihilo, knowledge of God, and divine providence."[35] It is precisely these three theological topics that, according to esoteric readings of Maimonides, best express the tension between the approach of the *Guide* and the traditional understanding of scripture. David Ben-Zazon has studied the different textual versions of Don Isaac's commentary on the *Guide of the Perplexed*, showing how different variants belonged to different periods of Don Isaac's life (those he spent in Portugal, Castile, Monopoli, and Venice). He identifies ideological and exegetical continuity that, while it can certainly be called conservative or harmonistic, really strives to achieve "perfection of knowledge," in the vein of Sephardic Iyyun. But despite the relative constancy of his approach, Ben-Zazon also noted important developments in Abravanel's attitude towards Maimonides:

> At first, Abravanel regarded himself a student in comparison to Maimonides; he felt the need to justify the very thought of disputing Maimonides. Over the years, however, his esteem for Maimonides waned to some extent. While he continued to regard Maimonides's opinion as fundamental . . . sometimes, he would inveigh against it. Toward the end of his life, his own independent opinion had already begun to occupy a place of honor, and Maimonides's opinion

was rejected in favor of it. [At this point] he treated Maimonides's view as one important approach among many—one which the inquirer must know on his path toward the truth.[36]

We have noted several examples of the difficulty in separating Abravanel's more conservative side (in comparison with Maimonides and his radical interpreters) from his innovative side. However, more important than the divide between conservative and radical interpreters of Maimonides's writings is the fact that that Don Isaac's harmonistic approach to Maimonides demonstrates the historical and cultural gap that separated him from the earlier stages of Jewish philosophy.

The Death of Don Isaac Abravanel

In the same letter to Hakohen from 1507, Don Isaac, then seventy years old, describes his old age: "Now that I am plentiful in years, my hand is heavy from age, and the light of my eyes has also fled."[37] In November 1508, Don Isaac Abravanel passed away. As Forti describes it, "Our luster has departed, our majesty has departed, and Isaac expired, and died, and he was gathered unto his people in the year 268 [269]. His sun set in this world, but his contribution is in the World to Come. And the officers of the city and the leaders of the Jews paid him great respect upon his death, and they brought him to Padua to be buried among the ancient graves."[38] The honors paid to Don Isaac upon his death by "officers of the city" of Venice and "the leaders of the Jews" attest to his exalted status, both among the leaders of the Venetian Republic and within the local Jewish community. Of course, the perspectives of the Jewish and Christian elites may very well have been different—just as Don Isaac's words to Venice's Council of Ten were different from his commentary on the Tower of Babel. "At that time," Forti continues, "eight days later, the light of the great leader, Rabbi Judah Mintz, was extinguished . . . and the two were buried one alongside the other." The great Italian Ashkenazic rabbi was buried next to the Sephardic court Jew and exegete.

Forti notes that Don Isaac was buried in Padua and not Venice—at that time, Jews could not be buried in the city. Forti adds that a year later, "the war was pitched around the walls of Padua, and this was the reason that these graves were destroyed, so much so that no one knows where his own relatives are buried until this very day."[39] In 1509, Emperor Maximillian, the Catholic Monarchs, Louis XII, the pope, and the Italian city-states forged an alliance and attacked Venice. As a result, Venice lost control of the cities adjacent to it. During the war, the Jewish cemetery in which Don Isaac was buried was destroyed. The historical irony is that this war was also one of the causes that led to a change in the Republic's attitude toward Jewish merchants and led to the official settlement of Jews in Venice. During the sixteenth century, a Jewish community was established—and even flourished—in the city, one of its most prominent trades being the Hebrew printing press.

In 1579, some seventy years after Don Isaac's death, the Christian printer Juan Bragadin, in collaboration with the Jewish scholar and writer Rabbi Samuel Archivolti, printed the complete commentary of Abravanel on the Pentateuch in Venice, the city in which the majority of the commentary had originally been composed. On the title page, the following words appear: "The commentary on the Pentateuch by the perfect sage, Don Isaac Abravanel (may the memory of a righteous man be for a blessing). It should rain down like dew upon grass, to bring forth the sprouting of blossoms and flowers, on the five books of the Torah."[40]

AFTERWORD

DON ISAAC ABRAVANEL IN THE TWENTIETH CENTURY

As I have tried to show throughout this book, Don Isaac Abravanel was a complex historical and intellectual figure. Although he participated in the economic, political, and cultural trends of his time, he also was at pains to defend his community from these influences—as we saw, for example, in his apologetic writings (those composed before and especially those composed after the expulsion from Spain). This complexity is undoubtedly the reason Don Isaac's character elicited such interest in the first centuries after his death. In the sixteenth century, at least seventeen editions of his writings were printed, encompassing the majority of his literary oeuvre.[1] And in the seventeenth century, Hebrew printers continued to print Abravanel's commentaries, especially in Amsterdam and Germany, while Latin translations of his writings began to make an appearance as well. The seventeenth-century Christian Hebraists found much of interest in his books, be it due to the works' polemical, anti-Christian character, or because they regarded Abravanel as one of the more prominent Jewish exegetes. Translations in Latin were usually of specific exegetical discussions excerpted from the full works.[2] For example, the Hebraist Johannes Buxtorf the younger (1559–1664), one the most famous translators of Abravanel's writings into Latin, translated many excerpts taken from Abravanel's commentaries. The selective nature of Buxtorf's translation can be seen in his *Dissertationes Philologico-Theologicae*, which was published in Basel in 1662.[3] Containing eighty pages of translation, it offers the Christian intellectual an anthology of Abravanel's discussions on various topics such as the monarchy, the stopping of the sun at Gibeon, the division of scripture into Torah, Prophets, and Writings, idolatry, and more. Preceding him was the Christian Hebraist Constantijn L'Empereur (1599–1648), who translated passages from Abravanel's commentary on Isaiah. Similarly, at the end of the seventeenth century and the beginning of the eighteenth, full translations of Abravanel's commentaries on Jonah, Habakkuk, and Nahum were published. In 1711, the German Hebraist Johann Heinrich May (1688–1732) published a complete translation of *Yeshuʿot meshiho*.

Through the medium of these translations, Christian intellectuals engaged with Abravanel's views. To name one example, the Bible scholar Richard Simon (1638–1712) looked favorably upon Abravanel's assertions about the late editing of the Former Prophets.[4] Abravanel's positive reception among Christians was considerable, perhaps as a consequence of his cultural affinity for Christian discourse (that is, his use of and participation in scholasticism, humanism, and religious polemics).

If we add to this the wide dissemination of Abravanel's commentaries in manuscript form and the references to his works in the early modern literatures of Jews and Christians alike, it can be argued that Jewish and Christian scholars from the sixteenth to the eighteenth centuries were very interested in the character and writings of Don Isaac. In Italy, Prague, the Low Countries, England, and (later) Germany, his works—conveyed through various channels—left a mark on the history of Jewish thought as well as Christian scholarship on Jewish subjects.

However, if we turn to the reception of Don Isaac's thought in later centuries, we find a very different picture. The complexity of his historical and intellectual profile seems to have severely obstructed attempts by readers in the nineteenth and twentieth centuries, chief among them historians and scholars, to characterize his life and works. It appears that as modernization progressed—with all the difficult experiences that it entailed—scholars in various historical disciplines eagerly searched for revolutionary figures such as Maimonides or Baruch Spinoza. Such figures, they hoped, could serve as founding fathers or forerunners of the modern condition—or, at the very least, of a more rational approach to religion. Faced with this historical and scholarly orientation, Don Isaac's complex character, a mosaic of innovation and conservatism, was regarded as incomprehensible and, most importantly, unappealing. In the last few pages of this book, I would like to offer a summary of the changes in the approach to Don Isaac Abravanel among modern scholars. This discussion will allow us to see how his reception fluctuated throughout the twentieth century and to evaluate recent scholarly insights raised at beginning of the twenty-first.

From Traditional Praise to Critical Examination

More than a century ago, Jacob Guttmann published *Die Religionsphilosophische Lehren das Isaak Abravanel*,[5] which subjected Abravanel's writings to scholarly philological analysis. In his study, Guttmann reached two major conclusions: (1) Abravanel was not an innovative thinker, and (2) he rep-

resented the end of medieval Jewish philosophy. These assertions were intended to dissuade the community of scholars of Jewish philosophy from
wasting their time on Abravanel's works and convince them instead to seek
interesting philosophical conceptions in the works of other Jewish thinkers. Evidence of the success of Guttmann's approach is the negligent treatment of Abravanel by his son, Julius Guttmann, in his renowned 1933 *Die
Philosophie des Judentums*.[6] It is clear that at the dawn of modern scholarship on Abravanel, the scholars of the nineteenth and twentieth centuries
eschewed the traditional early modern image of Don Isaac as a defender
of the Spanish exiles, an advocate of their cause and the cause of Judaism
in general, and a heterogeneous thinker who eclectically combined various
ideas and conceptions.

In 1937, Yitzhak Baer's "Don Isaac Abravanel and His Approach to the
Problems of History and the State" was published in the Israeli Hebrew
journal *Tarbiz*.[7] From the very first sentence of the article, the shift in perspective is evident: "Isaac Abravanel is one of the few Jewish political leaders of the Middle Ages to whom it is worthwhile and possible to devote an
entire book."[8] The drive behind this reevaluation is, as the title of Baer's
article suggests, a shift in scholarly interest from philosophical discussions
to political and historical ones. Baer correctly recognized Guttmann's utter
disregard for the historical and political dimension of Abravanel's writings,
and his article was intended as a corrective. In the wake of Baer's extensive
research on Spanish Jewish society from the twelfth to the fifteenth centuries, which he published in his famous two-volume work *Die Juden im
Christlichen Spanien*, he found much historical interest in Abravanel.[9] Baer
viewed Abravanel as the court Jew par excellence as well as the forerunner
of a new model, the Jewish humanist. In the first paragraph of his article,
Baer writes, "If we could succeed in understanding at least one of these Jews
whose continual work and employment were the service of kings, we could
then remove the veil obscuring the real face of this typical Jewish figure
[the court Jew], a figure responsible for great disasters, but also a source of
great consolations."[10]

Baer's primary innovation, as we have noted several times in this book,
is his focus on the humanistic aspects of Abravanel's writings. Baer based
this claim on three arguments: (1) Abravanel was versed in humanistic literature and availed himself of it, (2) he adopted a pragmatic and literary
approach toward the interpretation of scripture, and (3) he was the first to
develop a historical exegesis of the Bible. Ultimately, Baer wished to high-

light the two contradictions that characterized Abravanel's biography and his exegetical oeuvre: Abravanel served kings all of his life yet developed acutely antimonarchical and antipolitical views, and he wrote many messianic commentaries but did not adopt the lifestyle of a messianic preacher eagerly awaiting the eschaton. While Baer offered no independent explanation for these contradictions, there is no doubt that they are related to his overarching conception of the historical phenomenon of the court Jew and the role this figure played in the decline of Spanish Jewry.[11]

The same year that Baer published his article, Leo Strauss published an important article on the political philosophy of Abravanel, "On Abravanel's Philosophical Tendency and Political Teaching."[12] Strauss responded to Baer's article on Abravanel's humanism, but like Guttmann, he focused on Abravanel's relationship with Jewish medieval rationalism and particularly with Maimonides. Like Guttmann, Strauss viewed Abravanel as the last of the medieval Jewish philosophers—that is, a symbol of the final deterioration and decline of Jewish philosophy. Strauss did agree with Baer that Abravanel's writings articulate ideas with no precedent in medieval Jewish philosophy. However, unlike Baer, Strauss attributed these elements to Abravanel's assimilation of medieval Christian doctrines and not to any authentic predilection for humanism. These two key assumptions led Strauss to portray Abravanel as the end of the Jewish philosophical enterprise, because Strauss looked upon Abravanel's works as a confused admixture of traditionalism, Christian views, and superficial humanism.

One can summarize this stage in the modern study of Abravanel and his writings as follows: Early twentieth-century scholars concluded that Abravanel was primarily interesting due to the evidence his writings and life provided about the end of medieval Jewish philosophy, as well as the small amount of information that could be gleaned from his works about the history of Iberian Jewry. The Jewish intellectuals of the nineteenth and early twentieth centuries did not seem particularly impressed by the great esteem once shown to Don Isaac by both his coreligionists and Christians, during his life and afterward. Their chief concern was whether Don Isaac Abravanel was an original philosophical and social exemplar with relevance for the Judaism of their own time.

Negative Image

Benzion Netanyahu's *Don Isaac Abravanel: Philosopher and Statesman* (first published in 1953)[13] represents a pivotal stage in the study of Abravanel and his works. About forty years after Guttmann's book appeared, Netanyahu published a detailed biography of Abravanel that included a methodical discussion of his religious and philosophical thought. The two approaches adopted by previous studies—historical and philosophical—were unified by Netanyahu in an attempt to make an exhaustive statement about Abravanel's character within the context of Jewish history.

Following in the footsteps of Guttmann, Baer, and Strauss, Netanyahu characterized Abravanel as responsible for bringing an end to the heritages of Iberian Jewish leaders and medieval Jewish philosophy. However, unlike his predecessors, Netanyahu went a step further: he attempted to prove that Abravanel created a messianic historical movement, laying the ground for the cultural and political backwardness of early modern Jewry. This is in stark contrast to the fundamental changes undergone by European states in the early modern era. Thus, for Netanyahu, the historical value of Abravanel's life and writings is not only in the light they shed on the end of the Jewish Middle Ages, but also—and primarily—in helping us understand the historical failure of Judaism at the beginning of the modern era. Based on assertions made by Guttmann and Strauss about the anti-rationalist character of Abravanel's philosophy, Netanyahu made sweeping claims about Abravanel's role in distancing Jews from modern—as opposed to medieval—rationalism and political philosophy. Netanyahu's intellectual biography of Don Isaac reaches two major conclusions: (1) Abravanel was a leader with exceptional political and economic talents; (2) however, as a leader of Jewry, he failed to guide his people toward the hoped-for historical change—that is, the political change proposed by Zionism four centuries later. Netanyahu seems to have concentrated into the biographical portrait of a single man all the problems that he saw in modern Jewish history. With the publication of Netanyahu's biography, modern Jewish scholarship undermined Abravanel's traditional image, supplanting it with a negative historical image that catered to the needs of a modern Judaism seeking to disengage from the failed models of the early modern era.

Ephraim Shmueli continued this orientation in his important 1963 Hebrew book, *Don Isaac and the Expulsion from Spain*,[14] published ten years after Netanyahu's book. Shmueli presented Abravanel as a "figure overcome by tension"[15] and especially as an example of the tension between *homo economicus* and *homo politicus*, on the one hand, and *homo religiosus*, on the other hand. "[Within him] the master of Torah and the master of finances engaged in a brutal and harrowing debate," Shmueli writes in an attempt to pigeonhole Don Isaac sociologically and historically.[16] This characterization is meant to reinforce Shmueli's negative characterization of the activities of Abravanel and other members of the Iberian Jewish elite. "The economic and religious leadership of [Iberian] Jewry," Shmueli asserts, "was unable to withstand the mighty lords of the state [Castile, Aragon, and Portugal] when they plotted against the [Jews]. They lacked not only political power but also political training."[17] In Shmueli's understanding of the expulsion, which is based on a conscious comparison to the Holocaust in Germany, Don Isaac serves as a perfect example of the historical failures of the Jewish people: "Twice Don Isaac Abravanel, one of the greatest leaders of the generation of the expulsion, failed—once in Portugal (a private failure) and once in Spain (a general failure). In what follows we will observe this failure of those who were wise and instructed many . . . without casting blame and without debating their positions."[18]

Late Adoption

The next phase in the study of Abravanel sought to integrate him into the intellectual and literary traditions of the Renaissance, while examining the literary character of his writings more closely. This trend is expressed in the studies by Moshe Idel, Eleazar Gutwirth, Seymour Feldman, Ram Ben-Shalom, Eric Lawee, Abraham Melamed, Menachem Kellner, Aviezer Ravitzky and others.

Moshe Idel's 1985 article "Kabbalah and Ancient Philosophy in the Thought of Isaac and Judah Abravanel" is an excellent example of the scholarly shift in the treatment of Abravanel.[19] The article uncovers the influence of Marsilio Ficino's notion of *Prisca Theologia* on the writings of Don Isaac and his son Judah. In the view of Ficino and his companions, the conceptual affinities between various philosophical systems points to an ancient theology that underwent various metamorphoses over the course of history, becoming corrupted as a result. In this study, Idel has shown how Don Isaac and his son offered a Jewish interpretation of this notion. Idel's main innovation is to provide a definition of the literary and philosophical context of Abravanel's writings. Instead of vaguely defining Renaissance literature as essentially rationalistic—the prevailing assumption in most scholarship up to that point—Idel compared the indisputably Renaissance conception of Ficino with works written by Abravanel and his son Judah that are clearly in dialogue with this approach. Thus, Idel has shown how the Platonic and hermetic approaches of the Renaissance were adopted by the Abravanels, thereby laying the ground for a serious scholarly discussion of Abravanel's relationship with Renaissance literature. Furthermore, what Guttmann, Strauss, and Netanyahu characterized as Abravanel's anti-philosophical proclivities—for example, his interest in natural magic—is viewed by Idel as a mark of Renaissance literature and its influence. Thus, Abravanel is not presented as yet another thinker who opposed his cultural environment, but rather as one who internalized it, reworking it to fit his religious and social needs.

The studies by Eleazar Gutwirth published since the late 1980s represent a literary and rhetorical shift in discussions of Abravanel's writings.[20] Gutwirth dedicated an entire study to Abravanel's letter to the Count of Faro, putting special emphasis on its cultural and literary context—as clearly suggested by the article's title, "Consolatio: Don Ishaq Abravanel and the Classical Tradition." According to Gutwirth, Abravanel's letter is a prominent example of the social and literary activity of epistolary writing, a practice of the Christian elites in the fifteenth century. On this basis, Gutwirth concluded that Abravanel was a pivotal figure in the internalization of humanistic writings by the Jewish elites of the time. Thus, Gutwirth instigated a second revolution in the study of Abravanel, inverting the priorities of earlier studies—especially the precedence given to philosophical and theological issues over literary ones. Like Idel, Gutwirth endeavored to connect Abravanel with his cultural surroundings and to characterize him as a way station in the long cultural process of Jewish integration into European humanism.

A Complex Figure? A Modern Figure?

In 2001, about fifty years after the publication of Netanyahu's monograph, Eric Lawee published *Isaac Abarbanel's Stance toward Tradition: Defense, Dissent and Dialogue*.[21] If Netanyahu's book consolidated and summarized the scholarly conclusions of his predecessors, then Lawee's book internalized the innovative approaches to Abravanel articulated by scholars in the 1980s and 1990s, using them to create a completely new portrait of Don Isaac. The originality of Lawee's approach is expressed not only in his rejection of the negative orientations of Guttmann, Strauss, and Netanyahu—who based their discussion on a dichotomy between rationalism and traditionalism—but also in his refusal to ignore Abravanel's more conservative side. Without a doubt, Lawee's greatest contribution is his analysis of Abravanel's attitude toward talmudic and midrashic literature. Unlike most studies that had focused on Abravanel's relationship to philosophical, kabbalistic, or humanistic discourse, Lawee presents the wide range of strategies adopted by Abravanel to approach classical rabbinic literature and its medieval interpretations. Thus, Lawee succeeds in showcasing Abravanel's exegetical innovativeness without necessarily tying it to philosophical innovation. Furthermore, Lawee shows that the humanistic elements in Abravanel's writings are not linked to an unambiguously rationalistic approach, but rather to a new literary and historical approach that drew inspiration from Iberian and Italian humanism as well as medieval Jewish exegesis. The book's conclusion—that Abravanel was a transitional figure between the Middle Ages and the modern era—further contributes to a discussion of the full scope of Abravanel's oeuvre. This image is intended to put an end to the proposed tension between innovation and traditionalism that had dominated previous studies of Abravanel.

On the basis of this very brief review of almost a century of scholarship, we can summarize the history of Don Isaac's reception among scholars and intellectuals in the twentieth century as follows: The approach accepted by most early scholars was clearly articulated in Netanyahu's work, emphasizing the contradiction between Abravanel's successful political and economic career and the conservatism emerging from his writings, as well as their lack of philosophical interest. This contradiction served as the backdrop for speculative discussions about the end of Jewish philosophy, the end of Iberian Jewry, and the backwardness of Judaism at the dawn of the modern era. The prominent common denominator of studies in recent years is their tendency to eschew overarching or essentialist descriptions of Abravanel and his writings as proffered by their predecessors and instead to offer a collection of analyses on specific subjects, tying different parts of Abravanel's oeuvre to contemporaneous literary developments. As a result of these new studies, a new image of Abravanel emerged, as described by Lawee in his book. Abravanel is an especially interesting transitional figure who changed the face of Jewish exegetical literature from within by virtue of his ability to innovatively combine elements of the Middle Ages with those of humanism and other emerging trends of the Renaissance. One can thus see in the second phase of scholarship an attempt to resolve the tension between Abravanel's political and economic career and his literary endeavors, by uncovering the spirit of the Renaissance inherent in both. Over the course of a century, Abravanel has been transformed from a failed philosopher and leader into a successful cultural agent.

In retrospect, it seems that twentieth-century scholars unraveled the relatively positive reception that Abravanel enjoyed from the sixteenth century until the eighteenth. This was due to their adoption of new methodologies as well as their search for innovative and revolutionary figures. However, in the second half of the twentieth century and the first half of the twenty-first, it seems that scholars, who have begun to adopt more nuanced and multifaceted views on the transition to modernity, rediscovered a fondness for the personality and works of Don Isaac Abravanel. As modernity has begun to lose its image as a sharp break with and disengagement from the past, interest has grown in the complexity and contradictions that characterize cultural and historical figures such as Abravanel. In this sense, Abravanel has resumed his place as one of the heroes of early modern Jewry, and perhaps he is now a historical and cultural figure with whom readers in the twenty-first century can identify.

NOTES

1. Publisher's introduction in Isaac Abravanel, *Ma'ayanei hayesh'uah*, 2. The translation is my own.

2. For the historical background and context of this biography, see Benzion Netanyahu, *Toward the Inquisition*, 99–125; Samuel Hirsch Margulies, "La famiglia Abravanel in Italia"; Renata Segre, "Sephardic Refugees in Ferrara."

3. The literature on this historical episode is extensive. It is summarized in António Henrique Rodrigo de Oliveira Marques, *Portugal na Crise dos Sécuos XIV e XV*.

4. The details of the Abravanel family's arrival in Portugal is shrouded in mystery. For a summary of the pertinent documents, see Maria José Pimenta Ferro Tavares, *Os Judeus em Portugal no Século XV*, 1:235.

5. The literature on the Avis literary output is extensive. For an overview, see Aida Fernanda Dias, *Historia Critica da Literatura Portuguesa*, 1:307–75; José Gama, "A Geração de Avis"; Pedro Calafate, "O Infante D. Pedro"; Manuel Lopez de Almeida, *Obras dos Principes de Avis*; Saul António Gomes, *D. Afonso V O Africano*, 141–64.

6. De Oliveira Marques Marques, *Portugal na Crise dos Sécuos XIV e XV*, 408–19; Nuno J. Espinosa Gomes da Silva, "João Das Regras e Outros Juristas Portugueses da Universidade de Bolonha"; Virginia Rau, "Alguns Estudantes e Eruditos Portugueses em Italia no Século XV."

7. De Oliveira Marques, *Portugal na Crise dos Sécuos XIV e XV*, 530–64.

8. Ibid., 279–315; João José Alves Dias, *Portugal*, 337–58.

9. On this issue, see Elias Lipiner, *Two Portuguese Exiles in Castile*.

10. For a discussion of the relationship between the houses of Bragança and Abravanel, see Benzion Netanyahu, *Don Isaac Abravanel*, 3–33.

11. For further details about this work, see the critical edition (Dom Duarte, *Leal conselheiro*).

12. The Portuguese words *leal*, *lealdade*, and *lealmente* used in this passage evoke the dual meaning of the word: faithful and loyal. Thus, both the personal aspects of the obligation (faithfulness and sincerity) and the normative aspects (loyalty to God, the king, and the law) are implied.

13. Dom Duarte, *Leal conselheiro*, 7–9. The translation is my own.

14. For Dom Afonso's early life and rule, see Gomes, *D. Afonso V*, 32–90.

15. While the Reconquista campaign in North Africa could celebrate some victories, such as the conquest of Seuta in 1415, the Portuguese forces suffered a crippling defeat during the siege of Tangier in 1437. Dom Fernando, son of Dom João, was taken captive and died some years later in Fez. He was remembered as a martyr who had died for his faith and became a popular saint (Infante Santo). See de Oliveira Marques, *Portugal na Crise dos Sécuos XIV e XV*, 542–52.

16. Rui de Pina, *Chronica de el Rey D. Affonso V*, 2:119–20.

17. See ibid.; Sousa Viterbo, "Occurencias da Vida Judaica," 185–86. In his article, Sousa Viterbo enumerates various decisions made by Afonso V in response to special requests made by the Jewish communities in Portugal (ibid., 178–82).

18. For a discussion of this historical episode and its portrayal in historiography, see Gomes, *D. Afonso V*, 7–32 and 60–79.

19. See Lipiner, *Two Portuguese Exiles in Castile*, 46–79.

20. For further information on this text, see the critical edition (Dom Pedro and Frei João Verba, *Livro da Vertuosa Benfeytoria*).

21. Ibid., 15. The translation is my own.

22. Ferro Tavares, *Os Judeus em Portugal no Século XV*, 1:75; see also 43–105.

23. Ibid., 1:300–310.

24. De Oliveira Marques, *Portugal na Crise dos Sécuos XIV e XV*, 150–80; Alves Dias, *Portugal*, 232–39; Virginia Rau, *Portugal e o Mediterrâneo no Século XV*, "Uma Familia de Mercadores Italianos em Portugal no Século XV," and "Bartolomeo di Iacopo di Ser Vanni Mercador-Banqueiro Florentino 'Estante' em Lisboa nos Meados do Século XV."

25. Most of this information appears in chapters 4 and 5 of Ferro Tavares, *Os Judeus em Portugal no Século XV*, 1:215–395.

26. For an edition of this document, see Cedric Cohen Skalli, *Isaac Abravanel*, 169–77. For a discussion of the document's significance, see Ferro Tavares, *Os Judeus em Portugal no Século XV*, 1:280–281, and "Subsidios para o Estudo da História Monetaria do Século XV," *Nummus* 4–6 (1981–1983): 9–59.

27. Cohen Skalli, *Isaac Abravanel*, 174.

28. Isaac Abravanel, *'Ateret zeqenim*, 2. The translation is my own.

29. Isaac Abravanel, *Peirush Abravanel 'al nevi'im*, vol. 1: *Yehoshu'a-Shoftim*, 2. The translation is my own.

30. Publisher's introduction in Abravanel, *Ma'ayanei hayesh'uah*, 2. The translation is my own.

31. Isaac Abravanel, *Peirush Abravanel 'al nevi'im*, vol. 7: *Trei 'asar*, 497. The translation is my own. Don Isaac finished writing the commentary in 1499. For further details, see Gregorio Ruiz, *Don Isaac Abravanel y Su Comentario al Libro De Amos*, 246.

32. Fritz Baer, *Die Juden im Christlichen Spanien*, 2:246. See also Yitzhak Baer, *A History of the Jews in Christian Spain*, 2:93–94; Netanyahu, *Toward the Inquisition*, 99–125.

33. Netanyahu, *Toward the Inquisition*, 109–22.

34. Y. Baer, *A History of the Jews in Christian Spain*, 2:93–94.

35. Menahem Ben Zerah, *Tsedah laderekh*, 5. The translation is my own. See also Netanyahu, *Toward the Inquisition*, 99–100.

36. Ben Zerah, *Tsedah laderekh*, 5. The translation is my own.

37. For example, the chronicler Abraham Zacuto introduces Samuel as "Don Samuel Abravanel whose name was changed to Juan Sanchez de Sevilla during the persecution [*shemad*]" (*Sefer yuhasin*, 224).

38. Publisher's introduction in Abravanel, *Ma'ayanei hayesh'uah*, 2. The translation is my own.

39. See Dom Henrique's will from 1437, in Antonio Caetano de Sousa, *Provas da História Genealógica da Casa Real Portugueza*, 507.

40. De Oliveira Marques, *Portugal na Crise dos Sécuos XIV e XV*, 550–51.

41. See also Cohen Skalli, *Isaac Abravanel*, 69–70 and 169–75.

42. The second volume of Ferro Tavares's book provides an index that includes most of the extant documents that contain Isaac Abravanel's name. (*Os Judeus em Portugal no Século XV*, vol. 2).

43. The translation is my own. For a transcription of these Portuguese letters, see Lipiner, *Two Portuguese Exiles in Castile*, 104–9.

44. De Sousa, *Provas da História*, 507.

45. See Anselmo Braamcamp Freire, "Os Sessenta Milhoes Outogados em 1478"; Ferro Tavares, *Os Judeus em Portugal no Século XV*, 1:176 and 182–83.

46. Ferro Tavares, *Os Judeus em Portugal no Século XV*, 1:296.

47. Ibid., 1:327–28.

48. Ibid., 1:279–94.

49. Anselmo Braamcamp Freire, "Maria Brandoa, a do Crisfal," 362–63 and 437–38.

50. Cohen Skalli, *Isaac Abravanel*, 45 and 181–82; Rau, "Alguns Estudantes"; Ferro Tavares, *Os Judeus em Portugal no Século XV*, 1:290.

51. Garcia de Resende, *Cancioneiro Geral Lixboa 1516*, 7 verso. The translation is my own.

52. Ibid.

CHAPTER 2

1. For the details about and context of these letters, see Cedric Cohen Skalli, *Isaac Abravanel*, 1–78.

2. Hitherto, the most extensive discussion of Isaac's learning has been Jacob Guttmann's 1916 list of authors quoted in Abravanel's writings (*Die Religionsphilosophischen Lehren des Isaak Avravanel*, 22–47). See also Avraham Gross, "Rabbi Hayun verabi Yitshak Abravanel"; Eric Lawee, *Isaac Abarbanel's Stance toward Tradition*, 27–56.

3. For the dating of the letter, see the convincing arguments of Joaquim de Carvalho, "Una Epistola de Isaac Abarbanel," 3:119. For an edition of the letter, see Cohen Skalli, *Isaac Abravanel*, 81–97.

4. The text appears in the Alcobascense codex 475/297 at the Biblioteca Nacional of Lisbon. See Gabriel Pereira, *Os Codices 443 e 475*. See also the codex C III 2–20 at the Biblioteca Publica of Evora.

5. Elias Lipiner, *Two Portuguese Exiles in Castile*, 107.

6. For an extensive discussion and a bibliography, see George W. McClure, *Sorrow and Consolation in Italian Humanism*.

7. The translation is based on Cicero, *Tusculan Disputations*, trans. J. E. King (Cambridge, MA, 1966), 224–33.

8. Ibid., 314–18.

9. Seneca, *Ad Lucilium Epistulae Morales*, 3:2–4.

10. The scholarship on the development of humanistic literature in the Iberian peninsula is vast. See, for example, Saul António Gomes, *D. Afonso V O Africano*, 141–64; Nuno J. Espinosa Gomes da Silva, *Humanesimo e Direito em Portugal no Século XVI*; Joaquim de Carvalho, *Estudos Sobre a Cultura Portuguesa del Seculo XV*; Ottavio di Camillo, *El Humanismo Castellano del Siglo XV*; Ángel Gómez Moreno, *España y la Italia de los Humanistas*; Fernando Gómez Redondo, *Historia de la Prosa Medieval Castellana*, vol. 3; Jeremy Lawrance, "Humanism in the Iberian Peninsula" and "On Fifteenth-Century Spanish Vernacular Humanism"; Guillermo Serés, "La Autoridad Literaria Círculos Intelectuales y Géneros en la Castilla del Siglo XV."

11. For the historiographical background to this discussion, see Cedric Cohen Skalli, "Discovering Isaac Abravanel's Humanistic Rhetoric.". For a discussion of the Iberian humanism evident in the letter, see Eleazar Gutwirth's groundbreaking "Don Ishaq Abravanel and Vernacular Humanism in Fifteenth Century Iberia."

12. Cohen Skalli, *Isaac Abravanel*, 81–84.

13. In this respect, Abravanel followed in the footsteps of Profiat Duran, who adopted similar motifs in the opening of a letter of lamentation and eulogy sent to Abraham ben Isaac Halevi of Gerona. He opens that letter as follows: "That which results from the pains and occurrences of the soul are similar to the pains and occurrences of the body. And the stronger pain will conceal and hide the weaker one" (Profiat Duran, *Sefer ma'aseh efod*, 188). For the literary and historical context of consolation letters in the fourteenth and fifteenth centuries, see Ram Ben-Shalom, "The Consolatory Letters of a Jewish Communal Scribe in Montalbán, Aragon"; Eleazar Gutwirth, "Religion and Social Criticism in Late Medieval Rousillon," 145–50 and "Duran on Ahitophel." The collection published by Haim Beinart contains two lamentation hymns that bear certain similarities to Abravanel's Portuguese consolatory epistle (*Pirqei sefarad* 106–8).

14. For a critical edition of the text, see Pétrarque, *Lettres Familières: Livres I–III, Rerum Familiarium libri I–III*, 128–29.

15. For a discussion of the reception of Petrarch in Portugal, see Teófilo Braga, *Historia da Literatura Portuguesa, Edade Media* (Porto, 1909), 141–42, 397, and 414–16; Aida Fernanda Dias, "Um Libro de Esperitualidade," 230–35.

16. Enrique de Villena, *Obras Completas*, 1:225. The translation is my own.

17. For a discussion of the textual affinities between passages in Abravanel's commentaries and de Villena's work on the twelve labors of Hercules, see Ram Ben-Shalom, "Mitos umitologia shel Yavan veRoma betoda'ah hahistorit shel yehudei Sefarad bimei habeinaim." (To give one example, it is interesting to compare Abravanel's description of the

centaurs in his commentary on Joel 2:4 to the first chapter of de Villena's *Los Doze Trabajos de Hercules*.) Abravanel's many references to the trials of Hercules in his commentaries strengthen the argument that he was familiar with de Villena's book, which was printed in Zamora, Castile, in 1483—the same year that Abravanel arrived in the city. See Pedro M. Catedra and Paolo Cherchi, *Los Doze Trabajos de Hercules* (*Zamora, por Anton de Centenera, 1483*).

18. Cohen Skalli, *Isaac Abravanel*, 84.

19. Ibid., 88–91. See also Isaiah 38:5. For further examples of the literary and philosophical motif of the loan, it is worth comparing Abravanel's Stoic statements with the account of Rabbi Meir's sons in *Midrash Mishlei* 38. See Azariah Beitner, *Sipurei yavne*, 221–27.

20. Pétrarque, *Lettres familières*, 130–31. The translation is from Francesco Petrarca, *Rerum Familiarium Libri I–VIII*, 58.

21. Compare this to a similar passage in De Villena, *Obras Completas*, 1:243. In terms of mourning, this can be compared to a passage in Abravanel's commentary on Deuteronomy, written concurrently with this letter. See Shaul Regev, "Nusah rishon shel peirush Abravanel lesefer Devarim," 358–59.

22. Pétrarque, *Lettres familières*, 130–31. The translation is from Petrarca, *Rerum Familiarium*, 58.

23. Seneca, *Moral Essays*, 2:28–32. I have made minor adjustments to the translation for purposes of clarity.

24. For a discussion of the *consolatio* genre in Iberian literature, see Gonzalo Ponton, *Correspondencias*, 86–108; Pedro Catedra, "Una Epistola 'Consolatoria' Attribuida al Tostado," "Prospeccion Sobre el Género Consolatorio en el Siglo XV," and "Modos de Consolar por Carta"; Jeremy Lawrance, "Creación y Lectura."

25. See José Gama, "A Geração de Avis."

26. Cohen Skalli, *Isaac Abravanel*, 88–89.

27. See Eleazar Gutwirth, "Hercules Furens and War."

28. Seneca, *Hercules*, 29.

29. Karl Alfred Blüher, *Seneca in Spanien*, 86–117; Gómez Redondo, *Historia de la Prosa Medieval Castellana*, 3:2420–54 and 2598–2630; Moreno, *España y la Italia de los Humanistas*, 133–52; Helen Nader, *The Mendoza Family in the Spanish Renaissance*, 58–100.

30. For a discussion of the Castilian translations of Seneca's tragedies, see Blüher, *Seneca in Spanien*, 95–96 and 114–15. It is important to note that Iberian authors and humanists were particularly fond of Seneca because he was born in Cordoba on the Iberian peninsula. See ibid., 57–65 and 125–75; Moreno, *España y la Italia de los Humanistas*, 135–37.

31. There is an extensive literature describing the complex series of events that led to the revival of learning and imitating Cicero. See, for example, Ronald G. Witt, *In the Footsteps of the Ancients*.

32. Cohen Skalli, *Isaac Abravanel*, 93–94.

33. See Sebastião Tavares de Pinho, "O Infante D. Pedro e a 'Escola' de Tradutores da Corte de Avis"; Aires Nascimento, "As Livrearias dos Principes de Avis"; Joseph M. Piel, *Libros dos Officios de Marco Tulio Cicera o Qual Tornou em Langagem o Infante Dom Pedro*; María Morras, *Alonso de Cartagena, Libros de Tulio*; Moreno, *España y la Italia de los Humanistas*, 75 and 203.

34. Alexander Lee, *Petrarch and St. Augustine*, 63–112; Blüher, *Seneca in Spanien*, 13–81 and 125–75; Juan de Dios Mendoza Negrillo, *Fortuna y Providencia en La Literatura Castellana del Siglo XV*.

35. Cohen Skalli, *Isaac Abravanel*, 92–93.

36. Seneca, *Moral Essays*, 2:66–67.

37. Quoted in Cohen Skalli, *Isaac Abravanel*, 93–95.

38. Pétrarque, *Lettres familières*, 130–31. The translation is from Petrarca, *Rerum Familiarium*, 58.

39. Cohen Skalli, *Isaac Abravanel*, 94–95.

40. Ibid., 94–97.

CHAPTER 3

1. An allusion to this appears in Rabbi Gedalia ben David ben Yahia's letter to Isaac Abravanel. See Y. M. Toledano, *Otzar genazim*, 37–40.

2. For editions of the letters, see Cedric Cohen Skalli, *Isaac Abravanel*, 100–165.

3. Ibid., 25–68.

4. There is an extensive literature on the da Pisa family. See, for example, Umberto Cassuto, "Sulla Famiglia Da Pisa"; David Kaufmann, "La Famille de Yehiel de Pise"; Michele Luzzati, *La Casa dell'Ebreo*, and "Banchi e Insediamenti nell'Italia Centro Settentrionale fra Tardo Medioevo e Inizi dell'Età Moderna"; Cedric Cohen Skalli and Michele Luzzati, *Lucca 1493*; Fabrizio Lelli, "Pico, i Da Pisa e 'Eliyya Hayyim da Genazzano."

5. For a discussion of Feltre's invectives against Jewish bankers, see, for example, Vittorino Meneghin, *Bernardino da Feltre e i Monti di Pietà*; Renata Segre, "Bernardino da Feltre"; Giacomo Todeschini, *La Richezza Degli Ebrei*, 155–80.

6. See Joseph Hacker, "Qevutsat igrot 'al gerush hayehudim misfarad umesitzilya ve'al goral hamegurashim"; Moshe Idel, "'Igarto shel R' Yitshak mePisa (?) bishlosh nusha'oteha"; Yael Nadav, "Igeret shel hamequbal Yitshak mar Haim 'al torat hatsahtsahot"; Albert W. Greenup, "A Kabbalistic Epistle by Isaac B. Shmuel B. Hayyim Sephardi."

7. See Umberto Cassuto, *Gli Ebrei a Firenze nell'Età del Rinascimento*, 141–46.

8. Cohen Skalli, *Isaac Abravanel*, 101.

9. Ibid., 103.

10. Ibid., 103–5.

11. On the conquest of Arzila and the king's policy in Africa, see Saul António Gomes, *D. Afonso V O Africano*, 177–98.

12. Cohen Skalli, *Isaac Abravanel*, 107.

13. Rui de Pina, *Crónicas de Rui de Pina*, 822. The translation is my own. The dobra was an important gold coin in fifteenth-century Portugal. The amount mentioned here is equivalent to about a million ducats.

14. Ibid., 822–23. For a description of the conquest, see ibid., chapters 163–65. See also the short description of the battle in João II's chronicle, including praise of the prince's brave actions, in Garcia de Resende, *Crónica de D. João II e Miscelânea*, 5.

15. The Reconquista campaign in North Africa is discussed in chapter 1. See also de Oliveira Marques, *Portugal na Crise dos Sécuos XIV e XV*, 542–52.

16. Museu Nacioanal de Arte Antiga, *A Invenção Da Gloria: D. Afonso V e as Tapeçarias de Pastrana*.

17. For a description of the role played by the conquest of Arzila in constructing the identity of João II, see Luís Adão da Fonseca, *D. João II*, 32–35.

18. See Benzion Netanyahu, *Don Isaac Abravanel*, 18–20; Cohen Skalli, *Isaac Abravanel*, 31–41.

19. Cohen Skalli, *Isaac Abravanel*, 108–10.

20. The collection published by Haim Beinart also includes three letters about the ransom (*Pirqei sefarad*, 66–67, 72, 74–75, and 87–88).

21. Cohen Skalli, *Isaac Abravanel*, 110–12.

22. For the historical background of this conception, see Ram Ben-Shalom, "Hahatsran 'keshevet Yehuda.'"

23. Cohen Skalli, *Isaac Abravanel*, 114.

24. Visconde de Santarem, *Quadro Elementar das Relações Politicas e Diplomaticas*, 85–86.

25. Cohen Skalli, *Isaac Abravanel*, 118–21.

26. Lope de Almeida, *Cartas de Itália*; Virginia Rau, *Portugal e o Mediterrâneo no Século XV*, 3–31, and *Estudos de História Medieval*, 66–80.

27. Almeida, *Cartas de Itália*, 4. The translation is my own.

28. Nuno J. Espinosa Gomes da Silva, *Humanesimo e Direito em Portugal no Século XVI*, 111–37.

29. Joao Teixeira, *Oraçam que teve Ioam Teyxeira*, 13–14. The translation is my own.

30. Cohen Skalli, *Isaac Abravanel*, 120–21.

31. Ibid., 136–37.

32. Ibid., 181–82.

33. Ibid., 122.

34. For a discussion of these two works, see Shaul Regev, "Nusah rishon shel peirush Abravanel lesefer Devarim," 359. See also ibid., 287–304; Shaul Regev, "Re'iyat bnei yisrael (shemot 24:9–11) befilosofia yehudit biymei habeinayim"; Eric Lawee, *Isaac Abarbanel's Stance toward Tradition*, 59–82.

35. Abravanel often refers to Profiat Duran in his writings, though rarely to Joseph Ibn Shem Tov. See, for example, Abravanel's *Peirush Abravanel 'al nevi'im rishonim*, 4, 56, 137, 272, 285, 354, 356, and 367.

36. Cohen Skalli, *Isaac Abravanel*, 142–45.

37. For a description of the spread of this phenomenon in the Iberian peninsula, see Aires Nascimento, "As Livrearias dos Principes de Avis"; Gomes, *D. Afonso V*, 151–58; Ángel Gómez Moreno, *España y la Italia de los Humanistas*, 44–45; Mario Schiff, *La Bibliothèque du Marquis de Santillane*; Jeremy Lawrance, "Nuevos Lectores y Nuevos Generos," "The Spread of Lay Literacy in Late Medieval Castile," and "Nuño de Guzmán and Early Spanish Humanism"; Helen Nader, *The Mendoza Family in the Spanish Renaissance*, 95–97; María Concepción Quintanilla Raso and Miguel Ángel Ladero Quesada, "Bibliotecas de la Alta Noleza Cstellana en el Siglo XV."

38. Isaac Abravanel, *Peirush Abravanel ʿal neviʾim*, vol. 1: *Yehoshuʿa-Shoftim*, 2. The translation is my own.

39. Cohen Skalli, *Isaac Abravanel*, 181–82.

40. Virginia Rau, "Alguns Estudantes e Eruditos Portugueses em Italia no Século XV," 49 and 80, and "Italianismo na Cultura Juridica Portuguesa do Século XV," 200–201.

41. On Bartolo da Sassoferato's works in Portuguese legal learning, see Nuno J. Espinosa Gomes da Silva, "Bártolo na História do Direito Português."

42. Cohen Skalli, *Isaac Abravanel*, 125–27.

43. Elijah Haim da Genazzano, *Lettera Preciosa, Introduzione, Edizione e Traduzione a Cura di F. Lelli*, 140, see also 154–61, and 166–71; Eric Lawee, "Abravanel in Italy."

44. Cohen Skalli, *Isaac Abravanel*, 126–29.

45. The original is: "Sclavam unam nigram nomine Biccinai da Guinea . . ., etatis annorum otto vel novem, nondum baptizzata." An edition of the text appears in Cohen Skalli, *Isaac Abravanel*, 179–80.

46. António Henrique Rodrigo de Oliveira Marques, *Portugal na Crise dos Sécuos XIV e XV*, 39–40.

47. On the Jewish perception of blacks in the early modern period, see Jonathan Schorsch, *Jews and Blacks in the Early Modern World*; Abraham Melamed, *The Image of the Black in Jewish Culture*.

48. For the historical and cultural background of Iberian Jewish courtiership and the elitist conceptions that were developed by it, see Beinart, *Pirqei sefarad*, 51–62; Ben-Shalom, "Hahatsran ʿkeshevet Yehudaʾ"; Haim Hillel Ben-Sasson, "Dor golei Sefarad al ʿatsmo."

49. As evidence, see Fabrizio Lelli, "Umanesimo Laurenziano nell'Opera di Yohanan Alemanno."

CHAPTER 4

1. He had yet to complete his commentary on Deuteronomy. See Cedric Cohen Skalli, *Isaac Abravanel*, 122–25.

2. The precise dating of the work is difficult to ascertain. However, we can establish a *terminus ante quem*: Don Isaac signed the 1472 Hebrew letter to Yehiel da Pisa as follows: "Isaac son of my Lord Don Judah Abravanel, may his memory be blessed in the world to

come, in Lisbon." By contrast, in the introduction to '*Ateret zeqenim* his father is described as still alive: "a valiant man, of mighty deeds, the prince Don Judah Abravanel, a pure Sephardi" (Isaac Abravanel, '*Ateret zeqenim*, preface, 28). We can roll the date back further by turning to manuscript evidence: a copy of the work from 1469 is extant. Thus, it seems the work was written in the 1460s. On the dating of '*Ateret zeqenim*, see Shaul Regev, "Nusah rishon shel peirush Abravanel lesefer Devarim," 289–91; Benzion Netanyahu, *Don Isaac Abravanel*, 13–17 and269–70; Eric Lawee, *Isaac Abarbanel's Stance toward Tradition*, 59 and 240 n. 1.

3. See Shaul Regev, "Re'iyat bnei yisrael (shemot 24:9–11) befilosofia yehudit biymei habeinayim."

4. Maimonides, *Guide of the Perplexed*, 1:29. See also ibid., part 1, chap. 28; part 2, chap. 26; and part 3, chapter.8. See also Rashi's commentary on Exodus 24:10–11; Leviticus 10:1–2; Numbers 11:1–2; 11:16. All translations from *The Guide of the Perplexed* are from the translation by Shlomo Pines cited in the bibliography.

5. Maimonides, *Guide of the Perplexed*, 1:29; Aristotle, *On the Heavens*, 202–5.

6. Maimonides, *Guide of the Perplexed*, 1:29.

7. On the limits of the human intellect, see Joseph Stern, "Maimonides on the Growth of Knowledge and Limitations of the Intellect."

8. Ex. 24:1.

9. Maimonides, *Guide of the Perplexed*, 2:369.

10. Ibid., 1:29.

11. Ibid., 1:30.

12. Numbers 1:3. The citation is from Tanhuma, Beha'alotkha; Leviticus Rabbah, xx.

13. Maimonides, *Guide of the Perplexed*, 1:30.

14. Abravanel, '*Ateret zeqenim*, preface, 27. The translation is my own.

15. Numbers 13:32 and 14:37.

16. Abravanel, '*Ateret zeqenim*, 28. The translation is my own.

17. On Isaac's self-perception as a nobleman, see Cedric Cohen Skalli, "Abravanel's Commentary on the Former Prophets."

18. For a discussion of Isaac Abravanel's complex relationship toward the rabbinic and medieval traditions in his '*Ateret zeqenim*, see Lawee, *Isaac Abarbanel's Stance toward Tradition*, 59–76. While he criticizes the model of Maimonides, in certain passages Abravanel seeks to "save [Maimonides] from the mouths of lions that think evil thoughts about him" ('*Ateret zeqenim*, chapter 8, 52).

19. Abravanel, '*Ateret zeqenim*, preface, 28–29. The translation is my own.

20. Ibid., 29.

21. It should be noted that Isaac Abravanel's attempt to undermine the philosophical model embodied by Maimonides was part of a larger trend that began in the fifteenth century and swas pearheaded by figures such as Hasdai Crescas. See Shaul Regev, "Hamahshava haratsional-mistit behagut hayehudit bame'ah hat"v"; Eric Lawee, "Sephardic Intellectuals";

Menachem Kellner, "*Gersonides and His Cultured Despisers*"; Seymour Feldman, *Philosophy in a Time of Crisis*, 33–150.

22. Dante Alighieri, *The Divine Comedy*, Vol. 1: *The Inferno*, 131–32 (ll. 73–95).

23. See Juan de Dios Mendoza Negrillo, *Fortuna y Providencia en La Literatura Castellana del Siglo XV*, 51–157.

24. Abravanel, *'Ateret zeqenim*, chapter 11, 61. Abravanel's approach to astrology has a complex and diverse background that is related to a renewed cultural interest in astrology in the fifteenth century as well as to the philosophical discourse of the Middle Ages (especially that of Gersonides and Ibn Rushd). See Regev, "Hamahshava haratsional-mistit behagut hayehudit bame'ah hat"v"; Gad Freudenthal, "Hatslaha nafshit ve'astronomia" and "The Medieval Astrologization of Aristotle's Biology"; Dov Schwartz, *Studies on Astral Magic in Medieval Jewish Thought*; Enrique de Villena, *Obras Completas*, 1:397–557; David Ruderman, "Hope against Hope."

25. Abravanel, *'Ateret zeqenim*, chapter 11, 61.

26. Ibid., chapter 12, 63. The translation is my own.

27. See Aristotle, *Metaphysics*.

28. On the astronomical views of Alfarabi, Ibn Sina, and Ibn Rushd, see Herbert A. Davidson, *Alfarabi, Avicenna, and Averroes on Intellect*. For Isaac Abravanel's approach to Ibn Sina, Ibn Rushd, and Gersonides, see Cedric Cohen Skalli and Oded Horezky, "A 15th-Century Reader of Gersonides."

29. Abravanel, *'Ateret zeqenim*, chapter 12, 66. The translation is my own.

30. Ibid., chapter 12, 70. The translation is my own.

31. *Mikra'ot gedolot haketer: Mahadurat yesod hadasha: Vayiqra*, 142–43.

32. *Mikra'ot gedolot haketer: Mahadurat yesod hadasha: Devarim*, 261.

33. Abravanel, *'Ateret zeqenim*, chapter 12, 71. The translation is my own. For a discussion of the philosophical sources of this passage, see Lawee, *Isaac Abarbanel's Stance toward Tradition*, 76–81; Cohen Skalli and Horezky, "A 15th-Century Reader of Gersonides."

34. Abravanel, *'Ateret zeqenim*, chapter 12, 71.

35. Ibid., chapter 18, 95.

36. Ibid., chapter 19, 97–98. The translation is my own.

37. See specifically Chapters 13 and 14. Abravanel explicitly refers to Judah Halevi's Kuzari a number of times in Chapter 13. For Judah Halevi's influence on Isaac Abravanel, see Liron Hoch and Menachem Kellner, "'The Voice is the Voice of Jacob, but the Hands Are the Hands of Esau': Isaac Abravanel between Judah Halevi and Moses Maimonides."

38. Abravanel, *'Ateret zeqenim*, chapter 16, 87. The translation is my own.

39. Ibid., chapter 25, 130. The translation is my own.

CHAPTER 5

1. For an analysis of these events, see John H. Elliott, *Imperial Spain*, 15–44; Saul António Gomes, *D. Afonso V O Africano*, 198–241.

2. For a detailed account of the journey, see Gomes, *D. Afonso V O Africano*, 216–29.

3. For a discussion of this transition, see ibid., 234–272; Luís Adão da Fonseca, *D. João II*, 35–58.

4. See Anselmo Braamcamp Freire, "Os Sessenta Milhoes Outogados em 1478"; Maria José Pimenta Ferro Tavares, *Os Judeus em Portugal no Século XV*, 1:296.

5. Cedric Cohen Skalli, *Isaac Abravanel*, 134–37.

6. On the circumstances of Afonso V's death, see Gomes, *D. Afonso V*, 268–72.

7. Modern historians have portrayed João II as a perfect Renaissance prince (*príncipe perfeito*). For example, the Portuguese historian João José Alves Dias describes him as follows: "In contrast to his father, João II was a typical Renaissance monarch, who, from the beginning of his reign, expressed through his projects a clear agenda to turn Portugal into a modern state" (*Portugal*, 701). The translation is my own.

8. On the significance of this oath, see Armindo de Sousa, "O Parlamento na Época de D. João II," 250–52.

9. See Garcia de Resende, *Crónica de D. João II e Miscelânea*, 32; José Corrêa da Serra, *Collecção de Livros Ineditos da Historia Portuguesa dos Reinados de D. João I, D. Duarte, D. Affonso V, a D. João II*, 2:18–23. For the symbolic significance of this act of bowing, see Rita Costa Gomes, "As Cortes de 1481–1482," in *O tempo de Vasco de Gama*, ed. D. R. Curto (Lisbon, 1998), 248–50.

10. See Costa Gomes, "As Cortes de 1481–1482," 251; de Sousa, "O Parlamento na Época de D. João II," 252.

11. For a discussion of the duke's sentence and his last days, see Anselmo Braamcamp Freire, "As Conspirações no Reinado de D. João II," 393–97; da Serra, *Collecção de Livros*, 2:42–52; Resende, *Crónica de D. João II*, 58–70.

12. In his book on King Dom João II, the historian Luís Adão da Fonseca offers a summary of most of the primary sources describing this episode as well as an overview of the modern scholarly discussions of it (*D. João II*, 66–80).

13. Elias Lipiner, *Two Portuguese Exiles in Castile*, 113. The translation is my own.

14. Ibid., 112. The translation is my own.

15. Ibid., 115. The translation is my own.

CHAPTER 6

1. Elias Lipiner, *Two Portuguese Exiles in Castile*, 117–18. The translation is my own.

2. Judah Abravanel, "A Complaint against the Times," trans. from the Hebrew by Dan Almagor, Barbara Garvin, and Dan Jacobson, in Barbara Gavin, "Yehuda Abravanel and Italian Jewry," 56.

3. Isaac Abravanel, *Peirush Abravanel 'al nevi'im*, vol. 1: *Yehoshu'a-Shoftim*, 197. The translation of the Hebrew text throughout this chapter is based on Lipiner, *Two Portuguese Exiles in Castile*, 55–60.

4. The word used in the original Hebrew is *haqdamah*, which can be translated as "in-

troduction," "preface," "preliminary remark," "premise," or "principle," according to the context. See Jacob Klatzkin, *Thesaurus Philosophicus Linguae Hebraicae et Veteris et Recentioris*, 131–32.

5. Abravanel, *Yehoshu'a-Shoftim*, 1.

6. Ibid., 1.

7. In his book *Sefer or hahaim*, Joseph Yaavetz portrays the intellectual encounters that took place in Don Isaac's home in Lisbon, describing the latter's lessons on Maimonides's *Guide of the Perplexed*: "I learned from his mouth some chapters of the Guide in which [Maimonides] surpassed in wisdom, all other men . . . and I and the scholars who heard from his mouth saw that the difference between gold and copper is the difference between his interpretation and that of others. . . . And after he had interpreted and explained well [Maimonides's] meaning he would say "this is the intention of our Rabbi Moses [Maimonides] but not of our teacher, [the biblical] Moses" (*Sefer or hahaim*, 69–70). The translation is my own.

8. Abravanel, *Yehoshu'a-Shoftim*, 1–2.

9. Ibid., 2.

10. Ibid.

11. Ibid.

12. For a summary of the various views of this episode, see Luis Adão da Fonseca, *D. João II*, 78–107.

13. Ex. 1:8.

14. Abravanel,, *Yehoshu'a-Shoftim*, 2–3.

15. Gen. 19:17.

16. Abravanel, *Yehoshu'a-Shoftim*, 2–3.

17. Ibid., 4–5. From here until the end of the chapter, the translations from the Hebrew are my own

18. Ibid., 5.

19. Ibid.

20. Ibid., 5–6.

CHAPTER 7

1. See Eric Lawee, *Isaac Abarbanel's Stance toward Tradition*, 169–202, and "Introducing Scripture"; Jair Haas, "Divine Perfection and Methodological Inconsistency" and "Writing by Divine Imperative as a Criterion for the Prophetic Authority of Texts in the Biblical Exegesis of Isaac Abarbanel."

2. Isaac Abravanel, *Peirush Abravanel 'al nevi'im*, vol. 1: *Yehoshu'a-Shoftim*, 7. The translation is my own.

3. Ibid., 9–10. The translation is my own.

4. See *Biblia Latina cum glosa ordinaria Walfridi Strabonis aliorumque*, 1:3–4.

5. Abravanel, *Yehoshu'a-Shoftim*, 10.

6. Ibid., 10–11.

7. Ibid., 11.

8. Ibid. The translation is my own.

9. Ibid., 12. The translation is my own.

10. See Joaquim Veríssimo Serrão, *A Historiografia Portuguesa: Doutrina e Crítica.* vol. 1, and *Cronistas do Século XV Posteriores a Fernão Lopes.*

11. For a Castilian translation of Livy prepared by a chronicler, see López de Ayala, *Las Decadadas de Tito Livio.*

12. Leonardo Bruni, *History of the Florentine People,* 1:3.

13. Ibid.

14. Livy, *History of Rome,* 1:6.

15. Cicero, *De Oratore,* 1:245.

16. Isaac Abravanel, *Peirush Abravanel 'al nevi'im,* vol. 3: *Melakhim,* 274.

17. Abravanel, *Yehoshu'a-Shoftim,* 14–15. The translation is from Eric Lawee, "From the Pages of Tradition: Don Isaac Abarbanel: Who Wrote the Bible?," 67–68.

18. Abravanel, *Yehoshu'a-Shoftim,* 15.

19. Yitzhak Baer, "Don Yitshaq Abarbanel veyahso el ba'yot historiah vehamedinah," 247.

20. Abravanel, *Yehoshu'a-Shoftim,* 15–16. The translation is from Lawee, "Who Wrote the Bible?," 70.

21. Abravanel, *Yehoshu'a-Shoftim,* 16. The translation is from Lawee, "Who Wrote the Bible?," 70.

22. Ibid.

23. Lawee, *Isaac Abarbanel's Stance toward Tradition,* 184.

24. Fernán Pérez de Guzmán, *Generaciones y Semblanzas,* 59–62. The translation is my own.

25. Abravanel, *Yehoshu'a-Shoftim,* 17.

26. Baer, "Don Yitshaq Abarbanel veyahso el ba'yot historiah vehamedinah," 245. The translation is my own.

27. On the Aristotelian physicians, see Nancy Struever, "Petrarch's Invective Contra Medicum," 661–66; Carol E. Quillen, "A Tradition Invented"; Paul Oskar Kristeller, "Petrarch's 'Averroists.'"

28. Francesco Petrarca, *Invectives,* 451. On the contents of the humanistic neo-Latin genres, see Ronald G. Witt, *In the Footsteps of the Ancients.*

29. Giannozzo Manetti, *A Translator's Defense,* 109.

30. Lorenzo Valla, *On the Donation of Constantine,* 71.

31. The translation is based on Cristopher S. Celenza, "Lorenzo Valla's Radical Philology," 373.

32. Marqués de Santillana, *Obras Completas,* 502. The translation is my own.

33. Avraham Gross, *Rabi Yosef ben Avraham Hayun,* 231. The translation is my own.

34. Ibid., 231–32.

35. Ibid., 172–78.

36. Lawee, *Isaac Abarbanel's Stance toward Tradition*, 169–202. The translation is my own.

37. Profiat Duran, *Sefer ma'aseh efod*, 40. The translation is my own.

38. According to Leo Strauss, Abravanel "is a humanist who uses his classical learning to confirm his thoroughly medieval conceptions" ("On Abravanel's Philosophical Tendency and Political Teaching," 128). See also Benzion Netanyahu, *Don Isaac Abravanel*, 125–29, 148, and 183–84.

39. Abravanel, *Yehoshu'a-Shoftim*, 26. The translation is my own.

40. See Nissim ben Reuben Gerondi, *Derashot haran*; Isaac Arama, *Sefer 'akedat Yitshaq*. See also Sara Heller-Wilensky, *Rabi Yitshaq 'Arama umishnato*; Aryeh Leib Feldman, "Derashot haran."

41. Abravanel, *Yehoshu'a-Shoftim*, 26. The translation is my own.

42. Daniel Boyarin, *Ha'iyun hasfaradi lefarshanut hatalmud shel megurashei sfarad*); Yisrael M. Ta-Shma, *Hasifrut haparshanit latalmud be'eropa uvetsefon afrika*, 2:141–44.

43. Mauro Zonta, *Hebrew Scholasticism in the Fifteenth Century*.

44. Isaac Canpanton, *Darkhei hatalmud* 43. The translation is my own.

45. Yoel Marciano, "Hakhamim besfarad bame'ah hahamesh-'esreh."

46. Duran, *Sefer ma'aseh efod*, 4. The translation is my own.

47. Hasdai Crescas, *Sefer or Adonai*, introduction, 2. The translation is my own.

48. Ibid., 4.

49. Haas, "Divine Perfection and Methodological Inconsistency."

50. Abravanel, *Yehoshu'a-Shoftim*, 108 and 143.

51. Isaac Abravanel, *Peirush Abravanel 'al nevi'im*, vol. 2: *Shmu'el*, 95.

CHAPTER 8

1. Isaac Abravanel, *Peirush Abravanel 'al nevi'im*, vol. 1: *Yehoshu'a-Shoftim*, 33–34. The translation is my own.

2. Ibid., 35.

3. Ibid., 12. The translation is my own.

4. Ibid., 108.

5. Levi Gersonides, *Sefer milhamot Hashem* (Berlin, 1923), 445. The translation is based on Levi Gersonides, *The Wars of the Lord*, 3:473.

6. Gersonides, *Sefer milhamot Hashem*, 446. The translation is my own.

7. Ibid., 111–12. The translation is my own.

8. Hasdai Crescas, *Sefer or Adonai*, introduction, 5. See also Zev Warren Harvey, *Rabbi Hasdai Crescas*, 40–53.

9. Isaac Abravanel, *'Ateret zeqenim*, chapter 12, 64. The translation is my own.

10. Ibid., chapter 12, 74–75. The translation is my own.

11. Ibid., chapter 12, 64 and 69.

12. Abravanel, *Yehoshu'a-Shoftim*, 112. The translation is my own.

13. Yitzhak Baer, *A History of the Jews in Christian Spain*, 2:258.

14. See Shaul Regev, "Hamhashava haratsional-mistit behagut hayehudit bame'ah hat"v."

15. Abravanel, *Yehoshu'a-Shoftim*, 113–14. The translation is my own.

16. Ibid., 112.

17. Ibid., 123.

18. Ibid., 118.

19. Ibid., 221–22. The translation is my own.

20. Ibid., 232. The translation is my own.

21. Ibid.

22. Isaac Abravanel, *Peirush Abravanel 'al nevi'im*, vol. 2: *Shmu'el*, 16. The translation is my own.

23. Ibid. The translation is my own.

24. Ibid., 24–25. The translation is my own.

25. Ibid., 124–25. The translation is my own.

26. Ibid, 125.

27. Ibid.

28. Ibid.

29. Ibid.

30. Ibid., 158. The translation is my own.

31. Ibid., 191. The translation is my own.

32. Abravanel, *Yehoshu'a-Shoftim*, 5.

33. Abravanel, *Shmu'el*, 200. The translation is my own.

34. Marsilio Ficino, *Three Books on Life*, 360–61.

35. Abravanel, *Shmu'el*, 200.

36. Ibid., 203.

37. Maimonides, *Mishneh torah, Hilkhot yesodei hatorah*, chapter 7 Halakha 4.

38. See the discussion of the practical elements of Solomon's wisdom in chapter 13.

39. Abravanel, *Shmu'el*, 201.

40. Ibid., 202.

41. Ibid., 512. The translation is my own.

42. Ibid., 512–13. The translation is my own.

43. Ibid., 513. The translation is my own.

CHAPTER 9

1. Leo Strauss, "On Abravanel's Philosophical Tendency and Political Teaching," 128.

2. Benzion Netanyahu, *Don Isaac Abravanel*, 100, 105, 126, and 128.

3. Ibid., 95–194; Strauss, "On Abravanel's Philosophical Tendency," 95–129.

4. Isaac Abravanel, *Peirush Abravanel 'al nevi'im*, vol. 2: *Shmu'el*, 90.

5. BT Sanhedrin 20b.

6. Abravanel, *Shmu'el*, 91.

7. Nissim ben Reuben Gerondi, *Derashot haran*, 189–93. The translation is based on Avi Sagi, "Natural Law and Halakhah," 79.

8. Gerondi, *Derashot haran*, 189.

9. Aristotle, *Politics*, 127.

10. Abravanel, *Shmu'el*, 93.

11. *Biblia Latina cum glosa ordinaria Walfridi Strabonis aliorumque*, 2:71v.

12. Abraham Melamed, *The Philosopher-King in Medieval and Renaissance Jewish Political Thought* and *Wisdom's Little Sister*.

13. Abravanel, *Shmu'el*, 95.

14. Aquinas, *Political Writings*, 11.

15. Abravanel, *Shmu'el*, 96. See also Michael Walzer et al., *The Jewish Political Tradition*, 1:150–54. On the reception of ancient and Renaissance republicanism in Abravanel's writings and the early modern Jewish reception of republicanism in general, see Strauss, "On Abravanel's Philosophical Tendency"; Aviezer Ravitzky, "Kings and Laws in Late Medieval Jewish Thought."

16. Melamed, *Wisdom's Little Sister*, 272–304.

17. Arthur Lesley, "The Song of Solomon's Ascents by Yohanan Alemanno330–31.

18. On this, see Ronald G. Witt, *In the Footsteps of the Ancients*.

19. See Quentin Skinner, *The Foundations of Modern Political Thought*, vol. 1: *The Renaissance*.

20. For the Latin text, see Hans Baron, *From Petrarch to Leonardo Bruni*, 232–63. For the historical, philological, and intellectual context of the work, see Baron, *The Crisis of the Early Italian Renaissance*; Eugenio Garin, *La Cultura Filosofica del Rinascimento Italiano*, 3–37; James Hankins, *Renaissance Civic Humanism*); Gordon Griffiths, James Hankins, and David Thompson), *The Humanism of Leonardo Bruni*; Witt, *In the Footsteps of the Ancients*, 392–442.

21. Leonardo Bruni, "Panegyric to the City of Florence," 169. For the Latin original, see Baron, *From Petrarch to Leonardo Bruni*, 259. On the "idealized," "rhetorical," or "ideological" presentation of the Florentine regime, see John N. Najemy, "Civic Humanism and Florentine Politics."

22. Isaac Abravanel, *Peirush Abravanel 'al nevi'im*, vol. 1: *Yehoshu'a-Shoftim*, 3.

23. Ravitzky, "Kings and Laws."

24. Abravanel, *Shmu'el*, 96–97.

25. Ravitzky, "Kings and Laws."

26. Abravanel, *Shmu'el*, 96.

27. Ibid., 97.

28. Yitzhak Baer, "Don Yitshaq Abarbanel veyahso el ba'yot historiah vehamedinah," 256.

29. Strauss, "On Abravanel's Philosophical Tendency," 121–27.

30. Ravitzky, "Kings and Laws," 75–76.

31. Aquinas, *Political Writings*, 15–16.

32. Bruni, "Panegyric to the City of Florence," 151. For the Latin original, see Baron, *From Petrarch to Leonardo Bruni*, 245.

33. Leonardo Bruni, *History of the Florentine People*, 1:109–11.

34. Abravanel, *Shmu'el*, 98.

35. James Hankins, "Rhetoric, History, and Ideology."

36. Abravanel, *Shmu'el*, 98–99.

37. Ibid., 99.

38. *Biblia Sacra*, 2:71.

39. Abravanel, *Shmu'el*, 100. The reference is to 1 Kings 11:15.

40. Abravanel, *Shmu'el*, 101.

41. Ibid.

42. *Biblia Sacra*, 2:71.

CHAPTER 10

1. The value of a golden *real* was a little more than thirty maravedi.

2. For the documents, see Haim Beinart, *The Expulsion of the Jews from Spain*, 522–40.

3. On the Mendoza family, see Helen Nader, *The Mendoza Family in the Spanish Renaissance*.

4. See Mario Schiff, *La Bibliothèque du Marquis de Santillane*.

5. Ibid., 1–7.

6. See Luis Suárez Fernández, *Documentos Acerca de la Expulsion de los Judios* and *La Expulsión de los Judiós de España*; Beinart, *The Expulsion of the Jews from Spain*; Yitzhak Baer, *A History of the Jews in Christian Spain*, vol. 2; Henry Kamen, "The Mediterranean and the Expulsion of the Jews in 1492"; Maurice Kriegel, "La Prise d'une Decision."

7. Quoted in Beinart, *The Expulsion of the Jews from Spain*, 10.

8. Benzion Netanyahu, *Don Isaac Abravanel*, 40.

9. Ibid., 50.

10. Quoted in Beinart, *The Expulsion of the Jews from Spain*, 49–52.

11. Baer, *A History of the Jews in Christian Spain* 2:437.

CHAPTER 11

1. Elijah Capsali, *Seder eliyahu zuta*, 1:212.

2. Solomon Ibn Verga, *Shevet Yehuda*, 123.

3. On the Jewish community in Naples, see Giancarlo Lacerenza, "Lo spazio dell'Ebreo Insediamenti e Cultura Ebraica a Napoli (Secoli XV–XVI)."

4. See Robert Bonfil, "The History of the Spanish and Portuguese Jews in Italy."

5. Judah Messer Leon, *The Book of the Honeycomb's Flow* and *Nofet tsufim*.

6. Charles Berlin, *Hebrew Printing and Bibliography*, 111–38.

7. Jerry H. Bentley, *Politics and Culture in Renaissance Naples*.

8. Isaac Abravanel, *Haggada shel Pesah . . . 'im Zevah Pesah*, 3. The translation is my own.

9. Lacerenza, "Lo spazio dell'Ebreo Insediamenti e Cultura Ebraica a Napoli (Secoli XV–XVI)," 407–8.

10. For more information on Jews in Naples at that time, see Viviana Bonazzoli, "Gli Ebrei del Regno di Napoli all'Epoca della Loro Espulsione."

11. Quoted in Leone Ebreo (Yehuda Abravanel), *Dialoghi d'Amore*, 1:577.

12. Cesare Colafemmina, *Documenti per la Storia degli Ebrei in Puglia Nell'Archivio di Stato di Napoli*, 206–7, 212–13, 277–78, and 308.

13. Quoted in Joseph Hacker, "Igeret Rabi Meir 'Arama neged Rabi Yitshak Abravanel vehitqablutah," 509. Hacker presents a critical edition of the letter.

14. Sara Heller-Wilensky, *Rabi Yitshaq 'Arama umishnato*, 51.

15. Quoted in Hacker, "Igeret Rabi Meir 'Arama," 515.

16. Heller-Wilensky, *Rabi Yitshaq 'Arama umishnato*, 50–57.

17. Shaul Regev, "Nusah rishon shel peirush Abravanel lesefer Devarim."

18. Quoted in Hacker, "Igeret Rabi Meir 'Arama," 515. The translation is my own.

19. David Ben-Zazon, *Nevuhim hem*, 72–74.

20. Isaac Abravanel, *Peirush Abravanel 'al nevi'im*, vol. 1: *Yehoshu'a-Shoftim*, 3.

21. Moritz Steinschneider, "Zur Frauenliteratur."

22. David Messer Leon, "'Ein Haqoreh," folio 127v, Neubauer 1263, Bodleian Library, Oxford.

23. Ibid., folio 61r.

24. Ibid., folio 57r. The translation is my own.

CHAPTER 12

1. Isaac Abravanel, *Peirush Abravanel 'al nevi'im*, vol. 3: *Melakhim*, 1. Unless otherwise stated, all of the translations in this chapter are my own.

2. Ibid.

3. Ibid.

4. Eleazar Gutwirth, "Abraham Seneor" and "Don Yizchaq Abravanel"; Francisco Cantera Burgos, "Don 'Ishaq Braunel.'"

5. Abravanel, *Melakhim*, 1–2.

6. Elijah Capsali, *Seder eliyahu zuta*, 1:204–6; Joseph Hacker, "Kroniqot hadashot 'al geirush haYehudim miSefarad, sibotav vetotsa'otav"; Solomon Ibn Verga, *Shevet Yehuda*, 120–22; Joseph Hakohen, *'Emeq habakha*; Abraham Zacuto, *Sefer yuhasin*, 227; Gedalia ibn Yahya, *Shalshelet hakabalah*, 156–57; Alexander Marx, "The Expulsion of the Jews from Spain"; Samuel Usque, *Consolacion às Tribulações de Israel*, 2:195–200.

7. Miguel Ángel Ladero Quesada, *La España de los Reyes Católicos*, 13–59 and 99–154.

8. For the providentialist ideology of the Catholic Monarchs, see José Manuel Nieto Soria, *Fudamentos ideológicos del poder real en Castilla*, 49–78.

9. Abravanel, *Melakhim*, 2.

10. See especially Haim Beinart, *Moreshet Sepharad: The Sephardi Legacy* (Jerusalem, 1992), 1:31.

11. Ibn Verga, *Shevet Yehuda*, 120–22.

12. Capsali, *Seder eliyahu zuta*, 1:208–9.

13. Antonio Possevino, *Apparatus sacer ad scriptores Veteris et Novi Testatamenti*, 2:492.

14. On the issue of Queen Doña Isabel's role in the expulsion, see Hacker, "Kroniqot hadashot," 209–13; Haim Beinart, *The Expulsion of the Jews from Spain*, 1–54; Yosef Hayim Yerushalmi, *The Lisbon Massacre of 1506 and the Royal Image in the Shevet Yehudah*, 35–66, Luis Suárez Fernández, *Isabel*, 187–212; Haim Hillel Ben-Sasson, "Dor golei Sefarad 'al 'atsmo"; Capsali, *Seder eliyahu zuta*, 1:205–6.

15. Abravanel, *Melakhim*, 2.

16. See, for example, Ben-Sasson, "Dor golei Sefarad 'al 'atsmo"; Reuven Michael, *Haketiva hahistorit hayehudit meharenasans 'ad ha'et hahadashah*, 17–71; Yitzhak Baer, *A History of the Jews in Christian Spain*, 2:439–43; Beinart, *The Expulsion of the Jews from Spain*, 520–26; Robert Bonfil, "The History of the Spanish and Portuguese Jews in Italy"; Joseph Hacker, "Teguvot haMegurashim legeirush Sefarad uleshemad Portugal"; Yosef Hayim Yerushalmi, *Zakhor*, 56–75; Eleazar Gutwirth, "Italy or Spain?"

17. Abravanel, *Melakhim*, 3.

18. Ibid.

19. On the history of this image, see Jean-Christoph Attias, "Isaac Abravanel (1508–1992)."

20. See Capsali, *Seder eliyahu zuta*, 1:204–6; Ibn Verga, *Shevet Yehuda*, 120–22; ibn Yahya, *Shalshelet hakabalah*, 156–57; Usque, *Consolacion às tribulações de Israel*, 1:195–200.

21. For a description of the Sephardic exiles in Italy, see ibn Yahya, *Shalshelet hakabalah*, 91 and 157; Sara Heller-Wilensky, *Rabi Yitshaq 'Arama umishnato*, 50–57; Bonfil, "The History of the Spanish and Portuguese Jews in Italy"; Giancarlo Lacerenza, "Lo spazio dell'Ebreo Insediamenti e Cultura Ebraica a Napoli (Secoli XV–XVI)"; Hava Tirosh Rothschild, *Between Worlds*, 24–33 and 52–54.

22. Abravanel, *Melakhim*, 3.

CHAPTER 13

1. Isaac Abravanel, *Peirush Abravanel 'al nevi'im* vol. 3: *Melakhim*, 14. Unless otherwise stated, all of the translations in this chapter are my own.

2. Ibid., 42.

3. Ibid., 45.

4. See BT Horayot 12a.

5. Abravanel, *Melakhim*, 47.

6. Ibid., 49.

7. Ibid., 49–50.

8. Ibid., 53.

9. Ibid., 52.

10. Ibid., 77.

11. Ibid., 89.

12. Ibid., 94. See also Yehuda Halper, "In One Sense Easy, in Another Difficult."

13. Abravanel, *Melakhim*, 95.

14. Ibid., 96.

15. Ibid.

16. Ibid.

17. Ibid.

18. Ibid., 99.

19. Ibid.

20. Ibid., 99–100.

21. Ibid., 101.

22. Ibid., 106.

23. Ibid.

24. Ibid., 109.

25. Ibid.

26. Ibid., 110.

27. Marsilio Ficino, *Three Books on Life*, 359. For the history of the text, see ibid., introduction.

28. See Moshe Idel, "Hermeticism and Judaism"; Fabrizio Lelli, "Un Collaboratore Ebreo di Giovanni Pico della Mirandola." See also Yohanan Alemanno, *Heshek Shlomo le-rabi Yohanan Alemano*.

29. Abravanel, *Melakhim*, 110–11.

30. Ibid., 111–12.

31. Ibid., 113.

32. Ibid., 117.

33. Ibid., 118.

34. Ibid.

35. See Eugenio Garin, *Emertismo del Rinascimento*.

36. Giovanni Pico de Mirrandola, *Syncretism in the West*, 495–98.

37. Ibid., 499.

38. Abravanel, *Melakhim*, 115–16.

39. Flavius Josephus, *Jewish Antiquities*, 595–97.

CHAPTER 14

1. Isaac Abravanel, *Peirush Abravanel ʾal neviʾim*, vol. 3: *Melakhim*, 125. Unless otherwise stated, all of the translations in this chapter are my own.

2. Ibid., 126.

3. Ibid., 127.

4. Ibid., 133.

5. Ram Ben-Shalom,"Dimui hatarbut hanotsrit betoda'ah hahistorit shel yehudei sefarad veprovans," 144–52.

6. Abravanel, *Melakhim*, 212.

7. Ibid., 154.

8. Ibid., 152.

9. Ibid.

10. Ibid., 199.

11. Ibid., 198.

12. Ibid., 170.

13. Ibid.

14. Ibid.

15. Ibid., 150.

16. Ibid.

17. Ibid., 200.

18. Ibid., 204.

19. Ibid., 204–5.

20. Ibid., 205.

21. Ibid., 207.

22. Ibid.

23. Ibid., 208.

24. Ibid.

25. Ibid.

26. Ibid.

27. Ibid., 217.

28. Ibid., 3.

29. Ibid., 159.

30. Ibid., 275.

31. Ibid., 276.

32. Ibid., 590.

33. Ibid., 591. The translation is from Ram Ben-Shalom, "The Myths of Troy and Hercules as Reflected in the Writings of Some Jewish Exiles from Spain," 241–42.

34. Yitzhak Baer, *A History of the Jews in Christian Spain* 1:15–23; Haim Beinart, *Pirqei
sefarad*, 13–35; Ben-Shalom, "The Myths of Troy and Hercules."

35. For a review and study of these sources, see Ram Ben-Shalom, *Medieval Jews and the
Christian Past*, 177–238.

36. Abravanel, *Melakhim*, 592.

37. Ibid., 592–93.

38. Ibid., 1.

CHAPTER 15

1. Isaac Abravanel, *Rosh amanah*, 156.

2. Ibid., 39. The translation is my own.

3. Francesco Guicciardini, *Storia d'Italia*, 1:7–8. The translation is from Guicciardini, *The History of Italy*, 8.

4. See Niccolò Machiavelli's critique of these policies in "Dell'Arte della Guerra." See also Niccolo Machiavelli, *The Art of War*, 183–212.

5. See David Abulafia, *The French Descent into Renaissance Italy*.

6. Eric Lawee has correctly noted that Abravanel's flight to Sicily with Alfonso II attests to his rapid rise in the ranks of Neapolitan society and the hierarchy of the court (*Isaac Abarbanel's Stance toward Tradition*, 19). See also Benzion Netanyahu, *Don Isaac Abravanel*, 67–74; Isaac Abravanel, "Ma'ayanei hayesh'uah," 269.

7. Niccolo Ferorelli (*Gli Ebrei nell'Italia Meridionale dall'Eta Romana al Secolo XVIII*, 199–206), Salo Baron (*A Social and Religious History of the Jews*, 11:256–57 and 412–13, n. 81), and Cecil Roth (*The History of the Jews in Italy*, 279–81) all note that the anti-Jewish riots broke out after the death of King Ferrante of Naples. Furthermore, the parliament decided to expel the majority of Naples's Jewish population and to impose harsh regulations on those who remained, such requiring them to have as separate living quarters and wear a Jewish badge. The three historians also note that the French invasion provided an opportunity for anti-Jewish riots throughout the kingdom, in which French troops participated. See Menachem Dorman, "Mavo," 59–63; Robert Bonfil, *Jewish Life in Renaissance Italy*, 21–29; Lawee, *Isaac Abarbanel's Stance toward Tradition*, 20–21 and 226, nn. 99–100; Netanyahu, *Don Isaac Abravanel*, 67–71; Giancarlo Lacerenza, "Lo spazio dell'Ebreo Insediamenti e Cultura Ebraica a Napoli (Secoli XV–XVI)," 415–17; Viviana Bonazzoli, "Gli Ebrei del Regno di Napoli all'Epoca della Loro Espulsione," 499–506.

8. Ferorelli, *Gli Ebrei nell'Italia*, 211; David Abulafia, "Insediamenti, diaspora e tradizione ebraica"; Lawee, *Isaac Abarbanel's Stance toward Tradition*, 20–23; Netanyahu, *Don Isaac Abravanel*, 70, 78–81, and 286–88, nn. 64–68; Carl Gebhardt, "Regesten zur Lebensgeschichte Leone Ebreo," 20–21.

9. After Naples was annexed by Castile and Aragon, members of the Abravanel family played prominent roles in the local Jewish community up until the expulsion. Especially notable was the leadership of Samuel Abravanel and his wife, Benvenida. See Dorman, "Mavo", 43–95; Lacerenza, "Lo spazio dell'Ebreo Insediamenti e Cultura Ebraica a Napoli (Secoli XV–XVI)," 413–27; Samuel Hirsh Margulies, "La Famiglia Abravanel in Italia"; Ferorelli, *Gli Ebrei nell'Italia*, 226–33; Bonazzoli, "Gli Ebrei del Regno di Napoli"; Abulafia, "Insediamenti, diaspora e tradizione ebraica."

10. Regarding his wish to reach Salonika, Abravanel writes: "Salonika, whither I thought I would go due to the weight of the war" ("Teshuvot lesh'elot," 3: 18). Corfu played a pivotal role in Venice's war with the Ottoman Empire as well as the conquest of the port cities on

the Adriatic coast (Monopoli, Brindisi, and Otranto). See Carol Kidwell, "Venice, the French Invasion and the Apulian Ports."

11. Refugees who made their way to the Ottoman Empire included David Messer Leon and David ben Solomon ibn Yahya. See Ferorelli, *Gli Ebrei nell'Italia*, 119–218; Hava Tirosh Rothschild, *Between Worlds*, 53–55; Robert Bonfil, "The History of the Spanish and Portuguese Jews in Italy"; Joseph Hacker, "The Sephardim in the Ottoman Empire in the Sixteenth Century."

12. Meir Benayahu has noted that Rabbi Joseph Fassi's yeshiva was the continuation of the great yeshiva of Rabbi Isaac Abuhav in Guadalajara, an institution with which Abravanel had had ties before the expulsion ("Beit Abravanel beSaloniki"). See also Renata Segre, "Sephardic Settlements in Sixteenth-Century Italy," 132–33.

13. Isaac Abravanel, *Peirush hatorah lerabenu Yitshak Abravanel*, vol. 5: *Sefer Devarim.*, 5.

14. Isaac Abravanel, "Teshuvot lesh'elot," 3:2–3.

15. Isaac Abravanel, *Nahalat avot*, 8.

16. Most of the family remained in Naples. Judah Abravanel wandered between various cities in Italy. His brother Joseph settled in Venice, where he worked as a physician. Another branch of the family resided in Salonika and other parts of the Ottoman Empire. See Benayahu, "Beit Abravanel beSaloniki"; publisher's introduction in Isaac Abravanel, *Ma'ayanei hayesh'uah*, 3–4; Cecil Roth, *Jews in the Renaissance* (Philadelphia, 1959), 8, 10, 22, 34, 39–40, 45, 54, 108–9, 118, 128–36, 148, 228, 234, 262, and 310; Renata Segre, "Sephardic Refugees in Ferrara"; Aron di Leone Leoni, "Nuove notize sugli Abravanel" and "Per una storia della nazione portoghese ad Ancona e a Pesaro."

17. Isaac Abravanel, *Peirush hatorah lerabenu Yitshak Abravanel*, vol. 5, *Devarim*, 5.

18. Isaac Abravanel, "Zevah pesah," 4. The translation here and below is my own.

19. See Joseph Hacker, "Gaon vedika'on."

CHAPTER 16

1. See Abraham Yaari, *Hadefus ha'ivri bekushta*, 17–21 and 60–61; Adri K. Offenberg, *A Choice of Chorals*, 102–32; Allan Nigel, "A Typographical Odyssey"; Cedric Cohen Skalli, "On a Rhetorical Trend in Isaac Abravanel's First Edition in Constantinople 1505."

2. See the items in the previous note.

3. For further information on the first printed books by the Nahmias brothers see note 1. See also Shimon Iakerson, *Catalogue of Hebrew Incunabula from the Collection of the Library of the Jewish Theological Seminary of America*, 2:603–8.

4. Isaac Abravanel, *Rosh amanah*, 68. The translation is based on Abravanel, *Principles of Faith*, 82–83.

5. Abravanel, *Rosh amanah*, 86. The translation is based on Abravanel, *Principles of Faith*, 108–9.

6. Abravanel, *Rosh amanah*, 86–87. The translation is based on Abravanel, *Principles of Faith*, 108–9.

7. Seymour Feldman, "A Debate Concerning Determinism in Late Medieval Jewish Philosophy."

8. Hasdai Crescas, *Sefer or Adonai*, II, 5, chapters 5–6.

9. Abravanel, *Rosh amanah*, 87. The translation is based on Abravanel, *Principles of Faith*, 109.

10. Isaac Abravanel, "Zevah pesah," 4. The translations here and below from this work are my own.

11. Isaac Abravanel, *Rosh amanah, Zevah pesah, Nahalat avot*, 117.

12. Abravanel, "Zevah pesah," 5.

13. Avraham Gross, "Gerush sefarad viytsiratam hasifrutit shel hamegorashim."

14. Abravanel, "Zevah pesah," 4.

15. Shaul Regev, "Meshihiyut ve'astrologia behaguto shel Rabbi Yitshaq Abravanel," 187.

16. Abravanel, "Zevah pesah," 133.

17. Ibid., 134.

18. The verb used by Abravanel is *l.q.h.* It is used in the Talmud to describe a solar or lunar eclipse but also connotes violence and divine retribution: "Our Rabbis taught, When the sun is stricken it is a bad omen for idolaters; when the moon is stricken, it is a bad omen for Israel" (BT Sukah 29a).

19. Abravanel, "Zevah pesah," 134.

20. Ibid.

21. Ibid., 166.

22. Michael A. Shmidman, "An Excerpt from the *Avot* Commentary of R. Mattathias ha-Yizhari"; Joseph Hacker, "The Intellectual Activity of the Jews of the Ottoman Empire during the Sixteenth and Seventeenth Centuries."

23. Isaac Abravanel, *Nahalat avot*, 6. The translations here and below from this work are my own.

24. Ibid., 29.

25. Ibid., 29–30.

26. Ibid., 93.

27. Ibid., 133.

28. Ibid.

29. Ibid., 168.

30. Ibid.

31. For a comprehensive study of humanistic discussions of the dignitas hominis, see Charles Trinkaus, *In Our Image and Likeness*.

32. Lotario dei Segni (Pope Innocent III), *De miseria condicionis humane*.

33. Leone Ebreo, *Dialogues of Love*, 274.

34. Ibid., 275.

35. Isaac Abravanel, *Peirush Abravanel 'al nevi'im*. vol. 5: *Yirmiyahu*, 18.

36. Moshe Idel, "The Myth of the Androgyne in Leone Ebreo's 'Dialoghi d'Amore' and Its Cultural Implication"; Abraham Melamed, "The Myth of the Jewish Origins of Philosophy in the Renaissance."

37. See the overview in Trinkaus, *In Our Image and Likeness*.

38. Giovanni Pico della Mirandola, *On the Dignity of Man*3.

39. Ibid., 4.

40. Ibid., 5.

41. Ibid., 4–5.

42. Maimonides, *The Guide of the Perplexed*, 1:22. See also Yair Lorberbaum, *In God's Image*.

43. Abravanel, *Nahalat avot*, 169.

44. Ibid., 170.

45. Ibid.

46. Ibid.

47. Ibid., 170–71.

48. Ibid., 171.

49. Ibid., 181.

50. Crescas, *Sefer or Adonai*, II, 1, chapters 4–5.

51. Abravanel, *Nahalat avot*, 190.

52. Feldman, "A Debate Concerning Determinism," 40.

53. Crescas, *Sefer or Adonai*, II, 5, chapter 3.

54. Abravanel, *Nahalat avot*, 179.

55. Isaac Arama, *Sefer 'akedat Yitshaq*, 1:215.

56. Pico della Mirandola, *On the Dignity of Man*, 5.

57. Abravanel, *Nahalat avot*, 190–92.

CHAPTER 17

1. Isaac Abravanel, "Ma'ayanei hayesh'uah," 421. The translations here and below from this work are my own.

2. Yitzhak Baer, "Don Yitshaq Abarbanel veyahso el ba'yot historiah vehamedinah," 257.

3. Benzion Netanyahu, *Don Isaac Abravanel*, x.

4. Ibid., ix.

5. Girolamo Savonarola (1452–98) was a messianic Christian preacher and leader who was active in Florence. See Donald Weinstein, *Savonarola*.

6. Netanyahu, *Don Isaac Abravanel*, 249.

7. Ibid., 255.

8. Dov Schwartz, *Messianism in Medieval Jewish Thought*, 219.

9. Ibid.

10. Ibid., 63.

11. Ibid., 219.

12. Isaiah Tishby, *Meshihiyut vedor geirushei Sefarad vePortugal*, 52. The translation is my own.

13. Ibid., 660.

14. Gershom Scholem, *The Messianic Idea in Judaism*, 33.

15. Ibid., 41.

16. Moshe Idel, *Messianic Mystics*, 1–37.

17. Eric Lawee, *Isaac Abarbanel's Stance toward Tradition*, 127–68, and "The Messianism of Abravanel."

18. Joseph Hacker, "The Intellectual Activity of the Jews of the Ottoman Empire during the Sixteenth and Seventeenth Centuries," 112.

19. Quoted in ibid., 111.

20. Ibid., 112.

21. Abravanel, "Ma'ayanei hayesh'uah," 275.

22. Ibid.

23. Ibid.

24. Ibid.

25. Ibid., 282.

26. Abraham Bar Hiyya, *Sefer megilat hamegaleh*, 1.

27. Abravanel, "Ma'ayanei hayesh'uah," 283.

28. Ibid.

29. Ibid.

30. Ibid.

31. Ibid.

32. Ibid., 283–84.

33. Ibid., 284.

34. Ibid., 294.

35. Ibid.

36. Ibid.

37. Ibid.

38. Ibid. 297.

39. Ibid.

40. Ibid.

41. Ibid., 335.

42. Ibid.

43. Ibid., 401.

44. Ibid.

45. David Ruderman, "Hope against Hope."

46. Abravanel, "Ma'ayanei hayesh'uah," 401.

47. Ruderman has shown that 1503 CE was a favored date for more than a few Christian

and Jewish writers: it was a matter of consensus of learned prognosticators from both religions ("Hope against Hope").

48. Julius Guttmann, "Über Abraham bar Chijja's 'Buch der Enthüllung.'" See also Jacob Guttmann, *Die Religionsphilosophischen Lehren des Isaak Abravanel*, 98–108; Julius Guttmann, "Mavo," xxvi–xxvii.

49. Abravanel, "Ma'ayanei hayesh'uah," 410.

50. Ibid., 409.

51. Ibid., 412.

52. Netanyahu, *Don Isaac Abravanel*, 251.

53. Isaac Abravanel, *Yeshu'ot meshiho*.

54. Isaac Abravanel, *Mashmi'ah yeshu'ah*.

55. The original is: "Teshuvot lesh'elot: Ma'amarim ve'iyunim besefer Moreh nevukhim." Isaac Abravanel, "Teshuvot lesh'elot," 3:12.

56. Abravanel, "Ma'ayanei hayesh'uah," 401.

57. David Ben-Zazon, *Nevukhim hem*, 36.

CHAPTER 18

1. Publisher's introduction in Isaac Abravanel, *Ma'ayanei hayesh'uah*, 4. The translation is my own.

2. Ibid.

3. Isaac Abravanel, "Ma'ayanei hayesh'uah," 401.

4. Benzion Netanyahu, *Don Isaac Abravanel* 82–85.

5. David Kaufmann, "Don Isaac Abravanel et le Commerce des épices avec Calicut," 148. The translation is my own.

6. See Benjamin Ravid, "The Legal Status of the Jews in Venice to 1509."

7. Judah Abravanel, "A Complaint against the Times," translated from the Hebrew by Dan Almagor, Barbara Gavin, and Dan Jacobson, in Barbara Gavin, "Yehuda Abravanel and Italian Jewry," 56.

8. Ibid.

9. David Ben-Zazon, *Nevukhim hem*, 36.

10. Isaac Abravanel, "Teshuvot lesh'elot," 3:12.

11. Isaac Abravanel, *Peirush Abravanel 'al sefer Moreh Nevukhim*, 2:54b.

12. Abravanel, "Teshuvot lesh'elot," 3:12.

13. Yitzhak Baer, "Don Yitshaq Abarbanel veyahso el ba'yot historiah vehamedinah," 245–53.

14. Isaac Abravanel, *Peirush hatorah lerabenu Yitshak Abravanel*, 1:156. The translations here and below from this work are my own.

15. Maimonides, *The Guide of the Perplexed*, 1:25.

16. Abravanel, *Peirush hatorah lerabenu Yitshak Abravanel*, 1:207.

17. Ibid., 1:320.

18. Ibid., 1:319.

19. Seneca, *Ad Lucilium Epistulae Morales*, 2:407–9.

20. Ibid., 2:405.

21. Ibid., 2:412–13.

22. Ibid., 2:396–7.

23. Isaak Heinemann, "Abravanels Lehre vom Niedergang der Menschheit."

24. Ibid., 386. The translation is my own.

25. Flavius Josephus, *Josephus*, 4:29.

26. Augustine, *City of God against the Pagans*, 639.

27. Ibid., 426–27.

28. Abravanel, *Peirush hatorah lerabenu Yitshak Abravanel*, 1:320.

29. Ibid., 1:314.

30. Ibid.

31. Ibid., 1:322.

32. Leone Ebreo, *Dialogues of Love*, 286.

33. See Seymour Feldman, *Philosophy in a Time of Crisis* and "A House Divided."

34. Abravanel, "Teshuvot lesh'elot," 3:11b.

35. Ibid.

36. Ben-Zazon, *Nevukhim hem*, 348.

37. Abravanel, "Teshuvot lesh'elot," 3:11a–b.

38. Publisher's introduction in Abravanel, *Ma'ayanei hayesh'uah*, 4.

39. Ibid.

40. Abravanel, *Peirush hatorah*, volume 1, title page.

AFTERWORD

1. For a list of these printed editions, see Marvin J. Heller, *The Sixteenth Century Hebrew Book*.

2. See Aron L. Katchen, *Christian Hebraists and Dutch Rabbis*, 65–75, 84–87, 105, 195, and 231–46; Isaac Abravanel, *De capite fidei* and "D. Isaaci Abravanielis & R. Mosis Alschechi Comment"; Johannes Buxtorf Filius, *Dissertatio de Sponsalibus et Divortiis*, 169–95, and *Liber Cosri*. See the translations of Abravanel's texts in the section titled "Mantissa aliquot Dissertassionem ad quorundam locorum ulteriorem illustrationem," in Buxtorf, *Liber Cosri*, 389–415 and 431–55.

3. Johannes Buxtorf, Filius, *Dissertationes Philologico-Theologicae*.

4. Richard Simon, *Histoire Critique du Vieux Testament*. The second chapter of Simon's works even contains explicit references to Abravanel's *Preface to his ommentary on Former Prophets* and a long discussion of his views. Abravanel's text thus serves as an important backdrop to Simon's own views on the Prophets as public writers, that is, chroniclers and archivists of the ancient Hebrew state.

5. Jacob Guttmann, *Die Religionsphilosophische Lehren das Isaak Abravanel*.

6. Julius Guttmann, *Die Philosophie des Judentums*, 266–68. See also Julius Guttmann, *The Philosophies of Judaism*, 287–91.

7. Yitzhak Baer, "Don Yitshaq Abarbanel veyahso el ba'yot historiah vehamedinah."

8. Ibid., 241.

9. Fritz Baer, *Die Juden im Christlichen Spanien*. See also Yitzhak Baer, *A History of the Jews in Christian Spain*.

10. Baer, "Don Yitshaq Abarbanel veyahso el ba'yot historiah vehamedinah," 241.

11. Yitzhak Baer, "Todros Ben Yehudah vezemano," "Hamegamah hadatit-hevratit shel 'sefer hasidim,'" and "Hareka hahistori shel 'Raya mehemna.'"

12. Leo Strauss, "On Abravanel's Philosophical Tendency and Political Teaching."

13. Benzion Netanyahu, *Don Isaac Abravanel*.

14. Ephraim Shmueli, *Don Yitshaq Abravanel vegeirush sefarad*.

15. Ibid., 7.

16. Ibid, 8.

17. Ibid, 10.

18. Ibid.

19. Moshe Idel, "Kabalah ufilosofia qedumah etsel R. Isaac veyehudah Abravanel."

20. Eleazar Gutwirth, "Don Ishaq Abravanel and Vernacular Humanism in Fifteenth Century Iberia," "Consolatio," "Duran on Ahitophel," "Italy or Spain?," "Hebrew Letters, Hispanic Mail," "Medieval Romance Epistolarity," "Abraham Seneor," "Conversions to Christianity amongst Fifteenth-Century Spanish Jews," and "Don Yizchaq Abravanel."

21. Eric Lawee, *Isaac Abarbanel's Stance toward Tradition*.

BIBLIOGRAPHY

EDITIONS OF ISAAC ABRAVANEL'S WORKS CITED

ʿAteret zeqenim. Tzurot hayesodot. Jerusalem, 1993.

"D. Isaaci Abravanielis & R. Mosis Alschechi Comment." In Constantijn L'Empereur, *Esaiae Prophetiam 30.* Lyon, France, 1631.

De capite fidei. Translated by G. Vossius. Amsterdam, 1638.

"Maʿayanei hayeshʿuah." In Isaac Abravanel, *Peirush ʿal neviʾim ukhetuvim,* 267–421. Jerusalem, 1960.

Mashmiʿah yeshuʿah. In Isaac Abravanel, *Peirush ʿal neviʾim ukhetuvim,* 425–608. Jerusalem, 1960.

Nahalat avot. In Isaac Abravanel, *Pirqei avot ʿim peirush rabenu Moshe ben Maimon veʿim Nahalat avot mehasar hagadol rabenu Don Yitshaq Abravanel.* New York, 1953.

Peirush Abravanel ʿal neviʾim. Vol. 1: *Yehoshuʿa-Shoftim.* Jerusalem, 2009.

Peirush Abravanel ʿal neviʾim. Vol. 2: *Shmuʾel.* Jerusalem, 2010.

Peirush Abravanel ʿal neviʾim. Vol. 3: *Melakhim.* Jerusalem, 2011.

Peirush Abravanel ʿal neviʾim. Vol. 5: *Yirmiyahu.* Jerusalem, 2014.

Peirush Abravanel ʿal neviʾim. Vol. 7: *Trei ʿasar.* Jerusalem, 2015.

Peirush Abravanel ʿal neviʾim rishonim. Jerusalem, 1955.

Peirush Abravanel ʿal sefer Moreh Nevukhim. Prague, 1831.

Peirush hatorah. Edited by S. Archevolti. Vol. 1. Venice, 1579.

Peirush hatorah lerabenu Yitshak Abravanel. Vol. 1: *Sefer Bereishit.* Jerusalem, 1997.

Peirush hatorah lerabenu Yitshak Abravanel. Vol. 5: *Sefer Devarim.* Jerusalem, 2007.

Principles of Faith. Translated by M. Kellner. Rutherfor, NJ, 1982.

Rosh amanah. Edited by Menahem Kellner. Ramat Gan, Israel, 1993.

Rosh amanah, Zevah pesah, Nahalat avot. Istanbul, 1505.

"Teshuvot leshʾelot: Maʾamarim veʾiyunim besefer Moreh Nevukhim." In Isaac Abravanel, *Ketavim bemahshevet Yisraʾel,* 3:2a–21b. Jerusalem, 1967.

Yeshuʿot meshiho. Königsberg, 1861.

"Zevah pesah." In Isaac Abravanel, *Haggada shel Pesah . . . ʿim Zevah Pesah.* Bnei-Brak, Israel, 1962.

PRIMARY SOURCES

Alemanno, Yohanan. *Heshek Shlomo lerabi Yohanan Alemano.* Edited by Daphna Levin. Tel Aviv, 2019.

Alighieri, Dante. *The Divine Comedy.* Vol. 1: *The Inferno.* Translated by Marc Musa. New York, 1984.

Aquinas. *Political Writings.* Edited and translated by R. W. Dyson. Cambridge, 2002.

Arama, Isaac. *Sefer ʿakedat Yitshaq.* 6 vols. Jerusalem, 1984.

Aristotle. *Metaphysics: Book Lambda*. Translated with an introduction and commentary by Lindsay Judson. Oxford, 2019.

———. *On the Heavens*. Edited and translated by W. K. C. Guthrie. Cambridge, MA: 1960.

———. *Politics*. Edited by R. F. Stalley. Translated by E. Bekker. Oxford, 1998.

Augustine. *City of God against the Pagans*. Translated by R. W. Dyson. Cambridge, 1956.

Bar Hiyya, Abraham. *Sefer megilat hamegaleh*. Edited by Y. Guttmann. Berlin, 1924.

Ben Zerah, Menahem. *Tsedah laderekh*. Ferrara, Italy, 1554.

Biblia Latina cum glosa ordinaria Walfridi Strabonis aliorumque, et interlineari Anselmi Laudunensis. et cum postillis ac moralitatibus Nicolai de Lyra. et expositionibus Guillelmi Britonis in omnes prologos S. Hieronymi et additionibus Pauli Burgensis replicisque Matthiae Doering. 6 vols. Basel, 1498.

Bruni, Leonardo. *History of the Florentine People*, Vol. 1: *Books I–IV*. Edited and translated by James Hankins. Cambridge, MA, 2001.

———. "Panegyric to the City of Florence." Translated by Benjamin G. Kohl. In *The Earthly Republic: Italian Humanists on Government and Society*, edited by Benjamin G. Kohl, R. G. Witt, and E. B. Welles, 135–74. Philadelphia, 1978.

Buxtorf Filius, Johannes. *Dissertatio de Sponsalibus et Divortiis cui Accessit Isaaci Abravanelis Diatriba de Excidii Poena, Cujus Frequens in Lege & in Hac Materia Fit Mentio*. Basel, Switzerland, 1652.

———. *Dissertationes Philologico-Theologicae*. Basel, Switzerland, 1662.

———. *Liber Cosri*. Basel, Switzerland, 1660.

Capsali, Elijah. *Seder eliyahu zuta*. 3 vols. Jerusalem, 1976.

Cicero. *De Oratore*. Translated by E. W. Sutton. Vol. 1. London, 1976.

———. *Tusculan Disputations*. Translated by J. E. King. Cambridge, MA, 1966.

Corrêa da Serra, José, ed. *Collecção de Livros Ineditos da Historia Portuguesa dos Reinados de D. João I, D. Duarte, D. Affonso V, a D. João II*. Vol. 2. Lisbon, 1792.

Crescas, Hasdai. *Sefer or Adonai*. Jerusalem, 1971.

Da Genazzano, Elijah Haim. *Lettera Preciosa, Introduzione, Edizione e Traduzione a Cura di F. Lelli*. Florence, 2002.

De Almeida, Lope. *Cartas de Itália*. Edited by R. Lapa. Lisbon, 1935.

De Almeida, Manuel Lopez, ed. *Obras dos Principes de Avis*. Porto, Portugal, 1981.

De Ayala, López. *Las Decadadas de Tito Livio*. 2 vols. Edited by Curt J. Wittlin. Barcelona, 1982.

De Guzmán, Fernán Pérez. *Generaciones y Semblanzas*. Edited by José Antonio Barrio Sánchez. Madrid, 1998.

De Pina, Rui. *Chronica de el Rey D. Affonso V*. Vol. 2. Lisbon, 1901.

———. *Crónicas de Rui de Pina*. Edited M. Lopes de Almeida. Porto, Portugal, 1977.

De Resende, Garcia. *Cancioneiro Geral Lixboa 1516*. Reprint, New York, 1976.

———. *Crónica de D. João II e Miscelânea*. Preface by J. V. Serrão. Lisbon, 1973.

De Santarem, Visconde. *Quadro Elementar das Relações Politicas e Diplomaticas de Portugal,* vol. 9, Lisbon, 1864.

De Santillana, Marqués. *Obras Completas: Poesía, Prosa.* Edited by A. G. Moreno and M. P. A. M. Kerkhof. Madrid, 2002.

De Villena, Enrique. *Obras Completas.* Edited by Pedro Catedra., Vol. 1. Madrid, 1994.

Dei Segni, Lotario (Pope Innocent III). *De miseria condicionis humane.* Edited and translated by Robert E. Lewis. Athens, GA, 1978.

Dom Duarte. *Leal conselheiro.* Edited by Maria Helena Lopes de Castro. Lisbon, 1998.

Dom Pedro and Frei João Verba. *Livro da Vertuosa Benfeytoria.* Edited by Adelino Almeida Calado. Coimbra, Portugal, 1994.

Duran, Profiat. *Sefer ma'aseh efod.* Vienna, 1865.

Ebreo, Leone (Judah Abrabanel). *Dialoghi d'Amore.* Edited by G. Manuppella. Vol. 1 Lisbon, 1983.

———. *Dialogues of Love.* Edited by R. Pescatori; translated by Cosmos D. Bacich. Toronto; Buffalo; London, 2009.

Ficino, Marsilio. *Three Books on Life: A Critical Edition and Translation with Introduction and Notes.* Edited and translated by C.V. Kaske, and J.R. Clark. Tempe, 1998.

Gerondi, Nissim ben Reuben. *Derashot haran.* Edited by A. L. Feldman. Jerusalem, 1977.

Gersonides, Levi. *Sefer milhamot Hashem.* Berlin, 1923.

Gersonides, Levi. *The Wars of the Lord,* Vol. 3. Translated by S. Feldman. New York; Jerusalem, 1999.

Guicciardini, Francesco. *The History of Italy.* Edited and translated by Sidney Alexander. Princeton, NJ, 1984.

———. *Storia d'Italia.* Edited by E. Mazzali. Vol. 1. Milan, 1988.

Hakohen, Joseph. *'Emeq habakha.* Jerusalem, 1993.

Ibn Verga, Solomon. *Shevet Yehuda.* Edited by Y. Baer. Jerusalem, 1947.

Ibn Yahya, Gedalia. *Shalshelet Hakabalah.* Warsaw, 1977.

Josephus, Flavius. *Jewish Antiquities.* Translated by Ralph Marcus. London, 1950.

———. *Josephus.* Vol. 4: *Jewish Antiquities, Books I–IV,* translated by H. Thackeray. Cambridge, MA, 1961.

Livy. *History of Rome.* Vol. 1: *Books I–II.* Translated by B. O. Foseter. Cambridge, MA, 1998.

Machiavelli, Niccolo. *The Art of War.* Translated by E. Farneworth. New York, 1965.

———. "Dell'Arte della Guerra." In Niccolò Machiavelli, *Tutte le Storiche e Letterarie di Opere di Niccolo Machiavelli,* 353–67. Florence, 1929.

Maimonides, Moses. *The Guide of the Perplexed.* 2 vols. Translated by Shlomo Pines. Chicago, 1963.

Manetti, Giannozzo. *A Translator's Defense.* Edited by M. McShane. Translated by M. Young. Cambridge, MA, 2016.

Messer Leon, Judah. *The Book of the Honeycomb's Flow.* Edited and translated by Isaac Rabinowitz. Ithaca, NY, 1983.

———. *Nofet tsufim.* Edited by Robert Bonfil. Jerusalem, 1981.

Mikra'ot gedolot haketer: Mahadurat yesod hadasha: Devarim. Edited by Menahem Cohen. Ramat-Gan, Israel, 2011.

Mikra'ot gedolot haketer: Mahadurat yesod hadasha: Vayiqra. Edited by Menahem Cohen. Ramat-Gan, Israel, 2013.

Morras, María, ed. *Alonso de Cartagena, Libros de Tulio: De Senectute De los Oficios.* Alcala de Henares, Spain, 1996.

Petrarca, Francesco. *Invectives.* Edited and translated by D. Marsh. Cambridge, MA, 2008.

———. *Rerum Familiarium Libri I–VIII.* Translated by Aldo S. Bernardo. Albany, NY, 1975.

———. See also *Pétrarque.*

Pétrarque, *Lettres Familières: Livres I–III, Rerum Familiarium libri I–III.* Introduction by Ugo Dotti. Translated by Frank La Brasca. Paris, 2002.

Pico della Mirandola, Giovanni. *On the Dignity of Man.* Translated by C. G. Wallis, P. J. W. Miller, and Douglas Carmichael. Indianapolis, IN, 1998.

———. *Syncretism in the West: Pico's 900 Theses (1486): The Evolution of Traditional Religious and Philosophical Systems.* Edited and translated by Stephen A. Farmer. Tempe, AZ, 1998.

Possevino, Antonio. *Apparatus sacer ad scriptores Veteris et Novi Testatamenti. Eorum interpretes. Synodos et patres Latinos ac graecos. Horum versions. Theologos scholasticos. . . .* Vol. 2. Cologne, 1608.

Seneca. *Ad Lucilium Epistulae Morales.* Translated by Richard M. Gummere. Vol. 2 Cambridge, MA, 1970.

———. *Hercules, Trojan Women, Phoenician Women, Medea, Phaedra.* Edited and translated by John G. Fitch. Cambridge, MA, 2018.

———. *Moral Essays.* Translated by J. W. Basore. Vol. 2. Cambridge, MA, 1958.

Simon, Richard. *Histoire Critique du Vieux Testament.* Amsterdam, 1685.

Teixeira, Joao. *Oraçam que teve Ioam Teyxeira Chancarel mòr destes Reynoos em tempo del Rey dom Ioam o segundo de Portugal. . . .* Coimbra, Portugal, 1562.

Usque, Samuel. *Consolacion às Tribulações de Israel.* 2 vols. Introduction by Y. H. Yerushalmi and J. V. de Pina Martins. Lisbon, 1989.

Valla, Lorenzo. *On the Donation of Constantine.* Translated by G. W. Bowersock. Cambridge, MA, 2007.

Yaavetz, Joseph. *Sefer or hahaim.* Przemyśl, Poland, 1926.

Zacuto, Abraham. *Sefer yuhasin.* Jerusalem, 1963.

SECONDARY SOURCES

Abulafia, David, ed. *The French Descent into Renaissance Italy: 1494–95: Antecedents and Effects.* New York, 1995.

———. "Insediamenti, diaspora e tradizione ebraica: Gli ebrei del regno di Napoli da

Ferdinando il Cattolico a Carlos V." In *Carlos V, Napoli e il Mediterraneo*, edited by G. Galapro and A. Muji, 171–202. Naples, 2003.

Alves Dias, João José. *Portugal: Do Renasciemnto à Crise Dinastica*. Lisbon, 1998.

Attias, Jean-Christoph. "Isaac Abravanel (1508–1992): Essai de Mémoire Comparée." In *Mémoires Juive d'Espagne et du Portugal*, edited by E. Benbassa, 273–308. Paris, 1996.

Baer, Fritz, *Die Juden im Christlichen Spanien, Erster Teil Urkunden und Regesten*. Vol. 2: *Kastilien Inquisitionsakten*. Berlin, 1936.

Baer, Yitzhak. "Don Yitshaq Abarbanel veyahso el ba'yot historiah vehamedinah." *Tarbiz* 8, nos. 3–4 (1937): 241–59.

———. "Hamegamah hadatit-hevratit shel 'sefer hasidim.'" *Zion* 3 (1938): 1–50.

———. "Hareka hahistori shel 'Raya mehemna.'" *Zion* 5 (1940): 1–44.

———. *A History of the Jews in Christian Spain*. 2 vols. Translated by Louis Schoffman. Philadelphia, 1961 and 1966.

———. "Todros Ben Yehudah vezemano." *Zion* 2 (1937): 19–55.

Baron, Hans. *The Crisis of the Early Italian Renaissance: Civic Humanism and Republican Liberty in an Age of Classicism and Tyranny*. Princeton, NJ, 1955.

———. *From Petrarch to Leonardo Bruni: Studies in Humanistic and Political Literature*. Chicago, 1968.

Baron, Salo. *A Social and Religious History of the Jews*. Vol. 11: *Citizen or Alien Conjurer*. Philadelphia, 1952.

Beinart, Haim. *The Expulsion of the Jews from Spain*. Oxford, 2002.

———. *Moreshet Sepharad: The Sephardi Legacy*. Jerusalem, 1992.

———. *Pirqei sefarad*. Jerusalem, 1998.

Beitner, Azariah. *Sipurei yavne: Biqur holim venihum avelim*. Ramat-Gan, Israel, 2011.

Benayahu, Meir. "Beit Abravanel beSaloniki." *Sefunot* 12 (1971–78): 9–67.

Ben-Sasson, Haim Hillel. "Dor golei Sefarad 'al 'atsmo." *Zion* 26 (1961): 23–64.

Ben-Shalom, Ram. "The Consolatory Letters of a Jewish Communal Scribe in Montalbán, Aragon: Political Implications and Historical Context." *Dimensões* 33 (2014): 123–60.

———. "Dimui hatarbut hanotsrit betoda'ah hahistorit shel yehudei Sefarad veProvans (hame'ot hashteim esrei 'ad hamesh esrei). PhD diss., Tel Aviv University, 1996.

———. "Hahatsran 'keshevet Yehuda': Ha'igrot veshirei hashevah lahatsranim shel Yom Tov ben Hana, sofer kehillat Montalben shebisfarad." *Mikan* 11 (2012): 196–224.

———. *Medieval Jews and the Christian Past: Jewish Historical Consciousness in Spain and Southern France*. Oxford, 2016.

———. "Mitos umitologia shel Yavan veRoma betoda'ah hahistorit shel yehudei Sefarad bimei habeinaim." *Zion* 66, no. 4 (2001): 468–80.

———. "The Myths of Troy and Hercules as Reflected in the Writings of Some Jewish Exiles from Spain." In *Jews, Muslims, and Christians in and around the Crown of Aragon:*

Essays in Honour of Professor Elena Lourie, edited by H. J. Hames, 229–54. Leiden, the Netherlands, 2004.

Bentley, Jerry H. *Politics and Culture in Renaissance Naples.* Princeton, NJ, 1987.

Ben-Zazon, David. *Nevuhim hem: Masa bebi'uro shel Don Yitshaq Abravanel laMoreh Nevuhim.* Jerusalem, 2015.

Berlin, Charles, ed. *Hebrew Printing and Bibliography.* New York, 1976.

Blüher, Karl Alfred. *Seneca in Spanien Untersuchungen zur Geschichte der Seneca-Rezeption in Spanien vom 13. Bis 17. Jahrhundert.* Munich, 1969.

Bonazzoli, Viviana. "Gli Ebrei del Regno di Napoli all'Epoca della Loro Espulsione." *Archivio Storico Italiano* 502 (1979): 495–559, and 508 (1981): 179–287.

Bonfil, Robert. "The History of the Spanish and Portuguese Jews in Italy." In *Moreshet Sepharad: The Sephardi Legacy*, edited by Haim Beinart, 2:217–39. Jerusalem, 1992.

———. *Jewish Life in Renaissance Italy.* Berkeley, CA, 1994.

Boyarin, Daniel. *Ha'iyun haSfaradi lefarshanut haTalmud shel megurashei Sfarad.* Jerusalem, 1989.

Braamcamp Freire, Anselmo. "As Conspirações no Reinado de D. João II: Documentos." *Arquivo Historico Portuguez* 1 (1903): 389–97.

———. "Maria Brandoa, a do Crisfal." *Archivo Histórico Portuguez* 6 (1908): 295–442.

———. "Os Sessenta Milhoes Outogados em 1478." *Archivo Historico Portuguez* 4 (1906): 425–38.

Braga, Teófilo. *Historia da Literatura Portuguesa, Edade Media.* Porto, Portugal, 1909.

Calafate, Pedro. "O Infante D. Pedro." In *História do Pensamento Filosófico Português*, edited by Pedro Calafate, 1:411–44. Lisbon, 1999.

Canpanton, Isaac. *Darkhei hatalmud.* Jerusalem, 1981.

Cantera Burgos, Francisco. "Don 'Ishaq Braunel' (alguns precisions biograficas sobre su estancia en castilla)." In *Salo Wittmayer Baron Jubilee Volume*, edited by Saul Lieberman, 1:237–50. Jerusalem, 1974.

Cassuto, Umberto. *Gli Ebrei a Firenze nell'Età del Rinascimento.* okFlorence, 1918.

———. "Sulla Famiglia Da Pisa." *Revista Israelitica* 5 (1909): 227–38; 6 (1909): 21–30, 102–13, 160–70, and 223–36; and 7 (1910): 8–16, 73–86, and 146–50.

Catedra, Pedro. "Modos de Consolar por Carta." In *Actas del VI Congreso Internacional de la Asociacion Hispanica de Literatura Medieval*, edited by J. M. Lucia Megias, 469–87. Alcala de Henares, Spain, 1997.

———. "Prospeccion Sobre el Género Consolatorio en el Siglo XV." In *Letters and Society in Fifteenth-Century Spain*, edited by A. D. Deyermond and J. Lawrance, 1–16. Oxford, 1993.

———. "Una Epistola 'Consolatoria' Attribuida al Tostado." *Atalya* 3 (1992): 165–76.

Catedra, Pedro M., and Paolo Cherchi. *Los Doze Trabajos de Hercules (Zamora, por Anton de Centenera, 1483): Estudios.* 2 vols. Santander, Spain, 2007.

Celenza, Cristopher S. "Lorenzo Valla's Radical Philology: The 'Preface' to the Annotations to the New Testament in Context." *Journal of Medieval and Early Modern Studies* 42 (2012): 365–94.

Cohen Skalli, Cedric. "Abravanel's Commentary on the Former Prophets: Portraits, Self-Portraits, and Models of Leadership." *Jewish History* 23 (2009): 255–80.

———. "Discovering Isaac Abravanel's Humanistic Rhetoric." *Jewish Quarterly Review* 97 (2007): 67–99.

———, ed. *Isaac Abravanel: Letters*. Berlin, 2007.

———. "On a Rhetorical Trend in Isaac Abravanel's First Edition in Constantinople 1505." *Hispania Judaica Bulletin* 5 (2007): 153–75.

Cohen Skalli, Cedric, and Oded Horezky. "A 15th-Century Reader of Gersonides: Don Isaac Abravanel, Providence, Astral Influences, Active Intellect and Humanism." In *Gersonides through the Ages*, edited by O. Elior, G. Freudenthal, and D. Wirmer, 159–226. Leiden, the Netherlands, 2020.

Cohen Skalli, Cedric, and Michele Luzzati. *Lucca 1493: Un Sequestro di Lettere Ebraiche: Edizione e Commento Storico*. Naples, 2014.

Colafemmina, Cesare. *Documenti per la Storia degli Ebrei in Pugli Nell'Archivio di Stato di Napoli*. Bari, Italy, 1990.

Costa Gomes, Rita. "As Cortes de 1481–1482." In *O Tempo de Vasco de Gama*, edited by D. R. Curto, 245–64 .Lisbon, 1998.

Da Fonseca, Luís Adão. *D. João II*. Rio do Mouro, Portugal, 2005.

Da Silva, Nuno J. Espinosa Gomes. "Bártolo na História do Direito Português." *Revista da Faculdade de Direito da Universidade de Lisboa* 12 (1960): 5–49.

———. *Humanesimo e Direito em Portugal no Século XVI*. Lisbon, 1964.

———. "João Das Regras e Outros Juristas Portugueses da Universidade de Bolonha." *Revista da Faculdade de Direito da Universidade de Lisboa* 12 (1960): 5–35.

Davidson, Herbert A. *Alfarabi, Avicenna, and Averroes on Intellect: Their Cosmologies, Theories of the Active Intellect, and Theories of Human Intellect*. New York, 1992.

De Carvalho, Joaquim. *Estudos Sobre a Cultura Portuguesa del Seculo XV*. Coimbra, Portugal, 1949.

———. "Una Epistola de Isaac Abarbanel." In Joaquim de Carvalho, *Obra Completa de Joaquim de Carvalho*, 3:115–25. Lisbon, 1982.

De Oliveira Marques, António Henrique Rodrigo. *Portugal na Crise dos Sécuos XIV e XV*. Lisbon, 1986.

De Pinho, Sebastião Tavares. "O Infante D. Pedro e a 'Escola' de Tradutores da Corte de Avis." *Biblos* 69 (1993): 129–53.

De Sousa, Antonio Caetano. *Provas da História Genealógica da Casa Real Portugueza*. Lisbon, 1739.

De Sousa, Armindo. "O Parlamento na Época de D. João II." In *Congresso Internacional Bartolomeu Dias Actas*, 1:231–61. Porto, Portugal, 1989.

Di Camillo, Ottavio. *El Humanismo Castellano del Siglo XV*. Valencia, Spain, 1976.

Di Leone Leoni, Aron. "Nuove notize sugli Abravanel." *Zakhor* 1 (1997): 153–206.

———. "Per una storia della nazione portoghese ad Ancona e a Pesaro." in *L'Identita' Dissimulata*, edited by P. C. Ioly Zorattini, 27–97. Florence, 2000.

Dorman, Menachem. "Mavo." In Yehuda Abravanel, *Sihot 'al ahavah*, edited and translated by Menachem Dorman, 11–182. Jerusalem, 1983.

Elliott, John H. *Imperial Spain: 1469–1716*. London, 2002.

Feldman, Aryeh Leib. "Derashot Haran: Haderush ha'asiri nosah bet." *Sinai* 75 (1973): 9–51.

Feldman, Seymour. "A Debate Concerning Determinism in Late Medieval Jewish Philosophy." *Proceedings of the American Academy for Jewish Research* 51 (1984): 15–54.

———. "A House Divided." In *Crises and Creativity in the Sephardic World: 1391–1648*, edited by B. R. Gampel, 38–58. New York, 1997.

———. *Philosophy in a Time of Crisis: Don Isaac Abravanel: Defender of the Faith*. New York, 2003.

Fernanda Dias, Aida. *Historia Critica da Literatura Portuguesa*. Vol. 1: *Idade Média*. Lisbon, 1998.

———. "Um Libro de Espiritualidade: O Boosco Deleitoso." *Biblos* 65 (1989): 229–45.

Ferorelli, Niccolo. *Gli Ebrei nell'Italia Meridionale dall'Eta Romana al Secolo XVIII*. Naples, 1915.

Ferro Tavares, Maria José Pimenta. *Os Judeus em Portugal no Século XV*. 2 vols. Lisbon, 1982–84.

———. "Subsidios para o Estudo da História Monetaria do Século XV." *Nummus* 4–6 (1981–83): 9–59.

Freudenthal, Gad. "Hatslaha nafshit ve'astronomia: Milhamto shel haRalbag neged Talm'ai." *Daat* 22 (1989): 55–72.

———. "The Medieval Astrologization of Aristotle's Biology: Averroes on the Role of the Celestial Bodies in the Generation of Animate Beings." *Arabic Sciences and Philosophy* 12 (2002): 111–37.

Gama, José. "A Geração de Avis." In *História do Pensamento Filosófico Português*, edited by Pedro Calafate, 1:379–441. Lisbon, 1999.

Garin, Eugenio. *Emertismo del Rinascimento*. Pisa, Italy, 2012.

———. *La Cultura Filosofica del Rinascimento Italiano: Richerche e Documenti*. Bologna, 2001.

Gavin, Barbara. "Yehuda Abravanel and Italian Jewy." *Jewish Quarterly* 148 (Winter 1992–93): 51–59.

Gebhardt, Carl. "Regesten zur Lebensgeschichte Leone Ebreo." In *Leone Ebreo, Dialoghi d'Amore Hebräische Gedichte*, edited by Carl Gebhardt, 1–62. Heidelberg, 1929.

Gomes, Saul António. *D. Afonso V O Africano*. Rio de Mouro, Portugal, 2006.

Gómez Redondo, Fernando. *Historia de la Prosa Medieval Castellana*. Vol. 3: *Los Orígenes del Humanismo*. Madrid, 2002.

Greenup, Albert W. "A Kabbalistic Epistle by Isaac B. Shmuel B. Hayyim Sephardi." *Jewish Quarterly Review* 21 (1931): 365–75.

Griffiths, Gordon, James Hankins, and David Thompson, eds. *The Humanism of Leonardo Bruni: Selected Texts*. Binghamton, NY, 1987.

Gross, Avraham. "Gerush Sefarad viytsiratam hasifrutit shel hamegorashim." *Peamim* 75 (1998): 75–93.

———. "Rabbi Hayun verabi Yitshak Abravanel: Yehasim intelektualim." *Michael* 11 (1989): 23–33.

———. *Rabi Yosef ben Avraham Hayun: Manhig qehilat lisbon viytsirato*. Ramat-Gan, Israel, 1993.

Guttmann, Jacob. *Die Religionsphilosophischen Lehren des Isaak Avravanel*. Breslau, German Reich, 1916.

Guttmann, Julius. *Die Philosophie des Judentums*. Munich, 1933.

———. "Mavo." In Julius Guttmann, *Sefer megilat hamegaleh*, ix–xli, Berlin, 1924.

———. *The Philosophies of Judaism: The History of Jewish Philosophy from Biblical Times to Franz Rosenzweig*, translated by David W. Silverman. Philadelphia, 1964.

———. "Über Abraham bar Chijja's 'Buch der Enthüllung.'" *Monatsschrift für Geschichte und Wissenschaft des Judentums* 47 (1903): 446–68.

Gutwirth, Eleazar. "Abraham Seneor: Social Tensions and the Court-Jew." *Michael* 11 (1989): 169–229.

———. "Consolatio: Don Ishaq Abravanel and the Classical Tradition." *Medievalia et Humanistica* 27 (2000): 79–98.

———. "Conversions to Christianity amongst Fifteenth-Century Spanish Jews: An Alternative Explanation." In *Shlomo Simonsohn Jubilee Volume*, edited by Daniel Carpi, 97–121. Tel Aviv, 1993.

———. "Don Ishaq Abravanel and Vernacular Humanism in Fifteenth Century Iberia." *Bibliothèque d'Humanisme et Renaissance* 60 (1998): 641–71.

———. "Don Yizchaq Abravanel: Exegesis and Self-Fashioning." *Trumah* 9 (2000): 35–42.

———. "Duran on Ahitophel: The Practice of Jewish History in Late Medieval Spain." *Jewish History* 4 (1989): 59–74.

———. "Hebrew Letters, Hispanic Mail: Communication among Fourteenth-Century Aragon Jewry." In *Communication in the Jewish Diaspora: The Pre-modern World.*, edited by S. Menache, 257–82. New York, 1996.

———. "Hercules Furens and War: On Abravanel's Courtly Context." *Jewish History* 23, no.3 (2009): 297–300.

———. "Italy or Spain? The Theme of Jewish Eloquence in Shevet Yehudah." In *Daniel Carpi Jubilee Volume: A Collection of Studies in the History of the Jewish People Presented to Daniel Carpi upon His 70th Birthday by His Colleagues and Students*, 35–67. Tel Aviv, 1996.

———. "Medieval Romance Epistolarity: The Case of The Iberian Jews." *Neophilologus* 84 (2000): 207–24

———. "Religion and Social Criticism in Late Medieval Rousillon: An Aspect of Profyat Duran's Activities." *Michael* 12 (1991): 145–56.

Haas, Jair. "Divine Perfection and Methodological Inconsistency: Towards an Understanding of Isaac Abarbanel's Exegetical Frame of Mind." *Jewish Studies Quarterly* 17 (2010): 302–57.

———. "Writing by Divine Imperative as a Criterion for the Prophetic Authority of Texts in the Biblical Exegesis of Isaac Abarbanel." *Jewish Studies* 9 (2010): 293–325.

Hacker, Joseph. "Gaon vedika'on: Kotavim behavayatam haruhanit vehahevratit shel yots'ei Sefarad vePortugal ba'Imperiah ha'Othmanit." In *Tarbut vahevrah betoldot Yisra'el beyemei habeinayim*, edited by R. Bonfil, M. Ben-Sasson, and J. Hacker, 541–86. Jerusalem, 1989.

———. "Igeret Rabi Meir 'Arama neged Rabi Yitshak Abravanel vehitqablutah: Hidah sheba'ah 'al pitronah." *Tarbiz* 66 (2007): 501–18.

———. "The Intellectual Activity of the Jews of the Ottoman Empire during the Sixteenth and Seventeenth Centuries." In *Jewish Thought in the Seventeenth Century,* edited by I. Twersky and B. Septimus, 95–135. Cambridge, MA, 1987.

———. "Kroniqot hadashot 'al gerush haYehudim miSefarad, sibotav vetotsa'otav." *Zion* 44 (1978): 201–28.

———. "Qevutsat igrot 'al gerush haYehudim miSfarad umeSitzilya ve'al goral hameegurashim." In *Peraqim betoldot hahevra haYehudit biymei habeinaim uva'et hahadasha*, edited by I. Etkes and Y. Shalmon, 67–97. Jerusalem, 1980.

———. "The Sephardim in the Ottoman Empire in the Sixteenth Century." In *Moreshet Sepharad: The Sephardi Legacy*, edited by Haim Beinart, 2:109–33. Jerusalem, 1992.

———. "Teguvot hameegurashim legeirush Sefarad uleshemad Portugal." In *Dor geirush Sefarad*, edited by Yom Tov Assis and Joseph Kaplan, 223–45. Jerusalem, 1999.

Halper, Yehuda. "In One Sense Easy, in Another Difficult: Reverberations of the Opening of Aristotle's Metaphysics α ἔλλατον in Medieval and Renaissance Hebrew Literature." *Revue d'Etudes Juives* (forthcoming).

Hankins, James, ed. *Renaissance Civic Humanism: Reappraisals and Reflections.* Cambridge, 2000.

———. "Rhetoric, History, and Ideology: The Civic Panegyrics of Leonardo Bruni." In *Renaissance Civic Humanism: Reappraisals and Reflections*, edited by James Hankins, 143–78. Cambridge, 2000.

Harvey, Zev Warren. *Rabbi Hasdai Crescas.* Jerusalem, 2010.

Heinemann, Isaak. "Abravanels Lehre vom Niedergang der Menschheit." *Monatsschrift für Geschichte und Wissenschaft des Judentums* 82 (1938): 381–400.

Heller, Marvin J. *The Sixteenth Century Hebrew Book: An Abridged Thesaurus.* 2 vols. Leiden, the Netherlands, 2004.

Heller-Wilensky, Sara. *Rabi Yitshaq 'Arama umishnato*. Jerusalem, 1957.

Hoch, Liron, and Menachem Kellner. "'The Voice is the Voice of Jacob, but the Hands Are the Hands of Esau': Isaac Abravanel between Judah Halevi and Moses Maimonides." *Jewish History* 26 (2012): 61–83.

Iakerson, Shimon. *Catalogue of Hebrew Incunabula from the Collection of the Library of the Jewish Theological Seminary of America*. Vols. 1 and 2. New York, 2005.

Idel, Moshe, "Hermeticism and Judaism." In *Hermeticism and the Renaissance: Intellectual History and the Occult in Early Modern Europe*, edited by Ingrid Merkel and Allen G. Debus, 59–76. Washington, 1988.

———. "Igarto shel R' Yitshak mePisa (?) bishlosh nusha'oteha." *Qovets 'al Yad* 10 (1982): 161–214.

———. "Kabalah ufilosofia qedumah etsel R. Isaac veyehudah Abravanel." In *Filosofiat ha'ahavah shel Abravanel*, edited by Menachem Dorman and Ze'ev Levy, 73–112. Tel Aviv, 1985.

———. *Messianic Mystics*. New Haven, CT, 2001.

———. "The Myth of the Androgyne in Leone Ebreo's 'Dialoghi d'Amore' and its Cultural Implication." *Kabbalah* 15 (2006): 77–102.

Kamen, Henry. "The Mediterranean and the Expulsion of the Jews in 1492." *Past and Present* 119 (1988): 30–55.

Katchen, Aron L. *Christian Hebraists and Dutch Rabbis*. Cambridge, MA, 1984.

Kaufmann, David. "Don Isaac Abravanel et le Commerce des épices avec Calicut." *Revue des Etudes Juives* 38 (1899): 145–49.

———. "La Famille de Yehiel de Pise." *Revues des Etudes Juives* 26 (1893): 83–110 and 220–39; 29 (1894): 142–47; 32 (1896): 130–34; and 34 (1897): 309–11.

Kellner, Menachem. "*Gersonides and His Cultured Despisers: Arama and Abravanel.*" *Journal of Medieval and Renaissance Studies* 6 (1976): 269–96.

Kidwell, Carol. "Venice, the French Invasion and the Apulian Ports." In *The French Descent into Renaissance Italy: 1494–95: Antecedents and Effects*, edited by David Abulafia, 295–308. New York, 1995.

Klatzkin, Jacob. *Thesaurus Philosophicus Linguae Hebraicae et Veteris et Recentioris*. Leipzig, Germany, 1928.

Kriegel, Maurice. "La Prise d'une Decision: L'expulsion des Juifs d'Espagne en 1492." *Revue Historique* 527 (1978): 49–90.

Kristeller, Paul Oskar. "Petrarch's 'Averroists': A Note on the History of Aristotelianism in Venice, Padua, and Bologna." *Bibliothèque d'Humanisme et Renaissance* 14 (1952): 59–65.

Lacerenza, Giancarlo. "Lo spazio dell'Ebreo Insediamenti e Cultura Ebraica a Napoli (Secoli XV–XVI)." In *Integrazione ed Emarginazione*, edited by L. Barletta, 357–427. Naples, 2002.

Ladero Quesada, Miguel Ángel. *La España de los Reyes Católicos*. Madrid, 1999.

Lawee, Eric. "Abravanel in Italy: The Critique of the Kabbalist Elijah Hayyim Genazzano."
    Jewish History 23 (2009): 223–53.

———. "From the Pages of Tradition: Don Isaac Abarbanel: Who Wrote the Bible?"
    Tradition 30, no. 2 (Winter, 1996): 65–73.

———. "Introducing Scripture: The *Accessus ad Auctores* in Hebrew Exegetical Literature
    from the Thirteenth through the Fifteenth Centuries." In *With Reverence for the Word:*
    Medieval Scriptural Exegesis in Judaism, Christianity, and Islam, edited by J. D. McAuliffe,
    B. D. Walfish, and J. W. Goering, 157–79. Oxford, 2003.

———. *Isaac Abarbanel's Stance toward Tradition: Defense, Dissent, and Dialogue*. Albany,
    NY, 2001.

———. "The Messianism of Abravanel, 'Father of the [Jewish] Messianic Movements of
    the Sixteenth and Seventeenth Centuries.'" In *Jewish Messianism in the Early Modern*
    Period, edited by R. H. Popkin and M. Goldish, 1–38. Dordrecht, the Netherlands,
    2003.

———. "Sephardic Intellectuals: Challenges and Creativity." In *The Jew in Medieval*
    Iberia, edited by J. Ray, 350–92. Boston, 2012.

Lawrance, Jeremy. "Creación y Lectura: Sobre el Genero Consolatorio en el Siglo XV."
    In *Studies on Medieval Spanish Literature in Honor of Charles F. Fraker*, edited by
    M. Vaquero and A.D. Deyermond, 35–61. Madison WI, 1995.

———. "Humanism in the Iberian Peninsula." In *The Impact of Humanism on Western*
    Europe, edited by A. Goodman and A. MacKay, 220–58. London, 1990.

———. "Nuevos Lectores y Nuevos Generos: Apuntes y Observaciones sobre la
    Epistolografia en el Primer Rinacimento Español." In *Literatura en la Época del*
    Emperador, edited by V. G. de la Concha, 81–99. Salamanca, Spain, 1988.

———. "Nuño de Guzmán and Early Spanish Humanism: Some Reconsiderations."
    Medium Aevum 51 (1982): 55–85

———. "On Fifteenth-Century Spanish Vernacular Humanism." In *Medieval and*
    Renaissance Studies in Honour of Robert Brian Tate, edited by I. Michael and R. A.
    Cardwell, 63–79. Oxford, 1986.

———. "The Spread of Lay Literacy in Late Medieval Castile." *Bulletin of Hispanic Studies*
    62 (1985): 79–94.

Lee, Alexander. *Petrarch and St. Augustine: Classical Scholarship, Christian Theology and*
    the Origins of the Renaissance in Italy. Leiden, the Netherlands, 2012.

Lelli, Fabrizio. "Pico, i Da Pisa e 'Eliyya Hayyim da Genazzano." In *Giovanni Pico e la*
    Cabbala, edited by Fabrizio Lelli, 93–122. Florence, 2014.

———. "Umanesimo Laurenziano nell'Opera di Yohanan Alemanno." In *La Cultura*
    Ebraica nell'Epoca di Lorenzo il Magnifico, edited by I. Zatelli and D. Liscia, 49–67.
    Florence, 1998.

———. "Un Collaboratore Ebreo di Giovanni Pico della Mirandola: Yohanan
    Alemanno." *Vivens Homo* 5 (1994): 401–30.

Lesley, Arthur. "The Song of Solomon's Ascents by Yohanan Alemanno: Love and Human Perfection according to a Jewish Colleague of Giovanni Pico della Mirandola." PhD diss., University of California, 1976.

Lipiner, Elias. *Two Portuguese Exiles in Castile: Dom David Negro and Dom Isaac Abravanel.* Jerusalem, 1997.

Lorberbaum, Yair. *In God's Image: Myth, Theology, and Law in Classical Judaism.* New York, 2015.

Luzzati, Michele. "Banchi e Insediamenti nell'Italia Centro Settentrionale fra Tardo Medioevo e Inizi dell'Età Moderna." In *Gli Ebrei in Italia,* edited by C. Vivanti, 1:175–235. Torino, Italy, 1996–97.

———. *La Casa dell'Ebreo.* Pisa, Italy, 1985.

Margulies, Samuel Hirsch. "La famiglia Abravanel in Italia." *Rivista Israelitica* 3 (1906): 97–107 and 147–54.

Marx, Alexander. "The Expulsion of the Jews from Spain. Two New Accounts." *Jewish Quarterly Review* 20 (1908): 240–70.

Marciano, Yoel. "Hakhamim besfarad bame'ah hahamesh-'esreh: Hinukham, limudam, yetsiratam, ma'amadam udmutam." PhD diss., Hebrew University, 2010.

McClure, George W. *Sorrow and Consolation in Italian Humanism.* Princeton, NJ, 1990.

Melamed, Abraham. *The Image of the Black in Jewish Culture.* London, 2003.

———. "The Myth of the Jewish Origins of Philosophy in the Renaissance: From Aristotle to Plato." *Jewish History* 26 (2012): 41–59.

———. *The Philosopher-King in Medieval and Renaissance Jewish Political Thought.* Albany, NY, 2003.

———. *Wisdom's Little Sister: Studies in Medieval and Renaissance Jewish Political Thought.* Boston, 2012.

Mendoza Negrillo, Juan de Dios. *Fortuna y Providencia en La Literatura Castellana del Siglo XV.* Madrid, 1973.

Meneghin, Vittorino. *Bernardino da Feltre e i Monti di Pietà.* Vicenza, Italy, 1974.

Michael, Reuven. *Haketiva hahistorit haYehudit meharenasans 'ad ha'et hahadashah.* Jerusalem, 1993.

Moreno, Ángel Gómez. *España y la Italia de los Humanistas.* Madrid, 1994.

Museu Nacioanal de Arte Antiga, ed. *A Invenção Da Gloria: D. Afonso V e as Tapeçarias de Pastrana.* Madrid, 2010.

Nadav, Yael. "Igeret shel hamequbal Yitshak mar Haim 'al torat haTsahtsahot." *Tarbiz* 26 (1957): 440–58.

Nader, Helen. *The Mendoza Family in the Spanish Renaissance, 1350–1550.* New Brunswick, NJ, 1979.

Najemy, John N. "Civic Humanism and Florentine Politics." In *Renaissance Civic Humanism: Reappraisals and Reflections,* edited by James Hankins, 74–104. Cambridge, 2000.

Nascimento, Aires. "As Livrearias dos Principes de Avis." *Biblos* 69 (1993): 265–87.

Netanyahu, Benzion. *Don Isaac Abravanel: Statesman and Philosopher.* 5th rev. ed. Ithaca, NY, 1998.

———. *Toward the Inquisition: Essays on Jewish and Converso History in Late Medieval Spain.* Ithaca, NY, 1997.

Nieto Soria, José Manuel. *Fudamentos ideológicos del poder real en Castilla.* Madrid, 1988.

Nigel, Allan. "A Typographical Odyssey: The 1505 Constantinople Pentateuch." *Journal of the Royal Asiatic Society* 3 (1991): 343–51.

Offenberg, Adri K. *A Choice of Chorals: Facets of Fifteenth-Century Hebrew Printing.* Nieuwkoop, the Netherlands, 1992.

Pereira, Gabriel. *Os Codices 443 e 475.* Coimbra, Portugal, 1910.

Piel, Joseph M., ed. *Libros dos Officios de Marco Tulio Cicera o Qual Tornou em Langagem o Infante Dom Pedro.* Coimbra, Portugal, 1948.

Ponton, Gonzalo. *Correspondencias: Los Orígenes del Arte Epistolar en España.* Madrid, 2002.

Quillen, Carol E. "A Tradition Invented: Petrarch, Augustine, and the Language of Humanism." *Journal of the History of Ideas* 53 (1992): 179–207.

Quintanilla Raso, María Concepción, and Miguel Ángel Ladero Quesada. "Bibliotecas de la Alta Noleza Cstellana en el Siglo XV." In *Livre et Lecture en Espagne et en France sous l'Ancien Régime: Colloque de la Casa de Velasquez,* edited by O. Bresson, 47–59. Paris, 1981.

Rau, Virginia. "Alguns Estudantes e Eruditos Portugueses em Italia no Século XV." *Do Tempo e Da Historia* 5 (1972): 29–99.

———. "Bartolomeo di Iacopo di Ser Vanni Mercador-Banqueiro Florentino 'Estante' em Lisboa nos Meados do Século XV." *Do Tempo e da História* 4 (1971): 97–117.

———. *Estudos de História Medieval.* Lisbon, 1985.

———. "Italianismo na Cultura Juridica Portuguesa do Século XV." *Revista Portuguesa de Historia* 12 (1969): 185–206.

———. *Portugal e o Mediterrâneo no Século XV.* Lisbon, 1973.

———. "Uma Familia de Mercadores Italianos em Portugal no Século XV: Os Lomellini." *Revista da Faculdade de Letras* 22 (1956): 5–32.

Ravid, Benjamin. "The Legal Status of the Jews in Venice to 1509." *Proceedings of the American Academy for Jewish Research* 54 (1987): 169–202.

Ravitzky, Aviezer. "Kings and Laws in Late Medieval Jewish Thought: Nissim of Gerona vs. Isaac Abrabanel." In *Scholars and Scholarship: The Interaction between Judaism and Other Cultures,* edited by L. Landman, 67–90. New York, 1990.

Regev, Shaul. "Hamahshava haratsional-mistit behagut hayehudit bame'ah hat"v." *Mehqerei Yerushalayim bemahshevet Yisrael* 5 (1986): 155–89.

———. "Meshihiyut ve'astrologia behaguto shel Rabbi Yitshaq Abravanel." *Asufot* 1 (1987): 169–187.

———. "Nusah rishon shel peirush Abravanel lesefer Devarim." *Kobez al Yad* 15 (2001): 285–380.

———. "Re'iyat bnei yisrael (shemot 24:9–11) befilosofia yehudit biymei habeinayim." *Mekherei yerushalayim bemahsevet yisrael* 4 (1985): 281–302.

Roth, Cecil. *The History of the Jews in Italy*. Philadelphia, 1946.

———. *Jews in the Renaissance*. Philadelphia, 1959.

Ruderman, David. B. "Hope against Hope: Jewish and Christian Messianic Expectations in the Late Middle Ages." In *Essential Papers on Jewish Culture in Renaissance and Baroque Italy*, edited by David B. Ruderman, 299–323. New York, 1992.

Ruiz, Gregorio. *Don Isaac Abravanel y Su Comentario al Libro De Amos*. Madrid, 1984.

Sagi, Avi. "Natural Law and Halakhah." In *Avi Sagi: Existentialism, Pluralism, and Identity*, edited by H. Tirosh-Samuelson and A. W. Hughes, 59–102. Leiden, the Netherlands, 2015.

Schiff, Mario. *La Bibliothèque du Marquis de Santillane*. Amsterdam, 1970.

Scholem, Gershom. *The Messianic Idea in Judaism: And Other Essays on Jewish Spirituality*. New York, 1971.

Schorsch, Jonathan. *Jews and Blacks in the Early Modern World*. New York, 2004.

Schwartz, Dov. *Messianism in Medieval Jewish Thought*. Translated by B. Stein. Boston, 2017.

———. *Studies on Astral Magic in Medieval Jewish Thought*. Leiden, the Netherlands, 2018.

Segre, Renata. "Bernardino da Feltre, I Monti di Pietà e I Banchi Ebraichi." *Rivista Storica Italiana* 90 (1978): 818–33.

———. "Sephardic Refugees in Ferrara: Two Notable Families." In *Crisis and Creativity in the Sephardic World: 1391–1648*, edited by B. R. Gampel, 164–85. New York, 1997.

———. "Sephardic Settlements in Sixteenth-Century Italy: A Historical and Geographical Survey." *Mediterranean Historical Review* 6 (1991): 112–37.

Serés, Guillermo. "La Autoridad Literaria Círculos Intelectuales y Géneros en la Castilla del Siglo XV." *Bulletin Hispanique* 109 (2007): 335–83.

Serrão, Joaquim Veríssimo. *A Historiografia Portuguesa: Doutrina e Crítica*. Vol. 1. Lisbon, 1972.

———. *Cronistas do Século XV Posteriores a Fernão Lopes*. Lisbon, 1989.

Shmidman, Michael A. "An Excerpt from the *Avot* Commentary of R. Mattathias ha-Yizhari." In *Studies in Medieval Jewish History and Literature*, edited by I. Twersky, 315–36. Cambridge, 1979.

Shmueli, Ephraim. *Don Yitshaq Abravanel vegeirush Sefarad*. Jerusalem, 1963.

Skinner, Quentin. *The Foundations of Modern Political Thought*. Vol. 1: *The Renaissance*. Cambridge, 1994.

Sousa Viterbo, Francisco Marques. "Occurencias da vida judaica." *Arquivo Historico Portuguez* 2 (1904): 178–200.

Steinschneider, Moritz. "Zur Frauenliteratur." *Israelietische Letterbode* 12 (1888): 49–95.

Stern, Joseph. "Maimonides on the Growth of Knowledge and Limitations of the Intellect." In *Maïmonide, Philosophe et Savant (1138–1204)*, edited by T. Lévy and R. Rashed, 188–91. Leuven, Belgium, 2004.

Strauss, Leo. "On Abravanel's Philosophical Tendency and Political Teaching." In J. B. Trend and H. Loewe, eds., *Isaac Abravanel: Six Lectures*, 195–227. Cambridge, 1937.

Struever, Nancy. "Petrarch's Invective Contra Medicum: An Early Confrontation of Rhetoric and Medicine." *MLN* 108 (1993): 659–79.

Suárez Fernández, Luis. *Documentos Acerca de la Expulsion de los Judios*. Valladolid, Spain, 1964.

———. *Isabel: Mujer y Reina*. Madrid, 1992.

———. *La Expulsión de los Judiós de España*. Madrid, 1991.

Ta-Shma, Yisrael. *Hasifrut haparshanit laTalmud be'Eropa uvetsefon Afrika: Korot ishim veshitot*. Vol. 2: 1200–1400. Jerusalem, 2004.

Tirosh Rothschild, Hava. *Between Worlds: The Life and Thought of Rabbi ben Judah Messer Leon*. Albany, NY, 1991.

Tishby, Isaiah. *Meshihiyut vedor geirushei Sefarad vePortugal*. Jerusalem, 1985.

Todeschini, Giacomo. *La Richezza Degli Ebrei*. Spoleto, Italy, 1989.

Toledano, Y. M. *Otzar genazim: Osef igrot letoldot Yisra'el mitokh kitvei yad 'atiqim*. Jerusalem, 1960.

Trinkaus, Charles. *In Our Image and Likeness: Humanity and Divinity in Italian Humanist Thought*. 2 vols. London, 1970.

Walzer, Michael, Menachem Lorberbaum, Noam J. Zohar, and Yair Lorberbaum, eds. *The Jewish Political Tradition*. Vol. 1: *Authority*. New Haven, CT, 2000.

Weinstein, Donald. *Savonarola: The Rise and Fall of a Renaissance Prophet*. New Haven, CT, 2011.

Witt, Ronald. *In the Footsteps of the Ancients: The Origins of Humanism from Lovato to Bruni*. Boston, 2000.

Yaari, Abraham. *Hadefus ha'Ivri beKushta*. Jerusalem, 1967.

Yerushalmi, Yosef Hayim. *The Lisbon Massacre of 1506 and the Royal Image in the Shevet Yehudah*. Cincinnati, OH, 1976.

———. *Zakhor: Jewish History and Jewish Memory*. Seattle, WA, 1996.

Zonta, Mauro. *Hebrew Scholasticism in the Fifteenth Century: A History and Source Book*. Dordrecht, the Netherlands, 2006.

INDEX

Abraham (biblical patriarch), 275, 277

Abravanel, Don Isaac: antimonarchism of, 142–43, 148, 153–55; and Arama, 171–72; autobiographical introduction, use of, 12, 88–89, 94–97; and Bragança, 7, 17, 21, 35, 74, 78–81, 90–93; and Catholic Monarchs, 158–61, 176–81, 187; childhood of, 16; Christian and Jewish audiences, approach to, 53, 73–74, 113–14, 140–41; completion of literary oeuvre, 268–69; conservatism of, 138, 231, 278–80; as court Jew, 11, 16–19, 61, 88–91, 95–97, 163, 176–77, 284–85; on death, 27–34, 91; death of, 280–81; economic and social rise in Portugal, 18; escape to Castile, 79–81, 85–97, 133–34; on exile and renaissance, 209–12; on father, 11–13; and Ficino, 195; and Forti's biography, 3, 13; on free choice/will, 222, 239; on freedom, 238–42; and French invasion of Italy, 215–16; funding of Dom Afonso V's war, 77; and Gersonides, 69, 113, 119–29; and Gonzalo da Cordoba, 216; and Hayyun, 110–11; historiosophy of, 71–75; on human dignity, 231–34; on human intellect, 64–65, 69, 191–92, 234–35, 239–41, 259–60; on Italian republics, 146–50; Jewish political thought, 154–55; in King Ferrante's service, 169; letter to Hakohen, 278–80; and liberation of Arzilan Jewry, 39–44; as mediator between Venice and Portugal, 265–67; as member of Jewish elite, 18–19, 37, 43–44, 48, 53, 58–61, 68, 90, 96; and Mendoza family, 156–58; as merchant, 156, 270, 276; Messer Leon's criticism of, 172–73; messianic writings, 243–64; and Naples, 167–73, 174, 183–85, 217–18; negative image of, 285–87; and Pico della Mirandola, 233–34; plagiarism accusations against, 170–73; and Spanish expulsion, 158–64, 174–85, 207, 211–12, 228–29, 248–49; tax farming, 17, 156; twentieth century reception of, 282–90; and Yehiel da Pisa, 36–39, 44, 47–53, 54, 77–78, 149–50, 218. *See also* leadership; philosophy; politics

Abravanel, Joseph (nephew), 85–86, 156, 216, 264, 265–68

Abravanel, Don Judah (father), 11–13, 15–16, 196, 267–68

Abravanel, Judah (son). *See* Ebreo, Leone

Abravanel, Don Samuel (grandfather). *See* Sevilla, Juan Sanchez de

Abravanel, Samuel (son), 85, 216, 228–29, 264

Abravanel family: and Avis dynasty, 4–5; in Castile, 13–16, 85–86; commercial dealings of, 156; expulsion from Spain, 163–64; immigration to Portugal, 12–19; in Lisbon, 15–16; in Naples, 167–73; in Neapolitan kingdom, 169–70; social position, 13; splitting of, 15, 264; and trade relations, 18

absolute monarchy, 141, 146

Active Intellect, 56, 120–22, 124–27

active life (*vita activa*), 34–35

Adam, 29, 270–71, 274–75, 278

Ad Convicendum Perfidiam Judaeorum (Santa Fe), 262

Additiones of Pablo de Santa Maria, 99

Ad Lucilium Epistulae Morale (Moral letters to Lucilius) (Seneca), 23–24

Afonso II, King of Portugal, 10

African slave trade, 50–51

Akiva, Rabbi, 230–31, 234, 237–38

Al-Andalus, 9

Alantansi, Eliezer, 220

Alemanno, Yohanan, 143, 195

Alfarabi, 66

Alfonso II, King of Naples, 169, 215–16

Alfonso V, King of Aragon, 168, 214

Almeida, Lopo de, 44–46

angels, 62–64, 69–74, 252, 257–59

anointing of kings and high priests, 134, 187–88

antimonarchism, 142–43, 148, 153–55

Antiquities of the Jews (Josephus), 199

apocalypticism, 244–46

apologetics: Christian, 257, 261–62; Jewish, 213, 228–31, 240–42, 247, 261–62

'Aqedat Yitshak (Arama), 170, 172, 239

Aquinas, Thomas, 114, 142, 148–49

Arabic (Islamic) philosophy, 66, 123–27

Arama, Isaac, 170–72, 239

Arama, Rabbi Meir, 170–72

Archivolti, Samuel, 281

Aristides, Aelius, 145

aristocracy: Christian, 52–53; Portuguese, 21, 78–79, 92–93, 151; relationship between the crown and, 7, 81. *See also* nobility

Aristotelian causes, 111, 120, 190–91

Aristotle: conception of God, 66; constitutional vs. absolute monarchy, 141, 147; and divine providence, 69; first mover, 66; on generation and corruption, 75; on gradual nature of the philosophical process, 54–55; and Ibn Rushd, 124–25; and messianic speculation, 251–52; and miracle of Gibeon, 123–24; on modesty, 55–57; on physics, 221

Aroyo, Isaac Ibn, 247

Arzila, conquest of, 40–45, 102

Arzilan Jewry, 39–44, 53

astral bodies: and Active Intellect, 120–21, 126; avoiding temptation to believe in, 71; God's disruption of influence, 226–28; influence on nations, 64–65, 67, 70, 237, 272

astrological determinism, 70, 260–61

astrology: God's disruption of influence, 225–28; intellect vs. forces of, 241; in messianic writings, 259–61; Solomon's knowledge of, 193; stars' influence on nations, 64–65

'Ateret zeqenim (Abravanel), 12, 50, 54, 58–69, 71–75, 94, 123–25, 127–29

Augustine, 153, 154, 274–75

Avis dynasty: centralization of power in, 7, 151; Dom Afonso V, 41, 76, 90; establishment of, 3–5; and historical writing, 102; and nobility, 4–8, 76; rise of merchant bankers, 11

Babylonian Talmud, 104, 140, 251

Bar Hiyya, Abraham, 226, 246, 250–51, 258

Barletta, Italy, 263–64

battle of Alfarrobeira, 7

Battle of Cerignola, 264

ben Zerah, Menahem, 14–15

Bible: consolation in, 22; Don Isaac's new approach to, 98–106, 139; Don Isaac's reliance on in Hebrew letter, 52; and exile, 184; judges, 129–30, 146–49, 152–53; man in God's image, 235; messianic prophecies, 262; and Stoicism, 30–32. *See also* commentaries; *individual books or divisions by name*

Biblia Sacra with the *Postilla* (Lyra), 99

black slave trade, 50–51

book collection, 49, 52

Book of Doctrines and Beliefs (Gaon), 245, 254

Bragança, house of, 7, 17, 21, 35, 74, 78–81, 90–93

Bruni, Leonardo, 103, 144–51

Burgos, Pablo de. *See* Santa Maria, Pablo de

Buxtorf, Johannes, 282

Cain, 274–75

Cambini, Francesco and Bernardo, 49

Cancioneiro Geral (de Resende), 18–19

Canpanton, Isaac, 111, 114–15

Capsali, Elijah, 167, 179

Cartagena, Alonso de, 30–31

Castile, 85–164; and Abravanel family, 15–16, 85–86; and Avis dynasty, 3–9; Dom Afonso V's failed attempt to invade, 76–77; Don Isaac's immigration to, 79–81, 85–97, 133–34; and expulsion of Jews, 158–64, 181–85, 241; Jewish community in, 15, 87, 95–97, 175–77, 241, 261; nobility in, 160–61; speculative method developed in, 115

Catholic Monarchs, 156–64, 176–81, 187, 215, 262–63, 267, 280–81

causality, 64–65, 68, 70–71, 193, 239

celestial spheres (bodies), 63, 66–70, 74–75, 128, 134–35, 240–41

centralization of power, 7, 95, 151

Charles VIII, King of France, 214–16

cherubs, 205–6

Christendom: vs. Ottoman Empire, 258; refutation as kingdom of Messiah, 256–57

Christian Hebraists, seventeenth-century, 282–83

Christianity: and antimonarchism, 153–55; apologetics, 257, 261–62; conversion to, 13–15, 86, 158–59, 162–64, 178, 215, 261, 268; counselor figure in, 74; division of canon, 99; exegetical dimension, 153–55;

and Jewish exile, 38–39; legends as result of expulsion, 179–80; literature, 30, 64, 141, 232; philosophical perspectives, 32, 65, 73–75, 126–27, 232–34; *providencia* and *fortuna*, 62–64; Reformation, 244

Christian society: churches and cathedrals, 201–3, 207–8; class system, 48, 52–53, 180; Don Isaac's approach to, 53, 73–74, 113–14, 140–41; fall of Constantinople, 258; literary culture, 35, 112–16; relationship to Jewish communities, 10–12, 37, 53

Chronicles, Book of, 186–87

Cicero, 22–25, 31–32, 65, 103, 107–8

City of God (De Civitate Dei) (Augustine), 274–75

civil liberties, 145–46

civitas Dei (the city of God), 153

civitas terrena (the hierarchical earthly city), 153

classical rabbinic literature, 115–16, 154–55, 250, 289. *See also* Talmud

commandments, 73–75, 139, 154, 206, 208, 237

commentaries: on Chronicles, 186–87; on Daniel, 69–70, 89–90, 243–59; on Deuteronomy, 50, 139–40, 150, 153–54, 216–18; Don Isaac's approach to, 87–88; on Genesis, 269–78; *The Guide of the Perplexed*, 58–61, 172, 234–37, 263, 269, 278–80; on Isaiah, 217, 263, 282; on Jeremiah, 232–33; on Joshua, 87–88, 96–97, 100–101, 104, 118–25, 128–30, 174–75; on Judges, 129–30, 139, 174–75; on Kings, 103–6, 174–85, 186–212; Pentateuch (as a whole), 99, 106, 170, 220, 268–69, 281; on Samuel, 116, 129–41, 147, 150–55. *See also* Former Prophets

conservatism, 138, 231, 278–80, 288–89

consolation *(consolatio)* genre, 21–29, 32–35, 38–39, 95–96

Constantinople, fall of, 258–59

constitutional monarchy, 5, 141, 147–49

conversion, 13–15, 86, 158–59, 162–64, 178, 215, 261, 268

Cordoba, Gonzalo de, 215–16, 263–64

Corfu, 216–19

coronation, 33–34, 187–88

Cortes (Portuguese assembly), 4–5, 7, 78, 151, 159

cosmological system: Active Intellect's role in, 124–25; astrological determinism, 70, 260–61; counselor figure for, 74, 125; and divine providence, 120–21; first cause of, 133–34; and human dignity, 231–34; and inductive reasoning, 192; in Jewish apologetics, 230–31; and Jewish relationship to God in exile, 68–70, 75, 242; relationship to God, 66–67, 71, 124–25, 128, 263; soul's relationship to, 65; and theological justification for monarchy, 142. *See also* astral bodies; astrology

Council of Ten (Consiglio dei Dieci), 266–67

counselor figure, 74, 125

Count (Conde) of Faro (Dom Afonso): consolatory rhetoric, 24–29; death of, 33–34; humanistic rhetoric, 52–53, 134; overview, 20–21

Count of Odemira. *See* Noronha, Dom Sancho de

court Jews, role of, 11, 16–19, 61, 88–91, 95–97, 163, 176–77, 284–85

covenantal regime, 152–53

creation, 128, 232, 235–36, 238–40

creation ex nihilo, 102, 126, 263

Crescas, Hasdai, 115–16, 122–23, 222, 238–39

crown and nobility, 7, 78–81, 92–93, 158–61. *See also* royals

curtain *(parokhet)* and wall *(kotel)* symbolism, 206

cyclical approach or process, 204, 209–11, 278

cyclical dimension of Jewish history, 229–30

Cynics, 274–75

Daniel, Book of (commentary), 69–70, 89–90, 243–59

Dante Alighieri, 62–63

Darkhei hatalmud (Canpanton), 114

David (biblical), 12–13, 130–37

death: Don Isaac on, 27–34, 91; Seneca on, 23–24

Deborah (biblical prophetess), 130

declining generations theme, 122–23

De falso credite et ementita Constantini donatione (Valla), 108–9

De miseria condicionis humane (On contempt for the world or on the misery of the human condition), 231

De Oratore (Cicero), 103

De Regimine Principium (Aquinas), 142

De Remediis Fortuitorum (Remedies for fortune) (Pseudo-Seneca), 30

De Senectute (On old age) (Cicero), 31

Deuteronomy, Book of (commentary), 50, 110–11, 216–18

De Vita (On life) (Ficino), 134–35, 194–95

Dialoghi d'Amore (Dialogues of Love) (Ebreo), 232, 277–78

dignity of man *(dignitas hominis)*, 231. *See also* human dignity

disputatio, scholastic methods of, 113–14

Dissertationes Philologico-Theologicae (Buxtorf), 282

Divine Comedy (Dante), 62–63

divine influence, 67, 70, 188, 205–6, 237, 240, 253–54

divine influx, 135–37

divine model of the world, 238–39

divine providence (intervention): and Arab philosophy, 123–24; vs. astrological determinism, 70, 260–61; in 'Ateret zeqenim, 62–64; and biblical judges, 130; and creation ex nihilo, 102, 126, 263; and David, 134–37; and disruption of astrological order, 225; in Don Isaac's flight-as-victory from Portugal, 93–97; and fate, 30, 89; and intellectual conjunction with God, 132–33; miracle at Gibeon, 119–21; and special status of Jews, 42–44, 52, 67–69, 72–73, 152, 225–27

divorce compared to monarchy, 154

Dom Afonso. See Count (Conde) of Faro

Dom Afonso Henriques, King of Portugal, 9

Dom Afonso V, King of Portugal, 7–8, 16–17, 21, 40–41, 74, 76–78, 90–91

Dom Duarte, King of Portugal, 5–7, 10

Dom Fernando, Duke of Bragança, 7, 15–17, 41, 78–79

Dom Fernando I, King of Portugal, 3

Dom Henrique, 7, 17

Dom João I, King of Portugal, 3–5, 7

Dom João II, King of Portugal, 8, 46, 76–81, 85–86, 91–95, 146, 151, 267–68

Dom Manuel. See Manuel I, King of Portugal

Dom Pedro, 6–9, 21, 30

Doña Beatriz, Queen of Portugal, 3–5

Dona Isabel, Queen of Castile, 76, 86, 156–59, 179–80

Doña Juana, Queen of Portugal, 76, 158

Dona Leonor, Queen of Aragon, 6–7

Don Enrique IV, King of Castile, 76

Don Fernando, King of Aragon, 76, 86, 156–60, 178–80, 215–16

Don Isaac Abravanel: Philosopher and Statesman (Netanyahu), 285–86

"Don Isaac Abravanel and His Approach to the Problems of History and the State" (Baer), 284

Don Isaac and the Expulsion from Spain (Shmueli), 286–87

Don Juan I, King of Castile, 3–5

dual exile, 185

Duke of Bourgogne, 77

Duke of Bragança (Dom Fernando), 7, 15–17, 41, 78–79

Duke of Infantando (Iñigo Lopez de Mendoza), 156–58

Duke of Viseu (Dom Diego), 78–79, 85

Duran, Profiat, 111–12, 115

Earthly City, 153, 274–76

Ebreo, Leone (Judah Abravanel) (son): on Adam's fall, 277–78; birth and family arrival in Castile, 85–86; captive grandson in Portugal, 267–68; dialogue on Plato, 232; and Ficino, 195; and Gonzalo de Cordoba, 264; as personal physician, 216; poetry of, 86, 220, 267–68; Renaissance literature, 287–88

'Ein haqoreh (Messer Leon), 172–73

elders of Israel, 54–61, 71–72, 139–41

elite, Jewish, 18–19, 37, 43–44, 48, 53, 58–61, 68, 90, 96

emanatory system, 66–69

Enrique III, King of Castile, 13

epistolary writing: Abravanel's, 24–27, 30, 35, 36–53, 288; Seneca's, 23–24

Ethics (Aristotle), 33

exile: and angel Michael, 69–71; and chain of tradition, 229–31; and Christianity, 38–39; Daniel, 248, 254–56; Don Isaac

on, 181–85; and fate, 268; of Iberian
Jewry, 161–64, 209–12; from Israel, 73,
174, 209; Jewish relationship to God in,
68–70, 75, 242; leadership in, 241; and
redemption, 75, 226–29, 254–56, 257;
spiritual needs in, 249–50. *See also*
Sephardic exiles

Exodus, 60, 100, 203–4, 223–28, 260–61;
15:27, 249–50; 23–24, 71; 23:20, 62; 24,
56, 60–61; 24:9–11, 54; 33:22, 38–39

expulsion of Jews from Iberia: causes of,
158–60; commentary on Kings as response to, 174–85; communal trauma
of, 175, 184–85; the decree, 161–63,
181–85; messianic connections, 243–49,
259, 261; need for leadership in response
to, 241; plans for exile, 163–64; as
prelude to redemption, 228–29

fate, 23–24, 30, 63–65, 69, 89–91, 268
Feltre, Bernardino da, 36
Ferrandino, King of Naples, 215–16
Ferrante, King of Naples, 167–69, 198
Ficino, Marsilio, 134–35, 194–95, 197–98,
232, 287
first cause, 66–68, 238
first intellect, 67–68, 70–71, 73, 123
First Temple, 13, 185, 209–11
Florence, 36, 38–39, 143, 144–46, 147–49,
151
Former Prophets, commentary on, 98–137;
autobiographical introduction, 174;
completion after expulsion, 174, 176;
Don Isaac's ability to interpret and
teach, 96; Don Isaac's oath to interpret,
184; and Gersonides vs. Don Isaac,
119–29; introduction to, 88–90; Joshua,
87–88, 96–97, 100–101, 104, 118–25,
127–29, 174–75; Judges, 129–30, 139,
174–75; Kings, 103–6, 174–85, 186–88,

190, 200–202, 205, 207–12; Samuel, 116,
130–37, 138–41, 147, 150–55

Forti, Barukh (Hezqeto), 3, 13, 15, 265–66,
280–81

fortune *(fortuna)*, 33, 62–64, 94, 97, 130, 237
four kingdoms vision, 254–55, 258
France, invasion of Italy, 77, 214–18, 223
freedom, 227, 234, 238–42
free will, 222, 239

Gama, Vasco da, 266
Gaon, Saadia, 245, 254, 258
Garden of Eden, 90, 115, 270–71
Genazzano, Elijah Haim da, 50
Generaciones y Semblanzas (Guzmán),
106–7
Genesis, Book of (commentary), 31, 269–78
Gerondi, Nissim R., 140
Gersonides, Levi, 69, 113, 119–29
Gibeon, miracle at, 119–29
God: addressed by Don Isaac, 94–95;
Aristotelian conception of, 66; connection to, 66–73, 119–24, 128–30,
135–37, 187–88, 209, 275–76; covenant
with Israel, 44, 62, 67–69, 72–73, 152–53,
225; divine model of the world, 238–39;
image of, 234–40; intellects and spheres,
67–68, 71, 132–33; Jewish relationship to
God in exile, 68–70, 75, 242; knowledge
of himself, 239; and man, 71–74, 124,
234–37; and nature, 275; omniscience
and free will, 238–40; relationship to
cosmos, 66–67, 71, 124–25, 128, 263;
tripartite connection, 66–68, 71–74.
See also divine providence

Gothic architecture, 201–2
governance: historical comparison of
systems, 146–51; hybrid government,
152–53; republicanism, 138–55; theocracy, 142, 151–53. *See also* monarchy

Granada, 156–57, 159–60, 177–79, 187
el Gran Capitán. *See* Cordoba, Gonzalo de
Greek Cynics, 274
Guicciardini, Francesco, 214
The Guide of the Perplexed (Maimonides),
    54–61, 172, 234–37, 263, 269, 270–71,
    278–80
Guzmán, Fernán Pérez de, 30, 106–7

Habakkuk, 38, 176, 282
Habsburg, Maximilian von, 215
Haggadah. *See* Passover Haggadah
Hakohen, Saul, 216–17, 269, 278–80
Halakhah, 115, 116, 154, 220
Halevi, Judah, 72, 276
Halevi, Solomon. *See* Santa Maria, Pablo de
Hayyun, Rabbi Joseph, 110–11, 114
Hebrew epistles, 36–53; consolatory genre,
    38–39; and exchange of manuscripts
    and gifts, 48–51; leadership and rhetoric
    in, 51–53; on liberation of Arzilan Jewry,
    39–44; politics of friendship and royal
    delegation to the pope, 44–47; on
    secret diplomatic mission to the pope,
    47–48
Hebrew manuscripts, 48–51
Hebrew rhetoric, 52
Hebrew scholasticism, 114
Hermetic texts, 197–98, 287–88
Hezekiah's prayer, 29–30
Hiel of Bethel, 175–76, 185
historical writing, 71–75, 102–3, 106–12,
    147–49
History of Rome (Livy), 103
History of the Florentine People (Bruni), 149
The History of the Jews in Christian Spain
    (Baer), 14, 127
Holy League, 215–16
homiletical exegesis, 87–88, 113, 170
human composite nature, 271–72

human dignity, 231–34
humanism: active life, 34–35; Don Isaac's
    seeming neglect of philosophers, 233;
    in historical writing, 103; humanistic
    learning, 29–32; and justification of
    Florence's government, 149; and polit-
    ical philosophy, 138–39, 148; republi-
    canism, 144–45; Teixeira and, 45–46
humanity: and death, 31–32; development
    of, 277–78; deviation from nature, 274;
    elementary components of, 64; in
    Genesis commentary, 269–72; Mai-
    monidean approach to, 237; Neopla-
    tonic discourse on, 234
human progress, 273, 278
hybrid government, 152–53

Iberian peninsula: Christian vs. Jewish
    cultures, 37, 53; court cultural of, 20–35;
    Jewry in, 160–61, 175–76, 185, 209–12,
    245, 285; nostalgia for life on, 223; shifts
    in power, 76–78; slave trade, 50–51. *See
    also* expulsion of Jews from Iberia;
    Portugal; Spain
Ibn Ezra, Abraham, 226
Ibn Rushd, 66–67, 124–25, 127
Ibn Sina, 66
Ibn Verga, Solomon, 167–68, 179
Ibn Yahya, David, 216–17
Ibn Yahya, Tam, 170
Ibn Yahya family, 9–11
Igeret hamudot (Genazzano), 50
Innocent III, Pope, 231
Inquisition, 158–64, 180
intellect(s): Active Intellect, 56, 120–22,
    124–27; conjunction with God, 67–68,
    71, 132–33; first, 67–68, 70–71, 73, 123;
    and free will, 239–41; and image of God,
    234–35; as independent of astrological
    influence, 64–65; and induction, 191–92;

intellectual identity, 60–61; and prophecy, 120, 197; separate, 63–64, 65, 66–67,
72–74, 121–22, 193–94; and spheres,
66–68
international trade, 10–11, 16–19, 196
Isaiah, Book of (commentary), 29–30, 217,
263, 282
Isaiah 7:19, 38–39
Islam, 159–60, 256, 258
Islamic philosophy. *See* Arabic (Islamic)
philosophy
Israel: and astrological order, 225–27;
covenant with God, 44, 62, 67–69,
72–73, 152–53, 225; elders and nobles of,
54–62, 71–72, 139–41; exile of, 73, 174,
209; historiosophy, 71–75; Jerusalem,
182–85, 209–12; Kings commentary,
186–87; nation of, 275–76; as nucleus,
277–78; prophets of, 237; Temple in
Jerusalem, 13, 182–85, 201–12, 257–59
Italy, 167–290; Abravanel family exile to,
163–64; Barletta, 263–64; collapse of
political equilibrium, 214–15; Florence,
36, 38–39, 143, 144–46, 147–49, 151;
French invasion of, 215–16; humanism,
24, 107–9, 199; and Jewish expulsion
from Spain, 267–68; merchants in, 11,
17–18; Mestre, 267; Milan, 214–15; military crisis in, 213–18, 258–64; Monopoli,
216–18, 219, 262–64; Naples, 167–73, 174,
183–85, 214–18, 223, 262–64; republican
model, 143–50, 153; Sephardic exiles in,
163–64, 167–69; Tuscany, 36–37, 49, 150;
Venice, 217, 262–64, 265–68, 276, 280–81
itinerancy, 61, 170, 206

Jeremiah, Book of (commentary), 232–33
Jeremiah 20:1, 59
Jeremiah 42:2, 182–83
Jerome, 108–9, 113

Jerusalem, 209–12
Jewish Antiquities (Josephus), 274
Jews: anti-Jewish activities, 9–11; apocalypticism, 244; apologetics, 240–42,
261; Aragon community, 163–64;
Arzilan, 39–44, 53; and astrological
order, 225–28; Castilian community, 15,
87, 95–97, 175–77, 241, 261; as children
of the Omnipresent, 237; chosenness
of, 276; and Christian society, 10–12, 37,
53; continuity of, 13–16, 72–75, 102, 149,
163, 188–89, 228–30, 279; conversion to
Christianity, 13–15, 86, 158–59, 162–64,
178, 215, 261, 268; in Corfu, 216–17; court
role of, 11, 16–19, 61, 88–91, 95–97, 163,
176–77, 284–85; and culture of Middle
Ages, 123; in Diaspora, 42–44, 70,
162–63, 174, 185, 209–10; in Egypt,
225–27; elitism among, 18–19, 37, 43–44,
48, 53, 58–61, 68, 90, 96; and European
humanism, 256, 284, 288; on Iberian
peninsula, 160–61, 175–76, 185, 209–12,
245, 285; migration to the West, 9, 12–19,
168, 210; Naples, community in, 168–70;
and Passover Haggadah, 224; pogroms
against, 86, 123, 127, 164, 215, 261; Portuguese community, 9–12, 43, 47–48,
89–90; Sephardic Jewry, 167–68, 174,
183–84, 223–24; Venetian community,
267, 280–81. *See also* divine providence;
exile; expulsion of Jews from Iberia;
leadership
Job, 26–27
Josephus, Flavius, 198–99, 202, 274
Joshua, Book of (commentary), 87–88,
96–97, 100–101, 104, 118–25, 128–30,
174–75
Judah (kingdom), 153, 174, 176, 186–87,
209–10
Judaism: Abravanel's writings added to

Jewish ritual, 220–21; apocalypticism, 244; and cosmological order, 227–28; Crescas on Jews' shift away from, 123; Don Isaac's defense of, 219–42; Maimonidean principles of faith, 213; messianic rhetoric, 246, 259; modern, 286–87; Passover Haggadah, 44, 169, 220, 223–25, 247, 269; superiority of, 201–3

Judeo-Arabic philosophical models, 123–27

Judeo-Christian texts in consolatory genre, 22

judges, biblical, 129–30, 146–49, 152–53

Judges, Book of (commentary), 129–30, 139, 174–75

kabbalistic mysticism, 69, 246

Kimhi, Rabbi David, 48–49, 111

kings, 119, 150–52, 187–88, 284–85. *See also* monarchy

Kings, Book of (commentary), 103–6, 174–85, 186–212

Kuzari (Halevi), 72, 276

Latin literature, 37, 144, 274

Latin of Cicero, 107–9, 145

Latin translations, 108, 197–99, 282–83

Latter Prophets: Isaiah, 29–30, 38–39, 217, 263, 282; Jeremiah, 59, 182–83, 232–33

Laudatio Florentinae Urbis (Bruni), 144–45

laws of causality, 68, 193

Lazzarelli, Lodovico, 198

leadership: Abravanel family's history of, 15–16; in *'Ateret zeqenim,* 71–75; Catholic Monarchs' challenge to Jewish, 178–81; Don Isaac as Jewish leader, 36–53, 172–73, 174, 183–85, 212, 249, 280; Don Isaac's conception of, 96–97, 170, 241; and exegetical treatment of Kings, 186–87; grief as teacher of, 33; in Hebrew epistles, 36–53; heritages of Spanish Jewish leaders, 286; Jewish merchant class as leaders, 20, 39; Joshua as leader, 118–25, 128–30; and messianism, 262; model of in Portugal, 90; Moses as leader, 226–27; prophetic, 128–29; of Samuel, Saul, and David, 129–37; Solomon's relationship to God, 208–9

Leal conselheiro (The loyal counselor) (Dom Duarte), 5–6

L'Empereur, Constantijn, 282

letters: of consolation, 21–29, 34–35, 37–39; to Count of Faro, 21–29, 34–35, 52–53, 64, 65, 74, 91, 134; to Hakohen, 278–80; and plagiarism accusation, 170–73; Seneca's, 23–24. *See also* epistolary writing

Leviticus 18:25, 69

Lisbon, siege of, 4

Livro da Vertuosa Benfeytoria (Dom Pedro), 8–9, 30

Livy, 103

loans, 11, 17, 163

Lopes, Fernão, 102

Louis XI, King of France, 77, 214

Louis XII, King of France, 264, 280–81

loyalty, 5–6, 75, 178, 214–15

Lucena, Vasco Fernandes de, 31

luxuries, and fall of man, 270–76

Lyra, Nicholas de, 99, 140–41, 152–54

Ma'ayanei hayeshu'ah (Abravanel), 217, 243, 247–50, 253, 259–61

The Mad Hercules (*Hercules furens*) (Seneca), 29–31

magic and alchemy, 197–99

magic of song, 194–95

magus, 197–98

Mahaze Shadai (a treatise on prophecy) (Abravanel), 269

Maimonides: and Arabic philosophy, 125; on authentic religious knowledge, 123; on cherubs, 205; on covenantal rule and monarchy, 153; on creation, 128; Cresca's criticism of *Mishneh torah,* 115; on God's image, 234–37; *Guide of the Perplexed,* 54–55, 58–59, 172–73, 234, 263, 269–71, 278–80; and Jewish elitism, 58–61, 68; on leadership, 132–33, 173; model of philosopher prophet, 190; philosophical model of, 54–58; on prophecy, 135; on sin of Adam, 274; thirteen principles of faith, 213, 220–22

Manetti, Giannozzo, 108–9

Manuel I, King of Portugal, 262, 266–68

manuscripts, exchange of, 48–51

maritime trade, 11–12, 217–18, 264–65

Mashmi'a yeshu'ah (Abravanel), 217, 262

Masoretic text, 111–12

May, Johann Heinrich, 282–83

Medici, house of, 143, 215

Medici, Lorenzo de', 36

Megilat hamegaleh (Hiyya), 246, 250–51, 254, 260

melancholy, 134–35

Mendes, Gonsalo, 49

Mendoza, Don Iñigo (Duke of Infantando), 156–58

Mendoza, Don Pedro Gonzalez, 156–57

Mendoza, house of, 156–58, 161, 177

mercantile dimension: international trade, 10–11, 16–19, 196; loans, 11, 17, 163; maritime trade, 11–12, 217–18, 264–65; tax farming, 11, 17, 156

Messer Leon, David, 172–73

Messer Leon, Judah, 168

messianic writings and perspectives, 243–64; commentary on Daniel,

243–59; Don Isaac's tenuous attachment to, 262–64; and faith, 250; *Ma'ayanei hayesh'uah,* 243–61; *Mashmi'a yeshu'ah,* 262; messianic eschaton, 278; redemption, 207, 257–61; and Spanish expulsion, 211; *Yeshu'ot meshiho,* 261–62

Mestre, 267

metaphysics, 56–58, 193–95

Metaphysics (Aristotle), 66

Michael (angel), 69–71

Mif'alot elohim (Abravanel), 217, 263

Milan, 214–15

Milhamot Hashem (Gersonides), 120, 121

Mintz, Judah, 280

miracle at Gibeon, 119–29

Mishnah, 229

Mishneh torah (Maimonides), 115

modernity: Don Isaac as transitional figure, 283, 286, 289, 290; messianism's impact on Jewish backwardness, 245, 286–87

modesty, 55–57

monarchy: absolute, 141, 146; ancient Israel's transition to, 140–41, 150; anointing of kings and high priests, 134, 187–88; antimonarchical position, 142–43, 148, 153–55; biblical exegesis on, 139–41, 186–99; comparison of systems of government, 146–51; constitutional, 5, 141, 147–49; coronation, 33–34, 187–88; and covenantal rule, 153; as sin, 153–55; and theocracy, 142, 151–53. *See also* royals

Monopoli, 216–18, 219, 262–64

Moses, 54–58, 62, 68–69, 71–73, 118–19, 129, 152, 226

music and song, 134–37, 194–95

Muslims, 9, 42, 122–25

Nachmanides, 69

Nahalat avot (Abravanel), 217, 219–20, 228–31, 238–41

Nahmias brothers, 219–20

Naples, 167–73, 174, 183–85, 214–18, 223, 262–64

nations, astral influences on, 64–75, 237

natural laws, divine intervention in, 120–21

natural magical, theory of, 198

nature, human separation from, 274–75

Nebuchadnezzar, 89

Neoplatonism, 66, 232–34

neo-Stoicism, 29, 33, 65, 73, 75

New Christians, 158–59, 162–63, 215

New Testament, 22, 99, 108–9

nobility: Avis dynasty, 4–8, 76; and centralization of power, 95, 151; Christian, 52, 180; conflict with, 79, 92; and crown, 7, 78–81, 92–93, 158–61; of Israel, 59–61; oath of fealty, 78

nobles of Israel, 59–61, 62

Noronha, Dom Sancho de, 21, 34

numerology, 257–58

1 Kings 6:11–13, 208

1 Samuel 8, 116, 138–41, 147, 150–55

1 Samuel 10:2–7, 131–32

On the Heavens (Περὶ οὐρανοῦ) (Aristotle), 55

Or Adonai (Crescas), 115, 122–23, 238–39

Oratio de Hominis Dignitate (Pico della Mirandola), 233–34, 239–40

Ordenaçoens do senhor rey D. Affonso V (The ordinances of Afonso V), 10

original sin, 274–75

Ottoman Empire, 163, 168, 215, 216–17, 258, 262–64

Padua, 280–81

Palaçano, Gedalia, 17

paschal sacrifice, 224–25, 227

Passover Haggadah, 44, 169, 220, 223–25, 247, 269

patristic literature, 22

Pentateuch (as a whole), 99, 106, 170, 220, 269, 281. *See also* Torah

perfection: and creation, 235–36; of the individual, 68; of knowledge in the vein of Sephardic Iyyun, 279; *Pirkei avot*, 230; self-perfection, 55–57; Solomon's, 208–9; of the soul, 115, 271

Petrarch, Francesco, 25–28, 32–33, 107–8

philosophy and theology, 54–75; antiphilosophical rhetoric or sentiment, 123, 127, 288; Arabic, 123–27; *'Ateret zeqenim*, 12, 50, 54, 58–75, 94, 123–25, 127–29; Christian, 32, 65, 73–75, 126–27, 232–34; Cicero, 22–23; compared to Solomon's wisdom, 189–99; in consolatory rhetoric, 27–29; and human progress, 273; Jewish, 65–66, 122–23, 125–27, 280, 284–89; Muslim, 122–25; Neoplatonism, 66, 232–34; political, 138–39, 155, 285; and religion, 126–27; and science, 190–92; Solomon's, 195, 196–99. *See also* Aristotle; humanism; Maimonides; Stoicism

Pichon, Joseph, 14

Pico della Mirandola, Giovanni, 195, 197–98, 233–34, 239–40

Pina, Rui de, 7, 40–41, 102

Pines, Shlomo, 55

Pirkei avot, 228–31, 247. See also *Nahalat avot*

Pixatrix (Ficino), 198

plagiarism by Abravanel, accusation of, 170–73

plague, 77–78, 91, 169

Plato, 56, 133, 138, 232–33

poetry, 18–19, 110

pogroms, 86, 123, 127, 164, 215, 261

politics: of Castile, 156–64; Don Isaac's achievements, 176–77; Don Isaac's philosophy, 138–39, 155, 285; Don Isaac's political orientation, 7–8, 118; of friendship, 44–47; political action, 34; political history, 155; in public life, 156; republicanism, 138–55; role of power in, 34, 43, 76–78, 92, 141, 146–51; utility of death and, 32–34

Poliziano, Angelo, 46

Pontanto, Giovanni, 169

Portugal, 3–81; Abravanel family's original immigration to, 9, 12–19; aristocracy, 21, 78–79, 92–93, 151; Arzilan Jewry, 39–44, 53; Avis dynasty, 3–8; captive grandson in, 267–68; court culture, 20–35; crown and nobility, 92–93, 158–61; Dom Afonso V, 7–8, 16–17, 21, 40–41, 74, 76–78, 90–91; Dom João II, 8, 46, 76–81, 85–86, 91–95, 146, 151, 267–68; and Don Isaac on monarchies, 146; Don Isaac's downfall and escape to Castile, 77–78, 79–81, 85–86, 133–34; humanist activity in, 45–47; Jewish community in, 9–12, 43, 47–48, 89–90; and sea route to India, 265–66; slave trade, 50–51; and Venice, 266–68, 276

power, political, 34, 43, 76–78, 92, 141, 146–51

prayer(s), 29–30, 128–29, 136

priesthood, 187–88, 199

primordial unity, 278

Prisca Theologia (the first theology), 197, 287

prophecy: connection between leader and God, 135; in Daniel, 248–49, 253–57; of elders, 72–73; and intellect, 120, 197; messianic, 262; and Moses, 68–69; and perfection of individual, 68–69; and philosophy, 190, 196–99. *See also* Former Prophets; Latter Prophets

providence. *See* divine providence

Psalms, 136–37

quadripartite division of scripture, 99–101

questions, role in exegesis, 113–14

rabbinic literature, 115–16, 154–55, 250, 289. *See also* Talmud

Radak. *See* Kimhi, Rabbi David

rationalism, 39, 73–74, 138, 245, 273, 285–89

Reconquista, 7, 9, 157, 159–60, 178, 180, 291n15

redemption: apocalyptic notions of, 245–46; arrival of, 250–52, 257–59, 263–64; and construction of Second Temple, 211; and exile, 75, 226–29, 254–56, 257; and Jewish elitism, 43–44; messianic, 207, 257–61

religion: adoption of belief, 221–22; authentic religious knowledge, 123; behavior and reward, 206; and death, 29–34; erosion of, 209; and forming of the Jewish individual, 221–22; and philosophy, 126–27; superiority of, 199; uniformity policy, 178. *See also* Christianity; Islam; Judaism

Renaissance: book collecting during, 49; consolatory literature, 21–22; Italian, 138; literary traditions of, 287–89; and melancholy, 134

republicanism, 138–55

Republic (Plato), 56, 133

Resende, Garcia de, 18–19

rhetoric: antiphilosophical, 123, 127, 288; consolatory, 24–29; in Hebrew epistles, 51–53; and leadership, 51–53; medical conception of, 25; messianic, 246, 259

Roman Empire, 144, 147–49, 258

Roman historians, 102–3

Roman Republic, 108, 147–49, 256

Rome, 44–45, 144

Rosh amanah (Abravanel), 170, 172, 213, 219–22, 228

royals: clerks, 200–201; court society, 4, 9, 15–19, 24, 75, 95, 157, 169–70, 176–77, 201; and delegation to the pope, 44–47; monetary policy, 11–12, 16; nobility and crown, 7, 78–81, 92–93, 158–61; policy toward Jews, 160; power of, 76, 92, 146–51, 196; properties of, 5. *See also* Catholic Monarchs; *individual monarchs by name*

Salutati, Coluccio, 145
Samuel, Book of (commentary), 116, 129–41, 147, 150–55
Sanhedrin, 151, 251
Santa Fe, Jeronimo de (formerly Joshua al-Lorqui), 261–62
Santa Maria, Pablo de, 99, 140–41
Santillana, Marqués de, 110, 157
Saul, 130–36
scholasticism, 111–16
science, 126, 190–92, 197, 206
Second Temple, 204, 210–11, 257–59
Seder eliyahu zuta (Capsali), 179
Segura de la Orden, 86–88, 96
Seneca, 8–9, 22–25, 27–32, 65, 272–74, 276
separate intellects, 63–64, 65, 66–67, 72–74, 121–22, 193–94
Sephardic Diaspora, 174, 247
Sephardic exiles: competitive consciousness among, 237; destinations for, 163; Don Isaac as leader of, 179–81, 183–84; expulsion from Spain, 211–12; Israel as nucleus of, 277; and Jewish apologetic approach, 213; messianic consciousness of, 262; and redemption, 226–28; and Venetian sea trade, 217–18; *Zevah pesah*, 223–24
Sephardic Iyyun, 114–16, 279
Sephardic Jewry, 167–68, 174, 183–84, 217, 224, 226, 259–60

Sevilla, Juan Sanchez de (Samuel Abravanel) (grandfather), 13–16
Seville, 13–16
Sforza, Ludovico (Duke), 214
Shamayim hadashim (Abravanel), 217, 263
Shevet Yehuda (Verga), 179
Shir hama'alot leshlomo (The Song of Solomon's Ascents) (Alemanno), 143
Simon, Richard, 283
sin: of Adam, 274–75; avoidance of, 230; of the elders, 140–41; of monarchy, 153–55; original, 274–75; of Saul, 133; at Tower of Babel, 272
Sixtus IV, pope, 44
slavery, 41–44, 50–51
Solomon, commentary on, 187–209
Solomon's Temple, 13, 182–85, 201–11
song, 134–37, 194–95
soul, 22–26, 65, 115, 133–35, 222, 271
Spain: founding of, 211–12; inquisition in, 158–59; Jewish community in, 13–14, 178–79, 210–11; Seville, 13–16. *See also* Castile; expulsion of Jews from Iberia
spheres, 66–68, 74–75, 123–26
spiritual thirst, 249–50
stars. *See* astral bodies
Stoicism: active life, 34–35; biblical sources, 30–32; conception of fate, 30, 91; in consolatory literature, 25–26, 28–29, 32; and death, 29; model of the Stoics, 275–76; neo-Stoicism, 29, 33, 65, 73, 75
Storia d'Italia (Guicciardini), 214
Strabo, Walafrid, 99
Strauss, Leo, 138, 148, 152–55, 274, 276, 278, 285
sublunar world, 63–66, 120–21, 125, 230, 236–38
Summa Theologica (Aquinas), 114
Symposium (Plato), 232

Talmud, 104, 111, 114–16, 140, 247, 251–52, 261

Tangier, 44–45

al-Tansi, Eliezer, 216–17

tax farming, 11, 17, 156

technological development, 269–73, 276–77

Teixeria, João, 44–49

"Teluna 'al hazman" ("A Complaint against the Times") (Judah Abravanel), 86, 267–68

Temple in Jerusalem, 13, 182–85, 201–12, 257–59

theocracy, 142, 151–53

Tolomeo da Lucca, 148–49

Torah: allegorical exegesis, 204–6; children of the omnipresent, 237; connection between God and Israel, 72–73; division of canon, 98–99; Genesis, 269–74, 276, 278; *Guide of the Perplexed*, 279; historical continuity of, 229; itinerancy, 61; law of the king, 140; Leviticus 18:25, 69; perfection, 115–16; and Plato, 232. *See also* Exodus; Pentateuch

Torquemada, Tomas de, 159–60, 179–80

Tower of Babel, 271–72

trade, 10–12, 16–19, 196, 217–18, 264–68

translations, 108, 197–99, 282–83

Treaty of Lodi, 214

tripartite structures and divisions, 24–25, 73, 98–99, 133

Trismegistus, Hermes, 197–98

Troy, fall of, 210

Tsedeq 'Olamim (Abravanel), 170

Tuscany, 36–37, 49, 150

Tusculanae Disputationes (Tusculan Disputations) (Cicero), 22

Twelve Minor Prophets, 13, 217, 263

2 Samuel 22, 136

Tzedek 'olamim (Abravanel), 269

Valla, Lorenzo, 108–9

Venetian Republic, 262–68

Venetian sea trade, 217–18

Venice, 217, 262–64, 265–68, 276, 280–81

Verba, Frei João, 8

vernacular humanist movement, 62–63

Villena, Enrique de, 26–27

Viseu, house of, 79, 81, 92–93

Vulgate Bible (Jerome), 108–9

wisdom of Solomon, 189–99

wisdom vs. the studies of philosophers, 190

Writings: Chronicles, Book of, 186–87; Daniel, Book of (commentary), 69–70, 89–90, 243–59; Job, 26–27; Psalms, 136–37

Yehiel ben Isaac da Pisa, 36–51, 52–53, 54, 77–78, 149–50, 218

Yemot 'Olam (Abravanel), 170, 269

Yeshu'ot meshiho (Abravanel), 217, 246–47, 261–62, 282

yoqer ma'alato, 231

Zevah pesah (Abravanel), 169, 217, 219–20, 223–28

Zohar, 252

Zurara, Gomes, 102